TURNING THE BLACK SOX WHITE

TURNING THE
BLACK SOX
WHITE

THE MISUNDERSTOOD LEGACY OF
CHARLES A. COMISKEY

TIM HORNBAKER

FOREWORD BY BOB HOIE

SPORTS
PUBLISHING

Sports Publishing books may be purchased in bulk at special discounts for sales
promotion, corporate gifts, fund-raising, or educational purposes. Special editions can
also be created to specifications. For details, contact the Special Sales Department,
Sports Publishing, 307 West 36th Street, 11th Floor, New York,
NY 10018 or sportspubbooks@skyhorsepublishing.com.

Sports Publishing® is a registered trademark of Skyhorse Publishing, Inc.®, a Delaware
corporation.

Visit our website at www.sportspubbooks.com

10 9 8 7 6 5 4 3 2 1

Library of Congress Cataloging-in-Publication Data

Hornbaker, Tim.
    Turning the Black Sox White : the misunderstood legacy of Charles A. Comiskey/
Tim Hornbaker ; foreword by Bob Hoie.
        pages cm
    Summary: "Charles Albert "The Old Roman" Comiskey was a larger-than-life figure–a
man who had precision in his speech and who could work a room with handshakes and
smiles. While he has been vilified in film as a rotund cheapskate and the driving force,
albeit unknowingly, behind the actions of the 1919 White Sox, who threw the World
Series (nicknamed the "Black Sox" scandal), that statement is far from the truth"–
Provided by publisher.
    ISBN 978-1-61321-638-5 (hardback)
    1. Comiskey, Charles A. 2. Baseball team owners–United States–Biography. 3.
Chicago White Sox (Baseball team) I. Title.
    GV865.C644H67 2014
    796.357092–dc23
    [B]
                2013041431

Cover design by Richard Rossiter
Cover photo courtesy of the Chicago History Museum, SDN_000904, Chicago Daily
News, Inc.

Paperback ISBN: 978-1-68358-276-2
eBook ISBN: 978-1-61321-667-5

Printed in the United States of America

To my father, Tim, a lifelong baseball fan, for teaching me the benefits of hard work and for his willingness to always play catch, regardless of how tired he was.

To my sister, Melissa, for her insightful and imaginative perspective and for her unwavering encouragement throughout the years.

Praise for *Turning the Black Sox White*

"Hornbaker makes a sound case for why Comiskey has long been an inappropriate fall guy for the [1919 'Black Sox'] scandal. . . . His depth of knowledge of this era of baseball history shines through."

—*Kirkus Reviews*

"It is engrossing and provides a much-needed reassessment of the man and his impact on the sport. Verdict: A worthy read for Black Sox buffs and baseball history fans.

—*Library Journal*

"In *Turning the Black Sox White*, Tim Hornbaker reviews Comiskey's entire career and restores his reputation to its former state, with clear eye, fair mind, and thorough study."

—John Thorn, Official Historian of Major League Baseball and author of *Baseball in the Garden of Eden*

"I've always been a sucker for stories about Charles Comiskey and the 'Black Sox' scandal of 1919. Tim Hornbaker takes a new and different look at the situation. It's a pleasure to come along for the ride."

—Leigh Montville, *New York Times* bestselling author of *Ted Williams and The Big Bam*

"Charlie Comiskey is one of the giants of baseball history: a remarkable innovator as a player, manager, and mogul; a fierce competitor yet an extraordinarily charismatic fellow. In this richly detailed work, Tim Hornbaker makes an open-and-shut case that, contrary to modern depictions of Comiskey as a greedy villain, he deserves to be remembered as a good as well as a great man."

—Edward Achorn, author of *The Summer of Beer and Whiskey* and *Fifty-nine in '84*

"As a portrait of a major league baseball mogul in the early 20th century and as a cutaway view of the game before World War II, *Turning the Black Sox White* works well."

—Allen Barra, *Chicago Tribune*

"Those who revile Comiskey see this as a gross injustice. After reading this book, they just might change their minds."

—Paul Hagen, MLB.com

"Succeeds in humanizing an important-yet-oversimplified figure in baseball history."

—*SBNation*

CONTENTS

CONTENTS

FOREWORD

In Ken Burns' *Baseball* documentary, Daniel Okrent said the White Sox players "were abused horribly by Charles Comiskey, who was a man of small mind, tight fist and a nasty temperament."

Bill James, in his *Historical Baseball Abstract*, wrote in a chapter on the teens that "The arch-villain of this villainous era was Charles Albert Comiskey. He had no reason in the world not to deal fairly with his players. The White Sox drew the largest crowds in baseball in this period—even larger than the Giants—yet the White Sox were one of the worst paying teams. Comiskey had all the power in the relationship and he had to rub their noses in it. . . . Put Joe Jackson in the Hall of Fame? How about if we kick Comiskey out?"

Marvin Miller echoed this in his memoir, *A Whole Different Ball Game*, regarding the 1919 World Series. "[We do] not know to what degree the tightfistedness, mean-spirited and questionable tactics of the Chicago owner, Charles Comiskey, contributed to the condition that made the players susceptible to gamblers but I've always maintained that the question 'Why isn't Joe Jackson in the Hall of Fame?' should be supplemented with 'Why isn't Charles Comiskey out?'"

In his introduction to the 1987 paperback edition of Eliot Asinof's *Eight Men Out*, paleontologist and baseball fan Stephen Jay Gould wrote,"We feel that, whatever [the 'Black Sox'] did, they were treated unfairly both before and after. Sox owner Charles Comiskey was not only the meanest skinflint in baseball, but a man who could cruelly flaunt his wealth, while treating those who brought it to him as peons."

Virtually everything Okrent, James, Miller, and Gould wrote about Comiskey is based on Asinof's book. In *Eight Men Out*, Asinof wrote "[In

1919] the club owners had agreed to cut the ballplayers' salaries to the bone, despite the fact that they extended the season. Charles Comiskey, owner of the White Sox, had been especially loyal to the agreement. His ballplayers were the best and were paid as poorly as the worst."

Donald Honig, in his book *Baseball America,* wrote "the smug, portly, penurious Charles Comiskey was reason enough to make a man swindle his own ethics. . ."

In literally hundreds of books and thousands of articles about Charles Comiskey none of the authors have the slightest idea who or what Charles Comiskey really was. They have read *Eight Men Out*, embellished it characterizations of Comiskey, the cheap tyrant, and as a result what is largely nonsense persists as the prevailing view of Comiskey.

In Ken Burns' *Baseball*, narrator John Chancellor intones "No team played better than the Chicago White Sox . . . and few teams were paid as poorly. . . . The White Sox were heavily favored to beat the better paid but far weaker Cincinnati Reds in the World Series . . . Comiskey was among the game's most parsimonious executives."

In fact, in 1919 the White Sox went into the World Series with the highest payroll in baseball: $93,053; Cincinnati was eighth at $76,870.

In *Eight Men Out*, Asinof provided some salary comparisons between the White Sox and Reds. Joe Jackson's salary was $6,000, Edd Roush, the leading Reds hitter "though some 40 or 50 percentage points below Jackson made $10,000. Heinie Groh, at third base, topped [Buck] Weaver's salary by almost $2,000." And Dutch Ruether was getting almost double Eddie Cicotte's $5,500 salary.

In reality, Edd Roush, while playing on a two year, $5,000 per year contract, led the National League in batting in 1917 with a .341 average, and in 1918 he hit .333, finishing 2 points behind league leader Zach Wheat. In those same seasons, Jackson was playing on a two year, $6,000 per year contract extension he had signed with Cleveland a few days before he was sold to the White Sox in 1915. In 1917, he had to hit .444 in the final month of the season to raise his average to a career low .301. In 1918, he jumped the Sox three weeks into the season to work and play ball for the Harlan Shipyards in Wilmington, Delaware, and a few weeks after that, induced his friends Lefty Williams and Byrd Lynn (the Sox only backup catcher) to join him in Wilmington. Should it surprise anyone that in 1919, Roush signed for $6,500 and Jackson for $6,000? In 1919, Roush led the National League with a .321 average. Jackson finished fourth in the American League batting race at .351 (30 not "40 or 50" points higher than Roush), 33 points behind the leader Ty Cobb.

By any objective standard, Heinie Groh was a much better third baseman and better player than Buck Weaver. Groh was named third baseman on *Baseball Magazine's* "All America" team four times, Weaver none. Weaver was a singles hitter that seldom walked, while Groh hit a lot of doubles and drew a lot of walks, which gives him a huge edge in the various matrices (Bill James' Win Shares, Pete Palmer's Batter/Fielder Wins, Baseball-Reference Wins Above Replacement, etc.). Yet in 1919, contrary to Asinof's assertion, Weaver had a higher salary than Groh: $7,250 to $6,500.

In 1919, Cicotte had a base salary of $5,000 and in addition earned a $3,000 performance bonus. Ruether's salary was $2,340 less than half Cicotte's salary and less than a third of Cicotte's total earnings. The White Sox had eight World Series eligible pitchers and all but two of them had higher salaries than Ruether. In 1918–19, Cicotte's contracts including earned bonuses totaled $15,000. The only pitcher in the majors who made more in those years was Walter Johnson at $19,000 (Grover Alexander spent most of 1918 in the Army). From 1918–20, Cicotte's contracts including earned bonuses totaled $25,000, again second only to Johnson's $31,000.

While Ray Schalk repeatedly refused to talk to Asinof, Asinof apparently was able to channel him near the end of the 1920 season, writing that "[Schalk] didn't like Comiskey. . . . Comiskey was cheap, Comiskey underpaid him. Every year, Schalk hated to face signing that skimpy contract."

In 1919, Schalk was on the final year of a three year contract that paid $7,083 per year. This made him the highest paid catcher in the American League and the thirteenth highest paid player. In 1920, he got a raise to $10,000, which made him, by far, the highest paid catcher in baseball and the sixth highest paid player in the American League.

In 1919, there were fifteen players in the American League who had salaries of $6,000 or more and five of them were with the White Sox. In 1920, there were seventeen players in the American league that had salaries of $7,000 or more and seven (41 percent) were with the White Sox.

At a preliminary hearing and jury selection for the 1921 "Black Sox" trial, defense lawyers raised a number of issues that tended to make Comiskey the villain. Low salaries, players receiving only $3 a day meal money when other clubs got $4, and having to wear filthy uniforms.

From an interview Asinof had with Felsch, it is possible to deduce the meal money issue. There was no set amount for meals, but prior to the 1919 season, the standard for many years had been $3 per day; however due to inflation some clubs raised the amount to $4 in 1919. The White Sox opened the season on the road where they played 10 of their first 14 games and continued to pay the players $3. When they returned home, they acquired pitcher Grover Lowdermilk from the St. Louis Browns. When the White Sox began a long road trip on June 1 and the traveling secretary gave the players their meal money at the usual rate of $3/day, Lowdermilk said that they were getting $4 with the Browns. The players complained to Manager Kid Gleason and their meal money rate was changed to $4.

The filthy uniform story seems to be another event of rather short duration. At the time, the standard player contract required that the players pay a $30 deposit which would be returned at the end of the season or when they were released or traded. The clubhouse then and now was responsible for cleaning the uniforms; the clubhouse personnel might be paid employees of the club, but they survive on tips or what are now called clubhouse dues. The players claimed that they had paid to have their uniforms laundered but it got to be such an expense that they wore them dirty rather than pay. At some point, management went through the players lockers, laundered all the dirty uniforms, and "docked" the amount (50 cents) from their salaries. The only possible reference to this event came in mid-June 1918, when there was a 1917 World Championship flag raising ceremony at Comiskey Park. There are apparently no photographs of the players at the event, however for the next two days, the Sox played in road uniforms as the home uniforms were in the laundry. Otherwise the only contemporary references to dirty uniforms were those that noted how Buck Weaver stood out from his teammates because of his dirty uniform. Nelson Algren, in a hyperbolic rewrite of *Eight Men Out* that appeared in his book *The Last Carousel*, wrote: "Eastern fans began jeering Mr. Comiskey's players as 'Black Sox' before that appellation signified anything more scandalous than neglecting to launder their uniforms. The old man was so begrudging about laundry bills that his players looked as if they put on their uniforms opening day in the coal yard behind Mr. Comiskey's park; and hadn't changed them since." Thus creating the urban legend that the White Sox were already known as the "Black Sox" before the scandal. This tale found its way into a *Freakonomics* blog. The authors questioned the validity of the story and offered a *Freakonomics* T-shirt to the first person who could provide hard evidence that the White Sox were ever known as the "Black Sox" before the scandal . . . they are still waiting.

In 1922, Ray Cannon, a Milwaukee lawyer, claimed that in 1917, Comiskey had offered to give each player $5,000 in lieu of whatever their World Series shares might be. Their shares came out to $3,669, thus he owed the players $1,331 which Cannon rounded up to $1,500. Asinof wrote that Comiskey's bonus turned out to be a case of champagne. Actually there was no evidence that Comiskey made the offer. In fact, Comiskey knew that such an offer would have been in violation of Baseball Rules and he would know, because he was one of the reasons for the rule. In the early days of the World Series, owners frequently added the club's share to the player's share. In 1903, when Barney Dreyfuss did this for his club, it resulted in the Pirates losing share being greater than that of the Red Sox winning share. In 1905, Connie Mack did the same for his winning Athletics, and in 1906, Charles Comiskey did it for his winning White Sox, which gave them shares more than four times that of the losing Cubs. After 1907, when Tigers owner William Yawkey and Cubs owner Charles Murphy added their club's share to the player's shares, the National Commission adopted a rule that banned clubs giving or paying a bonus or prize to any or all of its players before or after the completion of the series. There was some talk that late in the 1917 season, Sox coach Kid Gleason was talking about a bonus, but this was most likely telling the players that Comiskey had given his 1906 club a bonus and might do it again, not knowing there was a rule that prohibited it. Now to the case of champagne. In his 1956 *Sports Illustrated* interview, Gandil said "I remember only one act of generosity on Comiskey's part. After we won the World Series in 1917, he splurged with a case of champagne." But no act of generosity by Comiskey can go unchallenged, Stephen Longstreet in his book *Chicago 1860–1919*, wrote "[Comiskey] had promised fine bonuses to the team if they won the American League pennant [in 1917] and with what did he pay off? A case of cheap horse-piss tasting champagne for the whole team—that was all." This story eventually found its way into Donald Gropman's book, *Say It Ain't So, Joe*.

Probably the most memorable line in *Eight Men Out* the movie, is when Eddie Cicotte who had been promised a $10,000 bonus if he won 30 games went to Comiskey's office said he won 29 even though he was benched two weeks and deserved the bonus. Comiskey told him "29 is not 30."

In *Eight Men Out* the book, Asinof wrote that the $10,000 bonus for winning 30 games came in 1917, and that Comiskey ordered that Cicotte be benched to keep him from winning 30. The problem with this version is that Cicotte did not miss any starts in the last two months of the season and in addition, made several long relief appearances. This story fails at several levels. Prior to 1917, Cicotte had never won more than 18 games. In the previous three seasons, he had averaged 13 wins a year. So why would he be offered a bonus if he won 30? And then the amount of the bonus; bonuses were always some fraction of the base salary, not multiples of it. Also, with the White Sox bonuses were usually incremental, for example, X if he wins 15, Y more if you win 20, etc.

If it did happen in 1919 during the Sox last eastern trip, Cicotte missed a couple of weeks due to a cold that settled in his arm and shoulder. Once recovered, he started and won against the Red Sox in a game that clinched a tie for the pennant and gave Cicotte 29 wins. He then received permission to leave the club and return to his farm in Michigan. Five days later, the White Sox still hadn't clinched the pennant so they requested that Cicotte rejoin the team. He started against the St. Louis Browns, pitched 7 innings, and left the game trailing 5–2. The Sox came back to win and finally clinched the pennant with Dick Kerr getting the decision. Why would Cicotte ask to go home when he still needed one win to get his bonus? Why did the White Sox recall him when a win by him would cost them $10,000? After all the "magic number" was one with five games to go.

The reality is there never was a $10,000 bonus. After winning 28 in 1917, Cicotte was given a contract with a base salary of $5,000, a $2,000 signing bonus, and an additional agreement that he would receive a $3,000 bonus if he had another season similar to 1917. He went 12–19 in the War short-ened season of 1918. In 1919, he again signed for $5,000, but the $3,000 bonus was carried over so by the start of the eastern road trip he had 28 wins, thus assuring that he would get the bonus.

When Bill James wrote that in the teens the White Sox drew the largest crowds in baseball—even more than the Giants—he apparently was using attendance as a substitute for revenues. In the first half of the decade (1910–14), the White Sox had a losing record (371–393). In the same span, the Giants won three pennants and had a 478–286 record—107 games ahead of the Sox (21.5 per season), yet the Sox outdrew the Giants at home by 32,000. They both played in new steel and concrete stadiums, and the Polo Grounds had a slightly higher seating capacity than Comiskey Park. The only advantage the Sox had was Sunday baseball. The Cubs also had Sunday baseball, but their park was not nearly as nice and had less capacity than Comiskey. They did, however, have a far superior team, going 453–312; 81.5 games better than the Sox, yet the Sox outdrew them at home by 513,000. So on an annual basis, the Sox were 16.5 games worse, but outdrew them by 102,600.

For the entire decade, the Giants won 91 more games than the White Sox and the Cubs won 18 more, yet the Sox outdrew the Giants by 229,000 and the Cubs by 1,440,000. How can this be? How can the inferior White Sox consistently outdraw the Giants and Cubs? Simple. The White Sox had a much lower price scale for tickets. At Comiskey Park, bleacher seats were 25 cents and grandstand seats 75 cents. At the Polo Grounds, they were twice as much—bleachers, 50 cents, grandstand $1.50. Box Seats were about a dollar higher than at Comiskey. So even though the White Sox outdrew the Giants, their revenues were much lower.

According to Charles Alexander's authoritative biography of John McGraw (titled *John McGraw*), the Giants returned an average annual profit of $250,000 in the period of 1912–17. Based on court records, from 1915–17, the White Sox net profits totaled $141,000 with Comiskey taking an average annual salary of $10,000.

Too many people have consumed the Kool-Aid served up by Westbrook Pegler, Eliot Asinof, and their acolytes when we have reached the point that charging low prices for tickets becomes evidence of greed.

What we really need is a clear, accurate, and coherent biography of Charles Comiskey. And thankfully, Tim Hornbaker has written it.

Charles Comiskey was an innovative first baseman and manager. He was one of only two men who managed ten or more years in the majors who had a career winning percentage over .600 (Joe McCarthy was the other).[1] He was one of the founders of the American League and the only major league player who became sole owner of a major league baseball franchise. He built the finest stadium of its time. He celebrated his sixtieth birthday shortly before the end of the 1919 baseball season. His team was in first place and he might soon win his third World Series as an owner. He could have looked back at a great, perhaps unprecedented career, but that was seemingly forgotten when members of his club threw the World Series. In time, he became seen not as a victim, but a facilitator of the fix. He had the highest paid team in baseball, but he was called a cheapskate.

Tim Hornbaker covers all this and much, much more in this excellent biography of Charles Comiskey. Read, learn, and enjoy!

—**Bob Hoie, November, 2013**

ENDNOTE

1 In twelve seasons as a manager, Comiskey finished with an 840–541 record (.608 winning percentage). This included winning four pennants and one World Championship (1886).

INTRODUCTION

INTRODUCTION

Adorned in a three piece suit, a distinguished gentleman watched workers prepare the ball field from a seat in the empty grandstand. He tapped his right foot relentlessly, as his anxieties were heavy on his mind. The day was like any other, but he felt the pressure of getting everything exactly right. That meant the conditions of the diamond, the comfort of his patrons, and the competitiveness of his players. His heart raced as if his entire being was wrapped up in the game and he made a mental list of the chores that still needed to be administered. Despite what people thought of "The Old Roman" Charles Albert Comiskey, his life was not full of bliss. In fact, he was working really hard to hold it together in spite of increasing pressure.

A century ago, in his heyday as an owner, Comiskey was one of the most beloved men in baseball. He possessed an uncanny ability to connect to people and had turned his White Sox ballpark into a warm and welcoming venue that was the envy of his peers. Brimming with a genuine affection for his clientele, he always wore a smile and constantly mingled amidst the people before and after games. In turn, his supporters were the most loyal in baseball, turning out regardless of whether the Sox were winning or losing. His friendly discord was contagious and dedicated rooter organizations contributed to many memorable occasions, both before the public and behind the scenes.

But as time went by, Charles Comiskey recoiled from his public position as baseball's ambassador, and the man that people had come to know and love, mysteriously vanished.

The fact is that Comiskey experienced an abnormal evolution. A combination of personal struggles and the heaviness of the crooked 1919 World Series turned his fun-loving personality into utter bitterness. His charming qualities gave way to unrelenting stubbornness and his rigid personal code and narrow perspective turned longtime friends into resentful enemies.

The "Black Sox" scandal terrorized him at the core, destroying his spirit and capping a nightmarish scenario that no baseball leader could ever live down. Comiskey knew all about the gambling element. He heard the rumors of thrown games and various stories of crooked ball players. He just never thought he'd be the man torn down by the ill institution; left eternally humiliated and shamed in the biggest swindle in Major League Baseball history.

To this day, the damage of the conspiracy still taints the Comiskey legacy, negating over fifty years of positive contributions to America's National Pastime.

Nevertheless, on a wall at the National Baseball Hall of Fame and Museum in Cooperstown, New York, resides a plaque bearing Comiskey's name. It commemorates his innovations as a first baseman, his accomplishments as a manager, and the legacy he established as the owner of the Chicago White Sox. The Old-Timers Committee in 1939 was fully convinced that he deserved to be immortalized forever among the greatest baseball figures in history.

However, Comiskey's complicated story and portrayals of his so-called nefarious actions have turned a segment of the baseball populace against him. These individuals believe that his purposefully despicable behavior warrants removal of his hall of fame credentials. Many of these critics would rather see "Shoeless Joe" Jackson acknowledged than honor Comiskey because of the latter's alleged wrongdoings.

A mangled form of the "truth" has been circulating for decades, told over and over to the point of exhaustion. These stories have been accepted by the mainstream media, whether in book or movie form, and have crucified Comiskey. His reputation has depreciated a stunning amount by a revision of history.

Instead of attempting to separate fact from fiction, writers have embraced the standard theories of Comiskey and labeled him a scoundrel on par with the "Black Sox" conspirators themselves. It is easy today to be affected by the standard lore surrounding Comiskey, but everything is not always as it seems. The deeper clarification of his career and the circumstances of the 1919 World Series have been ignored for far too long. In Jimmy Breslin's book, *Can't Anybody Here Play This Game?*, about the 1962 New York Mets, he makes this point clear, stating: "You see, most of the stories which have been handed down over the years about ballplayers or teams are either vastly embellished or simply not true at all."[1]

Finally, after almost 100 years of misrepresentations, the truth about Charles Comiskey can be made known.

ENDNOTE

1 Breslin, Jimmy, *Can't Anybody Here Play This Game?*, p. 18.

1

BASEBALL OR BUST

Nearly two decades before Charles Comiskey stepped onto a makeshift baseball diamond for the first time, his father was confronted with a life or death decision that changed the future of his family forever. Dire conditions had poisoned his homeland of Ireland due to the Great Famine of the 1840s, and John Comiskey was forced to leave his birthplace of Crosserlough, County Cavan, to escape the rampant disease and death.[1] About twenty-one years of age in 1848,[2] he journeyed outside of his familiar surroundings for a mysterious new world and would soon embrace the opportunities that America provided.[3]

The move was out of necessity, but John was a determined soul, hard worker, and a man unwilling to remain idle for any period of time. His courage as a young man was remarkable, and after arriving in the United States, he labored in the lumber industry around New Haven, Connecticut.[4] Seeking better employment in a city of real prospects, he made his way farther west to Chicago, where he landed in the autumn of 1853, settling on the quiet western side.[5] At the time, the city's population was just over 60,000, and because of its prime location in terms of land and water transportation, Chicago's growth was about to boom.[6]

Shortly thereafter, Comiskey wed Mary Ann Kearns and the couple had two sons, Patrick and James.[7] Their third child was born on August 15, 1859, and they named him Charles Albert.[8] He was followed by siblings Francis Josephine, the only girl of what would be eight children, which also included Edward, Edmond, Joseph, and Ignatius.[9] To support his sizable clan, John worked as a clerk for the Chicago and Rock Island Railroad Company, handling countless tasks in the company's freight department.

In his Tenth Ward neighborhood and around his home on South Union, Comiskey freely comingled with fellow Irish countrymen and Germans, making many friends.[10] Despite the appearance of a satisfactorily peaceful melting pot, there were signs that the various ethnicities felt more trust among their own than others of different backgrounds. That was especially the case when it came to politics, which in Chicago was tumultuous, at best. It was a fiery environment for anyone to thrive, and the exact reason why John Comiskey entered that spectrum is anyone's guess. Perhaps he felt a burning desire to at least try and better the conditions around him, or maybe it was a natural inclination. Whatever the motive, John threw his hat into the race for city alderman representing the Tenth Ward in 1859.

Dennis Coughlin was one of the key Irish leaders in the "Bloody Tenth." He was popular among like-minded citizens and had considerable pull throughout the city. He had many connections in the community of Bridgeport, south of his neighborhood, where the composition was mostly Irish. He had the kind of loyal friends he could count on to vote in his ward—illegally—to pad his numbers.[11] Using his affinity to attract supporters, unscrupulous methods, and a sharp tongue to lash out at adversaries, Coughlin gained an aldermanship in 1857, representing the Democratic Party. Two years later, in March of 1859, with many of the ruthless practices established as the "norm," Comiskey replaced Coughlin and was elected to his first term on the Common Council of Chicago.[12]

The *Chicago Press and Tribune,* a pro-Republican newspaper, cried foul, declaring that "an enormous amount of double voting" occurred and that "Celts voted from twice to ten times each" for Democratic candidates.[13] That same paper tied Comiskey to a "Long" John Wentworth undertaking to become City Printer in April of 1859.[14] Wentworth, a former Mayor of Chicago, was slick in the way he was able to juggle political allies—regardless if they were Republican or Democrat—to get what he wanted. In this case, he united his Democratic support against a Republican blockade which prevented him from winning the position.

Interestingly enough, Wentworth had given up his Democratic credentials a few years earlier and ran in the 1857 mayoral race as a Republican. He was also closely tied to Abraham Lincoln, the promising Republican leader from Springfield, Illinois. In spite of his qualifications, the current crop of Republican Aldermen united to keep him out because they didn't trust him. On the other hand, many Chicagoans did. He used his popularity to garner the Republican nomination for mayor again in 1860, and was reelected.

The shrewd actions of Wentworth, Coughlin, and others demonstrated the uneasiness of the Chicago political atmosphere, and to play ball in that company, an individual had to rise to the occasion—and often check their scruples at the door. Comiskey didn't write the unorthodox regulations used in the process of governing but needed to adhere to them if he wanted to remain afloat. Unsurprisingly, he fitted into his thorny surroundings like a puzzle piece and soon was acknowledged as one of the powerhouses of the Democratic landscape.

Comiskey was reelected in 1861 and was an instrumental figure in the development of Chicago into a flourishing metropolis.[15] The Board of Aldermen was responsible for everything from city taxes to the construction of bridges, tunnels, canals, sewers, streets, and sidewalks. They paid close attention to the railroad industry and waterways to ensure all transportation moved in and out of the city without obstruction. Additionally, they regulated salaries for city employees, set aside money for parks, and continuously labored to improve the lives of Chicago's citizens. The attractiveness of Chicago as a city of opportunity swelled the population to nearly 170,000 by 1864.[16]

When Democrat Francis Sherman became mayor in 1862, Comiskey's measure of influence grew significantly. He was named Sherman's "adviser," and played a central role in wrangling party aldermen, especially when contentious issues were on the table. The United States, by this point, was already embroiled in the Civil War, and the emotions of politics were running high. Democrats, with Sherman's approval, named the *Chicago Times* the city's official printer, a maneuver that received considerable condemnation.[17] The *Chicago Tribune* called the *Times* a "secession" newspaper for its backing of pro-slavery and Confederate interests.

Comiskey was dubbed "the most ultra Democrat in the city" by the *Tribune*, and the remark wasn't a compliment.[18] Based on the apparent sway of Comiskey and his fellow Tenth Ward alderman, Redmond Sheridan, it was alleged that the two men had, "in reality, been the Mayors of Chicago," and using Sherman as their puppet.[19] Comiskey tested his political capital by running for the Illinois House of Representatives for the 59th District in November of 1862, but finished fourth.[20]

As wartime politics intensified, Comiskey aligned with the Copperheads, a body of Democrats who desired for a simple and peaceful resolution to the conflict with the South. And if that meant giving up the fight to free slaves, some Copperheads were ready to accept that. Comiskey occasionally let his own frustrations over the war get the better of him, and he lashed out at the national government with harsh criticism.[21]

A few months later, Comiskey expanded his attack on the Lincoln Administration and commented that the original purpose of the war had shifted to strictly appease the Abolitionists.[22] He blamed the government for the heinous New York riots and lashed out at the *Chicago Tribune* for its pro-Republican stance. The *Tribune*, in turn, called Comiskey's commentary "ridiculous balderdash." There was a general belief that many individuals from the Copperhead element of the Irish community had little sympathy for the plight of the slaves and Comiskey denied the Irish were at war with blacks.[23] In December of 1864, he did imply that there was a tendency of the Common Council to aid the cause of the black minority in Chicago but reminded his peers that because blacks were not citizens of the U.S., they weren't protected by the Constitution, nor by the State of Illinois.

The boundaries of the city wards were adjusted in 1863, and Comiskey was elected to his third term as an alderman for the new Seventh Ward.[24] Mayor Sherman was also reelected, continuing their Democratic reign. The verbal cannon fire continued over the next two years and the arguments in halls and on the streets sporadically broke out into violence. From time to time, Democrats and Republicans were able to put aside their differences to meet the call of the Union Army for soldiers.[25] And in Comiskey's Seventh Ward, just that occurred in October of 1864, when both parties met peacefully and worked out a way to meet their quota for manpower. The *Chicago Tribune*, after the accomplishment, noted that the men "be honored" for their work.

On April 18, 1865, only days after President Lincoln was assassinated and with the war coming to a conclusion, there was a massive surge of Republican support in Chicago, and Comiskey was voted from office.[26]

Pushed to the background of city politics, Comiskey retained his persuasion among Irish voters and sought to return to some form of civil service. It took him two years to battle his way back into the running for Alderman of the Eighth Ward. Yet again, the *Tribune* roasted him prior to the election, hoping to make an impression by threatening Republicans that if they didn't act, it would mark the "restoration of the Comiskey dynasty."[27] The attacks failed. On April 16, 1867, Comiskey was elected by a narrow margin and began his seventh year as a Chicago alderman.[28]

Before the end of 1867, Comiskey found himself treading in hot water over remarks he made about the leadership of Chicago's police department.[29] He alluded to corruption and his statements sparked a huge firestorm that demanded immediate clarification. Inquiries were made, but ultimately produced very little in terms of results, prompting a spiteful backlash by various press outlets.[30] The controversial matter didn't affect his standing amongst his loyalists in the long run, and in November of 1869, he was returned to the Council of the Ninth Ward.[31] His colleagues were equally forgiving and agreed to promote him to "Presiding Officer" of the Board of Aldermen, the first such appointment in the city's history.[32] It was a fitting tribute in what would be his final year as a fixture in the council.

Living on the western side of the city, the Comiskey family was spared any direct physical or financial loss from the Great Fire of 1871, but was unequivocally committed to helping the city recover in its aftermath.[33] The destruction covered 2,300 acres of land, with an estimated 17,500 structures being damaged or destroyed and over a hundred thousand people displaced from their homes. Comiskey used his power of influence and construction contacts to swiftly move in to help aid Chicagoans at their time of need. It was an opportunity to unite above and beyond the pettiness of political strife, and that was exactly what happened. Chicago rebounded bigger and better than ever before, turning the disaster into a positive period of growth.

Despite the assumptions that all men involved in the government were wealthy, the Comiskey's were working class through and through. After leaving the railroad business, John toiled as an assessor for the Internal Revenue Service (IRS) and then as a bookkeeper at the German Savings Bank from 1871–75.[34] He remained active in Democratic circles and friends tried several times to get him nominated for better paying civic positions, including city assessor, recorder, and tax commissioner. His bitter feud with the *Tribune* tapered off and the publication even threw him an unenthusiastic compliment by agreeing that he was a man of "some talent," although was rather "crotchety."[35] He made an unsuccessful bid for Cook County sheriff in 1874, and served as the clerk for the county commissioners for several years.

Charles Comiskey, a boy of eleven in 1870, was greatly influenced by his father's dedication to the community and ardent work ethic in supporting their family. He attended the Holy Family Parochial School for his early education and advanced to St. Ignatius College in time to be one of the first thirty-seven students to attend the newly constructed institution.[36] [37] [38] Accompanied by his brother James, who was just a year older, he participated in a preparatory class and learned the basics of writing, reading, and mathematics while receiving a "third premium" award for his efforts. The next school year he studied Latin, Greek, and Christian doctrine in addition to English and arithmetic, and added bookkeeping and penmanship the following term.

With an abundance of positive elements surrounding him, Comiskey shied away from the expected path and began to idolize a different group of people: baseball players. In his neighborhood, there were improvised teams of mostly older boys who got together and staged games.[39] As he watched them go through the motions, he found that the excitement and competition of baseball was much more enthralling to his soul than anything that could be found in a classroom.

"It became my dream day and night to do some of the things they did," Comiskey explained in 1916. "I just grew up in baseball. The sandlots of Chicago were my school. It was there the fascination of the sport gripped me for life."[40]

On corner lots in what was dubbed the "west side prairies," Comiskey joined kids in mimicking the more experienced players and he found that being a pitcher suited him the most of all positions. He was accompanied by James Hart, Jack Halpin, John Coughlin, Billy O'Grady, and others with names like "Yank," "Marsh," and "Swede."[41] [42] Comiskey practiced religiously and when there was no one to throw to or when the hands of one of his friends became too sore to catch his fastballs, he targeted the nearest wall with all his might. He developed his speed and accuracy, and, maybe even more importantly, gained self-confidence in his own leadership on the field. It was a crucial period of maturity and said a lot about his budding dedication to the craft.

"Comiskey was a born leader," Hart explained in 1917. "So, of course, he was the captain of our team. We had an awful time getting balls and bats. We sold junk and stuff of that sort to get money for balls and our bats consisted mainly of those cast off after having been broken by regular ball players. We would glue and screw the broken bats together and use them as long as possible. When our team played we would compete on the proposition that the losing team would forfeit a bat. We seldom lost a bat, but when we did or were threatened with a loss, Comiskey would start a row with the umpire or opposing players and break up the game before we lost our bats. He was the foxiest kid in Chicago in those days.

"Comiskey seldom went to school more than two months a year. He was always out on the baseball grounds figuring out plays. The only reason he went to school at all was the bad weather around Chicago."[43]

On June 25, 1873, when Charles was thirteen years old, his mother Mary Ann passed away at the age of thirty-seven.[44] It was a crushing loss to the entire family, and John was suddenly handicapped by the full responsibilities of maintaining the household and bringing in an income. Charles' annoying disinterest in formal school was anything but pleasing to his father. In fact, the considerable amount of time he was spending on the diamond was enough cause to ship him out of state for school.[45]

The location was St. John's College in Prairie du Chien, Wisconsin, a small town bordering the Mississippi River.[46] Little did John know that baseball was as popular there as in Chicago, and it wasn't long after Comiskey's arrival for the 1873–74 term that he caught the eye of the school's team manager, John English.[47][48] A few years older than Comiskey, English was a senior and headed for the priesthood. He prided himself on being a good judge of talent, having put together a successful crop of young players, and was mighty impressed by the athletic abilities of the tall newcomer.

Flashing a solid fastball and a hypnotizing curve, Comiskey was all too eager to continue playing ball under English's watchful eye. He later said, "My father was determined to give his children a thorough schooling and probably thought he would put me out of baseball by sending me away to college. As events proved, that move only served to bind me closer to the game."[49]

Comiskey polished his skills as much as the conditions around him would allow during his attendance at St. John's. There were limitations of his growth insofar as obtaining first-class instruction and facing real competition. English, in 1910, said: "I do not believe it is generally known that Comiskey had a college education. At college, he at once developed the qualifications of a leader and an organizer. He was resourceful, industrious, and an enthusiast. He was a good student, strong in mathematics and commercial law. As an athlete, he excelled all. He was a likeable character; affable, jolly and an all around good fellow, yet he was a stickler for discipline and compliance with the rules."[50]

He also had a "faculty to judge human nature correctly and win the confidence and esteem of his associates," an innate gift that would benefit him his entire life.

Still motivated to drive baseball from his system and hopefully inspire him to engage another line of interest, John sent Charles even farther away, this time to St. Mary's College in St. Mary's, Kansas.[51] John was familiar with the Jesuit program at that institution because he had sent his son James there a year earlier. It was a rewarding place of learning with comparatively small classrooms and professors from international locations like England, Germany, and Belgium.[52] Students were primarily from across the Midwest, and among those officially registered for the year beginning on September 11, 1874, were fifteen-year-old Charles Comiskey, his brother James, and Timothy "Ted" Sullivan.

Sullivan may have been the oldest student at St. Mary's in 1874, but since his birth year was anywhere between 1851 and 1856, it's hard to know for sure.[53] Regardless of his actual age, he was mature in mind and spirit and was a natural mentor to friends. Hailing from Milwaukee, Sullivan was the kind of man a person meets and never forgets. His outgoing personality and enterprising outlook were especially unique, and Sullivan and Comiskey immediately bonded over their shared passion: baseball.[54] With two school teams engaged in a heated rivalry, Sullivan snagged Comiskey for his squad, and Comiskey was all ears in learning the finer points of the sport.[55]

Charles joined his brother Jim, LeClaire Magill, Tom Ward, Will Stark, and others in the pursuit of gamesmanship on the field over and above any classroom learning.[56] Nevertheless, the proficient staff of professors and religious leaders under the management of Reverend Francis H. Stuntebeck, president of the school, was effective in rounding out the education of Comiskey. Lessons in philosophy, math, composition, debate, law, and history were instrumental in his later functionality as a business mogul. Comiskey's time at St. Mary's only lasted a single scholastic year—from September 1874 to June 1875—a ten month period that would essentially be his last full session of formal schooling.

The combination of worldly and intellectual minds at St. Mary's was stimulating, but no one was more influential as a teacher to Comiskey than Ted Sullivan. Sullivan was thinking about baseball as much as Charles was, perhaps even more, and for decades after leaving St. Mary's, he'd manage and develop leagues and organizations with more regularity than anyone else. He traveled the globe spreading the positive ideals of the sport and was always scouting for the next big superstar. Comiskey had never met anyone who talked endlessly about the tricks of the trade. The education he received from Sullivan was much different from what his father expected from St. Mary's.

"My father frowned on baseball as a sport for town boys and loafers," Comiskey later explained. "The game hadn't appealed to him as a worthy profession for any of his sons."[57]

But back in Chicago, baseball had crept into the Comiskey household by other means while Charles and James were away at college, much to John's dismay. In April of 1875, Patrick, his oldest son and a clerk by trade, had assumed the role of secretary for a local club known as the "Eclipse."[58] Also playing second base for the squad was "Comiskey," although it's not known which Comiskey brother this referred to. Charles remained in Kansas through the annual commencement ceremonies at St. Mary's in June, and upon returning home, received a reality check from his uncompromising father, who demanded he learn a stable occupation instead of continuing with this baseball tomfoolery.

Giving up his dream wasn't that easy; and frankly, Charles didn't want to. But as a dutiful son, he agreed to study as a plumber's apprentice under John's acquaintance, Cook County Plumber Joseph Hogan. The opportunity was stellar, but what didn't make sense to John at the time was that Charles didn't care about a trade or a decent-paying career. He would give it all up in a second to get back on the diamond and play ball. Money or no money, he wanted to invest his time in baseball, and proved that when Sullivan asked him to join a small-time Milwaukee team in 1876. Quickly induced, Comiskey left his plumber's tools behind and picked up his rightful equipment on a Wisconsin field.[59]

Sullivan demonstrated his cleverness in obtaining financial backing, and received it from a local man of importance, the future "Lord" Thomas Shaughnessy. Shaughnessy was a businessman and politician, and in a matter of years would assume the presidency of the Canadian Pacific Railroad. The Alerts—as the team was called—were a talented bunch and displayed a winning sensibility in area competition. Comiskey played the infield and gained experience as a pitcher. When the short engagement was up, his first professional baseball job was in the books, and he pocketed $50 a month for his much-enjoyed labor.[60]

Upon to returning to Chicago, he arrived home to uncomfortable family conditions. John was still not pleased with his continued direction, but Charles managed to return to his plumbing vocation going into 1877.[61] On the side, he earned a trial with a distinguished local amateur team known as the "Libertys," managed by Isaac "Ike" Fleming, a local journalist.[62] Needed as a pitcher, Comiskey took the pitcher's box at seventeen years of age and usually overcame any regular nervousness to shine . . . but he had his moments.[63] During one unspecific game, he lost control of a fastball which nearly beamed veteran Ed Duffy in the head.[64] Duffy reacted by trying to throw his bat at Comiskey, and it was only thanks to catcher Dan O'Day, who grabbed the bat, that it wasn't heaved. O'Day and Duffy had words, and the former made it clear that if Duffy wanted any piece of his pitcher, he had to go through him. Duffy declined and went back to the plate to continue his at bat.

With Comiskey playing well, the Libertys were right in the thick of the fight for the amateur championship. The *Daily Inter Ocean* newspaper of Chicago acknowledged that his "very swift ball" was "difficult to hit."[65] In June of 1877, the club began to fall apart when several players left for opportunities elsewhere. The White Stockings of the National League, the most high-profile organization in the city, made an effort to scour the amateur ranks for talent and collected several athletes from smaller leagues. Eager to get into the majors, Comiskey received a tryout, but was overlooked by White Stockings manager Al Spalding. The rejection stung, but with humility, he accepted the fact that he still had a lot to learn.[66]

Management for the "Bluff City" franchise in Elgin, Illinois, made up of employees of the National Watch Company, heard of Comiskey's reputation as a pitcher and inquired about his availability.[67] He was offered a flat salary of $45 to play the remainder of their local season, to which Comiskey agreed. He brought along his Chicago friend, catcher Rudolph Kemmler, and the two teenagers assumed the battery role for the Elgin club for 11 games. Teammates George Schaller, Cyrus Wilbur, George Vail, George Bullard, and manager Fred Warren benefitted greatly from the sound abilities of Comiskey on the mound, and the team reportedly went undefeated with him pitching.[68]

The decision was another disappointment to his father, but Comiskey was committed to a career in baseball, and, after leaving for Elgin, his "home ties were severed completely."[69] During his 11 games for Bluff City, he batted .333 with 27 base hits while making nine errors.[70] The club faced off against teams from St. Charles, Lawndale, and Batavia, and occasionally Comiskey returned to Chicago to continue his pitching role for the Libertys. It was 1877 when Charles realized he could play baseball for a living, and even against the strain of his fractured relationship with his father, he was going head-first into the sport, ready to make it or break it.

For John Comiskey, his standing in the world of Chicago politics evolved greatly as he got older and mellowed with age. He was no longer seen as the bulldog of the Democratic Party and complained about many of the ballot-stuffing tricks that used to be employed during his heyday. He feuded with the *Chicago Times*, a publication that was once his ally, spurned bribes, and acted as a peaceful diplomat when chaos erupted around him.[71][72] His trusted word and clean-cut dealings earned him the nickname "Honest John," and he was the living example of changing with the times and rejecting the old school methods of crooked politics that defined the era he lived through in Chicago.

For Charles Comiskey, the road to success was far from being defined. In fact, after Elgin, his next step as a professional baseball player was uncertain. He believed in the prospects of financial freedom away from the umbrella of his childhood home and the life of a plumber, but the exact route was indistinguishable to the teenager. He was willing to give it a shot and follow wherever baseball called him. One of his St. Mary's teammates, LeClaire Magill, later said that as early as Comiskey's time at college, he envisioned that one day he'd be a baseball team owner in Chicago.[73]

"Of course," Magill joyfully admitted, "we didn't take him seriously then."

ENDNOTES

1 *Chicago Daily Tribune*, January 9, 1900, p. 4.
   Interestingly, throughout Charles Comiskey's time in baseball, people occasionally figured he was of Polish ancestry because of his last name. On August 16, 1879, the *Dubuque Daily Herald* had a little fun with an erroneous report that stated he was originally from Warsaw, Poland, and noted from that point on that he would spell his name as "Comiski."

2 John Comiskey's birth year, depending on the source, ranged anywhere from 1825 to 1830. For instance, in the 1860 U.S. Federal Census, he was reportedly thirty years of age, whereas in 1870, he was forty-five, putting his year of birth around 1825. Ancestry.com.

3 Comiskey's exact year of migration from Ireland to the United States is unclear. His obituary in the *Tribune* specified 1848; however, there was an entry in the Ancestry.com records for a sixteen-year-old "John Comiskey" having arrived in New York on the *Colombo* on October 7, 1845. There isn't enough information to prove or disprove this as being him. *Chicago Daily Tribune*, January 9, 1900, p. 4; Ancestry.com.

4 Axelson, Gustave W., *Commy: The Life Story of Charles A. Comiskey*, p. 33.
It is believed that John Comiskey had at least one brother, Hugh, living in the United States Hugh and his wife, Bridget, also lived in Connecticut in the early 1850s, where two of their children were born, prior to moving to Chicago before 1860. Catherine Comiskey, who is assumed to be the mother of John and Hugh, lived with John's family in Chicago in 1860. She was seventy at the time, and young Charles had not even aged a year when the census was recorded in July 1860. See the 1860 and 1870 U.S. Federal Census at Ancestry.com.

5 *Chicago Tribune*, March 3, 1865, p. 3.
Comiskey, as part of a legal matter he was involved with, admitted that he first arrived in Chicago in the "fall of '53." *Commy* and other sources have cited the years 1852 and 1854. In a voter registration record from 1888 at Ancestry.com, it was noted that Comiskey had lived in Cook County, Illinois, for thirty-five years, which corresponds with 1853 as being his year of settlement in the "Windy City." There is no way to know for sure.

6 *Chicago Tribune*, November 15, 1864, p. 4.

7 Chicago vital records for this time period were destroyed in the Great Fire of 1871. In Axelson's book, "Annie Kearns" was said to be from Albany, New York. She was listed as being born in Ireland in the 1860 Federal Census and New York in the 1870 version. Her mother, Honora Kearns, died at the Comiskey home on August 5, 1872. *Chicago Tribune*, August 6, 1872, p. 1. Axelson, Gustave W., *Commy: The Life Story of Charles A. Comiskey*, p. 34. Ancestry.com.

8 Certain sportswriters also relished in calling him "Charles Augustus," which tied nicely with the "Old Roman" nickname.

9 Comiskey named his siblings in a biographical piece written by George S. Robbins in the *Chicago Daily News* and reprinted in the *Sporting News*, December 28, 1916, p. 7. He called his sister by the name "Mary," although she was listed as Francis in census records. In the 1870 Federal Census, she was incorrectly listed as "Frank" Comiskey. Her correct name was Francis Josephine Comiskey and in 1885, she married John M. Sexton. She passed away at twenty-nine years of age on June 22, 1892. Cook County Death Index, Ancestry.com.

10 According to Axelson's book, Comiskey was born at Union and Maxwell Streets in western Chicago. This data matches up with Chicago City Directory information at Ancestry.com, listing the Comiskey residence as being on South Union,

between Mitchell and Liberty Streets. Comiskey talked about the "little frame dwelling at Union and Maxwell" as being his birthplace. *Sporting News*, December 28, 1916, p. 7. In a separate article, Comiskey explained that he was born at 142 Lytle Street, a residence blocks away from the South Union address, just on the other side of the major east-west artery, West 12th Street, now known as Roosevelt Road. *Chicago Daily Tribune*, March 25, 1911, p. 19. It appears that the Comiskey family didn't move to the Lytle Street address until sometime between 1865 and 1869.

11 *Chicago Daily Tribune*, March 5, 1857, p. 1.

12 *Chicago Press and Tribune*, March 2, 1859, p. 1.

13 *Chicago Press and Tribune*, March 3, 1859, p. 1.

14 *Chicago Press and Tribune*, April 19, 1859, p. 1.

15 *Chicago Tribune*, April 18, 1861, p. 4.

16 *Chicago Tribune*, November 15, 1864, p. 4.

17 *Chicago Tribune*, May 21, 1862, p. 4.

18 Ibid.

19 *Chicago Tribune*, October 21, 1862, p. 4.

Throughout the tenure of Francis Sherman as the Mayor of Chicago from 1862 to 1865, the *Tribune* alluded to the fact that Comiskey was really in charge. The newspaper stated that Comiskey had the "ability to lead and influence better men," and that he carried "the Mayor and the Copperhead Aldermen in his breeches pocket." *Chicago Tribune*, February 6, 1864, p. 4. The *Tribune* also declared Comiskey "the most influential Copperhead in the Board," and that he was "in fact, the Mayor of the city of Chicago." *Chicago Tribune*, April 11, 1864, p. 4. It should be mentioned that Comiskey was a member of the "Invincible Club," a Democratic organization that was reputed to hold great levels of power within the political structure of Chicago. *Chicago Tribune*, March 29, 1867, p. 2.

20 *Chicago Tribune*, November 5, 1862, p. 4.

21 *Chicago Tribune*, March 24, 1863, p. 4.

22 *Chicago Tribune*, August 11, 1863, p. 4.

23 *Chicago Tribune*, December 30, 1864, p. 4.

24 *Chicago Tribune*, April 22, 1863, p. 4.

Notably, Comiskey was also elected in 1864, but it is not clear why he was forced to run again only a year after his 1863 victory when the term of an alderman was generally two years. The *Tribune* published a lot of anti-Comiskey material leading up to the 1864 race but Comiskey prevailed anyway. *Chicago Tribune*, April 20, 1864, p. 4.

25 *Chicago Tribune*, October 11, 1864, p. 4.

26 *Chicago Tribune*, April 19, 1865, p. 4.

Comiskey's final day as an alderman occurred on May 3, 1865. *Chicago Tribune*, May 4, 1865, p. 4.

27 *Chicago Tribune*, April 14, 1867, p. 2.

28 *Chicago Tribune*, April 17, 1867, p. 4.

Comiskey beat out Republican Isaac Wentworth to become alderman by 22 votes. Mayor Sherman lost in his reelection bid to John Rice. *Chicago Tribune*, April 20, 1867, p. 4.

29 *Chicago Tribune*, December 17, 1867, p. 4.

30 *Chicago Tribune*, March 4, 1868, p. 2.

The *Tribune*, which was one of his biggest critics, stated that Comiskey "would save what little remnant of credit" he had left by never mentioning the police investigation again after the topic was brought up late in the summer of 1868. *Chicago Tribune*, September 3, 1868, p. 2.

31 *Chicago Tribune*, November 3, 1869, p. 4.

Ward boundaries changed again in 1869 and Comiskey's district became in the "Ninth."

32 *Chicago Tribune*, December 7, 1869, p. 4.

Comiskey was voted into the position by the vote of 37–1. From that point forth he was referred to as "President Comiskey" in the council. In an 1870 editorial, the *Tribune* explained that Comiskey was not reelected, and that the Council, "with one year's experience of him as their President, [should] secure a different sort of presiding officer." *Chicago Tribune*, November 13, 1870, p. 2. Comiskey was defeated in the 1870 aldermanic race in the Ninth Ward. *Chicago Tribune*, November 10, 1870, p. 2. Altogether, he served over nine full years as a Chicago alderman.

33 "Richard's Illustrated and Statistical Map of the Great Conflagration in Chicago," University of Chicago Library website, uchicago.edu.

Also see: *Chicago Daily Tribune*, October 9, 1960, p. 40.

34 *Chicago Daily Tribune*, October 17, 1878, p. 8.

35 *Chicago Daily Tribune*, September 6, 1874, p. 5.

36 John Comiskey was one of the founding members of the Church of the Holy Family on 12th Street in his neighborhood and helped collect money for its construction in the late 1850s. A stained glass window of the church was dedicated to him. holyfamilychicago.org/newsroom/81204ComiskeyRelease.htm. The church continues to thrive today at 1080 West 12th Street (Roosevelt Road). Holy Family Parochial school was headed up by Reverend Thomas O'Neill at the time of Comiskey's attendance, and the building was at the corner of Morgan and Twelfth Street.

37 St. Ignatius College was just east of the Holy Family Church on 12th Street. A detailed description of the school appeared in the *Chicago Sunday Times*, June 22, 1873, p. 2. Interestingly, the school had an impressive 7,000-book library.

38 Archivist Donald Hoffman of St. Ignatius provided details of Comiskey's enrollment at the college, beginning in 1870, in correspondence, December 17, 2012. The school program Comiskey was involved with from 1871–72 was called the "3rd Humanities Class," and from 1872–73, it was known as the "2nd Humanities Class." While called a "college," St. Ignatius covered schooling that would equate to elementary studies all the way up to college level. James Comiskey left St. Ignatius after completing his schooling in 1872. ignatius.org/jesuit_history. aspx.

39 *Sporting News*, December 28, 1916, p. 7.

40 *Sporting News*, December 28, 1916, p. 7.
Comiskey used to work with his father to rebuild the burned-out areas of Chicago. In an often shared story about Comiskey's jaunt into the realm of baseball, one day he strayed away from transporting bricks to either watch or play in a game. When the opportunity rose, he also traveled downtown to see the organized teams play on the larger ball grounds.

41 *Chicago Daily Tribune*, January 28, 1912, p. C1.
Halpin, a catcher who played with Comiskey, became a police officer and rose up the ranks to become Chicago's Chief of Detectives.

42 John J. "Bath House" Coughlin served forty-six years as a Chicago alderman. In 1936, he protested the name change of the road Comiskey grew up on, Lytle Street, because the two had played ball there together when they were kids. *Chicago Daily Tribune*, October 8, 1936, p. 3. It isn't known if Coughlin had any relation to the early Irish leader, Dennis Coughlin, a friend of John Comiskey's.

43 *San Francisco Chronicle*, October 15, 1917.
Hart worked as an elevator man in Denver.

44 *Chicago Daily Tribune*, June 26, 1873, p. 8.
Charles Comiskey said that his mother was the "best friend" he had. *Sporting News*, December 28, 1916, p. 7. Prior to 1880, John Comiskey was remarried to Rose Riley of New Haven, Connecticut.

45 Axelson, Gustave W., *Commy: The Life Story of Charles A. Comiskey*, p. 41.

46 "College" in those days is not like the colleges or universities that we know today. Comiskey would have been enrolled in some type of schooling program that would have given him a degree, probably more closely related to a high school diploma, with some college-level learning thrown as he progressed. This explains the references to college and his age.

47 The school was regularly misidentified as the "Christian Brothers College" at Prairie du Chien. While the Christian Brothers ran the college, it was named "St. John's." Information was provided by Brother Robert Werle, FSC, an archivist of the De La Salle Christian Brothers at the Midwest District Archives through e-mail correspondence between December 11, 2012, and January 8, 2013. Comiskey's enrollment at the school from 1873–74 was also clarified. James McTague was a catcher at the college and worked as a battery with Comiskey. He settled in St. Louis and occasionally talked to the press about his school years alongside the famous White Sox owner. He specifically made note that he caught for Comiskey without using a glove or any other protection. *Sporting Life*, December 15, 1900, p. 6.

48 *Salt Lake Telegram*, January 14, 1910, p. 9.
An article was featured in newspapers across the country in January 1910 that discussed how Father John E. English, an Omaha Catholic priest, "discovered" Charles Comiskey at Prairie du Chien.

49 *Sporting News*, December 28, 1916, p. 7.

50 *Bellingham Herald*, January 23, 1910, p. 19.

51 Documentation regarding Comiskey's time at St. Mary's was located by researcher Abigail Lambke at the Midwest Jesuit Archives in St. Louis. Among

the resources used were school student ledgers from the 1870s, student publications such as *The Dial*, alumni records, and other files that gave confirmation of his attendance, important dates, and other materials. This research was completed between November and December 2012. It needs to be clarified that Axelson's book *Commy* and other publications have alluded to the fact that Comiskey attended the college at Prairie du Chien after his attendance at St. Mary's, when, according to records, it should have been the year before. Other crucial information about St. Mary's was provided by Judith Cremer, Director of the Pottawatomie Wabaunsee Regional Library in St. Marys, Kansas.

52 The 1875 Kansas State Census and the 1880 U.S. Federal Census offered a perspective on the nationalities and birthplaces of the faculty and students at St. Mary's. The students ranged in age from 12–23. Ancestry.com. St. Mary's was about twenty-four miles northwest of Topeka.

53 Many Internet sources proclaim Sullivan's birth year to be 1851. When his passport application to travel overseas was filled out in 1888, his birth date was listed as March 17, 1854. In 1916, it was recorded as March 17, 1856. In 1880, the U.S. Federal Census noted that Sullivan was born about 1853 in Wisconsin, while other resources cite New York or Chicago as his birth location. For one of the most interesting characters in baseball history, Sullivan's early years are difficult to track and nearly impossible to prove as a 100 percent accurate. Ancestry.com. According to the records at the Midwest Jesuit Archives, Sullivan attended St. Mary's for two years, 1873–74 and 1874–75.

54 An 1889 article from the *New York Sun* included part of a conversation between the two in which they discussed meeting at St. Mary's. Sullivan said to Comiskey, "You had just entered college and I was about to finish. We were out in the college yard one day tossing the ball about and I spotted you at once as a likely player, although you couldn't have been more than 14 years old at the time. I put you in to catch that day and afterward told you that I would get you on a professional team when you finished schooling. And I did so, too." Reprinted in the *Kansas City Times*, August 11, 1889.

55 Comiskey explained that he was associated with Sullivan on one team, while his brother Jim was allied with Stark on the other. *Sporting News*, December 28, 1916, p. 7.

56 Magill was another guy who claimed to have given Comiskey his big break in baseball. In 1917, he capitalized on the wave of interest in Comiskey after the White Sox won the World Series and told his story to the press. *Duluth News-Tribune*, October 14, 1917, p. 3.

57 *Sporting News*, December 28, 1916, p. 7.
Comiskey, in that same article, added that his father "didn't figure on [baseball] becoming the nation's greatest pastime, involving the expenditure of millions of dollars and appealing to millions of people as their principal form of entertainment." He declared: "I disobeyed my father on the subject of baseball. I have never regretted it."

58 *Daily Inter Ocean*, April 24, 1875, p. 2.

A newspaper in 1928 mentioned that Charles Comiskey was a pitcher for the Chicago Eclipse in 1875. *Chicago Daily Tribune,* April 20, 1928, p. 25.

59 The "Alert Baseball Association" franchise played in the 1875 season, and it is not known whether Sullivan was involved in the management at that time. Sullivan worked as the team's player-manager in 1876, and performed at shortstop. Also see: *Milwaukee Daily News,* May 5, 1876 and July 23, 1876. In addition to Comiskey and Sullivan, the other players were Parkinson, Gray, Forrest, Harper, Foley, Lee, and Mead. Notably, Mead was also listed on a Chicago "Eclipse" team roster along with one of the Comiskeys in 1875. *Milwaukee Daily News,* September 22, 1876.

60 *Sporting News,* January 4, 1917, p. 7.

61 Comiskey's occupation in the 1877 Chicago City Directory was listed as "plumber." Ancestry.com.

62 The only records of Comiskey playing for the Libertys were from 1877. The book *Commy* stated that Comiskey's first manager was Ike Fleming of the Libertys, when Sullivan would have predated him in 1876 at Milwaukee. Axelson, Gustave W., *Commy: The Life Story of Charles A. Comiskey,* p. 21.

63 Before the days of the pitcher's mound, a pitcher would release the ball while standing inside of a box, which was drawn on the ground.

64 *Sporting News,* November 2, 1889, p. 1.

65 *Daily Inter Ocean,* June 7, 1877, p. 2.

66 *Sporting News,* October 19, 1889, p. 5.

67 *Elgin Daily Courier,* June 10, 1914, p. 10.
   A series of articles about Comiskey's time in Elgin were originally dug up by historian E. C. Alft and obtained through the work of researchers David Siegenthaler of the Elgin Area Historical Society and William R. Blohm of the Gail Borden Public Library, Elgin, Illinois. In 1877, there were two semi-professional baseball teams in Elgin, the Bluff City Squad and the Quicksteps. Comiskey was hired to join the former along with Rudy Kemmler. The club played teams throughout the area, from Chicago to Rockford.

68 Axelson, Gustave W., *Commy: The Life Story of Charles A. Comiskey,* p. 43–44.

69 *Sporting News,* January 4, 1917, p. 7.

70 *Elgin Morning Frank,* May 27, 1883, p. 1.

71 *Chicago Daily Tribune,* April 25, 1876, p. 2.

72 *Chicago Daily Tribune,* October 8, 1876, p. 2.

73 *Duluth News-Tribune,* October 14, 1917, p. 3.
   Comiskey briefly talked about his early ambition of being a club owner, *Chicago Daily Tribune,* December 5, 1912, p. 12.

2

NORTHWESTERN LEAGUE CHAMPIONS

Nestled along the banks of the magnificent Mississippi River, the city of Dubuque, Iowa, was a rapidly growing urban center in the mid-to-late 1870s, and seeing an influx of people from other points on the Illinois Central Railroad. The serene location was ideal for tourists looking to see the beautiful countryside, and especially ideal for young hopefuls hoping to raise a family and benefit from the agricultural and commercial opportunities. The "American Dream" was being realized in Dubuque, and it was quickly developing into a first-class city with a little something for everyone.

The railroad carried many spirited entrepreneurs into town, and one of them was the engaging Ted Sullivan, the pride of St. Mary's College in Kansas.[1] He was commonly seen at his favorite local hotel, the Lorimier, and in early 1878, was motivated by the rumors circulating about the establishment of a local baseball franchise. In March of that year, businessmen met to discuss the potential concept and analyzed the factors involved in such an endeavor. Sullivan, who'd learned many lessons while with the Alerts in Milwaukee, knew what was necessary to run a club and took a dominant interest in the Dubuque faction.

On June 10, 1878, Sullivan was named a member of the Dubuque Baseball Club's board of directors during a meeting at the Key City House and was picked to be the initial manager for the club a few days later.[2] The business would sell 100 shares at $5 apiece, and within a short time, over fifty shares were sold. Notifications were sent out to nearby towns, informing them that a new team was being established, and positive responses came in from a number of cities displaying a willingness to venture to Dubuque to play ball. In the meantime, Sullivan began the arduous task of creating a team from scratch. One of the first people he reached out to was his longtime friend from college; a man whom a local paper called "the most expert pitcher ever seen in this city," Charles Comiskey.[3]

Comiskey joined over a dozen amateurs and professionals who'd now converged on the town with hopes of making Sullivan's club. Among them were Bill O'Rourke, Tom Burns, Frank Byrne, Will Phelan, and Tom Cooney. Little time was wasted in filling in the nine positions and implementing a practice schedule that continued without rest until their first game on July 2, against a "picked nine."[4] That afternoon, the team beat a random collection of opponents by a score of 22–0, but it wasn't considered to be much of a challenge. Two days later, they met the experienced semi-professional Chicago Oaklands on a makeshift field at the Driving Park, and an unimposing audience saw them defeated 6–3, then 8–7 the following day.

During the first game, Comiskey gave up the ball to switch positions with his catcher, O'Rourke, who suffered a serious finger injury, and exhibited fine skill despite the lack of experience behind the plate. Since there wasn't a back-up to step in, it was necessary for players to be versed in the finer points of every position on the field. Before the end of any game, players could be swapped numerous times and, as shown by this example, pitchers could end up catching for their own backstop. Before the end of the month, Sullivan signed catcher Jeff Dolan of Chicago to shore up that spot on the field, and Comiskey returned to the mound with O'Rourke moving to second base.

Organized leagues were few and far between leaving the Dubuque club to compete as an independent franchise. That meant it would essentially meet any challengers from the professional ranks down to ramshackle squads made up of amateurs. During the first few games on the home grounds, local enthusiasts displayed a remarkable appreciation for baseball, and were exceedingly respectful toward opposing teams, sometimes even applauding louder for rivals than their local representatives. People yearned for clean sportsmanship and exciting baseball, and not only did the crowd sizes increase, but the reputation of Dubuque as a pleasurable sports town was widely circulated. There was also the noted factor of baseball becoming a box office draw, and to out-of-town teams, the ability to make money on the road in Dubuque was now a possibility.

The well known Peoria Reds headed for Dubuque and the *Dubuque Herald* promised "one of the finest [games] of the season," on August 6, 1878, despite the outsiders being the heavy favorites. Comiskey threw well—

probably the best of the season—and shutout Peoria through eight innings.[5] In the ninth, however, the latter scored three runs and won the game, 3–1. The press lauded Dubuque's aptitude in the face of a top tier challenge, but questioned Ted Sullivan's role as captain of the team, thinking that Comiskey, Dolan, or first baseman Spike Brady would do a better job.

Even with the press questioning the team's skipper, replacing Sullivan wasn't an option on the table. In fact, he was the heart of the club, and the following day the team's board of directors unanimously voted to retain him as captain during a special session at the Key City House. The *Dubuque Herald*, on August 8, responsibly noted: "Our criticism regarding Sullivan may, and probably was, ill-advised, for anyone who understands the game saw he played his men for 'keeps,' and if he holds them to such an average as yesterday's play, he is worthy of all confidence reposed in him by the management."

The heavens opened up and a torrential downpour kept things lively for a rematch with Peoria on August 10.[6] Comiskey's pitching was hindered by the conditions and Peoria took the victory with nine runs on nine hits against Dubuque's one run and four hits. The ultra-competitive Davenport squad was the next to tour the city and entered with a considerable reputation. Winning and losing was a status symbol in baseball for these towns, and Davenport had already made personnel moves to ensure they had the right players on the field when matching up against the upstart Dubuque. It paid off and on August 15, after 13 innings, Davenport won 6–4.[7]

The sportsmanship between the Dubuque and Davenport clubs was befitting two honorable teams. While at the former, the latter received a special bouquet of flowers and were privy to "unequalled courtesy extended" by the citizens of Dubuque. Davenport captain William Bohn sent a letter of thanks for their treatment, stating that "of all the cities which we know, we would like to make a home in Dubuque." These courtesies were repaid when Dubuque went to Davenport later in August, when Comiskey and his mates were treated to fine entertainment on Offerman's Island.[8] On the field, they were pushed around, defeated 6–0 and 9–4.[9]

Upon returning home, talented batsman Spike Brady was arrested for exhibiting a disturbing aggressiveness toward women on the downtown streets, and it was revealed that the team had fired him a few days earlier.[10] Later, it was said that Brady had been let go because he reportedly sold games, but readers of the *Dubuque Herald* were provided no proof of the claim.[11] The *Davenport Democrat*, incidentally, responded to the accusation:

"The Dubuques were not sold out, but were simply outplayed; they cannot and never could beat the Davenports, because they do not play as well."[12]

The loss of Brady had little effect when Dubuque beat Forest City of Rockford on September 3. Captain Sullivan's time was becoming more and more divided between his business interest and baseball, and he was called away for the game with Dolan stepping in as the team leader.[13] It was also felt by many that Comiskey's arm needed a rest, and a third stringer named Knight stepped into the pitcher's role while Comiskey played second base and accounted for one of the 15 hits in a 9–4 victory. On the negative side, only 200 people were in attendance.

Rumors of the club breaking up in the aftermath of Brady's actions were dismissed, and, in fact, the opposite actually happened.[14] Instead of a mass exodus, there were two new signings. Sullivan had arranged for players from the Peoria Reds to join the team, and not only that, but for the 1879 season, up to a half dozen Peoria players were going to defect to Dubuque, giving the squad perhaps the best team west of Chicago.[15] The addition of Farrell and Billy Taylor were a superlative addition to the team, and the new lineup matched equally with the Milwaukee Grays of the National League in late September and early October of 1878. Milwaukee won both games, but it was the first opportunity for the Dubuque locals to see a league club in their city.

Errors played a big role in both losses, but the twenty blunders racked up by Dubuque in the second game was an embarrassment. Fans in the city were turning elsewhere to spend their money and baseball in Dubuque had lost its luster. The Milwaukee squad, although they'd finish last in the standings, were a team of significant note, and if their appearance couldn't draw an audience, just who could? Officials tried in vain to lure the Chicago White Stockings to Dubuque, but the negotiations failed to produce.

The lack of support was enormously evident when $7 was the full gate at a benefit game for the yellow fever sufferers in the south on October 10, 1878.[16] It was an undeniable fact that the season would close on a low note. While the team struggled, Comiskey did well for himself through all 21 games and ended up with a .905 fielding average, which was second best on the team.[17] While his batting had room for improvement (he batted .170 with 16 base hits in 94 plate appearances), there was no question that he was a major factor in the team's eight victories. Their 13 losses, however, were a disappointment.

All things considered, even with the friendship between Sullivan and Comiskey, the latter's job was not guaranteed going into 1879. The destruction of the Peoria team gave Dubuque a considerable opportunity to pick up talent, and six members of that club jumped sides. With three other players joining the squad—two from Worcester and another from Chicago—that meant the entire Dubuque team was being replaced. Interestingly enough, the situation in Peoria came to a head after the team incurred debts that couldn't be paid. They relied on a last-ditch road trip which was meant to help even things out, but it was a masterful failure. After the club folded, many players were stranded in town still trying to come up with a way to pay off the money they owed for food and lodging.

Sullivan was never satisfied. Despite the incoming talent, he still spent a lot of time on the road during the winter, coordinating games and searching for prospects. One thing Sullivan and Dubuque had to be exceptionally happy about was the signing of Thomas Joseph "Tom" Loftus, a skilled second baseman, formerly of the St. Louis Brown Stockings. Loftus was a baseball genius, a true leader, and without question the next captain of the Dubuque squad. Loftus fell in love with Dubuque, married a local girl, Anna Kirk, in 1883, and had two children (Frank and John).[18] Other than the baseball exploits that called him away from home, he lived the rest of his life in the city.

Sullivan and Loftus also became close friends. Add Comiskey, and they were a trio of the greatest young minds in the business. Loftus invested in two of Sullivan's business schemes; the first being the novel Base Ball Emporium at 530 Main Street in Dubuque.[19] Also known as "Baseball Headquarters," the shop served many functions. In addition to selling all types of playing equipment, exhibiting seating charts for the park, and generally being a great place to run into members of the team, it was a billiard parlor and cigar shop. There were also quarters for players of opposing teams to coordinate their efforts if space was needed. Simply, the establishment was a nice place to waste time telling stories about the sport they loved. Additionally, youths who idolized the players and women looking to catch a glimpse of the athletes were commonly in the vicinity of the locale.

A second venture, the investment in a lead mine in the Dubuque area, proved to be a smart deal for Loftus and Sullivan, and the two made five figures when they sold out in 1886.[20]

The central topic of discussion in January of 1879 was the formation of a Northwestern League made up of a number of towns from throughout the region.[21] In addition to Dubuque, teams from Davenport and Rockford were represented, plus an outside shot for membership from the severely damaged club in Peoria, Cedar Rapids, Marshalltown, and Omaha. Of the latter grouping, Omaha was the only one to successfully put together a playable squad and join the league. Once again, expectations were high and the various hype machines were into overdrive touting the prospects for the new season.

For Comiskey, he still needed to figure out what his role in the Dubuque franchise was going to be. If Sullivan and Loftus already had their team solidified, he had many other playing options; not only in the Northwestern League, but elsewhere. On February 12, 1879, Comiskey returned to Dubuque and received confirmation that the massive overhaul had occurred, and that he was in the running to be the ninth man on the field, or perhaps a backup spot.[22] Sullivan's confidence in Comiskey's value was resolute, and he knew that his friend could play a number of different positions. The *Dubuque Herald* even bragged about his throwing ability, saying that he was "one of the swiftest pitchers in the country."[23]

Between short jaunts to Rockford and Chicago, Sullivan was actively trying to find a more suitable location for home games in Dubuque. Envisioning a field with a large grandstand behind home plate, like in Chicago, Sullivan initially had three choices. He decided on a 600 x 300 foot area between 22nd and 24th Streets (at the time known as Sanford Avenue), just east of Jackson Street.[24]

Loftus arrived in the city on March 10, 1879, and others trickled in a little at a time.[25] Eleven days later, it was announced that Comiskey had officially been named the team's ninth man.[26] At this point, the *Dubuque Herald* citing *Spalding's Baseball Guide for 1879* as the source, claimed that Comiskey had batted .282 the year before with a .937 fielding average.[27] These numbers were far more impressive than earlier reports, especially the .170 batting average that Comiskey was said to have achieved. Comiskey was the only man from the '78 Dubuque team to make the club. Even Ted Sullivan himself was sitting out to concentrate on the managerial duties.

The lineup consisted of Charles Comiskey, Tom Loftus, the Gleason Brothers (Bill and Jack) of St. Louis, the speedster Harry Alvaretta, Tom Sullivan, William Lapham, Laurie Reis, and Charles Radbourn. Bill Taylor would serve as a substitute and play as needed. First baseman Lapham and catcher Sullivan were imports from the Worcester squad of '78, and Reis, who could pitch, had played in Chicago. Everyone else, besides Comiskey, had come in from Peoria. It was expected that Comiskey would occasionally be the team's pitcher, but mostly play right field.

Radbourn, who would ultimately win 309 games in his eleven-year National and Players League career (1881–1891) and was inducted into the National Baseball Hall of Fame in 1939, wasn't initially recognized as one of the team's regular pitchers, but rather as an outfielder.

The improved quality of the Dubuque club and the overall outlook for the Northwestern League itself generated a lot of attention. By-laws, rules, and a season schedule were drawn up, lasting from May 1 to September 1 of 1879.[28] Each of the four teams would play 36 games—72 total—and send $15 each to the league treasurer to create a pennant that would go to the winner of the championship. Another, more contentious, decision was made by the hierarchy of the organization, and that was to remove base hits and errors from the daily newspaper scoring. There was the impression that printing box scores of games loaded with errors would hurt their box office take. Loyalists to the sport hated the change.

Around April 11, Comiskey made his way back to Dubuque from Chicago and joined the club.[29] Practice went into full swing, and the uniforms (white flannel with the word "Dubuque" written in red across the chest, red trim, and stockings) were ordered from Spalding's of Chicago. All ten of the athletes, as a display of their personal code of honor and exceptional dedication to maintaining the integrity of the team, took what was called in the press to be a "total abstinence pledge."[30] They would collectively refrain from ungentlemanly behavior—which included alcohol—and represent the people of Dubuque to the best of their ability. The pledge was repeated mid-season.

The weather was hovering between the mid-to-high 60s on the afternoon of May 1, 1879, the auspicious debut for Dubuque in the Northwestern League, and Comiskey stood on guard in center field, ready for anything.[31] He impressed the audience by his catch of a pop-up and targeted throw to third base to double up a Rockford player. He didn't contribute any hits, but brought his "A" game to the field, and behind Reis' pitching, the club finished with an 8–0 victory. Two days later, Dubuque again conquered Rockford, 9–4, and Comiskey commenced a rally by leading off the eighth with a base hit, advanced on a wild pitch, took third on a hit by Reis, and scored when Jack Gleason smashed a double. It was a banner day for the entire team and it was hard not to be awed by their slick style of gamesmanship.

They were off to a good start and things got even better. During their first road trip, they won six league games: two at Rockford, three at Omaha, and one at Davenport. They also beat a semi-pro squad at Council Bluffs, 12–4. A sportswriter at the *Herald* was enjoying the run, telling the other teams in the league that "Second place is still open."[32] On May 16, the club returned home and was greeted by the Providence Grays of the National League, led by player-manager George Wright.[33] Providence was in the midst of a championship year and defeated Dubuque in an exhibition game topping the latter by the score of 16–2.

Comiskey took a seat on the bench several times during May because of Taylor's solid hitting, but the latter's eight errors in left field on May 21 against Davenport were eye-opening.[34]

In that same game, Comiskey committed a notable blunder of his own when he failed to touch first base after powering a well hit double and was declared out. Nevertheless, the team won their tenth straight in league competition, and followed up with a trio of wins in exhibitions in Wisconsin and Iowa, including a 34–2 victory over a team in Cresco. The unbeaten streak continued until losing their first league game to Omaha on June 3, but with a record of 12–1, they rested proudly at the top of the standings.[35]

Rockford was in second place, and if anyone had a chance to stop Dubuque's clear path to the pennant, it was them. Comiskey and his mates went to Rockford for a June 13 game, and were defeated, 12–3. The *Rockford Daily Register* reported that during the game, manager Ted Sullivan sat in the stands and yelled epithets at the crowd, actions that were "unbecoming a gentleman."[36] Conversely, Sullivan complained to the *Herald* that his team had been "treated disgracefully" by the audience, which vocalized thier insults at the top of their lungs and affected the confidence of his team.[37] The *Daily Register* responded by calling Sullivan's club the "Dubuque Babies," mocking them because they had been scared into a loss by the enthusiastic Rockford spectators.[38]

Despite their outstanding record, Sullivan was experiencing a lot of stress. The recent happenings, compounded on top of business demands calling him away from the game, were becoming too much to deal with. On June 22, it was announced that Sullivan, with great regret, had resigned as the manager of the team.[39] Not so surprisingly, owing to his splendid record, other cities almost immediately inquired about his future plans.

Although the local press sometimes went overboard in their cheerleading for the club, they weren't afraid to let the truth be known when the team played poorly. After a 6–3 loss to Detroit on June 21, 1879, the *Herald* noted that they lost because of their own "carelessness, negligence, and country playing." A few days later, they were back on the road in Omaha and Davenport, but left the latter on a controversial note which threatened their standing in the league.

Without the steady leadership of Sullivan by their side, the team went to the Davenport ball grounds and found that their opponents could only field six players.[40] In the end they were able to pick up a few amateur players and the game went ahead as scheduled. During the ninth inning of an unexpectedly competitive game, Dubuque received a terrible call from the umpire, walked off the field, and left the city that night, forfeiting three scheduled games. Their actions also violated league rules, and officials, pending an investigation, had the unfortunate task of deciding whether or not to punish them (with the most harsh punishment being thrown out of the league altogether). This issue was eventually brushed under the carpet as the season came to a close.

Comiskey and the team found their way back to Dubuque in early July 1879, and Sullivan decided to resume managerial duties in light of the Davenport disaster.[41] Whereas he may have believed the club was a well-oiled machine capable of running itself, it clearly wasn't. By July 6, Comiskey had only played in 13 of the 22 games that season—the lowest of any player on the team—and was batting .224 with a .925 fielding average.[42] His stellar fielding was a constant, regardless of the position. The only teammate with a better fielding percentage was Lapham with .973.

Around this time, versatile Bill Taylor was cut from the team, guaranteeing that Comiskey would play every day and, only nine or ten days after returning to the helm of the club, Sullivan again resigned.[43] Additionally, the first ten days of July saw the disbandment of both the Davenport and Omaha clubs from the Northwestern League, and the turmoil surrounding the Rockford team left little to be desired. On July 10, Dubuque was in Rockford for a scheduled game but a mutually acceptable umpire couldn't be agreed upon, so no game was played.[44] They proceeded to Milwaukee, where they beat up on the local independent team, 13–1.

Rockford, suffering from the same financial problems Davenport and Omaha succumbed to, was on its last leg. Finally, the team officially dissolved and the *Rockford Daily Register* blamed the "reprehensible conduct" of the Dubuque team for the failure of the Northwestern League.[45] The newspaper cited Dubuque's "trickery and bulldozing" as factors in the league's unpopularity and its July 14 edition stated that: "The Dubuques showed themselves pigs, and exhibited a swinish disposition to gobble all the honors of the league."

The last team standing—and the winner of the Northwestern League pennant—was Dubuque with a 17–7 record.[46] Rockford finished in second with a 15–9 record, and Davenport and Omaha had exactly the same record at 5–13. Although the season was mired by controversy and quarrels, it was a proud victory for Dubuque and one they truly cherished.

On July 29, 1879, the legendary Cap Anson-led Chicago White Stockings ventured to Iowa and beat Dubuque, 8–1 before one of the largest audiences of the year—2,000 people.[47] Dubuque pulled a shocker on August 4 when they won a rematch, 1–0, in what was called a "magnificent game" with Radbourn on the mound. Comiskey played second base for the exhibition and Anson sat out because of an illness. Later that week, Dubuque took two games from the well-known African American club, the Chicago Uniques, with the second by a score of 31–0. A number of exhibitions closed out the season, including five games with the famous Rochester Hop Bitters and two losses to the Chicago White Stockings in October.

During the apex of the 1879 season, there was already speculation that the entire club was signed for 1880, and that everyone was coming back for another run at the championship in a reorganized league. That couldn't have been any further from the truth.

The prospective outfit was going to field just three members from the season before: Tom Sullivan, Laurie Reis, and Tom Loftus. Rather than working to keep the nine men together, little was done in that regard and instead management felt that completely retooling the squad would give them the best chances for victory in 1880. Newcomers included John Troy, Charles Eden, John O'Connor, and E. C. Kent. Of the six players imported to Dubuque, most were from the New York-New Jersey area with Eden coming in from Cleveland. As expected, the *Herald* remarked that their city was going to be "favored with one of the best clubs in the country."[48]

Charles Comiskey, the twenty-year-old with big dreams, was now without a team. In fact, an injury to his pitching arm, his minimal batting average, and youthfulness were among the reasons he was purposefully ignored. The stronger elements brought into town were considered sure-fire talent, while he was, to some locals, just a friend of Sullivan's who had made the team because of their friendship. His contributions since 1878 were already forgotten and his future in baseball was certainly in doubt.

As an employee of Sullivan, Comiskey made around $150 a month as a clerk in the local Dubuque news office, and often worked as a salesman of cigars, newspapers, magazines, and even fruit on the Illinois Central Railroad between Chicago and Sioux City.[49] Sullivan's business commitments as boss of at least twelve news agents kept him away from active participation, but he remained a careful spectator, especially while in Chicago, where he was several times a week. While he was out of town, he had great trust that Comiskey could run his business evenly, and felt a certain responsibility in ensuring that the young man would find his way back onto the diamond to prove all the naysayers wrong.

Comiskey's morale was diminished by the turn of events—especially coming off the highs of 1879 and the championship season. Like the other members of the dismantled team, he could have sought placement on a squad elsewhere in the country, but he had a particular fondness for someone in Dubuque that kept him stabilized. Her name was Anna "Nan" Kelly, the third daughter of Lawrence and Catherine Downs Kelly; Irish immigrants that originally settled in Connecticut until moving to Dubuque. The relationship of Charles and Anna strengthened in light of his sudden departure from baseball. Between his job as a clerk and her work as a tailoress, they figured on solidifying their future together with a quiet life somewhere in the city.

Lacking the edge they once had, Dubuque was embarrassed in their home opener on April 13, 1880, by the Chicago White Stockings, dropping the game, 27–0.[50] On top of it, they made 17 errors. The loss hurt attendance in the rematch, which ended with Chicago winning again, this time by the score of 10–1. Dubuque's losing streak continued in Chicago, and a 22–2 result further hurt the confidence of the players and the team's ability to secure future high-profile games. The Dubuque "Reds," as they were called by the press, returned home and committed themselves to practicing for their next major tour two months later against the St. Louis Browns, an independent franchise of some repute. Loftus' team was successful in winning two straight, and then took two more games from Jefferson City, which included a 39–0 victory on June 16.[51]

Despite the renewed vigor, the team was officially disbanded by the Dubuque Baseball Association in July of 1880, as it couldn't secure enough games to sustain the players' contracts.[52] On July 24, 1880, Comiskey returned to the field as a first baseman for the "Easterns," with Sullivan as short, against the "Westerns," comprised of a mixture of professional and amateur athletes.[53] [54] Scoring two runs on two hits, Comiskey led his team to victory, and it was obvious that he was yearning to get back into a regular system of ball playing. Unfortunately for him, baseball in Dubuque was dying a slow death.

During the spring of 1881, another attempt to revive the sport was initiated and Comiskey was elected player-manager.[55] The vote of confidence was a remarkable turnaround after the previous year's snub. Surrounded by names such as Phelan, Lear, Brown, and the ever familiar Tom Loftus, Comiskey and his mates played decent ball and the lineup saw many small changes. In May, Al Spink of the St. Louis Browns sent an inquiry to Comiskey regarding the Dubuque team possibly traveling down river to play a series in the "Mound City."[56] Before that tour could be finalized, Dubuque beat the Ravenswoods, Lake Views, and Oaklands, all amateur and semi-pro teams from Chicago.

Comiskey's fielding remained impressive and he played errorless ball during a three-game series in St. Louis beginning on July 16, 1881.[57] Dubuque was swept by the more experienced professionals, but individually they stood out. Ted Sullivan, who could have been the rustiest player on the field, was lauded for his pitching in spite of the overall result. When the players weren't on the field, the Dubuque squad was escorted to the opera and other entertainment venues, regally honored by Spink and the St. Louis management. Two of the St. Louis victors were none other than Jack and Bill Gleason, the brother duo who'd formerly worn Dubuque colors and were close friends of Comiskey, Sullivan, and Loftus.

There was a lot of chatter amongst managers throughout August and September of 1881, but Comiskey couldn't nail down any game opportunities for the team. In November, Sullivan was back discussing the possibilities of Dubuque joining another new league—this one extending from Brooklyn to St. Louis—named the American Association.[58] Little did Comiskey know at the time that he would be playing for the new league, but not as a member of the Dubuque club. Sullivan made an inquiry to Spink and the St. Louis Browns management about the possibility of Comiskey joining the team.

Later in 1881, Spink agreed to give him a shot, asking Comiskey what his terms would be to join St. Louis. Unsure, Comiskey went to Sullivan, who advised him to ask for $75 a month, much less than he was making between his clerking and baseball play in Dubuque. But Sullivan was confident that Comiskey's skillful actions on the field would quickly earn him much more than that nominal amount. The humble salary request was smart—it guaranteed him a chance to break into a professional league, and in December of 1881, he was signed by the Browns.[59]

His next big game was not going to be on Sanford Avenue in Dubuque, but at Sportsman's Park in St. Louis, and his days of selling cigars and candy while moonlighting as a ball player were over. Comiskey was going full-time and head first into a new phase of his life . . . and his career would never be the same.

ENDNOTES

1 *Dubuque Telegraph Herald*, May 17, 1908.

2 *Dubuque Daily Herald*, June 11, 1878.
   Also see: *Dubuque Daily Times*, June 16, 1878.
   The local Dubuque club was reportedly known as the "Rabbits," but this name was seldom used by local sportswriters. The *Dubuque Daily Herald* was known as *The Daily Herald* or the *Dubuque Herald* during this period.

3 *Dubuque Daily Herald*, June 22, 1878.
   Comiskey's name was commonly misspelled in newspaper reports. "Commisky" was a favorite inaccuracy among scribes.

4 *Dubuque Daily Herald*, July 3, 1878.

5 *Dubuque Daily Herald*, August 7, 1878.

6 *Dubuque Daily Herald*, August 11, 1878.

7 *Dubuque Daily Herald*, August 16, 1878.

8 *Dubuque Daily Herald*, August 27, 1878.

9 *Dubuque Daily Herald*, August 29, 1878.

10 *Dubuque Daily Herald*, September 3, 1878.

11 *Dubuque Daily Herald*, September 7, 1878.
   Brady was the team's first baseman and was said to be from St. Louis. At the time of his departure, he was the Dubuque's top hitter with a .333 average and the club's best fielder. His numbers remained tops through the end of the season, and he batted over 70 points higher than the second best hitter on the team, Dolan, who had a .260 average. *Dubuque Daily Herald*, November 8, 1878.

12 Ibid.

13 *Dubuque Daily Herald*, September 4, 1878.

14 *Dubuque Daily Herald*, September 8, 1878.

15 *Dubuque Daily Herald*, September 19, 1878.

16 *Dubuque Daily Herald*, October 11, 1878.

17 *Dubuque Daily Herald*, November 8, 1878.

18 *Dubuque Telegraph-Herald and Times-Journal*, June 11, 1930.
   When Mrs. Anna Loftus passed away in 1930, J. Louis Comiskey attended her services.

19 *Dubuque Daily Herald*, February 1, 1879.
20 *Webster City Tribune*, February 10, 1886.
21 *Dubuque Daily Herald*, January 7, 1879.
22 *Dubuque Daily Herald*, February 13, 1879.
23 *Dubuque Daily Herald*, February 23, 1879.
24 *Dubuque Daily Herald*, April 1, 1879.
25 *Dubuque Daily Herald*, March 11, 1879.
26 *Dubuque Daily Herald*, March 21, 1879.
27 *Dubuque Daily Herald*, March 5, 1879.
28 *Dubuque Daily Herald*, April 3, 1879.
   Also see: *Dubuque Daily Times*, April 6, 1879.
29 *Dubuque Daily Herald*, April 11, 1879.
30 *Dubuque Daily Herald*, April 20, 1879.
31 *Dubuque Daily Herald*, May 2, 1879.
32 *Dubuque Daily Herald*, May 7, 1879.
33 *Dubuque Daily Herald*, May 17, 1879.
   The victors also got a good look at Radbourn on the mound. In 1881, Radbourn
   launched his Major League effort as a member of the Providence squad.
34 *Dubuque Daily Herald*, May 22, 1879.
35 *Dubuque Daily Herald*, June 4, 1879.
   There was some scuttlebutt about the exceedingly brief report in the *Herald*
   after Omaha ended the winning streak. The two-sentence comment on the loss
   was stunningly different from most game descriptions, and a lot could be read
   into it. However, the *Herald* claimed that due to a large write-up on the Masonic
   meeting, the paper just didn't have room for an account of the game. *Dubuque
   Daily Herald*, June 5, 1879. During the 1879 season, Dubuque press reporters
   were "at war" with newspaper writers from rivaling cities, specifically Davenport
   and scribes for the *Rockford Daily Register*.
36 *Rockford Daily Register*, June 14, 1879.
37 *Dubuque Daily Herald*, June 15, 1879.
38 *Rockford Daily Register*, June 17, 1879.
39 *Dubuque Daily Herald*, June 22, 1879.
40 *Dubuque Daily Herald*, July 2, 1879.
41 *Dubuque Daily Herald*, July 3, 1879.
42 *Dubuque Daily Herald*, July 6, 1879.
43 *Dubuque Daily Herald*, July 12, 1879.
44 *Dubuque Daily Herald*, July 11, 1879.
45 *Rockford Daily Register*, July 12, 1879.
46 *Dubuque Daily Herald*, July 16, 1879.
   Dubuque played 57 games in 1879 and won 43 of them. *Dubuque Daily Herald*,
   September 16, 1879.
47 *Dubuque Daily Herald*, July 30, 1879.
48 *Dubuque Daily Herald*, March 7, 1880.
49 Axelson, Gustave W., *Commy: The Life Story of Charles A. Comiskey*, p. 49–54.
   Also see: *Chicago Daily Tribune*, May 8, 1914, p. 16.

50 *Dubuque Daily Herald*, April 14, 1880.

51 *Dubuque Daily Herald*, June 20, 1880.

52 *Dubuque Daily Herald*, July 24, 1880.

53 *Dubuque Daily Herald*, July 25, 1880.

54 Comiskey, because of his height and wide reach, was a natural at the first base position.

55 *Cleveland Leader*, May 3, 1881, p. 2.

56 *Dubuque Daily Herald*, May 24, 1881.

57 *Dubuque Daily Herald*, July 20, 1881.

58 *Dubuque Daily Herald*, November 27, 1881.

59 *St. Louis Post Dispatch*, December 15, 1881, p. 5. The newspaper spelled his name "Cumisky," and noted that he was "one of the best general players in the country." The *Globe Democrat* spelled his name correctly and explained that Comiskey "won the respect of all, not only by his ability as a fielder, batsman and base runner, but by his steady and earnest play and gentlemanly qualities." *St. Louis Globe Democrat*, December 8, 1881, p. 3.

Also see: *St. Louis Globe Democrat*, December 15, 1881, p. 6.

3

A SENSATION IN ST. LOUIS

There were many memories in Dubuque for Charles Comiskey: especially the memorable championship season of 1879 and the legendary squad of talent that dominated the Northwestern League. He personally recalled the endless baseball stories recited at Ted Sullivan's emporium and channeled each bit of information into a different sector of his memory. He was, after all, still a student of the game. The advice he received, plus the bits of knowledge shared by the more experienced players, regardless of how trivial the instruction, was like gold to him. With his girlfriend Nan eternally supportive, Comiskey ventured to St. Louis with high hopes, ready to accept a new challenge.

Baseball in St. Louis was undergoing a metamorphosis under the leadership of Christian Von der Ahe, a local businessman. Von der Ahe, born in Germany in 1851, operated an unassuming grocery store before changing the direction of his life by leasing the baseball-friendly Grand Avenue Park in 1880.[1] He bought property on the corner of Grand and St. Louis Avenue near the ball grounds and opened up a saloon, anticipating a financial windfall from pedestrians attending games.[2] He also formed a new organization known as the Sportsman's Park and Club Association, which took an interest in the administration of the St. Louis Brown Stockings, an unaffiliated franchise that played its games at his stadium.[3]

Von der Ahe assumed the role of president for the Browns and spent liberally in upgrading the playing grounds.[4] As the leading force in the forward momentum of baseball in St. Louis, he was responsible for restoring the public's confidence after the aftermath of the 1877 scandal which involved several players throwing games for money.[5] The dreadful controversy had a lasting effect on the sport in the city, and to once again draw fans successfully, baseball needed to be spotless in terms of reputation—both on the field and off. Von der Ahe was the face of the new movement, and his players were under the microscope to produce a clean and enjoyable baseball experience for fans.

On November 2, 1881, Von der Ahe attended a meeting in Cincinnati to discuss the formation of a new league, the "American Association of Baseball Players," which also included teams from Philadelphia, Baltimore, Pittsburgh, Louisville, and Cincinnati.[6] For these clubs, it was a fresh start as a separate entity from the established National League and gave baseball enthusiasts in affiliated cities a structured system of competition that had potential to be just as spirited as the League itself.

Veteran outfielder Edgar "Ned" Cuthbert, who acted as director of athletics at Sportsman's Park for Von der Ahe, was named player-manager of the Brown Stockings going into the 1882 season. His aggregation included Eddie Fusselback, George Seward, Bill Smiley, and St. Louis boys, the Gleason Brothers, George "Jumbo" McGinnis, and Frank Decker. Twenty-eight-year-old McGinnis, who, for years played with local teams, was to be the team's star pitcher, and when Comiskey signed on, the press observed his previous work as a hurler and seemed to expect him to serve as a back-up for McGinnis on the mound.[7]

Comiskey's pitching ability dwindled during his years in Dubuque and his arm had lost its earlier zip. He was more confident at first base, but Von der Ahe and Cuthbert already had big Oscar Walker at that bag and wanted Comiskey to pitch and play the outfield. Comiskey was adamant, and marched up to the Browns' owner and demanded to play first base.[8] McGinnis remembered Comiskey's shift to the initial bag a little differently.[9] "The first day [Comiskey] started to play centerfield, he found himself unable to judge a fly ball and asked to be shifted to first base. I told Oscar Walker, our first baseman, to switch with 'Commy.'" That switch cost Walker his job, for 'Commy' played first base thereafter for the Browns.

There might have been truth in both stories. In his demonstration of protest to Von der Ahe, Comiskey was said to have earned the latter's utmost respect, and Von der Ahe was not easily impressed by ballplayers.[10] In fact, he was usually repelled by the behavior of his men and was frequently engaged in some sort of conflict with one or more of his players during the season. Von der Ahe was, at times, a difficult man to get along with and it was easy for an instigator to get the better of him. He'd quickly lose his cool and, in his curious dialect, he would shout and yell a variety of unintelligible words in a mix of broken English and his native German. He prided himself on promoting discipline and he levied so many fines on players for inconsequential matters that it became a joke.

Comiskey was different. He wasn't a troublemaker, and Von der Ahe's association with him matured differently from the others on the club. It was apparent to the Browns' president that his new player was quite distinctive and he'd come to rely on his leadership and advice. Comiskey was the perfect team loyalist and carried the enthusiasm of the St. Louis club to the highest degree each time he stepped on the field. Not before long, he became the team's most valuable player.

Comiskey figured out early on how to avoid detonating Von der Ahe's fury. He accepted his boss's personality defects and when bad news had to be shared, he had the ability to withhold information until the time was right—and when Von der Ahe was in a calm enough state to receive it. While it was hard not to be affected by his loud commentary, especially after a trying loss, Comiskey likely ignored much of Von der Ahe's outrageous spewing and assisted in redirecting the team's focus once the boss was out of the room.

Browns pitcher McGinnis discussed the team's first baseman's role, saying that Comiskey was "the first man to field the position as it should be covered." He made an interesting point that during the 1880s, three of Comiskey's future Hall of Fame peers at that position—Dan Brouthers, Cap Anson, and Roger Connor—were each physically sizable players.[11] They were terrific hitters—among the best in the business—but with Connor standing 6'3" and weighing 220, Brouthers at 6'2" and 207, and Anson weighing in excess of 225 (while being the same height, 6', as Comiskey), their mobility, McGinnis felt, was comparatively limited. Another star first baseman, Dave Orr, weighed a whopping 250 pounds. Conversely, Comiskey was about 180 pounds on his 6' frame and played the base with heightened versatility unlike anyone before; combining his great speed, reflexes, and intelligence.

Simply stated, he was a revolutionary in the field. As noted sportswriter Hugh Fullerton said, Comiskey "showed the possibilities of his position" and was the "first of the really great first basemen."[12]

That being said, the question remains: What exactly did Comiskey do to change the functions of the position?

In his own words, Comiskey said: "I always played my position ten or fifteen feet deeper than the other first basemen, and the pitchers had to get over to cover the bag." The pitchers "could not be sluggish," he added. "If I saw the pitcher was loafing on me, I fielded the ball and threw to first base whether anyone was there or not. Then the crowd saw who was to blame, and pretty soon the pitchers got into the habit of running over rapidly."[13]

Baseball historian Bill James in his authoritative *The New Bill James Historical Baseball Abstract* evaluated the long recycled tale that Comiskey was the originator of playing deep and having the pitcher cover first base.[14] He concluded that it was true; Comiskey invented the practice, basing his assessment on all available evidence and a review of the stats of putouts made by St. Louis pitchers during the era.

A witness to Comiskey's fielding during his heyday, Tom Brown was a member of three different American Association teams between 1882 and '86. He also played in the National League against Anson, the famous manager of the Chicago White Stockings. Brown was quoted in saying: "Never in my life did I regard Anson as a first-class first baseman, fit to rank among the tip-toppers. Anson was always slow in stooping for a low-thrown ball. He was a contrast to Charles Comiskey, who introduced deep playing at the first corner. Comiskey was a careful student of the various batsmen, and had a line on all the right field hitters. When these hitters to right came to bat, Comiskey backed twenty-five or thirty feet from his base, and depended on his pitcher to cover the base. He knocked these right field hitters out of many a hit by deep playing. In practice, he made the pitchers rehearse the play of covering the base, and this work resulted in his having the finest staff of fielding pitchers in the old association."[15]

During the 1882 season, Comiskey proved a natural amongst the fast company of the Association, and it only occasionally appeared that nerves got the better of him. Most of the time, he was sturdy as a rock, handling the bulk of put-outs for his club on a game-by-game basis. After the first 17 games of the season, he was batting .222 with a .970 fielding average, while the Brown Stockings were only winning a few more games than they were losing (10–7).[16] The team battled through various bumps and bruises and Comiskey himself briefly went out of action with a bad leg after an in-game collision.[17] Players had to be familiar with more than one position to cover for their injured brethren, and Cuthbert did his best to lead in spite of the adversity.

The pitching staff was also depleted due to injury, and Comiskey was thrust onto the mound for a July 8, 1882, game at Louisville, where he gave up eight runs on 12 hits in an 8–3 defeat.[18] As the season continued, the troubles for the Browns caused a fall from second place to a battle for fourth, and Von der Ahe went into rebuilding mode for the 1883 season long before the '82 race was decided. He signed pitcher Tony Mullane and third baseman Walter "Arlie" Latham, and cleaned house by releasing Seward (right field, batted .215), Smiley (second base, batted .213), and Fusselback (utility man, batted .228).[19] It was made known that lackluster play by others on the roster would lead to more discharges. However, the *St. Louis Globe Democrat* specifically mentioned Comiskey and Bill Gleason as being two members of the club who'd performed up to standard all season long.[20]

During the afternoon of September 3, 1882, before a mammoth crowd of almost 10,000 people at Sportsman's Park, Comiskey was singled out after the fifth inning and presented with a special, engraved gold watch and chain by fans, acknowledging his spectacular play throughout the championship grind.[21] As a reward for his absolute commitment to the team, he was granted a brief vacation to visit family in Chicago, and his imminent plans to wed Nan Kelly were undoubtedly a central subject of conversation.

Coordinated with a road trip by the Browns, the wedding occurred a few weeks later on September 29 in Dubuque, the day after an exhibition against the local franchise. Charles and Nan were married before Pastor Patrick Burke with teammate Jack Gleason acting as a witness.[22] The story was told in the press that Comiskey was hitched in the morning, played baseball in the afternoon, and kissed his wife in the evening as he left to rejoin the team, beating all previous records for the briefest honeymoon.[23] Despite early reports that they'd settle in St. Louis, the young couple maintained a home in Dubuque.

In 1883, Comiskey's mentor, Ted Sullivan, was named manager of the Browns[24] and immediately went east to secure several big names for his new club.[25] While the present season fizzled out with St. Louis finishing in fifth place (37–43), the talk of renowned athletes Charles Radbourn, Jerry Denny, Tom Deasley, and Jim Whitney joining the club was exciting news.[26] Of the four, pitching sensation Radbourn, a veteran of Sullivan's 1879 Dubuque nine, was the biggest catch. While there was much news on Sullivan's trip, he returned with only Deasley officially signed. Additionally, there was some mention that Tom Loftus, another former Dubuque colleague (and Comiskey's best friend), would be added to the roster but outside of a few appearances for the Browns, the plan fell through.

While Comiskey was considered a rookie in 1882, it was the best season of his short career, and although he hit only .244, his .970 fielding average led the Browns.[27] He received nearly a hundred dollar a month raise from Von der Ahe, while Tom Deasley, George McGinnis, Ned Cuthbert, and Arlie Latham still made $200 or more.[28]

The retooled 1883 Browns included newcomer Hugh Nicol, a speedy, 5' 4" outfielder who had previously played for the Chicago White Stockings, catcher Tom Dolan, outfielder Fred Lewis, and second baseman George Strief. Jack Gleason was ushered out of his third base job for a spot in the outfield but hit a rocky patch on offense early in season and was benched and later released.[29]

The American Association added two teams to its organization during the winter, and one of the new arrivals, the New York Metropolitans, were a great opponent for St. Louis in 1883. Their June 21, 1883, game, which lasted 13 innings, was called the "most exciting contest that has been played in St. Louis for many years."[30] Many times during the year, the Browns displayed unshakeable spirit in coming back from deficits, and proved that they would not accept a defeat until the last strike of the last out. Stunning base running highlighted their efforts, and Comiskey was relentless on the diamond. His energy was contagious, and he was becoming a leader by example with his stellar play.

In addition to the Metropolitans, the American Association also added the Columbus Buckeyes. Even with the new franchises in play, Comiskey's on the field presence was widely regarded. In fact, Columbus manager Horace Phillips was so impressed by Comiskey that he inquired about a potential deal for him, but Von der Ahe rejected the offer.[31] In the meantime, stemming from the great faith Von der Ahe had in him, Comiskey was promoted to team captain, and the twenty-three-year-old was bearing the responsibilities of a much more seasoned player.[32] Even with his age, Comiskey displayed the maturity and the will to be both a student and a teacher of baseball's finer points. His ascension was due to his attitude and workmanship, and his passionate commitment to the sport made up for any physical handicaps in terms of playing ability.

Sullivan's results were proving much more successful than the prior year and the Browns held a share of first place with 19 games to go. (They were 53–26 at that point in the season and tied with the 52–25 Philadelphia Athletics.) His managerial style butted with the personality of Von der Ahe, and the latter constantly interfered with the decision making In his usually abrasive way, Von der Ahe vocalized his complaints about the way Sullivan was enforcing team discipline and the two had a heated argument during the club's stay in New York in late August of 1883.[33] Sullivan promptly resigned from his position and Von der Ahe named Comiskey as the new temporary manager of the Browns.

The race was close until the very end and St. Louis remained only a game behind the newly crowned champion Philadelphia Athletics when the season concluded.[34] Comiskey, incidentally, was laid out by a serious illness in October, and, to make matters worse, he was given the news that Von der Ahe had hired James Williams to manage the Browns the following season.[35] After convalescing, Comiskey joined a make-shift travel winter squad led by Sullivan, and teamed with the likes of Charles Radbourn and Buck Ewing for games in New Orleans. In time for the holidays, he returned to Dubuque and spent some much needed time with Nan, who was pregnant with their first child.

On January 13, 1884, Charles A. Comiskey Jr. was born in Dubuque, Iowa. Sadly, he was exceptionally ill and died less than a week later.

Owing to understandable feelings of loss and yearning to remain with his wife as long as possible, Comiskey was the last man to enter Browns camp in late March of 1884. Von der Ahe's big concept for the new season was organizing a main roster of players and then a secondary team of reserves who'd be able to step in at a moment's notice in the case of injury or suspension.[36] In this situation, manager Williams had eighteen players to work with prior to the start of the new year, with a number of other potential recruits still being signed. Among the additions to the team were pitcher John "Daisy" Davis, outfielder Harry Wheeler, and second baseman Joe Quest. Von der Ahe was determined to give Williams all the assets he needed to win a championship, and the constant movement of talent demonstrated that.

Over the next couple of months, a trio of newcomers would stand out from the rest and establish themselves as significant players in the Browns' machine going forward. The trio consisted of James "Tip" O'Neill, Robert Caruthers, and David Foutz, who were all pitchers but versatile enough to also perform in the outfield. Foutz immediately made an impression, and the twenty-year-old Caruthers, who was such an unknown quantity, proved to be a star in the making. O'Neill was a better hitter than he was a pitcher, and, in time, became the everyday left fielder. Not only did Von der Ahe have high hopes for the trio, but he saw the combination as a solid group to make up for the loss of their star pitcher, Tony Mullane.

The Browns began the season poorly and were finding it difficult to rise above fourth place.[37] It was the exact opposite of what Von der Ahe expected, and he blamed the losses on the lack of discipline. Fred Lewis, who was suspended in September of 1883 for being intoxicated and breaking team rules, was seen as one of the primary troublemakers.[38] When Tom Dolan abruptly deserted the team, the players were noticeably demoralized and their collective attitude translated to losses on the field that should have been victories.[39]

Von der Ahe's wrath was being felt up and down the line, and on September 2, with just 23 games left in the 1884 season (the Browns had a 51–32 record), Williams tendered his resignation. Motivated to ensure his words were being heeded, Von der Ahe took the reins of the club with Comiskey maintaining the field generalship.[40] All the turmoil in the mix of heavy competition caused a failure to improve above fourth in the standings, and that's the way the season ended.[41]

A report in the *St. Louis Post Dispatch* indicated that Comiskey wasn't Von der Ahe's first choice to manage the Browns in 1885 and that he'd tried to hire Jack Chapman, an experienced National League leader, to run the club.[42] Chapman refused the job and eventually joined the Buffalo Bisons 24 games into the season, leaving Comiskey to perform the duties and coexist at the helm with Von der Ahe.[43] The standard approach of management for the championship race of 1885 was built around discipline and stability. Von der Ahe cast out any hooligans and brought in the wise veteran Albert "Doc" Bushong, a catcher formerly with Cleveland, and two players from the defunct Toledo Blue Stockings, Curt Welch and Sam Barkley.[44] He also picked up twenty-five-year-old William Robinson, a 5'6" scrapper who epitomized team loyalty.

Even though Comiskey injured his shoulder and missed part of spring training, he was still able to welcome the new additions to the Browns.[45] With Comiskey at the helm, the team was reenergized into a winning contingent and played every game in harmony without the outside distractions that crippled St. Louis in previous seasons. Beginning on May 5, the Browns went on an incredible 17-game winning streak, boosting their record to 23–5 and took a commanding lead in the pennant race. Being out in front didn't lessen the club's motivation to win, and Comiskey kept their spirits high. When asked about field captains in baseball, Von der Ahe happily replied, "They don't get any better than Charley Comiskey."[46]

While Von der Ahe stressed discipline, Comiskey preached what is commonly known today as "small ball." He thrived on bunting, sacrificing, and base running. He expected everyone on the team to hustle and be versatile enough to do what was needed to win. During the early years of the sport, games were not regularly won on big hits, but rather by getting players on the base paths and doing what was necessary to score runs. That entailed adhering to Comiskey's signals, and when he called for a steal or hit and run, it was an order to be followed. He'd prefer to see a nice sacrifice to get runners over than watch a player recklessly swing for the fences; and it didn't matter who the batter was—a perennial .300 hitter or a guy barely batting his weight. As a base runner himself, he possessed speed and an artistic sliding ability to bend his body out of the reach of the fielder's tag. He illustrated his points to his men by demonstrating what he wanted when he was in the field, and it was hard for the players not to be driven by their leader's eagerness. The games were not about individual records or the number of hits, but about achieving a victory by any means necessary. And with all of Comiskey's hard work and innumerable responsibilities, he was rewarded with a salary around $3,000 for the 1885 season, which was considered above average for the era.[47]

Without question, Comiskey was as hard on himself as his players, and took the majority of the blame for losses, believing every game was a winnable one. During the first inning of a game against Pittsburgh on August 8, 1885, his spirited play in the field caused him to suffer a broken left collarbone and he was not expected to return to the team for the remainder of the season (as both manager and player).[48] He went home to Dubuque to recover and fortunately arrived only a day or so before the birth of his son, John Louis Comiskey, on August 12. Named after his grandfather, John Louis would be affectionately known as "J. Louis" or "Lou" throughout his life.

Once his condition improved a bit, Comiskey rejoined the team as a bench manager and resumed playing on September 15 in a 3–2 victory over Philadelphia.[49] St. Louis was far enough ahead to claim the American

Association Championship, and Von der Ahe immediately went to work organizing a World Series against the National League kingpins, the Chicago White Stockings, owned by the influential Albert G. Spalding.[50] A seven game series was the proposed deal, with both magnates contributing to a $1,000 pot for the winners.[51] It should be noted that these games were considered "exhibitions" and the first official World Series did not occur until 1903.

Darkness forced a tie in the first game at Chicago (called after eight innings at 5–5) and controversy surrounded the second on October 15, 1885, in St. Louis.[52] Comiskey, in reaction to the erratic and unbalanced decisions of the umpire, pulled his men from the field in the sixth inning, effectively forfeiting the game to the White Stockings, 9–0.[53] It was apparent to pro-Browns supporters that Umpire Dave Sullivan was partial to the Cap Anson-led squad, and Comiskey, in disgust, responded to the unevenness in protest. Over the next two days, the Browns stormed out and took two victories from Chicago (first winning 7–4 and then 3–2) and led in the series, 2–1. The White Stockings won the next two games in Pittsburgh and Cincinnati, leaving the series at 3–2, with Chicago in the lead.

A report circulated nationally that an agreement had been reached between the two clubs to throw out the result of the forfeited game, ensuring that the last contest on October 24, 1885, in Cincinnati would be for the championship.[54] Under those circumstances, both teams had achieved two wins, and the last game would settle the championship. Comiskey's aggregation was inspired beyond belief and his Browns pummeled Chicago unmercifully, 13–4, and captured the highest honor in baseball.

Embarrassed, Spalding immediately denied that a decision had been made not to count the forfeited game.[55] In addition, he declared that the series itself, which had been touted as being for the championship, was actually not for any such distinction. The record books, even before they were written in ink, were amended to reflect a tie, 3–3–1, between the Brown and White Stockings in the 1885 World Series.

Following another winter tour of the south, Comiskey split his time between Dubuque and Chicago. It was during his stay in the latter city that he received word that pitcher Bob Caruthers, a 40-game winner for the Browns in 1885, was traveling to Europe in February of 1886 and wanted a significant raise.[56] Von der Ahe was inflexible and flatly refused to meet the athlete's demands. While Comiskey considered the loss of Caruthers and the vacancy it would leave on his pitching staff, he incidentally knew of a potential prospect that just happened to live down the street from his family's home in Chicago.

John and Margaret Hudson lived at 119 Lytle Street, a few houses away from the Comiskey's, with their two daughters and teenage son, Nathaniel.[57] By fifteen years of age, "Nat" was already a ballplayer of promise, coming into his own in the Colorado State and Western Leagues. Now only two years later, the young man was being scouted by Comiskey for the majors. Hudson was certainly no replacement for the battle tested Caruthers, but if he could eat up innings on the mound and do it effectively, his signing would be a success.

Caruthers ultimately agreed to a Browns contract without further dispute. The four-man rotation of George McGinnis, David Foutz, Nat Hudson, and Robert Caruthers was immensely formidable and gave St. Louis the strongest team in its history.

The general methods of the Browns noticeably evolved and their on-field customs inspired national recognition and commentary. It all started with Comiskey's own tendency to argue with umpires, a characteristic that developed through the years to a heightened pitch. He was relentless in his quarrels, bickering over bad calls and accumulating more than $200 worth of fines in a contentious verbal war with umpire Ben Young early in the 1886 season. Others also complained about Young and, shortly thereafter, the umpire was fired by the Association.[58]

It was understood that Comiskey didn't care about "kicking" to umpires at the risk of being fined, as Von der Ahe was paying the financial toll—and not him personally. The excessive complaining about officials and the callous attitude about being punished made many people in the Association angry. On top of that, St. Louis players were developing a reputation as ruffians.[59] In the course of a single game, they could be found purposefully preventing an opponent from throwing the ball, blocking bases, and intentionally being hit by a pitched ball to get on base by crowding the plate. These tricks and various others of the same ilk were overly aggressive in some opinions and completely unsportsmanlike.

Another tactic was perpetrated on a common basis by Comiskey, Latham, and Gleason.[60] Outside the diamond, while the Browns were on offense, they would coach base runners, but in the midst of doing so, became a complete and utter distraction to rival clubs. They would comment on the top of their lungs at times, using catchphrases and other diversionary remarks that affected—and occasionally—rattled opponents. The crowd was amused by the wordy players and enthused by the unusual outbursts. That is, until it became stale and perceived as a nuisance. But the trio didn't care; they kept it up and their scheme definitely made an impact.

Taking away the antics for a moment, the St. Louis Browns were near unbeatable and didn't need the unorthodox techniques to be successful. Comiskey was in rare form and for only the third time in his career, recorded 100 hits for the season.[61] [62] His teammate, "Tip" O'Neill, was leading in almost every offensive category, while the Browns pitchers were logging inhuman numbers with Foutz winning 41 games and Caruthers winning 30.[63] Overall, the Browns captured 93 victories and their second straight American Association title. When the season ended, St. Louis was a full 12 games ahead of their nearest rival.

Another World Series was arranged between the Browns and the National League Champion White Stockings. This time, however, all involved parties hoped for a clear resolution. Anson's slick ace John Clarkson, a 36-game winner and future Hall of Famer, earned a shutout in the first game at Chicago on October 18, 1886, defeating Foutz, 6–0.[64] The next afternoon, the Browns pulled off a shutout of their own as Caruthers dominated in a 12–0 victory. Clarkson worked his repeated magic in game three, and again was victorious, 11–4, giving his club a 2–1 advantage in the series.[65]

The animated competition lost some of its luster as the Browns won the next two games, and on October 23, at St. Louis, finished the White Stockings off with a dramatic tenth inning victory, 4–3, to annex the championship.[66] Curt Welch became an instant legend with his steal of home in what was known as the "$15,000 slide"—the amount in receipts won by St. Louis with the victory. Their achievement was entirely legitimate and there was nothing Spalding could say to diminish their grand success. Comiskey and his teammates were undoubtedly the best in the world.

For what the *St. Louis Post Dispatch* called "a very fair" increase in salary, Comiskey signed a contract with the Browns for the 1887 season, and his income was amply enhanced by a saloon he owned in Chicago.[67] [68] With two

American Association championships and a world championship under his belt, he was one of the most talked about player-managers in the business, and most certainly a coveted asset.[69] While he was indeed coveted, he was still committed to Von der Ahe and moved his family to St. Louis from Dubuque, settling into a home along Grand Avenue.[70]

Many of the Browns demanded a raise going into 1887, with several of them entering into disputed territory with Von der Ahe. Because of this, a number of individuals were signed to brief contracts pending the negotiations with the holdouts. Slowly, Foutz, Caruthers, Latham, and other stars agreed to terms, and the prospects of winning a third straight pennant were improved significantly. Jack Boyle joined the club as a backup catcher to Bushong and two familiar faces, McGinnis and Nicol, were released.

A best-of-nine spring series between St. Louis and Chicago was staged from April 7–14, and the White Stockings won four of the six games played. Three additional contests were also scheduled for the close of the regular season campaigns of both teams to definitively decide the championship.[71] Chicago would be playing at home and needed only one win to regain their lost crown.

Due to deficient pitching support, Von der Ahe went out and signed Charles Albert "Silver" King, a nineteen-year-old St. Louis prodigy, who'd briefly played with the Kansas City Cowboys of the National League in 1886.[72] King's acquisition was an unexpected blessing for the Browns and his marvelous pitching would quickly make him the sensation of the American Association.

Backed by an expert defense, King led St. Louis with 390 innings pitched and won 32 games. On offense, the Browns were remarkable, and it often appeared that they could score at will. Lopsided scores were customary with the likes of Latham, O'Neill, Robinson, Welch, and Caruthers relentlessly pounding the ball to all corners of the field. Comiskey, despite his inadvisably wide stance at the plate and weakness to swing and miss the high inside curve, was in on the action as well, batting .335 and amassing 180 hits.[73] [74] O'Neill was the real marvel, however, as he led the Association in nearly all offensive categories and achieved the illustrious Triple Crown. His batting average of .435 was, to date, the all-time baseball record and he added 14 home runs, 123 RBI, and 225 hits.

The Browns routed their league rivals and their closest adversary in the race, Cincinnati, was 14 games behind at season's end.[75] In the National League, Chicago failed to live up to expectations, coming in third place, and the planned continuation of the spring series was canceled. Instead, St. Louis faced the National League pennant winners, the Detroit Wolverines, in a World Series, best-of-fifteen match-up.

Comiskey, who was fully recovered from a broken thumb on his right hand suffered in a game against Philadelphia in September, was facing a rather different situation than in years past.[76] Whereas the Browns had seemed to naturally avoid inner-club turmoil, the whispers of disgruntled players were becoming louder and louder.[77] Bushong and Caruthers were two of the players alleged to have been peeved by their working conditions and perhaps at Comiskey and Von der Ahe as well. The team also changed certain aspects of its machinery, including considerably cutting back on the vocalized coaching that other clubs frowned upon. With all things considered, Comiskey wasn't leading a spirited bunch into the Series against Detroit, but rather a demoralized unit certain to lose.

And that's what occurred. Detroit dominated by capturing eight victories in eleven tries, and won the championship on October 21, 1887.[78] The overall tally was ten wins for Detroit and five for St. Louis. It was an embarrassing demonstration that was not fitting for the same Browns team that had dominated the Association all year long. The internal strife was acknowledged by Von der Ahe and he wasn't going to sit back and watch his franchise implode.

As Comiskey guided members of the Browns westward on a winter schedule in San Francisco, the owner of the Browns worked deals to sell five of his superstars, Caruthers, Foutz, Bushong, Welch, and Gleason for $22,000 in cash.[79 80 81]

Von der Ahe refused to part with Latham or Comiskey, and as much as $10,000 was being offered for the latter. But the losses sustained by the Browns were enough to spell doom in 1888 and prognosticators were expecting St. Louis to finish no higher than fifth place in the next championship race. Such a scenario was a drastic departure for the successful Browns, and although Comiskey was confronted by an ugly set of circumstances, he was ever the fighter. If he had a say in the matter at all, he wouldn't let the Browns crumble—and certainly would not concede the next Association pennant for fifth place.

ENDNOTES

1 Christian Von der Ahe was born on October 7, 1851 to Christian and Sruisa Pefer Von der Ahe. Missouri Board of Health Death Certificate.

2 *Sporting News*, September 17, 1942, p. 4.

3 The Sportsman's Park and Club Association was incorporated in March 1881. Von der Ahe reportedly bought $1,800 worth of stock in the previously established St. Louis Baseball Association in 1881, which gave him majority control over the Brown Stockings club. Al Spink, a sportswriter, had been a member of the Association and became secretary for the rejuvenated Browns. He was responsible for arranging games for the independent franchise with regional and national competitors. thisgameofgames.blogspot.com, maintained by Jeffrey Kittel.

Also see: St. *Louis Post Dispatch*, October 8, 1881, p. 2, and *Sporting Life*, June 14, 1913, p. 9.

4 *St. Louis Post Dispatch*, April 9, 1881, p. 9.

It was said that $5,000 was invested in the Grand Avenue Park to improve conditions.

5 The controversy involved players Jim Devlin, George Hall, Al Nichols, and William Craver, members of the Louisville club, who were banned from professional baseball for crookedness in making a deliberate effort to lose games. The revival of baseball in St. Louis was discussed in the *St. Louis Post Dispatch*, January 25, 1882, p. 5.

6 *Cincinnati Daily Gazette*, November 3, 1881, p. 11.

7 *St. Louis Globe Democrat*, December 18, 1881, p. 16.

8 *Sporting News*, September 17, 1942, p. 4.

9 Spink, Alfred H., *The National Game* (1911), p. 178.

10 Baseball owners were confronted by distracting personalities, heavy drinkers, gambling problems, and a general lackluster allegiance by players to their own ball clubs during the 1880s. There were the same types of player-owner disagreements over salaries that were later seen in the early 1900s and guys who begrudged management for their perceived financial slight. Behavior troubles and rowdiness were difficult issues to manage if owners did not take a direct and severe approach to the difficulties. Von der Ahe was known to dole out harsh punishments but sometimes his reprimands were excessive or for trivial things, which only turned his players against him. Comiskey lived a restrained lifestyle and saved his aggression for the ball field.

11 Spink, Alfred H., *The National Game* (1911), p. 178.

12 *Chicago Daily Tribune*, February 4, 1906, p. A2.

13 *Patriot* (Harrisburg, Pennsylvania), September 10, 1901, p. 8.

14 James, Bill, *The New Bill James Historical Baseball Abstract*, p. 42.

15 *St. Paul Globe*, June 7, 1897, p. 5.

At the time of his comments, Brown was still playing major league baseball and managing the Washington Senators. During the 1880s it was common to draw comparisons between the fielding of Cap Anson of Chicago and Comiskey, particularly surrounding their championship series in 1885 and '86. Anson, far and away, was the better hitter.

16 *St. Louis Globe Democrat,* June 10, 1882, p. 12.

17 *St. Louis Globe Democrat,* June 26, 1882, p. 3.

He missed the June 25 game due to his injury. According to baseball-reference. com, he only missed one or two games of the 80 scheduled during the entire season.

18 *St. Louis Globe Democrat,* July 9, 1882, p. 4.

Comiskey's throwing was called "wild and irregular all through," but the faded condition of his arm was the reason he wasn't pitching regularly. The Browns tried a number of pitchers during the season, including Shappert, Hogan, Doyle, Mitchell, and Dorr, but McGinnis proved to be the only mainstay.

19 *St. Louis Globe Democrat,* August 5, 1882, p. 7.

Mullane, who was the ace of the Louisville staff, signed with the Browns for $250 a month for the 1883 season.

20 *St. Louis Globe Democrat,* August 24, 1882, p. 7.

21 *St. Louis Globe Democrat,* September 4, 1882, p. 3.

The newspaper indicated that a "more deserved tribute was never paid to a player."

Also see: *St. Louis Post Dispatch,* September 4, 1882, p. 8.

22 Dubuque County Marriage Records, Carnegie-Stout Public Library, Dubuque, IA; research by Amy Muchmore, Adult Services Librarian. Notice of the marriage was made in the *St. Louis Globe Democrat* on September 29, 1882, p. 5 and the *St. Louis Post Dispatch,* same date, p. 8. It is unknown whether Comiskey's other teammates attended the ceremonies, although the team reportedly returned to St. Louis on September 30, making it certainly possible that they did. Gleason's name was specifically mentioned in the Dubuque marriage records as having attended, along with another individual, "Mary Kelly," who may have been Nan's sister. The aged record was difficult to decipher.

23 *St. Louis Globe Democrat,* October 1, 1882, p. 20.

24 After the 1882 season, the team changed their name from the Brown Stockings to the Browns.

25 *St. Louis Globe Democrat,* September 24, 1882, p. 6.

26 The Cincinnati Red Stockings won the American Association championship in 1882, finishing with a 55–25 record. Philadelphia came in second and Louisville third. St. Louis ended in fifth place with a 37–43 record.

27 *St. Louis Globe Democrat,* October 11, 1882, p. 5.

28 *St. Louis Post Dispatch,* June 29, 1883, p. 5.

Tom Deasley was the highest paid player on the Browns in 1883, making $250 a month. Comiskey was earning $171 monthly.

29 *St. Louis Post Dispatch,* May 19, 1883, p. 8.

There was some speculation whether John's brother Bill Gleason would also leave the Browns, but he remained.

30 *St. Louis Post Dispatch,* June 22, 1883, p. 3.

St. Louis was defeated by the Metropolitans by the score of 2–1.

31 *St. Louis Post Dispatch*, May 19, 1883, p. 8.

32 It is unclear exactly when Comiskey was promoted to "Captain" of the St. Louis Browns, and it may have taken place prior to the 1883 season. The earliest reference located was when he was referred to as "Capt. Comiskey" by the *St. Louis Post Dispatch*, July 18, 1883, p. 8. In an interview, Ted Sullivan said that Comiskey received an additional $600 for his labor as team captain in 1883. *Dubuque Herald*, January 13, 1884, p. 3.

33 *St. Louis Post Dispatch*, August 31, 1883, p. 8.

34 Philadelphia finished the season with a 66–32 record and St. Louis came in second with 65 wins and 33 losses. Tony Mullane was the team's foremost winner on the mound with 35 victories versus 15 losses and George McGinnis had a record of 28-16. Baseball-reference.com. Following the departure of Sullivan, the team went 12–7 under the management of Comiskey.

35 *St. Louis Post Dispatch*, October 27, 1883, p. 5.
    Williams was the secretary of the American Association and exceptionally knowledgeable about the game. Von der Ahe convinced Williams to join the team at a salary of $2,500, which was $500 more than Columbus had offered him.

36 *St. Louis Post Dispatch*, November 1, 1883, p. 2.

37 *St. Louis Post Dispatch*, July 5, 1884, p. 8.

38 *Boston Herald*, September 18, 1883, p. 4.

39 *St. Louis Post Dispatch*, August 25-26, 1884.
    Dolan complained about a lack of playing time over catcher Tom Deasley, prompting him to leave the Browns and, essentially, break his contract.

40 *St. Louis Post Dispatch*, September 4, 1884, p. 4.
    Comiskey has been commonly regarded as the manager of the Browns after the departure of Williams. However, it appears that Von der Ahe maintained tighter control over his club than usual, and at least coexisted with Comiskey at the helm of the franchise.

41 The New York Metropolitans won the American Association championship of 1884. Columbus came in second, Louisville third, and St. Louis fourth with a 67–40 record. Baseball-reference.com. Comiskey played in 108 games, had 109 hits, and ended the season with a batting average of .237. His .969 fielding average was again the best on the Browns.

42 In five season as a National League manager, Chapman had a 127–194 record (.396 winning percentage).

43 *St. Louis Post Dispatch*, March 21, 1885, p. 11.

44 *St. Louis Post Dispatch*, May 18, 1885, p. 5.
    The newspaper noted that the Browns didn't have "a single lusher" on the team, and that "their work shows it, too."

45 *St. Louis Post Dispatch*, April 13, 1885, p. 7.

46 *St. Louis Post Dispatch*, July 4, 1885, p. 10.

47 *St. Louis Post Dispatch*, July 11, 1885, p. 10.

48 *St. Louis Post Dispatch*, August 10, 1885, p. 5.

49 *Philadelphia Inquirer*, September 16, 1885, p. 3.

50 The Browns captured the American Association championship in 1885 with a 79–33 record. Cincinnati, the second place club, was 16 games back at the close of the season; baseball-reference.com.

51 *St. Louis Post Dispatch,* October 1, 1885, p. 8.

52 *Chicago Daily Tribune,* October 15, 1885, p. 6.
   The game ended at 5–5 at the end of the eighth inning.

53 *St. Louis Post Dispatch,* October 16, 1885, p. 8.

54 *Chicago Daily Tribune,* October 25, 1885, p. 11.
   The paper acknowledged that the St. Louis Browns were "Now Champions of the World." This result was also printed in *Sporting Life,* November 4, 1885, p. 2.

55 *Chicago Daily Tribune,* October 26, 1885, p. 2.
   Also see: *Sporting Life,* November 11, 1885, p. 3.

56 *St. Louis Post Dispatch,* February 15, 1886, p. 1.
   Caruthers wanted a $5,000 contract for 1886 and $3,000 in advance.

57 The Hudsons moved to Lytle Street in the early 1880s, as they had resided on East Indiana when the 1880 U.S. Federal Census was taken. Ancestry.com. Also see *Daily Inter Ocean* (Chicago, Illinois), September 1, 1887, p. 8 and the *Chicago Daily Tribune,* December 8, 1910, p. 11. Regarding the Hudson family, after his father John died suddenly in March of 1887, Nat was relied upon by his siblings to handle the crisis as his mother was also deathly ill. This caused uproar within the management of the Browns when Hudson delayed reporting and it was said that he was holding out for more money. He finally joined the team about a month into the 1887 season and his mother died that August. *Sporting News,* March 26, 1887, p. 5 and *St. Louis Post Dispatch,* May 25, 1887, p. 3.

58 *St. Louis Post Dispatch,* May 7, 1886, p. 5.

59 *St. Louis Post Dispatch,* May 17, 1886, p. 5.
   Also see: *St. Louis Post Dispatch,* June 10, 1886, p. 8.
   The latter article mentioned that Von der Ahe was refusing to pay the fines chalked up by his club and threatened to leave the American Association because of perceived unfair treatment. It was said that he was encouraging "ruffianism." Von der Ahe eventually paid the fines of Comiskey to settle the matter. One newspaper claimed that his fines amounted to $260; *Cincinnati Enquirer,* June 10, 1886, p. 2. In 1887, Cleveland manager Jimmy Williams wanted Comiskey's actions put to an end. Comiskey responded by saying that all was fair in war and baseball and that anything should be done to win a game. He went as far as to say that if he was allowed to tie an opponent up by his thumbs to prevent him from getting to a base, he'd do it. As for those who called him unsportsmanlike or a "hoodlum" for his on-field conduct, he didn't care because it was all part of the game. Off the diamond, he was a gentleman; *St. Louis Post Dispatch,* April 30, 1887, p. 12. Comiskey admitted playing a "rough-and-tumble game." *Sporting Life,* August 12, 1885, p. 4. Rough play and spiking was part of baseball culture in the '80s and '90s.
   Also see: James, Bill, *The New Bill James Historical Baseball Abstract.*
   Comiskey provided vast insight into his perspective of baseball in the *Sporting News,* April 27, 1889, p. 2. He said: "A winning team is made up of players who will 'turn tricks' when they see a chance—men who study points and work every

advantage to win. All is fair in love and in war, and the same may be said of base-ball. It is all right for a player to acquire the reputation of being a gentleman both on and off the field, but you can bet that when he stands ace high with his opponents, he is not giving his club much service. I go on a field to win a game of ball by any hook or crook. It is the game we are after, not reputations as society dudes. Now, understand me. I do not indorse leg-breakers, brutes and ruffians, who expect to win by injuring someone or indulging in profanity. There is nothing in such treatment. The St. Louis team never sent any players to the hospital. I do not indorse work of that kind. I instruct my men, however, to turn a trick every time they get a chance. I think that is part of the business. It is not so much in taking advantage of your opponents as it is getting away with it. I always make it a point to encourage a young player, especially a pitcher, and all the other members of my team do the same thing."

60 *St. Louis Post Dispatch*, July 24, 1886, p. 12.

61 *St. Louis Post Dispatch*, August 2, 1886, p. 7.

62 Comiskey collected 147 hits in 1886, and previously went over the 100-hit mark in 1883 (118) and 1884 (109).

63 St. Louis finished with a 93–46 record. Pittsburgh came in second place, possessing a record of 80–57. Comiskey batted .254 and had 147 hits on the year. He again led the team in fielding with a .972 average; baseball-reference.com. The Eugene Jaccard's jewelry company gave Comiskey a special medal for being tops in fielding amongst the Browns. *Sporting News*, October 18, 1886, p. 5.

64 *Chicago Daily Tribune*, October 19, 1886, p. 2.

65 *Chicago Daily Tribune*, October 21, 1886, p. 2.

66 *Chicago Daily Tribune*, October 24, 1886, p. 10.

67 *St. Louis Post Dispatch*, November 20, 1886, p. 10.

68 *Sporting Life*, February 17, 1886, p. 5.

69 *Sporting News*, February 5, 1887, p. 6.

70 *Sporting News*, February 26, 1887, p. 5.
A year later, his family moved down Grand Avenue, a little closer to the park and into a stone-front domicile. *St. Louis Post Dispatch*, March 20, 1888, p. 8. Another report claimed that Comiskey moved into "one of President Von der Ahe's new houses." *Sporting Life*, November 7, 1888, p. 3.

71 *St. Louis Post Dispatch*, April 21, 1887, p. 8.
There were reports that Chicago regained the world's championship following their four wins over the Browns in April 1887. However, that series was not yet completed, and Chicago needed one additional victory to officially claim the title.

72 *St. Louis Post Dispatch*, April 25, 1887, p. 5.

73 *St. Louis Post Dispatch*, July 24, 1886, p. 12. *Sporting News*, December 20, 1917, p. 8.

74 The 1887 season was the only time Comiskey would ever hit over .300. He finished his career with a .264 average in thirteen seasons.

75 St. Louis finished the 1887 season with a 95–40 record and won its third straight American Association championship. Cincinnati came in second with a record of 81–54; baseball-reference.com.

76 *St. Louis Post Dispatch*, September 13, 1887, p. 8.

77 *St. Louis Post Dispatch*, October 2, 1887, p. 10.

78 *Detroit Free Press*, October 22, 1887, p. 2.

79 A winter series of games was played at the Haight Street ball grounds in San Francisco involving representatives from Chicago, New York, St. Louis, and the local champions of the California league. Impressive crowds watched games from late November into December 1887, but the popularity waned into January 1888. During the vacation, Comiskey and Latham reportedly got into a physical altercation and Comiskey walked away with a "beautiful black eye." *Daily Inter Ocean*, January 29, 1888, p. 10. Latham said the talk of a fight was "all nonsense," and that he and Comiskey were "old friends and never had a fight in our lives." He also said: "Arthur Irwin, Bushong, and Comiskey had their families out west with them. Well, all their children got the measles together and Irwin thought that one of his was going to die. One doctor was attending to all of them, and he was taken down with black small pox and died in one week. The children finally got well." *St. Louis Post Dispatch*, January 28, 1888, p. 8.

80 *St. Louis Post Dispatch*, December 29, 1887, p. 8.

81 Von der Ahe sent Caruthers, Foutz, and Bushong to the Brooklyn Bridegrooms, and Welch and Gleason to the Philadelphia Athletics.

4

FROM MANAGER TO MAGNATE

Chris Von der Ahe, naturally, was the least popular man in St. Louis following the sale of five of his high-quality players. Yet for the athletes themselves who were being transferred elsewhere, they were content to be getting away from the contentious atmosphere created by the Browns' owner.[1] The decision had serious consequences for the club's future, but in Von der Ahe's opinion, he felt it was best to eliminate his problematic stars before their negative attitude destroyed the team. One newspaper claimed Charles Comiskey was "dead sore" at his boss for his impromptu actions and probably figured there was a better way to handle the situation that would've maintained the Browns' strength in 1888.[2]

In some minds, Von der Ahe killed baseball itself in St. Louis with his ill-advised deeds, and there was no way to resurrect his franchise with a bunch of unproven youngsters. But Von der Ahe expected a lot out of Comiskey and believed in his ability to transform players—regardless of their talent level—into winners. The new crop included outfielders Tom McCarthy and Harry Lyons, infielders Joe Herr and James McGarr, and catcher John Milligan. On the mound, Nat Hudson and Charles "Silver" King were joined by Ed Knouff and James Devlin.

The core of Charles Comiskey, Tip O'Neill, William Robinson, and Arlie Latham were resolute in their determination and led the Browns to five-straight wins over the world champion Detroit Wolverines during the first part of April 1888.[3] Although they were exhibition games, it was a clear signal that St. Louis wasn't going to roll over and die. Once the American Association race commenced, the strenuous effort of the Browns continued and a number of sportswriters who predicted their failure were forced to eat crow. A co-owner of the Baltimore club, B. F. Farron, told Von der Ahe:

"Say, Chris, if you were to pick up the thrown-aside talent of any club in the country, you and Comiskey would make winners out of them."[4] In a different report, it was remarked that Comiskey could gather a team of farmers and still win the title.[5]

Many people credited Comiskey with being the best manager in the country and what he was able to do in keeping St. Louis a contender was remarkable. Favored to win the Association title, the Brooklyn Bridegrooms, who had acquired three of Von der Ahe's castoffs, were the best team in the league through the latter part of June. . . . But Comiskey's men never gave up their fight and stampeded their way into the lead. Comiskey's intensity was never sharper and each game was played like it was the final of a championship series. However, there was a negative side to his ferocious attitude that became public in June of 1888.

After a heartbreaking 2–1 loss to Cincinnati on June 19, Comiskey unloaded on his players in the clubhouse and, according to the *St. Louis Post Dispatch*, his booming voice was "sentimental and full of tears."[6] He prodded O'Neill for a costly mistake and then focused on the twenty-two-year-old Harry Lyons. Along with Robinson and Latham, Comiskey got on the young man's case for not bunting the ball when told to do so. It wasn't borderline abuse, but a full-scale gang-style attack, and Lyons was so distraught by the confrontation that he wrote a letter to his father telling him he wanted to quit the Browns and return to his Pennsylvania home.[7]

"Why, I was never more surprised at anything in my life than when I read Lyons' childish effort," Comiskey later told a reporter. "I have done everything to encourage him, have reasoned with him and showed him the practical results of the system pursued by me for the past six years in the management of my men. I want him to 'sacrifice' wherever he has the chance and advance men on bases, but up to date, he has persistently refused to do it. As for any attempt to browbeat him, or keep him back in any way, there has been nothing of the kind done. When a ball player signs a contract to play with us, he does so with the understanding that he is to play ball to win at all times, obey the rules of the club, and follow out the instructions given him."[8]

He then added: "Let him carry out his threat of going home to his father. I hardly think the Browns will disband or fall to the rear in the race if Lyons goes home."

Von der Ahe admitted that he'd never heard a player talk about maltreatment by Comiskey. He was quoted with the following response: "Go ask

Welch, Gleason, Caruthers, Foutz, and Bushong what they think of Comiskey's management and whether or not they would not be glad at any time to play ball again under him. If Lyons wants sympathy, he is going about it the wrong way to get it."

The turmoil period was brief and Lyons remained with the Browns through the end of the season. For Comiskey, the negative stories highlighted his blistering frustrations with even a single defeat, his towering expectations of his athletes, and how seriously he enjoyed the competitive nature of baseball. His line of approach in dealing with players, particularly when overly agitated by a close defeat, wasn't always pleasing on the morale of those selected recipients.[9] He was much more reasonable in his teachings at any other time, not including those instances when his emotions got the better of him.

The Browns added Elton Chamberlain, a youthful right-hander formerly of the Louisville Colonels in September, and made a mad dash for their fourth straight Association championship.[10] With all the turmoil and issues both on and off the field, the Browns were, by season's end, able to achieve that honor. Hudson, a reliable hurler during the season, dropped off the roster due to injury as the Browns entered the World Series against the New York Giants in October of 1888. His loss, combined with less than stellar performances by a majority of the club, provided a 6–4 Series defeat for St. Louis.[11]

The publication *Sporting Life*, mentioned that, prior to the games, Von der Ahe made it known that he was going to give each player a $200 bonus check for their participation in the contests, win or loss.[12] But once it was over, no money was turned over, and it was blamed on a misunderstanding; albeit one that did more to demoralize the players than anything else. It was also explained that Von der Ahe's salary list was over $40,000 for 1888 and that he fully expected to reduce wages the following year.

Despite the Series loss, Comiskey's friends arranged a special tribute for him at the Grand Opera House in St. Louis on November 5, 1888, and the *Sporting News* called it the "most substantial testimonial ever given a professional player."[13] In addition to a lengthy speech by his pals extolling his virtues, he was presented with a gold ball holding $500 in $20 gold pieces. When it was his turn to speak, Comiskey talked only for a short time, enough to thank everyone who'd contributed. He also relayed his intentions to win a fifth straight American Association title, plus a World Series championship to boot. His never-failing enthusiasm was roundly appreciated.

During the offseason, Comiskey spent $2,200 to purchase a 25 x 111 foot range of land from his father, directly next to his childhood home on Lytle Street.[14] He immediately became engrossed in the construction of a three-story flat building on that piece of property and remained in Chicago as many of his teammates began to report for spring training in St. Louis.[15] Upon arrival, he was confronted with another new class of signees brought in by Von der Ahe to strengthen the club. William "Shorty" Fuller was to fill the weak shortstop position and Charles Duffee joined O'Neill and McCarthy in the outfield. Other newcomers who failed to produce were released.

The Browns started the 1889 season like a team possessed and commanded the first place position in the Association standings. As expected, Brooklyn was right on their heels and playing top-notch baseball. The rivalry was not only fiery on the field, but off as well, as Brooklyn owner Charles Byrne engaged Von der Ahe in a public war of words and their competition became immensely personal. By mid-season, St. Louis kept up their first place tempo, but began to face a series of odd problems starting with the claim that Arlie Latham, the longtime Browns' veteran, had been hanging out with a known gambler and allegedly worked to throw games.[16]

Sometimes rumors and innuendo were enough to displace a winning team, and the talk against Latham was detrimental to the momentum of the Browns. Nat Hudson was also becoming more of a problem, and Von der Ahe dealt with that situation by trading him to Louisville for Tom Ramsey.[17] The Browns' owner then received a $10,000 offer for Comiskey from Cincinnati and had to deny the gossip that he was moving his franchise to Washington, D.C.[18] A contentious near riot at Brooklyn that nearly saw several players injured and speculation about biased umpires added into a single melting pot that aided in the destabilization of the franchise on its march toward its fifth straight championship.[19]

Brooklyn overtook St. Louis in the standings, but the race remained close. Trying desperately to ensure the pennant, Brooklyn players began paying money to the opponents of the Browns as an extra incentive to win.[20] That news infuriated Von der Ahe and it seemed that he took out much of his frustrations on his own players. He levied suspensions on Latham and King for various infractions and had verbal spats with Chamberlain and Robinson. It was turning out to be an impossible situation with so many extenuating factors. Finally, Brooklyn eked out the pennant and a major chapter in St. Louis sporting history was coming to a close.[21]

For months, the Brotherhood of Professional Baseball Players (a union of National League ballplayers) fumed over the actions of owners to establish a salary classification system that narrowly segregated athletes into categories based on irregular logic.[22] Other grievances added to the increase of animosity and eventually led to a full-fledged mutiny by players in efforts to charter their own course outside the greedy will of League magnates. Nearly every single member of the National League joined the Brotherhood (also called the Players' League) and agreed to participate in a new, eight-team organization for the 1890 season. Leaders of the union found financial backers, arranged for ball grounds, and prepared for an all-out war against the National League.

Comiskey was asked what he thought about the Brotherhood movement and responded by saying, "I hope the Brotherhood will succeed in their fight." He added that he wanted to "see [Chicago White Stocking owner Al] Spalding knocked out," but denied he was leaving the Browns to join the faction.[23] That statement conflicted with a news item published in early November of 1889 that claimed Comiskey was, in fact, a member of the Brotherhood—joining the Chicago franchise as captain.[24]

Another winter tour was arranged for late 1889 and a combination of St. Louis players journeyed into Colorado and Texas.[25] While in Galveston, Comiskey frankly admitted that he was not going to rejoin the Browns and that he planned on becoming a member of the Brotherhood in Chicago.[26] He said: "I think the American Association is dead. I have played for many years in first-class company, and after attaining a leading position in the profession, I do not relish the idea of dropping into a second-class organization. Von der Ahe has made a mint of money with the St. Louis club, and while the dissolution of the Association will be a severe loss to him, he really has no kick coming."

On January 15, 1890, in a letter published in various newspapers, Comiskey officially announced that he was leaving the St. Louis Browns.[27] He explained that he had personal reasons for going to Chicago, specifically mentioning his family and the fact that he was raised there. Additionally, he was completely on the side of the players in their fight against the leaders of baseball, citing the reserve and classification rules as being against the best interests of athletes. He made mention of another aspect of his motivation, and that was the bad blood between himself and Von der Ahe, who was not named personally in the missive. Comiskey did say, "My relations with the management of the St. Louis club have during the last year been so unpleasant that I do not care to renew them."

Von der Ahe, of course, bitterly responded to the defection of Comiskey, saying: "There is a mistaken idea prevalent among baseball people that Comiskey was the entire St. Louis team in himself and that the club's success in the past was due entirely to his skill as a player and a field captain. Comiskey was no more to me than any of my other players, and I will show these people that I can successfully run a baseball team without him. In one respect, I am glad I am rid of him. Owing to his ugly temper and quarrelsome disposition on the field, he kept me in hot water all the time. No, I am not sorry Comiskey deserted me; neither do I mourn the loss of the other players who have been so ungrateful to me."[28]

He also added that Comiskey wasn't the one managing the team, and that he "allowed him to gain newspaper notoriety by claiming that he did."

The mutterings of Von der Ahe were inconsequential and after Comiskey signed a three-year Brotherhood contract to manage, captain, and play first base for the Chicago franchise, he solely focused on his new responsibilities.[29] In charge of a team of all-stars made up of former League and Association players, he was accountable for making them work together in harmony—a terrifically tough job. The roster included Silver King, "Tip" O'Neill, Arlie Latham, Mark Baldwin, Hugh Duffy, Ned Williamson, Fred Pfeffer, Frank Dwyer, and Jimmy Ryan. The men were professionals, but once the season got going, inklings of chaos became apparent.

Factions bloomed amongst the players, dividing the men up into cliques and hindering teamwork.[30] Like schoolchildren, they refused to talk to each other at times and did the bare minimum to earn their salaries. One group took stock in the belief that Comiskey was biased toward his fellow St. Louis brethren and others completely disregarded the manager's signals while on the field. Being out of shape was common as well. Altogether, the absence of discipline—a hallmark of Comiskey's managerial strategy—despite his best efforts to rectify the situation, eventually condemned the club to an unsuccessful pennant run.

In late August of 1890 in New York, Comiskey suffered a severe broken ring finger, tearing ligaments in the process, and missed weeks of playing

COMISKEY WRITES A LETTER.

He Outlines the Reasons Why He Joined the Brotherhood.

Capt. Comiskey embodied his sentiments in the following letter, which was received by the editor of the *Sporting News*

ST. LOUIS, Jan 15.—EDITOR SPORTING NEWS' During the past few weeks many interviews have appeared with me in the different newspapers of the country relative to my having signed a contract with the St. Louis and Chicago brotherhood clubs. Up to this writing I am mind and fancy free. But before Saturday night, January 18, I will have signed a contract to play at first base for the Chicago brotherhood team I take this step for the reason that I am in sympathy with the brotherhood. I believe its aims are the best welfare and interest of the professional players. I believe that if the players do not this time stand true to their colors and maintain their organization they will from this forward be at the mercy of the corporations who have been running the game who drafted the reserve rule and gave birth to the obnoxious classification system. I have taken all the chances of success and failure into consideration and I believe that if the players stand true to themselves they will score the grandest success ever achieved in the base ball world. But besides having the welfare of the players at heart I have other reasons for wanting to play in Chicago My parents and all my relatives reside there and all the property I own is located in that city I was raised there and I have a natural liking for the place. But outside of all these reasons my relations with the management of the St. Louis club have, during the past year, been so unpleasant I do not care to renew them. I have many friends in St. Louis and for their sake I hate to leave here, but the other reasons outbalance this friendship, and so I will cast my lines with the Chicago club This is the first letter I have written on a subject which seems to have interested the base ball world throughout the whole of the present winter. Yours respectfully,
CHARLES COMISKEY.

The original copy of the article written by Comiskey in the *Sporting News* on January 15, 1890.

action.[31] He finished with a .244 batting average and fewer than 100 hits, far less than his usual offensive production.[32] Even so, he still led the team in fielding. The club achieved a mediocre fourth place in the standings behind Boston, Brooklyn, and New York, and was ten games behind the leaders. Despite its promise, the Brotherhood lasted only one year and the *New York Times* blamed its failure on "mismanagement." Financial difficulties were rampant and left no possibility for survival beyond 1890. Comiskey was personally owed over $1,300 in salary.[33] He appeared ready to distance himself from the troubling conditions in Chicago and opened up talks with Von der Ahe about rejoining the Browns.

Comiskey agreed to a one-year agreement with Von der Ahe at $6,000 a year.[34] He was anxious to put the previous year behind him and to make champions out of the makeshift St. Louis team. Lacking "Silver" King on the mound and Latham at third base, Comiskey was surrounded by Tip O'Neill, old faithful Jack Boyle behind the plate, and Tommy McCarthy in the outfield. His pitching staff, which was defective from the start, included Jack Stivetts, Clark Griffith (in his major league debut), and a 5'6" teenager named Willie McGill from Atlanta. Stivetts was the load-bearer and worked 440 innings in 64 games through the 1891 season. His admirable work earned him 33 victories and over 250 strikeouts.

Instilling his brand of discipline to players that actually listened was an appreciated concept for Comiskey, and he got good play from many of his talented players. Outfielder William "Dummy" Hoy was not only fast in the field and on the bases, but he had a great eye at the plate. The combination of Hoy, McCarthy, and O'Neill was a superior hitting trio, and third baseman Denny Lyons more than held his own in that department. Comiskey's batting also returned, and he produced 148 hits. In general, Comiskey extracted the best from the men he had, but they were only able to carry home second place in the Association because they just weren't able to match the all-around power of the Boston Reds.[35]

Constant interference from Von der Ahe, and his protégé son, Edward, barely over twenty years of age, drove Comiskey into an inescapable corner and the team suffered for it.[36] The ill will between captain and president grew uncontrollably, and in the midst of their stubborn feud, the two refrained from talking for two months.[37] By about August, Comiskey was surveying his options for the future and met a receptive bidder for his services in John T. Brush, owner of the National League's Cincinnati Reds.[38] Brush was a successful businessman turned baseball magnate and was eager to transform his club into a winner. He offered Comiskey a three-year deal worth $20,000, plus a percentage of receipts.[39] Comiskey agreed, and for the first time in his career, was entering the heavy competition of the National League.

Logic would say that Comiskey's experience with a deeply involved owner like Von der Ahe had prepared him for anything. But Brush was a different kind of beast; one who also thrived on being a hands on kind of magnate. His involvement in the day-to-day management of the Reds over the next three years was going to limit the team's success and effectively damage Comiskey's reputation as a developer of baseball champions.

In the early stages of the Comiskey-Brush relationship, things were copacetic and their understanding of the path to success was jointly fused. It was reported that Brush was keeping his mouth closed in terms of offering advice about running the team.[40] With that said, many people believed that Comiskey was given full rein to sign and release players and do whatever was necessary to bring the League championship to Cincinnati.

Motivated to get to work, Comiskey started lining up a squad of competent men, including pitchers Tony Mullane and Willie McGill, two of his St. Louis teammates. That duo in addition to three other ex-Browns also on Cincinnati, Elton Chamberlain, Arlie Latham and "Tip" O'Neill, gave Comiskey a friendly set of warriors who already understood his methodical approach to the game. However, the Reds were full of veterans set in their ways and perhaps unwilling to listen to a newfangled system of base running, sacrifices, and small ball that were less about individual statistics and more about the team itself. That little fact increased the difficulty of Comiskey's job and made it virtually impossible to win.

Luck was simply not on his side at any point in 1892. Pitcher Billy Rhines, a 28-game winner in 1890, engaged in a drunken three-way brawl with fellow Reds Eddie Burke and Jerry Harrington outside a downtown saloon.[41] Days later, McGill, who Comiskey fought to sign, joined Harrington in a separate drunken escapade along the streets of Cincinnati, completely embarrassing the club and drawing attention to Comiskey's ability to discipline his players.[42] To set an example, Comiskey released both men immediately.

"Experimentation" was the keyword for the Cincinnati Reds from 1892 to '94 as Comiskey and Brush tested scores of players, trying to find the right combination on the field. Pete Browning, Curt Welch, Frank Genins, Mike Sullivan, and many others passed through the clubhouse in a sort of revolving door. Salary cuts approved by the League diminished morale by mid-season, and Mullane was so upset that he walked out on the team.[43] The press came down hard on slumping O'Neill and, considering the "disorganized" state of things, wondered when Comiskey's premier "executive ability" was going to kick in.[44]

Living out of the Grand Hotel locally, Comiskey briefly dealt with a serious issue back home in Chicago that trumped anything related to baseball. His young son, Louis, was afflicted by diphtheria, and for a time, his life was in jeopardy before turning a corner and regaining his health.[45] Comiskey also suffered from an illness in 1892 and lost considerable weight, appearing gaunt, with his lack of strength affecting his play.[46]

The trials and tribulations of the Reds equated to unexciting gamesmanship, and the drama between management and players off the field was sometimes more entertaining than the work on the diamond. To make matters just a little worse, the team was nearly silenced completely by a train wreck near Grafton, West Virginia, in September of 1892.[47] This time, the fortunes were on the side of the Cincinnati ballplayers, as injuries were scant. After the accident, Comiskey led a parade of his men to a nearby farmhouse where they were provided with a memorable breakfast—a timely feast in the aftermath of potential disaster.

The exhausting season finally concluded with Cincinnati holding down the fifth place position.[48] After much commiseration, the powers-that-be felt they knew what movable parts needed to be adjusted to become a winner in 1893. One of the priorities was the outfield, and O'Neill was released to make way for a rotation of different candidates to include ex-St. Louis Brown Bob Caruthers, Jim Canavan, Frank Ward, and Jack McCarthy. Shortly after the season began, a controversy sprung up when the ever-newsworthy Tony Mullane who had returned to Cincinnati, was suspected of throwing a game against Pittsburgh.[49] There was immediately talk of blacklisting the pitcher, but as quickly as the discussion arrived, it disappeared, and Mullane was not punished in any way.

Brush's obstructive actions were constantly undermining Comiskey's forward momentum.[50] While the latter was searching for the right team chemistry and working long hours with specific players to rebuild their confidence, the former would unceremoniously release them. All players were on rocky footing as a dozen new athletes were given regular season auditions to gauge their worth. Comiskey also concluded that the team would benefit more if he stepped off the diamond and managed from the bench. His offensive production was way down,[51] and his speed on the base-paths, which always inspired his teammates to follow suit, was missing.[52] He signed twenty-three-year-old Frank Motz to fill the first base role and played intermittently from that point on.

Fans of the Reds watched the team fall way out of contention and disappointment was rampant. Sportswriters regularly tagged Comiskey and Brush with criticism and there were unconfirmed reports that Comiskey planned to retire from baseball at the end of the season. And if that scandalous rumor wasn't true, gossipers definitely knew that Brush was getting rid of him to hire someone else. Both individuals made denials, and Brush specifically addressed the Comiskey story by saying, "I have no fault to find with him this year, and think that he has done the best he could under the circumstances."[53]

The 1893 season ended with Cincinnati finishing sixth in the standings, and despite the confident front shown by Cincinnati's leaders going into 1894, things weren't going to improve all that much. In fact, they weren't going to improve at all. Brush's financially liberal days were stifled and he was no longer willing to spend recklessly on talent like he did the two previous seasons. Comiskey's last major acquisition was outfielder William "Dummy" Hoy, a member of the 1891 Browns, and the kind of speedster he sought after.

League Park in Cincinnati underwent major renovations during the off-season and Brush went to great lengths to make opening day on April 19, 1894, an exceptionally special occasion. With Ohio governor and future president William McKinley in attendance, a Cap Anson-led Chicago Colts as their opponent, and an energized team ready to better their 1893 record, Brush's big day was instead washed out by Mother Nature and rescheduled for the next afternoon. By the time the game was actually played, the heavy anticipation had dimmed to a more ordinary level, and the Reds hoped their 10–6 victory was the sign of positive things to come.

By June 1, however, the team was seven games below .500 (11–18). Their dreadful record turned up the heat on Comiskey, and he displayed an irate side of his personality when the stress got the better of him. In Pittsburgh, he pulled and benched Chamberlain after the latter claimed to have been injured and pitched poorly in an 11–3 loss. Chamberlain received no pay during his time off the field in what amounted to be his final full season in the majors, ending with 10 wins, 9 losses, and a 5.77 ERA. In an embarrassing 15–6 loss on August 16 at Baltimore, he verbally confronted Arlie Latham on the field and pulled him from the game.[54]

When they lost, they lost big, and between August 12 and September 5, they dropped 17 of 21 games, losing by such one-sided scores as 18–3, 25–8, and 16–2 during that streak.[55] There was no way to upright the sinking ship for Comiskey, and the Reds ended with a 55–75 record, finishing in 10th place out of 12 teams in the National League.[56]

"My management was not a success," Comiskey explained, quoted in the December 8, 1894, edition of the *Hamilton Daily Democrat*, "and I hardly think it is worth while at this late day to explain why I did not secure better results. The club officials were ever ready to spend their money freely in securing desirable players, but unfortunately, they could not be had."

There were no more acceptable excuses, and Comiskey felt that he'd lost the support of local fans and the press; so much so that he desired to examine his other options in baseball. For him, it was a nice time to be reborn with a new set of responsibilities.

The Western League, a junior organization, was fast becoming one of the most touted baseball units in the country. With teams in eight Midwestern cities from Toledo to Kansas City, it had lineage back to 1885, but similar incarnations had launched and failed. Finally, in 1893, the current minor league organization was established and was making an impression under the leadership of Ohio native Byron Bancroft "Ban" Johnson, one of the wisest minds in the sport.[57]

Within weeks of its 1894 season ending, President Johnson called the leaders of the Western League to Chicago to discuss reorganization. It was revealed that nearly all teams in the league had made a profit but that the pennant winning Sioux City Cornhuskers only averaged about 700 people per game. Considering that larger, more profitable towns like Kansas City, Indianapolis, Detroit, and Minneapolis were also involved in the league, it was decided that Sioux City would be cast from the association to prevent them from winning again. There was speculation that Comiskey was planning to step in, take a bulk of the Sioux City players, and relocate them to Chicago or St. Paul, completing the organization's new circuit.

The speculation proved true, and Comiskey offered a formal application to the Western League for the St. Paul charter.[58] His wealth of experience and profuse knowledge of baseball was seen as a major benefit to the league, and he was approved for ownership on November 21, 1894.[59] [60]

"I regret to leave Cincinnati," Comiskey said, quoted in the December 8, 1894, edition of the *Hamilton Daily Democrat*, "chiefly on account of President Brush, Col. Ellison, and Treasurer Lloyd. They have been very kind to me, and I appreciate all they have done. My contract as manager of the Cincinnati club has expired, and there is nothing that can tie me to the league. I'll sail under the colors of a magnate now on a small[er] scale."

For the first time in his life, Charles Comiskey was a baseball club owner, and he could (and would) call all of the shots regarding his minor league team. There was no one to answer to and nobody looking over his shoulder. He absorbed the most constructive aspects of franchise management from Von der Ahe, Brush, and his mentor, Ted Sullivan, and was dead-set on running his own show from the top down. It was the logical progressive step.

"It has been my ambition for some years to get a baseball plant of my own in some good city," Comiskey said, "and this has seemed to me to be my opportunity ever since last fall. In applying for the franchise, I could offer nothing except the fact that I had the money to back the undertaking. Now that I have got it, I propose to go ahead and make the best of it. I will do my best to make the game popular in St. Paul, and hope that it will get the encouragement of the best classes. It goes without saying that I will try to get a winning team. If I have tried to do that as a manager, I shall try even harder as an owner."[61]

His anticipated arrival in St. Paul came on December 6, 1894, with his father John by his side.[62] Setting up an office and quarters for the players at the Windsor Hotel, he was warmly received by local authorities and the press. Comiskey said all the right things and made all the right gestures to the St. Paul population. Most of all, he promised to provide first-class baseball. On the surface, it seemed like the perfect fit.

Over the course of the first three months of 1895, Comiskey filled out his team nicely, signing a number of athletes to contracts and working to finalize his final roster. Among the signees were former members of the Sioux City squad, including catcher Frank Kraus, infielders Tim O'Rourke and Red Houlihan, outfielders Charles "Lefty" Marr and Lew Camp, and pitcher Henry Killeen. Marr was seen as the best of the bunch, having hit .378 the season before. He also signed Tony Mullane, who Comiskey still believed he could successfully manage, and second baseman Jack Pickett, the soon-to-be-named captain of the St. Paul club.

A major challenge that needed to be solved quickly was finding a place in St. Paul for the team to play. The *St. Paul Daily Globe* expressed the urgency of the matter, relaying the rumor that if Comiskey was unable to find a suitable location, he'd consider relocating elsewhere. Ultimately, an old circus grounds on Aurora Street was chosen and John Comiskey, who had intricate knowledge of the construction process due to his years of public office in Chicago, was placed in charge of the new park.[63] He worked closely with the architect and contractors to establish the best course of action.

After a preseason exhibition schedule in Cincinnati, Rockford, and Dubuque, Comiskey and his team arrived in St. Paul for the first time as a complete unit on April 21, 1895.[64] He had been so adamant about getting his men into condition that he got himself sick following a six mile run in bad weather. His training regimen was inflexible and he demanded that his players report promptly at 10:00 each morning and again at 2:00 in the afternoon. Applying all the tricks he'd picked up in previous years as a player and manager, he was completely hands-on as a motivational spirit, fitness guru, and baseball commander. The additional load of stress pertaining to the business side of the franchise was also being dealt with expertly.

The *Daily Globe*, on April 16, 1895, reported that the local team would be known as "Comiskey's Saints" from that point further. Throughout the year, however, the team was referred to as the "Saints" and the "St. Paul Apostles" by press reporters.

Shortly before opening day on May 1, Comiskey faced his first local condemnation in a growing movement to prevent Sunday baseball games at his new venue. The opposition party, many of whom lived around the park, were distressed by the so-called offensive behavior of enthusiasts and wanted them flushed from their neighborhood before things got out of hand. Unnerved by the complaints, Comiskey believed the objections should have been aired before the park was constructed, but finally accepted the fate of holding Sunday games at the West Side Ballpark.[65] At his own expense, Comiskey had that facility prepared for professional baseball. There was no shaking him from his course.

The Western League season began with a victory for St. Paul at Kansas City, taking a 4–3 win.[66] By May 7, the club was back at home in the midst of a serious frenzy of attention. Following a street parade featuring electric cars, trolleys, and bands, the home opener was played before a jovial audience at Aurora Park.[67] Smashing 18 hits and scoring 17 runs, St. Paul made a significant splash with area fans, and took the win from Milwaukee, 17–4.

Watching his team intently and looking for potential holes, he signed Charlie Irwin, recently of the National League's Chicago Colts, and shifted Lew Camp from short to the outfield. Despite his good intentions, the team wasn't strengthened by the maneuver and began to lose almost daily. They dropped to a 5–8 record, losing five in a row, and traveled eastward where their record dipped to 8–18. The combination of poor play and the political firestorm festering about Sunday baseball was weighing on Comiskey. As a player and manager, he was previously able to defer certain off the field aspects to ownership, but now as the head of the franchise, he was solely responsible to answer all charges and complaints. He was unquestionably held accountable for the showmanship of his ball club, and if they remained in last place, his financial investment and the future of his team in the city were in doubt.

There was still plenty of time to turn things around and Comiskey wasn't about to give up on his team. On June 1, 1895, he vocalized his sentiments about their current state of play and collective attitudes.[68] In a nutshell, he put everyone on notice, clearly telling them that if they figured their status on the club was secure and they could just wing it through the season, then they were sadly mistaken. Comiskey snapped at Captain Pickett and made it known that the latter's lack of leadership was one of the reasons for their dismal record. The team as a whole was void of enthusiasm and discipline, and one way or another, Comiskey barked, it was going to be a winner . . . with the current crop of players or without them.

The Saints began June in last place, and after an eight-game winning streak, they were in fourth, including a series of wins over the first place Indianapolis Hoosiers. As the team fought their way to above .500, Comiskey released "Lefty" Marr and Ollie Smith and signed Billy George, Scott Stratton, and Jim Burns. With the versatile Camp alternating between centerfield, first, and second base, the new trio became the team's primary outfielders. Bill Phyle, a hurler for Dubuque of the Independent League, was also picked up; as was Roger Denzer, and Comiskey's brother Ignatius even stepped in to pitch, throwing two scoreless innings against the Terre Haute Hottentots on July 29, 1895.[69]

The next day, St. Paul defeated Grand Rapids and slid into third place with a 44–34 record. Both Indianapolis and Kansas City were battling for the top spot, and Comiskey's outfit was quietly sneaking into position to challenge for the pennant.

Unfortunately for Comiskey, time ran out, and a week before the season ended on September 22, newspapers proclaimed Indianapolis the winners of the Western League championship, as their lead was too much to overcome. St. Paul played great baseball through the final weeks, winning 8 of their last 11 games, including a 22–6 win over Indianapolis on September 19. They amassed a record of 74–50 and held firm on second place as the last two games of the season were rained out at home.

Comiskey expressed confidence in keeping as many of his players going into 1896 as possible and planned a lengthy exhibition schedule through the first part of December.[70] Before meeting his team on the road in Montana, he went to Chicago to discuss the political happenings of the Western League. There was talk of reorganization, but the major theme was the heavy push of John T. Brush to oust President Johnson, heightening the animosity between the two. Not only did the future of the league depend on which side was victorious, but the direction of the sport was going to be influenced. It all depended on who attained the upper hand in the end.

ENDNOTES

1 *Daily Inter Ocean,* February 12, 1888, p. 12.
  Also see: *St. Louis Post Dispatch,* January 1, 1888, p. 6.
2 *Cleveland Plain Dealer,* December 17, 1887, p. 4.
3 The series began on April 2, 1888, in New Orleans and was scheduled to be best-of-five. After St. Louis won the third game at Memphis on April 5, there was talk that the Browns had regained the world championship. Comiskey said: "The game at Memphis yesterday settled the spring series for the world's [championship], and I think that winning the title back again was one of the easiest things I ever saw in my life." *St. Louis Post Dispatch,* April 6, 1888, p. 8.
  Also see: *St. Louis Post Dispatch,* April 15, 1888, p. 6.
4 *St. Louis Post Dispatch,* May 7, 1888, p. 5.
5 *St. Louis Post Dispatch,* April 21, 1888, p. 8.
6 *St. Louis Post Dispatch,* June 20, 1888, p. 8.
7 *St. Louis Post Dispatch,* July 2, 1888, p. 5.
8 *St. Louis Post Dispatch,* July 3, 1888, p. 8.
9 Comiskey was well-known for being able to seriously censure a player for an on-field mishap, and only moments later, reverse his explosive temperament to smooth things over with the browbeaten individual. It was a purposeful method he used to ensure that the player received both a critical lesson and a "kind remark" of some nature, preventing the athlete from being overly depressed by the forceful dressing-down. *Chicago Daily Tribune,* April 13, 1890, p. 32.

10 The Browns finished with a 92–43 record and Brooklyn came in second, 6.5 games back. Silver King won 45 games, Hudson 25, and Chamberlain added another 11 victories to catapult St. Louis to the championship for the fourth straight time (baseball-reference.com). Comiskey tied for eighth place among first basemen on defense, but once again led the Browns with a .972 fielding percentage. He batted .273 on the year, and had 157 hits and 77 stolen bases. *Sporting News*, November 24, 1888, p. 2.

11 *St. Louis Post Dispatch*, November 4, 1888, p. 16.

St. Louis batted .219 as a team in the World Series. Latham batted .219, Lyons .111, and O'Neill, a perennial .300 hitter, finished with a .263 average—the same as Comiskey.

12 *Sporting Life*, November 7, 1888, p. 3.

13 *Sporting News*, November 10, 1888, p. 2-3.

It was stated that: "$500 in gold was the largest ever given a professional player." *St. Louis Post Dispatch*, November 7, 1888, p. 8.

14 *Daily Inter Ocean*, April 25, 1889, p. 11.

When he sold the old family home at 142 Lytle Street and the three-flat property in 1911, Comiskey said: "When my father purchased the property he had in addition to the fifty-feet frontage on which the homestead stood, twenty-five feet to the south. With the first money I earned and saved in baseball, I purchased this little strip of land and erected a three story flat building." *Chicago Daily Tribune*, March 25, 1911, p. 19. By 1894, Comiskey owned three flat houses in Chicago and rented them out, earning $2,000 a year. *Cleveland Plain Dealer*, March 14, 1894, p. 5.

15 *St. Louis Post Dispatch*, March 10, 1889, p. 6.

16 *Sporting News*, July 20, 1889, p. 1.

Latham was suspended by Von der Ahe in August for unsatisfactory play and talk of his alleged crookedness increased.

Also see: *Sporting News*, August 17, 1889, p. 3 and the *Sporting News*, October 19, 1889, p. 5. Comiskey believed that Latham was "wholly responsible for the loss of sixteen" games they'd played, and, along with the rest of the team, endorsed his suspension. *Sporting News*, August 17, 1889, p. 5.

17 *Sporting News*, July 20, 1889, p. 7.

Pitcher Tom Ramsey was long affiliated with Louisville but his drinking problems were regularly a bone of contention.

18 *Sporting News*, July 27, 1889, p. 1.

19 *Sporting News*, September 14, 1889, p. 1.

20 *Sporting News*, October 19, 1889, p. 3.

21 Brooklyn won the Association championship with a 93–44 record. St. Louis finished in second place, 90–45, and was only two games back when the season ended. Comiskey was the top fielder for the Browns with a .970 average and batted .286. Baseball-reference.com.

22 *New York Herald*, December 17, 1888, p. 6. *New York Times*, September 23, 1889, p. 2. Also see: *Sporting News*, June 29, 1889, p. 1.

23 *Sporting News*, October 19, 1889, p. 5.

24 *New York Times*, November 2, 1889, p. 6.

Comiskey was visited by former White Stocking-turned-Brotherhood advocate, Fred Pfeffer, and the two discussed the advantages and pitfalls of the organization at Tony Faust's famous St. Louis restaurant. Pfeffer was financially involved in the new Chicago franchise and wanted Comiskey to sign. A "Windy City" sportswriter claimed Comiskey had officially affixed his signature to a contract after the meeting, but it was untrue. *Sporting News*, November 9, 1889, p. 1.

25 Comiskey led a combination outfit from November 1889 to January 1890 and traveled nearly 10,000 miles. The team journeyed to Texas, New Orleans, Denver, San Francisco, and Portland and Comiskey said: "It was the longest ever made on land by any club." *Chicago Daily Tribune*, January 18, 1890, p. 6.

26 *Sporting Life*, December 25, 1889, p. 6.

27 *Chicago Daily Tribune*, January 17, 1890, p. 6.

28 *Sporting Life*, February 5, 1890, p. 7.

29 The contract was signed on January 17, 1890. The Chicago member of the Brotherhood organization was commonly referred to as the "Chicago White Stockings," although it was also known as the "Chicago Pirates." When the *Tribune* acknowledged the signing of Comiskey, it was reported that he was joining the "White Stocking Base-Ball Club of Chicago." His salary was said to be $7,500 a year, although the figure wasn't officially announced at the time. *Chicago Daily Tribune*, January 18, 1890, p. 6. A list of salaries for the Chicago team was published in *Sporting Life*, February 5, 1890, p. 7.

30 *Chicago Daily Tribune*, November 30, 1890, p. 27;
Also see: *Chicago Daily Tribune*, September 3, 1890, p. 6 and *Philadelphia Inquirer*, October 20, 1890, p. 3.
Comiskey was said to have been so upset by the condition of his team that he was entertaining an offer of a three-year contract with Philadelphia at $10,000 annually. One local sportswriter noted that Comiskey was a "gigantic failure" in Chicago and wondered if the team needed him. Regardless, Comiskey already had a contract and wasn't going anywhere. *Philadelphia Inquirer*, September 13–14, 1890.

31 *Chicago Daily Tribune*, August 31, 1890, p. 2.

32 The Chicago Brotherhood franchise won 75 games in 1890 and lost 62 and placed fourth out of eight clubs. Notably, the team had two thirty-game winners in Baldwin and King. Baseball-reference.com.

33 Comiskey was owed $1,319.58 in salary, plus $500 in stock. *Chicago Daily Tribune*, December 30, 1890, p. 5.

34 *Chicago Daily Tribune*, November 6, 1890, p. 7.

35 St. Louis captured second place in the 1891 American Association race with an 85–51 record and were 8.5 games back from first place Boston. Baseball-reference.com.

36 Comiskey said that young Eddie Von der Ahe was the real power behind the St. Louis Browns. *Daily Inter Ocean*, November 1, 1891, p. 3.

37 *Boston Herald*, November 3, 1891, p. 8.

38 *Philadelphia Inquirer*, November 15, 1891, p. 3.

39 *Boston Herald,* November 5, 1891, p. 10.

Brush reportedly lost as much as $50,000 on the Cincinnati Reds in 1891. His salary list increased from $30,000 to $51,000 in 1892, and with Comiskey at the head of the club and after paying all that money, expected a championship contender. *Cincinnati Post,* July 5, 1892, p. 3.

40 *Cincinnati Post,* April 8, 1892, p. 4.

41 *Cincinnati Post,* May 5, 1892, p. 1.

For their actions, Comiskey suspended Rhines and fined both Burke and Harrington $100 each.

42 *Cincinnati Post,* May 11, 1892, p. 1.

43 *Cincinnati Post,* July 5, 1892, p. 3.

44 *Cincinnati Post,* August 18, 1892, p. 3.

45 *Cincinnati Post,* August 31, 1892, p. 4.

46 Comiskey played through sickness during the 1892 season and participated in 141 games. *Cincinnati Post,* March 27, 1893, p. 1.

47 *Cincinnati Post,* September 19, 1892, p. 1.

48 Cincinnati finished in fifth place in 1892 with 82 wins and 68 losses. They were 20 games behind Boston. Comiskey made 125 hits and had a .227 batting average. In the field, he led the team regulars on defense, achieving a .984 fielding average; baseball-reference.com.

49 *Cincinnati Post,* May 9, 1893, p. 4.

Mullane flatly denied throwing the game and claimed that his arm strength was gone.

Also see: *Cincinnati Post,* May 10, 1893, p. 4.

50 *Cincinnati Post,* May 27, 1893, p. 4.

51 Comiskey's avg. from 1889–93:

1889: .286; 1890: .244; 1891: .259; 1892: .227; 1893: .220

52 In 64 games, Comiskey batted .220 and had 57 hits. Baseball-reference.com.

53 *Cincinnati Post,* August 5, 1893, p. 3.

54 *Cincinnati Post,* August 17, 1894, p. 4.

55 The Reds lost both ends of a doubleheader to the Boston Beaneaters on August 21 by a combination of 43–11 (18–3 and 25–8). The 16–2 loss was against the New York Giants on September 3.

56 Cincinnati's top three pitchers, Frank Dwyer, Elton Chamberlain, and Tom Parrott each managed to attain an earned-run average greater than 5.00 on the 1894 season. That helped account for being 35 games out of first place; baseball-reference.com. An indication of his dedication to his job, Comiskey remained faithful to the Reds between the time he submitted his application for the Western League ownership position and the moment it was approved. Even knowing he was heading to a new team, he still worked to better Cincinnati's prospects for the 1895 season.

57 Ban Johnson, born in Ohio on January 5, 1865, was a former sports editor for the *Cincinnati Commercial Gazette.* In a story often recited in baseball circles, it was Comiskey who recommended Johnson for the Western League Presidency, having dealt with him on numerous occasions while manager of the Reds.

58 James Hart, owner of the Chicago Colts of the National League, was also pursuing membership in the Western League, hoping to establish a south side minor league club that would act as a reserve and proving grounds for his team. He said: "Few South Side people patronize the Polk Street Park—the distance is too great—and there are thousands of ball cranks in that district who would welcome a good club in their neighborhood. With a 25-cent admission, and a non-conflicting schedule, the new team ought to be a big success." *Chicago Daily Tribune*, September 23, 1894, p. 7. There were some fears within the Western League about Hart becoming a member and using his influence to rule the organization. That led to members voting for Comiskey instead.

59 Ban Johnson said: "We made a good move in securing him. He is a bright man, and his experience and sagacity will be of great benefit to us. He will also give St. Paul the best baseball that city ever had." *St. Paul Daily Globe*, November 22, 1894, p. 5.

60 *Chicago Daily Tribune*, November 22, 1894, p. 11.
Rumors circulated later on that John Brush of Cincinnati was Comiskey's silent partner and "money man" in St. Paul. Comiskey denied it wholeheartedly.

61 *St. Paul Daily Globe*, November 22, 1894, p. 5

62 *St. Paul Daily Globe*, December 7, 1894, p. 5.
His arrival had been delayed because of Nan Comiskey's illness.

63 *St. Paul Daily Globe*, March 19, 1895, p. 5.
It was a 600 x 330 foot region between Dale, Aurora, St. Albans, and Fuller Streets. Comiskey felt it was an "excellent" location and arranged for a lease on March 18, 1895. He said: "A more convenient spot for a ball park could not have been obtained in this city." The diamond, it was determined, would face southeast, and construction for a fence around the park, a stone foundation, wooden grandstand, bleachers, and overall improved conditions were to begin immediately with a plan from an experienced architect named William Kingsley. The development of the park took longer than expected and the location of the grandstand was shifted from the angle at Fuller and St. Albans Streets to St. Albans and Aurora.

64 *St. Paul Daily Globe*, April 22, 1895, p. 5.

65 *St. Paul Daily Globe*, April 27, 1895, p. 2.
Comiskey offered to appease the complainants by hiring extra security and improving the park to meet certain requests. Also, a petition signed by pro-stadium residents of the region around the venue was delivered to the mayor, but a judge was convinced to order an injunction preventing Sunday ball games until it could be hashed out in court.

66 *St. Paul Daily Globe*, May 2, 1895, p. 5.

67 *St. Paul Daily Globe*, May 7, 1895, p. 5.

68 *St. Paul Daily Globe*, June 2, 1895, p. 14.

69 *St. Paul Daily Globe*, July 30, 1895, p. 5.

70 *St. Paul Daily Globe*, October 1, 1895, p. 5.

5

THE COMPLEXITIES OF OWNERSHIP

At the conclusion of the 1895 season, the St. Paul Saints took to the road and played local teams as they crossed the Dakotas, Montana, and ventured into Oregon.[1] The barnstorming tour was the brainchild of Charles Comiskey and the former manager of the Minneapolis club, John S. Barnes. Barnes managed a second squad billed as the "All-Americas," and the usual scheme saw one of the two teams match up against a neighborhood franchise, then playing each other in the second game of the doubleheader. By mid-October, they all were expected in Northern California, where they'd be joined by two additional teams, one representing San Jose and led by Theodore Engel of Milwaukee, and the other in Los Angeles run by Joe Cantillon.

The lineups were arranged, leases and contracts signed, and the winter league began to a rousing reception. On October 27, 1895, an estimated 3,000 spectators attended the Central Park game in San Francisco between the local squad, formerly the All-America team, and the Oaklands, the West Coast version of the Saints.[2] Comiskey, in what was expected to be one of his final appearances on the diamond, played first base in support of Tony Mullane on the mound, but neither were successful. The owner accounted for three errors in the 15–2 loss. During the trip, Comiskey's younger brother Ignatius occasionally played right field for the Saints, while Pat Comiskey handled all the finances.

Sharp competition and the utmost professionalism of the players were anticipated, but for some, the "real world" of the Western League and the hustle and bustle of the sunny California market were too much for them to endure sober. Discipline was completely lost as players delved deep into alcoholic binges before, during, and after games. At one point, according to a story told by Barnes, twelve of the eighteen players in a game were smashed, causing hundreds of enthusiasts to leave disgusted. It didn't take long before baseball fans who expected to attend an entertaining game were completely turned off by the exhibitions of drunkenness. The behavior wasn't limited to any particular club, and Comiskey's outfit was just as guilty as the rest. But the trip became legendary for the failure that it was, both for its lack of quality play and gentlemanly conduct.

Of course, there were other claims that bad weather and a lack of larger venues inhibited audiences. Very quickly, news of the fiasco radiated across the country, and Comiskey's reputation took a significant hit. In the *Sporting News*, Cantillon and pitcher Alex Jones came to his defense.[3] [4] Because of his inside position in the league, Cantillon addressed the rumors, explaining that not only did Comiskey take care of his players on the trip, but he ensured that members of the Los Angeles squad stranded in that city received enough money to get home. In total, Comiskey was said to have lost between $1,000 and $2,500.[5]

In the midst of their dismal California experience, Comiskey fled to Chicago for a mandatory Western League meeting on November 21, 1895, and was probably happy to get away from the coast. Owners were confronted by an aggressive National League shift in rules relating to the minors that had severe consequences.[6] Instead of adhering to the previously established policy to pay $1,000 for all drafted players from Class A clubs, the National League wanted to reduce the fee to $500. The Western League, which had been in the Class B category in 1894 and subsequently promoted to "A," was going to be dramatically impacted by the reversal.

It was a hostile move toward the minor league owners. When the Western League operators met in Chicago, they had the opportunity to kick back at their counterparts. John T. Brush, owner of the Indianapolis franchise, was at the center of controversy, and his actions through the previous season had caused plenty of friction. In fact, he was the pariah of the organization because he jointly owned the Cincinnati Reds of the National League and was a supporter of the reduction of drafting prices that hurt every man at the table.

Over the previous months, Brush took advantage of his unique position as owner of both a major and minor league team by freely swapping players from club to club. If a position needed to be strengthened or an injury laid a man out, he could easily reach into his bag of alternates to fill the gap. The wide availability aided both clubs and to those who didn't have that same opportunity, it presented an unfair situation. Brush, given his position and overall power in the sport, felt entitled to benefit under existing rules and considered the minor league a breeding ground for talent. Players were at that level to be groomed for the big stage; nothing more and nothing less.

Among National League owners, there was an intrinsic belief that they were the kings of baseball; the ultimate class of dignitaries in a sport that worked from the top down, not the other way around. In its two brief seasons, the Western League had made significant progress and was constantly churning out excellent talent. Leaders Ban Johnson, Comiskey, and their peers were well regarded and had brought great credibility to their outfit, but were still of a lesser class, at least the National League believed so.

Playing both sides of the fence, Brush yearned to impose his will over the Western League, particularly when it came to dealing with the latter's president. Brush never wanted Johnson, who was from Cincinnati, to lead the organization in the first place. He wanted Johnson replaced by a man friendlier to his operations, further strengthening his own individual standing. How it impacted others in the Western, he didn't seem to care.

To Brush's dismay, Johnson wasn't going anywhere. He was completely supported by league owners to the point that members wanted to update the organization's constitution to pay Johnson a set salary so he could attend to the league year round. He was, after all, representing their interests full-time.

The National Agreement, which was initially created in 1883 to establish peace and cooperation between the National League and American Association and again revised following the Brotherhood war in 1890, was altered during the NL's February 1896 meeting in New York City, and the drafting decrease was ironed into law.[7] Once again, major league owners used the National Agreement to display their superiority over all minor organizations, spurning any thoughts that the Western or any other group was approaching an even par. Sportswriter T. H. Murnane of the *Boston Globe* predicted doom for the minor leagues and named Brush as the leading force behind the increasing pressure. It was clear that concessions by the major leagues needed to be enacted as soon as possible to resolve the crisis.

Proving to be no pushovers, the Western League took measures of its own, firing directly at Brush when it instituted a rule that any player shifted from the National to the Western must be unconditionally released first.[8] In effect, it opened the platform for other major league teams to jump in and sign the transferring player well before they got a chance to appear in a Western uniform. If a player was drafted or bought by a National League outfit, a payment had to be made to the treasury of the league beforehand. The era of casually loaning players between teams was over. These implementations were going to force Brush to handle the upcoming season a little differently.

For Comiskey, the looming 1896 season presented its own series of adjustments. During the winter, he made a decision to retire from active play, meaning that his appearances in California were to be his final on the professional diamond.[9] He told the press that he might occasionally work the baselines, and it would be many years before he'd give up his seat on the bench. On a different note, he was confronted by the loss of two of his best players in the major league draft, shortstop Charlie Irwin, and the promising backstop, Eddie Boyle. He told the *Sporting News* that he'd "much rather have Boyle this season than the $1,000 which [he] received from the Louisville club."[10]

Renowned shortstop Jack Glasscock of West Virginia, a rambunctious infielder who played for several major league clubs, was bouncing back from an arm injury and was interested in joining the league. He'd been written off as finished by nearly everyone, but to Comiskey, he possessed the right kind of hardnosed attitude his team needed. Based on his experience, there was a belief that he'd take over as team captain, especially since the 1895 leader, Jack Pickett, ran into some difficulties with Comiskey during the California trip.[11] But bygones were bygones, and Pickett was renamed captain. Glasscock assumed the first base role, while newcomer Frank Shugart took over at short.

Another importation was ex-longshoreman Sam "Sandow" Mertes from San Francisco, a young athlete with a lot of talent and a bright future.[12] Mertes had graduated from the Quincy club of the Western Association and proved his capable ability to hit, field, and run, and Comiskey was able to beat out Milwaukee for his rights, placing him in the centerfield position. Other fresh faces on the team included Henry Spies, a versatile catcher, and infielder Wallace Hollingsworth of Cedar Rapids. Returning were Tony Mullane and Bill Phyle on the mound, infielders Frank Kraus and Tim O'Rourke, and outfielders Billy George and Jim Burns.

During the evening of March 23, 1896, Comiskey returned to St. Paul with his family, as they planned to live in the city through the rest of the year.[13] He informed the press that the team would arrive for spring training by April 1. Upon arrival back in town, Comiskey knew that he definitely had his hands full. In addition to arranging a slew of exhibitions, a practice schedule in Dubuque, and finalizing the deal providing grounds for Sunday games at the West Side Park, he was facing quite a mess at the Aurora Street Stadium. An ice skating rink had been established during the off season, and it destroyed segments of the playing field.

Comiskey told the *St. Paul Daily Globe*: "You can bet that there will be no more skating rinks in Aurora Park as long as I have anything to do with it. It's an awful mess out there. I was out all day with eight men and two teams digging it out, and we did not miss what we took out at all when we got through. When we looked on the dumping ground across the street, we could see the work we were doing, but there are acres of ice still in the park to be removed. Six feet of ice at one end, and that right back of second base! All I want to do now is to get the diamond clear so the boys can get out to practice."[14]

Other parts of the stadium were getting an overhaul as well, including a restructuring of the grandstand and alterations to the press box; all in efforts to provide everyone with an improved view of the field. A stunningly popular new mode of transportation, bicycling, was also something to take into consideration as people were expected to ride their two wheelers to the park on a regular basis.[15] Parking for the many bicycles was just one more thing Comiskey had to worry about. After meeting the initial deadline for spring training, the club went to Dubuque, where it faced a consistent barrage of bad weather, slowing their practice schedule immensely.

Back in St. Paul, the team appeared for an exhibition on April 20 against the Minnesota Packing and Provision Company, also known as the "Packers."[16] The Saints displayed their power, winning 25–7, and in an attempt to keep the neighborhood kids from running off with the foul balls that rained down on the streets surrounding the park, Comiskey let them into the stadium for free after the third inning. The financial burden of lost balls during the course of a game or practice was a common thorn in the side of owners and special netting and other adjustments were made to limit the problem.

The season opened at Milwaukee on April 22, with a 6–5 victory in 10 innings. Unlike the year prior, this time around the clubs were fighting for a new prize, the *Detroit Free Press* Cup, worth several hundred dollars, and going to the championship victor.[17] Five games into the season, St. Paul was under .500 with a 2–3 record. Their home opener was rained out, but the impending weather of April 30, 1896, didn't stop a loud audience of just under 1,000 people from watching the Saints debut on the local grounds.[18] With a speech by Mayor Smith classing up the occasion, St. Paul went out and beat Kansas City 9–7 in an exciting game.

Over the next five months, enthusiasts were regaled by a roller coaster ride of remarkable ups and downs. There was rarely a dull moment for the players, fans, sportswriters, and Comiskey to relax and rest on their laurels. By mid-May, they were stuck in a battle between second and third place with Kansas City, lagging behind Detroit, the league leaders. Not unusual, the newspapers in rivaling cities chided the Saints for apparent wrongdoings, specifically dirty play, in what would become a running theme throughout the season. The *Milwaukee Journal* claimed a baseman for the team threw "dust" in the eyes of a Minneapolis runner.[19] Later, the *Indianapolis News* took great pride in condemning St. Paul for its actions, as did the *Kansas City Times* and *Kansas City World.* If there was an opening to bash Comiskey's squad, they jumped at it with a certain enjoyment that intensified the personal sentiment all around.

Batting over .360 as a team, the Saints powered past Grand Rapids on May 17, 35–6, and played well in the field, committing only two errors. Pitcher Phyle, whose record was unimpressive to date, was benched after what was dubbed a "disagreement" with Comiskey, and their intense relationship was beginning to stray from the tracks.[20] The owner was getting good ball from sophomore pitcher Roger Denzer, who was recruited from St. Peter, Minnesota, the season before, and continued his speedy development. Soon, Denzer was being scouted by as many as six major league clubs, but Comiskey refused to sell him because his team was still in the hunt for the pennant. His championship aspirations looked a little less probable after a harrowing twenty-game road trip to the east, where they won only five games.

It was a frustrating journey for everyone involved. At Columbus, Glasscock's irritations burst inappropriately when he launched a ball at the umpire while the latter's back was turned, and teammate Mertes was tossed from the game for abusive language.[21] Comiskey wasn't one to hide his anger and was visibly upset by the downturn in competitiveness shown by nearly all of his players. On June 12 in Milwaukee, he returned to the field for the first time in months, breaking his self-imposed "retirement" and played first base.[22] He only had one at bat and was hit by a pitch, then stole a base, showing his old-school fiery approach to ball playing. He was an inspiration to the younger guys but nothing could stop their free fall. By the end of the trip, they were three games under .500 and in fifth place. Trade talks were now ongoing, and Denzer was at the top of the list.

In a somewhat comedic fashion, a St. Paul enthusiast sent a telegram to Comiskey asking to take over the lease of the ball park and replace the Saints with his own group of players—obviously in the belief that they could do better than the faltering pros.[23] Comiskey, not amused by the offer, did not reply.

Home cooking was always a good remedy, and St. Paul gained momentum with a 34–21 defeat over Kansas City on June 21.[24] In the next series versus Milwaukee, they won a doubleheader on June 25, then a second doubleheader the following day, including a three-hit, 14–0 shutout by Phyle. Comiskey made his first major roster move when he traded the highly-touted "Sandow" Mertes to the Philadelphia Phillies for a pitcher, Willie McGill, and Tuck Turner, an outfielder.[25] McGill had previously played for Comiskey in St. Louis and Cincinnati.

The Saints fought their way back over .500 behind the outstanding hitting of Glasscock and Billy George, batting .411 and .431 respectively. The duo had powered for over 100 hits and was the core of their lineup. Another great offensive display was made on July 5, when St. Paul trounced Minneapolis, 41–8.[26] Included in St. Paul's box score were forty-five hits and nine home runs, and Glasscock reached base eight of his nine times at bat.

The winning continued and St. Paul worked their way back into third place. Through July 22, they rattled off sixteen straight victories and attained the second place position. They'd also gotten the upper hand in several games on the league's top team, Indianapolis. One of the darker moments of the stretch was an altercation between pitchers Mullane and James Johnston at a local St. Paul establishment, when the latter beamed an object at the former's head, smashing through a glass window.[27] For his actions, Johnston was benched and later farmed out to a team in Winona, Minnesota. In response to the loss, and in effort to strengthen the team, Comiskey added two pitchers, Hon Fricken and Bert Inks.

By August 2, the Saints were in first place, but with 55 games left, anything was possible. Needless to say, fans back home were ready to celebrate their heroes upon return, and a pennant was now within reach. But that was far from the truth. St. Paul's negative turnaround came quickly as they won only three out of the next 12 games, dropping back into third place. Embarrassed by the implosion of his club, Comiskey found himself before the press delivering a vitriolic assessment of things, and might have regretted his statements later.

"If I had the four best pitchers in the business, they could not win games with a lot of quitters laying down behind them," Comiskey told the *St. Paul Globe*.[28] "They're good runners, they are, on a street car. They're all right when they're on the home grounds, and twenty-five or thirty rooters behind 'em yell and stamp their feet as they come to bat. Why, they knock the cover off the ball, but get 'em away from home where the other man has to pay for the balls, and they handle 'em as though they were afraid a home run'd knock him in the hands of a receiver. Why, that outfield of mine was good for eight and ten hits a game when they were home. This trip, they haven't been good for that many hits in three weeks. Why this team could not win from a high school class in an institute for the shelter of cripples."

The "quitter" comment circulated wide and far and players were said to be justifiably upset by his candid statements. In terms of personnel, Comiskey benched Captain Pickett, recalled Bill Phyle and Wallace Hollingsworth, and signed Larry Twitchell as an outfielder, who recently resigned from the Milwaukee team under questionable circumstances. Altering the batting order to further shake things up, Comiskey rejoined the team as first baseman for a game against Milwaukee on August 17, and the club won 18–0.[29] The next day, St. Paul won again, this time by a score of 29–6. They were back in third place and Comiskey, with a .500 batting average, was leading the team. Of course, he'd only played in two games.

Fielding errors were a constant problem for St. Paul, and Twitchell ended up making 11 in 12 games before being precipitously released. In a surprising move, Pickett, the team's captain for the past two seasons, was traded to Minneapolis.[30] Comiskey exited the dugout two additional times to play first base on August 27 and 28, and St. Paul won both games against Detroit. He'd finish with a .167 batting average over the four games.

Small crowds plagued Comiskey at home into September, but he still expected to earn at least $15,000 in profits for the season.[31] On September 12, the Saints lost both games of a double header at Detroit, and repeated the dubious feat at Grand Rapids three days later. It happened again in Indianapolis on the final day of the season, September 23, and the team finished in fourth place with a 73–63 record. Minneapolis won the pennant and the *Detroit Free Press* Cup with a 4–2 series win over Indianapolis.

The Western League experienced another successful year, and shortly after the season concluded, the personal animosities of John Brush again came to the forefront. Teamed with John Goodnow of the Minneapolis franchise, he found a new way to lash out at Ban Johnson and league owners who'd acted against his wishes.[32] Citing an infraction of the National Agreement, Brush and Goodnow complained that when the league admitted Grand Rapids to play the 1896 season, it did so without the five votes needed to approve admittance. Behind the public grievance, there were several private issues that Brush was steamed about, among them the changes to the farming system rules and the fact that Tom Loftus was approved as owner of the Columbus club over the man he was pushing for. Already owner or partial owner of a number of teams, Brush wanted to add Columbus to his syndicate.

Even more shocking, Brush had already reached out to allies in several cities, setting up a game plan that would be enacted the moment the National Board of Arbitration lifted the "protection" of the Western League because of violations of the agreement. That would open the flood gates to strip the league of its star players by National League teams, without having to pay the $500 per player fee to do so. It was also setting up Brush's new Western League, an organization he controlled, and one that Johnson, Comiskey, and the others had no part of. "Brushism," as some called it, was in full effect. And if he had his way, the Western would never amount to anything more than a proving ground for future National League players.

Johnson promised to fight what Milwaukee owner Matt Killilea called, "the most high handed undertaking I ever heard of in all my life," and was going to throw every cent of the $15,000 in the league treasury at the battle. If the arbitration board failed to protect them, Johnson planned to take the case directly into the courts to safeguard the rights and investments of owners. On October 6, 1896, the National Board of Arbitration dismissed Brush's ploy because of a lack of jurisdiction. The unproductive attack was successful in strengthening the resolve of Johnson and his league owners, and they were learning that their cohesiveness and shrewd decisions were gaining respect in light of being known as a second-class operation.

While magnates were scrambling, Comiskey spent some much needed vacation time at Moose Lake, Minnesota, hunting.[33] His around-the-clock participation in all-things baseball would resume soon enough, but the peacefulness of the country gave him time to clear his head. In November of 1896, at the annual meeting in Chicago, he was named to the league's board of directors as Johnson was reelected president, secretary, and trea-surer.[34] Through the remainder of the year, Comiskey scouted talent, dis-cussed trades and contracts, and worked himself into a frenzy of his own. Along the way, he contracted a serious illness and was bedridden early in 1897 with what some newspapers called full-fledged pneumonia.[35]

Wheeling and dealing resumed in due time, and Comiskey was back on his feet evaluating talent from all corners of the baseball universe. Jack Glasscock, the major league veteran who'd been considered too old to bounce back from an arm injury, led the Western League in batting during the 1896 season with a .431 average, and an amazing 263 hits in 135 games.[36] Glasscock was a dynamo for his age and proved all the naysayers wrong. Comiskey, in honoring his achievements and great field presence, named him captain going into the 1897 season. As expected, Denzer was dealt away to Chicago of the National League, and was going from one baseball spe-cialist, Comiskey, to another, Cap Anson.

New signee Algernon McBride was going to center field, Walter Preston of Virginia into right, and Charlie Nyce was established at second, with another $800 being spent on Tom Parrott. Old favorites George, Mullane, Shugart, and Spies were returning, yet the popular third-baseman Tim O'Rourke would be sent to Kansas City in May. There were also several play-ers refusing to sign contracts based on the Western League's new salary limitations. Every individual team was capped at $2,400 a month, and despite the increase in attendance in most league cities, player salaries decreased.

Versatile Frank Kraus of Brooklyn wrote a letter to the editor of the *St. Paul Globe*, explaining that he'd already taken a cut in pay, and was now facing a second reduction.[37] Without advance money or a ticket to join the club, he was staying put for the time being. Within a few months, Kraus became deathly ill from consumption (tuberculosis) and although his con-dition was said to have improved during the summer, he passed away in September.

Ironically, Comiskey, after griping about the way Aurora Park had been turned into an ice skating rink the winter before, became a promoter for the same such events in late 1896 into '97. He was behind an entire winter carnival featuring skating races and polo matches. The change of heart was based on the fact that the Saints were not returning to the Aurora grounds for the 1897 season, but moving to a new park at the corner of University and Lexington Avenues.[38] The pioneering $75,000 venue, 660 x 600 feet in size, featured 2,000 opera-style seats in the grandstand, brand new amenities, and an upscale bicycle track. It was a remarkable achievement for baseball in St. Paul and helped create a wave of excitement throughout the Twin Cities.

People were inspired by the approaching season, but Comiskey saw another flaw in his team's approach that needed to be rectified. He implemented a no alcohol policy for players, promising bonuses for abstinence, and threatening fines to others. The renewed discipline policy targeted what he believed to be a consistent thorn in the team's side, and the boozing ultimately led to arguments and quarrels. He was having no more of any of it, and those who decided to break the team rule were going to feel his wrath.

Exhibitions in Cincinnati, Louisville, and St. Louis preceded the season opener on April 22, 1897, at Kansas City, won by the Saints, 10–7.[39] The next day the squad pummeled their rivals 29–4, but couldn't complete the sweep, dropping the finale on April 25, 14–11. After a stop in Milwaukee, the third place Saints returned home for its opener at Lexington Park on April 30, and Mayor Doran's speech was followed by a ceremonial first pitch.[40] An estimated 5,000 people—400 who rode to the park on bicycles—attended the game, which was won by the home team, 10–3. By May 7, St. Paul was atop the standings, and the pitching of Phyle, Mullane, and Fricken helped keep them in first place through most of the month. They endured two seven game winning streaks, but their first dreaded road trip began in early June.

With Columbus fast becoming the hottest team in the league, the Saints were losing more than they were winning, and dropped to third place. Fighting back, on July 5, 1897, they took both games of a doubleheader against Minneapolis, and Comiskey treated the entire team to a special evening at the California Wine House.[41] Spirits were high as St. Paul not only tied Columbus for first a few days later, but took them over with wins over Minneapolis and Milwaukee. The standings were tight amongst the top four clubs and changing almost daily.

Comiskey was still optimistic that his team was a contender. Reality was pulling them in the other direction, especially once Mullane's arm began to fail. On July 23, 1897, the veterans of the Saints teamed in a losing effort against the youngsters, billed as the "Colts" in an exhibition benefit for Frank Kraus.[42] Comiskey returned to the field and had two hits, while his brother Ignatius played for the "Kids." The final score was 3–2 and over 600 people were in attendance.

Instances of bad blood and dirty play appeared throughout the season. During a game against Kansas City, faithful catcher Spies rushed after a wild throw, only to see Jock Menefee kick the ball as he was reaching for it, scraping his knuckle at the same time. An argument ensued, but no punches were landed. Later that same game, Spies again went after a foul ball on the Kansas City side, but just as he was about to catch it, a rival player threw a glove, hitting him square in the stomach. Spies caught the ball, but no one admitted to the deed. In Indianapolis, on a different occasion, a local player and instigator named George Hogriever attempted to interfere with a play, again affecting Spies.[43] The dispute led to physicality, and saw Hogriever throw a bat at Spies, injuring the latter's leg. The crowd burst onto the field, and a riot nearly started before police calmed matters.

Also in Indianapolis, Comiskey was thrown out of a game for arguing a contentious play to the opposing manager, but he refused to leave the stadium.[44] Police were called in to escort him out, and players were preparing their bat bags to go with him. The fans in the seats around the visiting dugout surprisingly acted in the Saints favor, desiring nothing but fair play from both teams. They began to edge onto the field, creating a stressful situation for police, as Comiskey finally relented and left under his own accord. Glasscock convinced the players to finish the game. In all, Comiskey and Shugart were thrown out, while Glasscock and George were fined for their actions.

The Saints could never retain a position higher than third for the rest of the season, finishing 86–51 behind Indianapolis and Columbus. Phyle, who missed nine weeks due to his injury, returned on September 5, and was in condition to finish the year. He confronted Comiskey at the train depot as the team was preparing to depart for Milwaukee on September 17.[45] Loudly insisting that Comiskey pay on the promised bonus if he stayed sober during the season, former boxer Phyle took off his jacket and was ready to fight. Comiskey, a veteran of various physical confrontations over the course of his baseball career, proceeded to smack Phyle around, including "several well-directed kicks," according to the *St. Paul Globe*. Phyle ran off, and then briefly assaulted the team's treasurer.

Phyle finished the season with a 19–8 record, the best on the Saints, but was known for his late night extracurricular activities. In October, he was arrested with his brother Joseph for drunkenness in Minneapolis.[46] In spite of his own actions, Phyle knew one thing for sure; he wasn't going to play for Charles Comiskey again. He was reportedly drafted by the Brooklyn Bridegrooms of the National League and headed for the show.

Another year had passed and Comiskey wasn't able to achieve the championship of the Western League. However, he remained utterly respected for his abilities as a leader. Anytime the press caught wind of him commiserating with a major league owner, he was immediately rumored to be taking over as the manager of the latter said club. One story claimed Chris Von der Ahe was offering him $10,000 a year to again handle the Browns.[47] But Comiskey didn't want to backtrack to a managerial position. He was an owner, and the success of the Western League continued to build. As far as the current crop of team owners were concerned, the future of the Western was bright, and Comiskey wasn't going anywhere.

ENDNOTES

1 *St. Paul Daily Globe*, September 23, 1895, p. 5.

2 *San Francisco Call*, October 28, 1895.

3 *Sporting News*, December 21, 1895.

4 Ibid.

5 *Bismarck Tribune*, November 27, 1895.
  Also see: *Rockford Morning Star*, December 10, 1895, p. 5.

6 *Chicago Daily Tribune*, November 15, 1895, p. 8.

7 *Baltimore Sun*, February 25, 1896, p. 6.

8 *St. Paul Daily Globe*, March 3, 1896, p. 5.
  The rule change was adopted at a meeting in St. Paul. In other league news, Omaha was considered a replacement for the dissolving Terre Haute, but Columbus was added instead. Toledo also tried to reenter the league after dropping out mid-season in 1895, but was eventually rejected.

9 *Washington, D.C. Evening Star*, January 11, 1896, p. 20.

10 *Sporting News*, February 15, 1896.

11 *St. Paul Daily Globe*, February 23, 1896, p. 7

12 *St. Paul Daily Globe*, January 7, 1896, p. 5.

13 *St. Paul Daily Globe*, March 24, 1896, p. 5.

14 *St. Paul Daily Globe*, March 28, 1896, p. 5.

15 *St. Paul Daily Globe*, April 5, 1896, p. 11.

16 *St. Paul Daily Globe*, April 21, 1896, p. 5

17 *St. Paul Daily Globe*, March 3, 1896, p. 5

18 *St. Paul Daily Globe*, May 1, 1896, p. 5.

19 *St. Paul Globe*, May 15, 1896, p. 5.

20 *St. Paul Globe*, May 19, 1896, p. 5.

21 *St. Paul Globe*, June 4, 1896, p. 5.

22 *St. Paul Globe*, June 13, 1896, p. 5.

23 *St. Paul Globe*, June 17, 1896, p. 5.

24 *St. Paul Globe*, June 22, 1896, p. 5.

25 *St. Paul Globe*, June 24, 1896, p. 5.

26 *St. Paul Globe*, July 6, 1896, p. 5.

27 *St. Paul Globe*, July 14, 1896, p. 5.

28 *St. Paul Globe*, August 14, 1896, p. 5.

29 *St. Paul Globe*, August 18, 1896, p. 5.

30 *St. Paul Globe*, August 27, 1896, p. 5.

31 *St. Paul Globe*, August 21, 1896, p. 5.

32 *St. Paul Globe*, October 4–7, 1896.

33 *St. Paul Globe*, October 21, 1896, p. 5.

34 *St. Paul Globe*, November 13, 1896, p. 5.

35 *Philadelphia Inquirer*, January 3, 1897, p. 22.

36 The second best hitter, with over 100 games played, was Wilmot of Minneapolis, who bat .384 and had 210 hits. *St. Paul Globe*, January 21, 1897, p. 7.

37 *St. Paul Globe*, April 14, 1897, p. 7.

38 *St. Paul Globe*, March 14, 1897, p. 9.

39 *St. Paul Globe*, April 23, 1897, p. 1.

40 *St. Paul Globe*, May 1, 1897, p. 1.

41 *St. Paul Globe*, July 6, 1897, p. 5.

42 *St. Paul Globe*, July 24, 1897, p. 5.

　　At one point during the game, Ignatius Comiskey found great humor in watching his older brother Charles try to stretch a single into a double—only to be thrown out at second. Charles' intentions were good, but his tired legs no longer had the ability to execute that kind of play.

43 *St. Paul Globe*, September 5, 1897, p. 10.

44 *St. Paul Globe*, August 3, 1897, p. 5.

45 *Sporting News*, September 25, 1897.

46 *St. Paul Globe*, October 25, 1897, p. 2.

47 A report from St. Louis claimed Comiskey was worth "between $50,000 and $60,000" and that he was "grayer" than the last time he'd been around town. This story was picked up by the *St. Paul Globe*, October 12, 1897, p. 5.

6

BIRTH OF THE AMERICAN LEAGUE

Nurtured in a large household as a child, Charles Comiskey always took great delight in being surrounded by family—his siblings, nieces, nephews; the more the merrier. He placed such an emphasis on the welfare of his kin that shortly after the death of his brother-in-law, Augustus Fredericks in 1882, he and Nan began to care for their young niece, Mabel.[1][2] The Comiskey's raised her as their own daughter, living initially in Dubuque, then St. Louis, before settling in St. Paul with their son J. Louis. Both children attended local schools, and Lou even played baseball at St. Thomas College in 1897.[3] Their Fuller Street household was a regular den for baseball magnates, local politicians, and the social elite.

Also in the city lived Comiskey's two most trusted advisors, his father, John, and older brother, Patrick Henry. John was a frequent resident of downtown hotels, and a sportswriter for the *St. Paul Daily Globe* caught up with him one evening following the 1895 season.

"It has been a busy season for an old one like myself," John explained, "but when the baseball schedule ran out on Sunday, I began to feel a lonesome streak creeping over me. I am lonesome at the idea of leaving St. Paul. It has been very kind to Charlie, to me, and all concerned, and I have grown to love the town nearly as much as my old home in Chicago."[4]

John Comiskey managed the developments at Aurora Park for his son from 1895–96, and briefly held a city superintendent position for all baseball venues.[5] As for Patrick, he was Comiskey's right-hand man, working as the secretary for the Saints and handling most of the administrative duties that came along with it.[6] Seeing that his brother was consumed by the on-the-field play of the Saints, ever committed to making the team better,

Patrick filled a major void, relieving Charles from the paperwork that would've hounded him throughout the year.

In late 1897, Western League owners expressed a desire to update the National Agreement.[7] Unsatisfied with the drafting system, they proposed a two player limit, per club, to be promoted to the National League on a yearly basis. As it currently stood, there was no limit, and a major league organization could feasibly select half of the players—or more—from a single roster. Additionally, a regulation keeping a player in the minors for two years before being drafted was suggested, and Western League officials tried to sell the idea by saying it would give athletes time to develop instead of jumping to the majors too soon and possibly failing.

Compromises were reached at the National League meeting in Philadelphia, where owners agreed to the two drafting rule alterations the Western proposed.[8] That agreement was contingent on several other amendments being added to the constitution. National League magnates sought a thirty-day option to return a player to the minors if a major league trial didn't work out. Plus, they wanted the right to farm out athletes and then recall them on thirty-days notice. Without much of an alternative, the concessions were temporarily agreeable to Western League President Ban Johnson, who attended the convention.

Overall, the administrators of the Western League were not happy, and there were scattered reports by sportswriters that its best move would be to break away from the National League and sever all ties to the National Agreement. It was a drastic proposition, but in light of the continued anxieties, it was an option that could prove advantageous. At the moment, though, it wasn't the road they were ready to take.

Rumors that Cap Anson was thinking about joining the organization gave the Western League tremendous credibility in the press.[9] There was also renewed talks of Chicago joining the league, but the same problems that blocked Chicago Colts President James Hart's push for a local franchise three years earlier was still preventing him from obtaining one in 1897.[10] He wanted a minor league unit that would directly feed his Colts and give him total control over the club.

Other Western League owners were not going for it, and Chicago was kept from membership. The organization was faced with a decline in attendance for games in 1897 compared to the year before, and profits were way down. Grand Rapids, Minneapolis, and Kansas City suffered great financial losses, while the Connie Mack-led Milwaukee Brewers proved to be the most valuable. In need of steadying payments to players, owners agreed to impose a $2,000 a month limitation for the 1898 season.[11] The $2,000 was not for a single player, but for the entire roster, and was actually $400 less than the previous year. No single player, except for the captain of the team, could make more than $200 a month.

The intense pressures levied against Western organization owners by the National League combined with lower attendance, caused a similar strain on its own players by way of salary cuts. To supervise the new monthly salary limitation, Johnson was going to personally handle all player signings and the finances that went along with it. With Chicago out of the picture, Omaha, Toledo, Des Moines, and Grand Rapids were in competition for the eighth spot in the league, and Omaha eventually won out in February 1898, awarded with a three-year franchise.[12]

Comiskey was facing an uphill fight. His best hitter, Algie McBride, who led the league in 1897 with a .382 batting average and 199 hits, was sold to Cincinnati for $1,000. Billy George and Charlie Nyce, two other offensive weapons, also departed, along with pitcher Frank Isbell. Pick ups included Doggie Miller from Minneapolis, Eddie Burke from the Reds, and Phil Geier, a Philadelphia transplant. Comiskey remained confident that his newcomers would be fine replacements for the stars that he lost, asking the St. Paul Globe, "How can we lose?"[13]

He added, "If we can't win the pennant this year, we never can."

The salary limitations were hurting nearly every club in the league. Geier, incidentally, was one of many players to protest the meager pay, and briefly held out for more money before joining the team. By March 31, 1898, a day before players were scheduled to report, Comiskey only had seven players under contract: Miller, Burke, Walter Preston, Wallace Hollingsworth, Henry Spies, Hon Fricken, and Captain Jack Glasscock.[14] [15] Feeling the pinch, Comiskey said he'd do what was necessary to field a team, and play first base himself, at thirty-eight years old, if need be. He'd pick up a couple of amateurs as well. In an interview, he appeared convinced that players were going to arrive before the season officially launched.[16]

All owners, because of the reserve clause of the National Agreement, possessed a god-like ownership of the players under their rule. They were in

charge of their athletes' destinies; protected by the rules of Organized Baseball and empowered to buy, sell, and trade them with free will. The players,
conversely, were left with little recourse. If they protested their pay and
walked off the job, there was nowhere to turn within the structure of major
league baseball. They were prevented from going to another team because
they were "owned" by their current club, and they could either jump to an
outlaw franchise or retire from the sport. This system was one of the reasons
that fostered the belief that owners were nothing more than tyrants and
demonstrated that the rules were completely slanted against the players.

Bill Phyle, who reconsidered his vow never to return, and Roger Denzer
arrived at Lexington Park for the start of practice during the first week of
April 1898. Glasscock, Bob Glenalvin, Sam Gillen, Frank Shugart, and Lem
Cross also joined the club. Most players were in decent-to-good condition,
but the workout regimen Comiskey spent years modifying was going to get
everyone into playing shape.[17] One of his favorite routines was chasing a
street car that already had a half a block start. He firmly believed that running was the best way to work off excess weight.

Comiskey donned a uniform and glove to play in one intrasquad exhibition on April 14, but the team of "regulars" destroyed the "Yannigans,"
made up of substitute and trial players, of which Comiskey was a member,
45–1.[18] Decidedly to create a farm system of his own, Comiskey joined the
owner of Lexington Park, Edward Smith, and William White to form a St.
Paul amateur baseball league a few days later.[19] The secondary circuit was
going to be a valuable structure of training for potential future leaguers.
It was a smart organization to sponsor and demonstrated a measure of
forward thinking in the growth and prosperity of the St. Paul Saints.

Content with the playing schedule, particularly the range of home
games at the end of the year, Comiskey took his team to Omaha to christen
the latter's new baseball stadium during the season opener on April 21,
1898—a game which St. Paul won, 7–6, behind Denzer's pitching.[20] The
Saints took three of four games in Omaha, and were then victorious in two-
of-three in Kansas City, returning home on April 29 in third place. Only
1,800 fans turned out to see the start of the new season, but those in attendance were able to watch their heroes win their third straight game.[21]

The Saints went on an amazing streak, winning 12 in a row. Their initial
game against Minneapolis drew Lexington Park's largest crowd, an overflow audience of 7,000 people, on May 8.[22] Briefly rising to first place, they
were confronted by the fact that Indianapolis was playing even better ball

and remained in the top position for most of May. On May 30, Indianapolis beat St. Paul in both games of a doubleheader, and the embarrassing losses, stained by perplexing errors, depleted the confidence of Saints fans.[23] Their lack of competitiveness was startling and the team was in danger of alienating its remaining supporters.

A few days earlier, on May 27, Comiskey again returned to the field after Glasscock was called away because of an illness in his family, and played errorless ball against Columbus.[24] He had a hit, but saw his team shutout, 7–0.

Attendance was sporadically bad, and was usually blamed on concerns over the Spanish-American War. Comiskey, who was known to make changes to his lineup throughout the season, sold longtime favorite Tony Mullane to Detroit, and the latter would pitch against the Saints during a series in June. Following eight errors in a loss to Milwaukee on June 9, 1898, hometown fans outwardly jeered the Saints for their lackluster play, and by June 19, they were in fourth place behind Indianapolis, Columbus, and Kansas City.[25] Their home-stand, which usually afforded them a push in the standings, ended with eight losses and only seven wins. Additionally, the team average was much lower than previous seasons, at .271.

The race was full of energy and, by July, there were five teams less than .100 percentage points from first place. In any given day, a single loss could drop a team from second to fifth, but the Saints battled to remain in contention. They fought for a spot at the head of the pack, but on August 7, 1898, they were defeated in two games of a double-header at home. The *St. Paul Globe*, citing the recent bad play, including a heavy dose of errors, announced, "Good-bye pennant of 1898."[26]

Holding onto a positive attitude, Comiskey made some changes. He released Doggie Miller and signed Lewis Ritter, a catcher, and outfielder Charles Campau, in reaction to Eddie Burke's ankle injury. So far in the season there had been many glimpses of extraordinary athleticism. For instance, Geier's work in the field, Spies behind the plate—especially in chasing foul balls—and by Glenalvin, who was the first to reach 100 hits for the team. But they were unable to play with any consistency, losing games to inferior teams. They fell to fifth place, and when Sammy Gillen became ill, Comiskey rejoined the team at first base, gaining two hits in a loss to Kansas City on September 1.[27] He displayed great range in the field and played errorless ball.

The next day was a memorable one as Comiskey was in action for both games of a doubleheader against St. Joseph.[28] After sustaining a loss in the first contest, Comiskey led the fight in the second, powering a long drive that was a guaranteed inside-the-park home run. With his head down, he trotted as fast as he possibly could, but was not the runner he once was—and the heat was said to have been a factor in his failure to reach home. He landed safely on third and scored a brief time later in what would eventually be a victory. Comiskey's actions at the plate and in the field were admirable, but his club as a whole was playing like a fifth place team.

Captain Glasscock soon retired from the Saints and went back to West Virginia. His lack of offense and lackluster defense, in comparison to previous seasons, were disconcerting to him personally, and he knew it was time to throw in the towel. To everyone but his St. Paul teammates and the enthusiasts who treasured his loyalty and heart, Glasscock represented a disorderly style of play that was generally frowned upon. In fact, the Saints as a whole were regarded as a dirty team, and their methods were said to be condoned and applauded by Comiskey. The comments of unsportsmanlike conduct were almost always recited by a sportswriter representing a rivaling city, and their own objectiveness was certainly called into question.

Unscrupulous actions on the field were prevalent across the baseball landscape and it was easy to blame the manager of any team for the behavior of players. Comiskey, in this instance, was being called out for allowing a handful of his athletes to act in a questionable manner. He was passive as his players incited fights, abused umpires, and used foul language. And when his players weren't jumping down the throats of umps, he was doing it himself. Their combined antics had a resulting affect on the audience as well, and when the play was bad, St. Paul fans showered both visiting and the home teams with all types of maltreatment.

The Saints won their final nine games of the 1898 season, but finished in fourth place with a 81–58 record.[29] Without a doubt, Denzer was the star pitcher, winning 30 and losing 10, and Phyle, who was sold to Chicago before the season concluded, finished 18–15. Glenalvin batted .322 and had 165 hits in 131 games, while Glasscock was at .261 and Comiskey, over his five games, at .273. Western League President Ban Johnson called it the most exciting season in the history of the organization, and the top five teams each were in first place at one time or another.[30] Kansas City, on the last day of the season, secured the top spot and won the pennant over Indianapolis, with Milwaukee placing third.

Financially, Comiskey broke about even.[31] There were more rumors that he was dissatisfied in St. Paul and returning to the big leagues as a manager, but Comiskey didn't appear to be concerned by the reports.[32] He instead spent weeks hunting in the northern part of Minnesota.

But there was truth to the gossip, as Comiskey was, indeed, planning something big. His old St. Louis franchise was being sold at public auction on March 14, 1899, and Comiskey, along with Tom Loftus, were among the two busiest movers and shakers in the business leading up to the sale.[33] Together and individually, they met with financers, associates, Chicago Colts owner James Hart, and Western League President Ban Johnson. As Loftus was seen as taking the point position on the possible purchase, people speculated to Comiskey's interest in the matter and wondered if he was going to end up back in St. Louis as a part owner and manager. In terms of politics, there was a fear that National League magnates would work to block Loftus and Comiskey from ownership if they did score a winning bid.

The eyes of the baseball world were on St. Louis on March 14, and both Loftus and Comiskey were on hand, seemingly to make a move. In the end, neither made a bid, and a consortium representing creditors of Sportsman's Park and Club bought the franchise for $33,000.[34] Different stories of what happened behind-the-scenes surfaced but apparently Comiskey and Loftus were in cahoots with the creditors and decided against bidding because they didn't want to run up the price.[35] It was soon expected that they'd purchase the organization in a private sale, but were advised against the deal at the last minute by their attorney. Rather than working the matter out, they let the deal slip through their hands and would later regret it. The creditors didn't hesitate to sell the club to another buyer.

Heading into the new season, St. Paul pundits were anticipating Comiskey's Saints to be much improved over last year. Comiskey told the *Globe*, "I have no reason to fear that my team will rank up with the best of them this year," and that he thought he had "the best pitching staff in the league without exception. Roger Denzer is the best pitcher in this league today."[36]

He was even more confident after seeing his players practice at Kittsondale, saying: "The St. Paul ball team this season is an aggregation of pennant winners."[37] Among those returning were Denzer, Spies, Shugart, Burke, Glenalvin, Geier, and Isbell, who he expected great things from at first base. He traded Cross and Gillen for Dan Lally, a proven asset, and acquired pitcher Chauncey Fisher for $1,200. Fisher was one of the last holdouts for the season, but came to terms just as the Saints were appearing for their initial series at Kansas City on April 28, 1899.

A little over 1,900 people attended the Lexington Park opener on May 4, and the Saints prevailed over Kansas City, 11–3.[38] A classic 17-inning pitcher's duel occurred four days later against Milwaukee, when Denzer went the entire length of the game and secured a victory, 5–4.[39] The *Globe* compared his effort to that of the legendary Charles Radbourn, Comiskey's old teammate at Dubuque, and Denzer held his opponents to only six hits. In first place briefly in May and again in early June, the Saints had some interesting moments including the near riot at Lexington Park on May 14, when an estimated 1,000 spectators, spurred on by the captain of the Minneapolis team, nearly attacked the umpire after a forfeited game.[40]

Later in the month, Comiskey played the initial bag in a 3–1 victory over Indianapolis on May 30, committing two errors in the field, but beat out a bunt to first base, showing his continued vigor.[41] Admittedly, he'd gained weight since settling in St. Paul and wasn't the athlete he used to be. But Comiskey used all the tricks of the trade, blocking players from the bag at times and forcing outs that would normally be safe. It was nearly impossible to outwit him, and if a player wasn't on top of their game, thinking at all times, Comiskey would have the upper hand—either at bat or on the field. He'd seen it all before and knew all the various techniques to gain an advantage; and most of the time, the umpires would look the other way.

His style of play was infectious and invigorated the Saints on the field. For some of the younger athletes, it was hard not to be in awe of him, especially because of all the stories surrounding his great successes in the past. They were inspired by his hustle and dedication to hardnosed play, even while handling the responsibilities of an owner. It seemed that once he got back onto the field, contract talks and the overall bottom line meant little in comparison to what was most important: playing to win. The fans also respected his enthusiasm, applauding wildly when he came to bat.

Sinking in the standings, the Saints were at the mercy of better teams, falling to Rube Waddell and the Columbus franchise, their Twin Cities rival, Minneapolis, and the rest of the league. It was difficult to comprehend, but St. Paul was a fifth place franchise, and the hype of a pennant at the start of the season was quite exaggerated. Comiskey made additional changes, signing pitcher John Katoll, Charlie Frank, Arthur Ball, George Decker, "Lefty" Houtz, and Harry Vaughn, but not everyone survived the season.

Back in Chicago, Comiskey's father John was failing in health, and Charles was compelled to be at his bedside every chance he got. The *Milwaukee Sentinel* picked up on the story but didn't explain why he was spending so much time in the "Windy City." Instead, it stated that the Saints might have been playing better if he was around them more often.[42] Comiskey was also perpetually scouting for new talent and had real estate holdings in Chicago that required supervision. Now valued at $100,000, his time was in high demand and his focus was on many things, including the discussion of a secondary organization being formed in opposition to the National League.[43]

Needless to say, the St. Paul press searched for a reason for the team's lack of success. Some writers picked up on the speculation that excessive boozing by Saints players was to blame, and Comiskey planned to weed the partiers out. It was true that a lack of concentrated discipline was hurting the club, and Comiskey's regular absence was a likely contributor. "They have been batting like a lot of school boys," Comiskey told the *Globe*, "I cannot understand them. Last year several of these same men were batting around the .300 mark, and when the team lined up for work this spring, they looked like winners."[44]

But they were far from winners. The season ended on September 11, 1899, with St. Paul finishing in fifth place behind Indianapolis, Minneapolis, Detroit, and Grand Rapids, with a 57–69 record.[45] The team batted .263, led by Phil Geier and Dan Lally, but were last in fielding, having committed 412 errors, the most of any franchise in the league.

The baseball world was in turmoil. Earlier in the year, structural cracks in the foundation of the National League were apparent when a band of powerful owners aligned against the weaker representatives of the group, and a downsizing from twelve clubs to eight was expected. Some newspapers indicated that league owners were at war as President Johnson and the other Western League magnates sat idly by, waiting for the situation to resolve itself. If four teams were discarded from the majors, the Western was in a fine place to secure the disposed of players suddenly in need of employment. That would immediately improve the level of competition, and Comiskey was eagerly awaiting the prime opportunity to score big. To make matters worse for the National League, the American Association of Baseball Clubs was organized in Chicago on September 17, and among its list of powerbrokers were Cap Anson and H. D. Quinn.[46] In possession of substantial aspirations, the new organization was seen as a threat to the National League's dominance, while others felt it was all just a bluff to throw off the plans of other competition.

In response, Chicago Colts/Orphans owner James Hart, trying to protect his territory from the threat of the Association, urged a strengthening between the National and Western Leagues by admitting a second club to operate in his city.[47] The new Chicago club would be run by Tom Loftus and operated under the direction of his franchise. It was a last-ditch effort to control the Western League before it expanded on its own and into his backyard without his endorsement. Not so shockingly, his partner in the scheme was John T. Brush of Cincinnati-Indianapolis.

Neither Johnson, Comiskey, nor any of the other members of the Western League wanted to bow to Hart or Brush. That was apparent when the Western League unanimously approved its next move, changing the organization's name to the "American League," during its annual meeting at the Great Northern Hotel in Chicago, on October 11, 1899.[48] Seen by some observers as a move further bonding to the former Western to the National League, it was an aggressive maneuver, and along with repeated requests to change the National Agreement, the prospects for a cohesive and strong partnership were in full doubt. Hart, for one, was not content with the adjustments and could plainly see the writing on the wall.

Continued denials appeased the St. Paul public that Comiskey wasn't packing up and leaving town in spite of many new claims to the contrary. Although he wasn't as boisterous as in previous years, he expressed a desire to upgrade his stadium from Lexington Park to another venue, claiming that the decline in attendance was because of the poor location of the grounds. Comiskey was biding his time before making the big announcement; a declaration that would forever change things for him personally, and for the course of baseball forever. The great "Comanche," as some reporters called him, was moving up in the world.[49] But in reality, his life was coming full circle. Comiskey was going back home.

On the evening of November 20, 1899, it was finally announced that the American League was launching a club in Chicago in 1900 and the team would be under the ownership of Charles Comiskey.[50]

The big question was whether or not the encroachment of the American League into Chicago—a sacred National League town—violated the National Agreement. To Hart, of course it did. In his view of the rules, territories were protected from invasion, and because of this, Comiskey had no basis to enter his region without his approval. Comiskey, on the other hand, was not in the mood to play games, and told the *Chicago Daily Tribune* just that: "We mean business, and you will see an American league club in Chicago next year."[51]

He continued: "We have waited long and patiently for the National League club to act reasonably and to meet its promises. We do not want a baseball war, but we do not propose to be frozen out of our rights any longer. There is not an impartial baseball man or enthusiast in Chicago who will say that an additional club here will hurt the National League club. There will be plenty who will say it will help the league club. We are willing to go in and arrange everything that can be arranged so as to meet the mutual interests of both teams."

"I think that the two clubs," Johnson added, "will live in peace and harmony."

Back in St. Paul, Patrick Comiskey worked to unload the local club to an area buyer.[52] Edward Smith, to whom Comiskey was paying $2,000 annually to lease Lexington Park, was a prime candidate, but backed out once negotiations failed. According to reports, Comiskey was looking for anywhere from $12,000 to more than $15,000 for the team, thousands of dollars more than Smith thought it was worth.

Boston owner Arthur Soden told the press that the new American Association, not the American League, would benefit greatly if it picked up the cast-off franchises of the National League; indicating that the latter would work in partnership with the new organization.[53] To this, Johnson was furious. After years of paying protection money to the National League, his teams were now subjected to favoritism from a league which hadn't yet played a single game. For years, the majors had tried to dominate the Western, acting in a tyrannical and bullying fashion, and as the new American League grew in stature, threatening its territory, the National League was doing everything its power to limit the potency of the intimidating force.

Johnson knew that the National League, for years, failed to compromise despite their pleas. Their appeals to change the drafting rules went unheard, and, time after time, the Western accepted the tight stipulations imposed by the major clubs. If they had to break from the National Agreement, they were prepared to do so. It hadn't benefited them anyway, seeing that it was strictly controlled by the National League itself. Peace and harmony was no longer expected.

"There is no use fooling over this any longer," Comiskey explained. "I am going to have a club of my own in Chicago next season. Hart says we cannot get a club in here without getting his permission. Well, we don't want his permission. It is not needed. Mr. Hart has assured some innocent reporter that the president of the Chicago club will have the say so in the matter and that unless we want to break the national agreement, the talk of a second club is all bosh. Well, all this may be a pleasant reverie for Mr. Hart, but did you ever give a thought to what may happen when he wakes up? I think that the American League managers are perfectly willing to break that agreement. It never did us a particle of good, and we will be much better off without it."[54]

In an interesting sidebar that had potential to resolve the problems in Chicago, Comiskey's best friend, Tom Loftus, was named the new manager for Hart's Orphans.[55] Loftus was a smart baseball leader and was willing to hang up his duties as owner of the Columbus-Grand Rapids franchise to enter the realm of the National League. In that position, having the ear of Hart, he could potentially smooth things over with Comiskey and end the Chicago war.

Even if he wasn't able to, local fans were going to be the recipients of two professional baseball outfits during the 1900 season. They were certainly familiar with the Orphans, but the Chicago White Stockings, run by native son Charles Comiskey, were a brand new product. While the addition was an exciting one, the team's stability, especially for the long run, still remained to be seen.

ENDNOTES

1 *Dubuque Herald*, March 7, 1882.
   Fredericks was twenty-eight years old when he passed away from consumption. He was a well-liked former pressman, and had married Katherine "Kate" Kelly, the sister of Comiskey's wife Nan, about five years earlier. They had two young children, Charles and Mabel.

2 *St. Paul Globe*, April 14, 1899, p. 2.
   Also see: *Dubuque Herald*, April 16, 1899.

3 *St. Paul Globe*, April 6, 1897, p. 7.

4 *St. Paul Daily Globe*, September 29, 1895, p. 14.

5 By 1897, he had relocated back to Chicago.

6 He resided at 547 Martin Street with his wife and two daughters, and was instrumental in the growth and prosperity of the Saints. Had he not passed away in
1900, he would have undoubtedly been a significant behind-the-scenes factor in
the success of the White Sox.

7 *St. Paul Globe,* November 1, 1897, p. 5.

8 *New York Tribune,* November 10, 1897, p. 3.

9 *Chicago Daily Tribune,* December 21, 1897, p. 4.

10 *Chicago Daily Tribune,* December 22, 1897, p. 4.

11 *St. Paul Globe,* November 28, 1897, p. 10.

The team captain's wages was whatever the owner wanted it to be and the
amount did not count against the salary limit. Any teams found to be over the
$2,000 limit would be fined by President Johnson.

12 *Chicago Daily Tribune,* February 25, 1898, p. 10.

13 *St. Paul Globe,* March 2, 1898, p. 3.

14 *St. Paul Globe,* March 31, 1898, p. 5.

15 Glasscock batted third in the league in 1897 with a .373 average.

16 *St. Paul Globe,* March 27, 1898, p. 10.

17 *St. Paul Globe,* April 7, 1898, p. 5.

18 *St. Paul Globe,* April 15, 1898, p. 5.

19 *St. Paul Globe,* April 17, 1898, p. 10.

20 *Omaha World Herald,* April 22, 1898, p. 2.

21 *St. Paul Globe,* April 30, 1898, p. 5.

22 *St. Paul Globe,* May 9, 1898, p. 5.

23 *St. Paul Globe,* May 31, 1898, p. 5.

24 *St. Paul Globe,* May 28, 1898, p. 5.

25 *St. Paul Globe,* June 10, 1898, p. 5.

26 *St. Paul Globe,* August 8, 1898, p. 5.

27 *St. Paul Globe,* September 2, 1898, p. 5.

28 *St. Paul Globe,* September 3, 1898, p. 5.

29 *St. Paul Globe,* September 21, 1898, p. 5.

30 *St. Paul Globe,* September 22, 1898, p. 5.

31 *St. Paul Globe,* September 16, 1898, p. 5.

32 *St. Paul Globe,* November 30, 1898, p. 5.

33 *Cleveland Plain Dealer,* February 18, 1899, p. 8.

34 *Cleveland Plain Dealer,* March 15, 1899, p. 8.

35 *St. Paul Globe,* March 18, 1899, p. 5.

36 *St. Paul Globe,* March 31, 1899, p. 5.

37 *St. Paul Globe,* April 13, 1899, p. 9.

Although it is unclear, it seems that Comiskey relied on veteran Glenalvin as
the team's player-captain, while he directed all happenings from the bench as
manager.

38 *St. Paul Globe,* May 5, 1899, p. 5.

Neither the Minnesota governor nor St. Paul mayor attended the festivities,
despite invitations.

39 *St. Paul Globe,* May 9, 1899, p. 5.

40 *St. Paul Globe*, May 15, 1899, p. 5.
   Walt Wilmot of the Millers was said to have instigated pro-Minneapolis fans against umpire Al Mannassau. Police prevented things from getting too far out of hand.
41 *St. Paul Globe*, May 31, 1899, p. 5.
42 *St. Paul Globe*, July 29, 1899, p. 5.
43 *St. Paul Globe*, July 20, 1899, p. 5.
   The report of his finances originally came from the *Buffalo Commercial* newspaper. The said amount was likely far too inflated at this point in Comiskey's career as an owner. That is also considering that his baseball business in St. Paul was not earning him an exceptional living. It is more reasonable to theorize that Comiskey's real estate holdings were more profitable to him in 1899 than his baseball interests.
44 *St. Paul Globe*, August 8, 1899, p. 5.
45 *St. Paul Globe*, September 12, 1899, p. 5.
46 *Cleveland Plain Dealer*, September 18, 1899, p. 6.
47 *St. Paul Globe*, September 21, 1899, p. 5.
48 *St. Paul Globe*, October 12, 1899, p. 5.
49 Comiskey was frequently referred to as "Comanche" by sportswriters in St. Paul.
50 *St. Paul Globe*, November 21, 1899, p. 5.
51 *Chicago Daily Tribune*, November 22, 1899, p. 6.
52 *St. Paul Globe*, November 22, 1899, p. 5.
53 *St. Paul Globe*, December 1, 1899, p. 5.
54 *St. Paul Globe*, December 21, 1899, p. 6.
55 *Chicago Daily Tribune*, November 29, 1899, p. 6.

7

THROUGH TRAGEDY TO TRIUMPH

Charles Comiskey was not bluffing about his strategy for Chicago, nor was he striving to provoke a deliberate rivalry against James Hart, president of the Orphans and local representative for the National League. The decision to break into the "Windy City" was instigated by the other factors in baseball, generally the quick rise of the ballyhooed American Association and the perceived demise of the National. Although the American League was still considered the minors, it was rapidly making headway to becoming a peer of the National League. Ban Johnson knew the time was right to strengthen its circuit and Chicago was natural choice for expansion. If they hesitated, there was a possibility that they'd lose all the ground they'd worked for, and remain regulated to second class status.

Of course, there were private reasons for Comiskey as well. Being in his hometown, for one; but the promise of making a success of it as an owner in a big-time city was a challenge he aspired to. His experiences in St. Paul were a revelation as he was confronted by the fundamental duties of a club boss for the first time in his life. He planned to continue moving forward with the same ideals, notions, and wisdom he'd garnered throughout his career, and was firmly confident that he was going to a find a way to be successful.

The united front of the American League seemed like it could topple any problem and overcome all adversity. Aside from the excitement presented by relocating to Chicago and starting with a fresh perspective, Comiskey was going to face a number of personal trials in 1900 that came at regular intervals through the year, taxing his mind and spirit. His inner strength was going to be tested during a time that was supposed to be enjoyable, and the unfortunate realities were criminally painful to his heart and soul. All things considered, the first happening, shortly after the New Year arrived, was somewhat expected.

At his Lytle Street home, where he'd lived for decades, "Honest" John Comiskey passed away on the morning of January 8, 1900.[1] The venerable former Chicago alderman with the distinguished gray beard had been in decreasing health for some time and his death sent a cold shutter through the bodies of everyone he'd touched. Charles and his father didn't always see eye to eye, but the elder was a substantial influence on the way he worked in a diplomatic fashion, played hardball when necessary, and sought ways to compromise in thorny situations. If John had his way, his son would've become a plumber, but Charles found his own path and followed his dreams without that early fatherly guidance. They later reconciled and John was an important counselor in all areas of his life, both business and personal.

John's funeral was attended by current members of the Chicago City Council, friends, and admirers. He was survived by seven of his children and, at the time, no one could have known or imaged the fate of the Comiskey family in the coming months.

Comiskey maintained a strong front in the public eye, keeping the strain of the loss quiet and resuming his demanding workload. Constant uproar in the press flaunted the growing muscle of the American Association and in January of 1900, the National League formed a symbolic alliance with the Association that was supposed to keep the peace.[2] Essentially, the Association was manipulated into becoming a puppet organization for National League magnates, and if it was able to get off the ground, it would always be a secondary outfit. Ultimately, the dreams of the Association sank into the abyss and only the National and American Leagues played ball in April.

But before that could come to fruition, there were still plenty of decisions yet to be made. Comiskey laughed off claims that he was relocating to Kentucky and Johnson continued to sell the reasoning for having two clubs in Chicago.[3] [4] He explained that the city housed two million people and that there was no reason why one man should have exclusive rights to such a massive region. Additionally, playing to the fears of National League owners, he reiterated the fact that by having the American League operating in Chicago, it would eliminate the threat of an outside organization running in opposition.

Showing his lighter side, Comiskey told the *Chicago Daily Tribune* that if he didn't successfully achieve a franchise in the city, he was going to take a surprising new occupation: "I will either have a team in Chicago or else go on the police force. I think I can pass a good enough civil service examination to get a job as desk sergeant. I shouldn't want to travel a beat, but I guess I could if worst came to the worst. I am pretty near six feet tall and weigh over 180 pounds. I ought to be able to qualify as a policeman. That is the proposition so far as I am concerned."[5]

Tom Loftus, the man with the plan, went to work to settle all lingering questions. As the new manager of the Chicago Orphans, he had a direct line to President Hart and he arranged a special meeting at the Great Northern Hotel on March 13, 1900 to be attended by Hart, Johnson, and Comiskey.[6] The atmosphere was pleasant, the individuals respectful and friendly, and although a deal wasn't reached that day, it was a few days later when certain stipulations were reached that were favorable to all parties.[7] Officially, with the National Agreement unbroken, Comiskey was the owner of the second Chicago professional baseball franchise.

Comiskey was thrilled that things had been smoothed over. He'd agreed to only play ball in the city when the Orphans were out of town, and the accord also gave him—and all other American League clubs—access to buy reserve players held by National League squads. It was imperative to put a competitive team on the field for the 1900 season, as anything less would be damaging to the league's credibility and an embarrassment to Comiskey. Spending a small fortune, he obtained William "Dummy" Hoy, Dick Padden, Fred Hartman, Herm McFarland, Dick Buckley, Tommy Dowd, Joe Sugden, and Steve Brodie, while bringing over Roger Denzer, Frank Isbell, Dan Lally, Frank Shugart, and John Katoll from the St. Paul club. Pitchers Chauncey Fisher and Willie McGill, formerly of the Saints, held out for more money but came around just after the season began.

In picking a name for his club, Comiskey chose the "White Stockings," a designation with special heritage in Chicago going back several decades, and his selection was lauded by enthusiasts who appreciated the historical connotations of its resurrection.[8]

Also on his agenda was the selection of appropriate grounds for a makeshift stadium. With the relocation of the Wanderers Cricket and Athletic Club from an area at 39th Street and Wentworth Avenue, the latter became available for Comiskey to lease.[9] The South Side location for years featured amateur and professional sports from cricket to football and rested four blocks south of where Comiskey had played as a member of the Brotherhood squad. Once it was selected as the site for American League baseball,

Comiskey went right to work arranging for a grandstand to be erected on the southwest corner. Fencing and bleachers were established, and by mid-April, only a paintjob was needed.

The White Stockings reported on Monday, April 2, 1900, and went directly to Champaign, Illinois, where they began spring training under the leadership of new catcher, Dick Buckley.[10] For reasons that were well understood, Comiskey, who remained the club's manager, was unable to join the team because of troubling news on the home-front.

His fourteen-year-old son, Louis, was battling pneumonia at their home on Wabash Avenue and 44th Street in Chicago, and his condition was considered severe.[11] The unpredictability of the illness was heartbreaking for members of the Comiskey family, who felt helpless and at the mercy of its curse. Baseball was pushed out of the way as Charles remained steadfast in his duties to his son Louis' health improved steadily, and after a few days he completely recovered. Still, Comiskey refrained from heading south as his team played exhibitions against the University of Illinois, and supervised the construction of his park. He also ordered uniforms and made preparations for an extravagant opening day, including invitations to local and state politicians, the customary fare.

On April 18, 1900, Comiskey was hammered again with more distressing news.[12] His older brother, Patrick, who'd been so instrumental in the administration of the Saints, was on his deathbed in St. Paul. Dropping everything (again), he rushed to his brother's side, but Patrick passed away during the afternoon of April 19 of Bright's disease.[13] Patrick had been sick for some time but had appeared to be recovering when his final downturn came.

Opening Day for the White Stockings was delayed because of muddy conditions at the stadium, and the postponement allowed Comiskey to attend to private family matters.[14] The American League's Chicago franchise took the field for the first time in a game that actually counted on April 21 under cloudy skies. They were greeted as heroes by a little over 5,000 in attendance; a crowd that was aware of the game's significance. The Milwaukee Brewers were less impressed and, after 10 innings, won 5–4.

While early season injuries were a literal pain in the neck, the White Stockings were still able to display a good symmetry of hitting and fielding. Pitcher Isbell was using his curve ball to silence batters, while Katoll was fast becoming the ace of the staff. McFarland smashed the ball with frequency, including a couple of the club's earliest home runs.[15] After six games at home, it was reported that paid attendance for the club had risen above

21,000, and Comiskey admitted that the total had nearly eclipsed the entire season figures for St. Paul in 1899.[16]

Huge throngs of people turned out for games at Milwaukee, and the April 29 presentation against Chicago drew over 15,000 people, the largest crowd on record for baseball at the Lloyd Street Grounds.[17] Isbell pitched impressively and the Stockings scored two runs in the eighth, enough to win the game, 2–1. A lack of practical playing experience as a cohesive unit was blamed for mistimed errors in the field, and Dick Padden, the man Comiskey personally selected to captain the squad, was commended for his ability to fuse the different talents into a flowing organism. Padden, originally from West Virginia, played three years with the Pittsburgh Pirates before landing in Washington in 1899. He was arguably Comiskey's biggest addition during the offseason and the most important player on the White Stockings.

Able to size up critical circumstances during the extent of a game, Padden was usually cool under pressure and expertly directed the team in Comiskey's absence. Comiskey, however, made his presence felt from time to time by scheduling extra batting practice and giving speeches on tactical play, including tricks to being better base runners.[18] He changed the batting order, shifted players around, and clearly imparted his demands to Padden on the field. It was fast becoming rare to see Comiskey on the bench at all; a definite change over previous years.

The reigning champion Indianapolis Hoosiers came to Chicago for a key four game series beginning on June 14, 1900, and the White Stockings took three of four from the first place team.[19] More importantly to note was that each game ended in a shutout, but a reversal came on June 16, when Winford Kellum of Canada no-hit Chicago 6–0 at the South Side grounds.[20] The *Tribune* stated that the White Stockings "had not the slightest license to win," and had been haunted by bad fielding and, of course, a lack of offense. Their three victories in the series were significant in shifting momentum in the league, as Chicago had only one direction they planned on going—up.

Eleven thousand spectators watched the final game against Indianapolis, and several hundred sat along a fence on the field itself. The team went on a terror, winning 13 of 14, and then entered first place on June 24. Their home stand ended with victories in 20 of 27 games.[21]

Things changed on the road, but the decline was again overshadowed by a significant personal crisis in the life of Charles Comiskey. His youngest brother, Ignatius, passed away unexpectedly at the age of twenty-eight at

Charles' home in Chicago during the overnight hours of July 3, 1900.[22] Ignatius played for a number of different semi-pro baseball teams, even performing in exhibitions for his brother while in Minnesota. He was a versatile athlete and his death was stunning considering most felt he was in premier physical shape.

The first year of the American League saw the deaths of Comiskey's father and two of his closest brothers. The family once again came together to pay respects to their loved one, and Comiskey put himself back to work as soon as possible, trying to cope with all the losses in his own way.

In Detroit on July 14, 1900, the worst kind of example of fan involvement in the on-the-field happenings surfaced when hundreds of fans raced onto the field after Chicago beat the local team, 4–2.[23] The angry mob, which had been throwing bottles at White Stockings players during the course of the game, quickly moved to surround umpire Joe Cantillon, collectively fuming at the latter's decision making. Shouts of lynching the official were among the outrageous bellows, and even after police stepped in to protect Cantillon, taking him to a nearby station, the furious horde waited outside for him to reappear. The same kind of riotous behavior occurred at the umpire's hotel later on, as the crowd seemingly wouldn't pardon his apparently unforgiveable actions. President Ban Johnson suspended a Detroit player and fined another for prompting the affair.

Johnson, notably, didn't have many friends in the Detroit franchise at the time, and there was a growing animosity between him and the team's owner, James Burns. Burns had a perspective about the hierarchy of the American League, and was quoted as saying: "It is my opinion that Mr. Comiskey is at present the power behind the throne and has a firm hand on the throttle that is running the league."[24]

Others probably thought the same way, seeing how close Comiskey and Johnson were. Nevertheless, the players of the White Stockings weren't engaged in the politics of the league, but overcoming long odds to perform at a championship level. Despite numerous injuries, and doing what needed to be done to win, Chicago was in fine position going into the final weeks. A pennant was expected and even before the title was officially won, Comiskey took steps to display the championship banner—preordering a 300 foot tall flag pole and flag.[25]

Even with Comiskey's confidence, there was still an outside chance that the White Stockings could finish second. It was unlikely, but a complete meltdown was still possible. In some circles, the celebration commenced early and on September 15, 1900, Comiskey pronounced it "Padden Day," in recognition of his captain's outstanding leadership.[26] Six thousand people turned out and a band enlivened the festivities. On the field, Buffalo took the victory, 5–4. Chicago also lost the season finale against Indianapolis on September 18, but it didn't matter; the White Stockings had clinched the American League pennant with a 82–53 record, giving Chicago its first championship in fourteen years.[27]

President James Hart pushed for a best-of-seven series between his National League Orphans and the White Stockings to begin on October 1, but Comiskey explained that his men were no longer bounded to him once the season was over and were going their separate ways.[28] Most of them were going back to their hometowns and were finished with baseball for the year. Then Hart asked Johnson to put together an all-star squad made up of any set of players from the American League. With respect, Johnson replied that because of the timing of the issue, a series could not be arranged.[29] He then joined Comiskey aboard a train headed to Minnesota, where they planned to fish and hunt for the next ten days.[30]

A new round of tension spread through the National League as Johnson made it known that the American League was likely going to expand further in 1901. The surprising success of the White Stockings in Chicago made it evident that certain cities were able to support two ball clubs at the same time. Sponsoring a clean style of play, supported by Johnson's staunch discipline, heavy competition, and respectable management, the American League was in a position to overtake the National League in terms of popularity in some regions. In fact, the National League was losing money in most of its cities and the reputations of many of its owners were in the toilet. The prospects of a second major league organization successfully challenging the Nationals for superiority were again high.

And it was also apparent that Johnson was possibly angling the American League in that direction. To do so, the league would have to declare its independence and break from the National Agreement. Although that threat had been made in previous years, the American League had reached its zenith in terms of respect and achievement and now it was all very serious. Johnson had manipulated the league into the perfect position and possessed the right kind of leverage to make substantial changes to the baseball landscape.

Having been bullied and maneuvered into unfair contracts for years, players in the National League were excited by the arrival of a new organization. The enthusiasm grew when Johnson agreed to negotiate a refined contract with the Protective Association of Professional Ball Players, a union formed on June 10, 1900, in an effort to straighten out a slew of grievances by the athletes themselves.[31] One of the most important proposed alterations was limiting the lifetime reserve rule to three years, meaning that a player would be free of all binding obligations after that time. As it stood, players were considered a "slave" to team owners for an infinite period, and a change to the regulation was music to their ears.

The American League voted to approve expansion into Eastern cities and banned the dreaded farming system at the annual fall meeting in October 1900 in Chicago.[32] Other judgments were either delayed for a future conference or made in secret. A special Circuit Committee was formed, made up of Comiskey, Johnson, James Manning of Kansas City, and Charles Somers of Cleveland, and on October 30, a vote of 3–1 favored league clubs in Philadelphia and Washington, D.C., replacing Minneapolis and Kansas City.[33] Baltimore was soon added as well, while Indianapolis, the multiple-time pennant winner for the Western League, was dropped.[34]

Johnson was becoming more and more appreciated for his calculated decision making and was seen as a much better leader than President Nick Young, a pawn of scheming National League owners. On October 31, 1900, Johnson sent a notification to Young stating that the American League wanted a redesign of the National Agreement and that they would not be signing the contract as it currently stood. Plus, the league was not going to remit annual dues (protection money) for 1901 until the agreement was updated.

Johnson went east to personally supervise the efforts in Philadelphia, Washington, D.C., and Baltimore. On November 12, 1900, a meeting was held in Baltimore that saw the preliminary circuit of the eight team American League announced.[35] The teams would be:

East	West
Baltimore Orioles	Chicago White Sox
Washington Senators	Detroit Tigers
Philadelphia Athletics	Cleveland Blues
Buffalo Bisons	Milwaukee Brewers

With the ending of its five-year agreement, the American League was ripe to be reorganized and accepted as an equal to the National League—signi-

fying that it was now a major league organization. The 1901 season represented the start of a new era.

Comiskey, always devoted to his playing grounds, spent more money reno-
vating his ballpark during the off season.[36] Additional box seats were added
to the grandstand and the field itself was raised more than a foot. Plus, the
first baseline bleachers were shifted nearly 50 feet closer to the diamond,
giving fans a better perspective of the action. Plotting a spring training to
remember, he announced a planned trip to Mexico and the Southwestern
United States, an idea that was later scrapped because of the cost involved.
His back up location was Arkansas, but that also fell through. The team
would end up training in Excelsior Springs, Missouri, a relaxing region
known for its high mineral spring water.

Politics and war dominated baseball headlines between December and
April of 1901. Because the American League refused to sign the National
Agreement, it was effectively an independent organization free from
National League cooperation.[37] In the press, National League owners, even
Hart in Chicago and President Young, kept a positive attitude, saying that
the two organizations could get along and there was no reason to expect a
drawn out, combative situation. Privately, National League bigwigs were
steaming mad at the fact that Johnson had announced they were expanding without asking permission to do so. It was considered a sign of disre-
spect and the air of peacefulness was quickly diminishing.

The Protective Association of Professional Baseball Players was on the
verge of a strike because of the National League's apathy to its demands.
Although the American League was promising considerations, the National
was demonstrating a real lack of management and its true selfish nature by
further straining its ties to the player union—a move it would later regret.
The *Tribune* compared the two organizations, explaining that the American
had a much better record to build upon as it tried to strengthen the sportsmanship and overall reputation of baseball.[38] Behind stringent Johnson as
the chief disciplinarian, it was rooting out the problems more often seen in
the National League, including fighting, obscene language, and abuse of
umpires.

These efforts were earning the praise of the public and influential
sportswriters across the nation, and by adding the support of the players, it

was becoming an unbreakable force. Soon, Buffalo was replaced by the Boston Americans (later to be known as the Red Sox), and the circuit for 1901 was complete.

In response to the building momentum against it, the National League came up with a plan to resurrect the American Association yet again; this time to run opposition in American League cities.[39] That meant that in Boston, Philadelphia, and Chicago, there would be *three* professional clubs, restricting attendance for everyone. The Association squads would be financed by the National League and made up of the latter's reserve rosters. It was an odd reaction, but nevertheless was intended to pressure Johnson and his cohorts as they labored to expand. When all was said and done, the National League proved to be all talk, refusing to finance the Association, and the plan demonstrated more poor judgment.

The great personal loss of Comiskey's two brothers and father over the previous year was made even worse when another brother, James Comiskey, died in Kansas City on January 2, 1901.[40] A former postmaster in St. Mary's, Kansas, James was survived by his wife and six children. Charles rushed to Kansas City to attend the services for his lost sibling.[41]

In early February, Comiskey battled a harsh winter cold, but went to St. Louis on January 21 to discuss a proposition made by Charles Daniels to promote a soccer game between teams made up of baseball players.[42] [43] The suggestion initially seemed like a good idea with March 17 being picked as the date of a scheduled match-up, but the game never came to fruition. Comiskey's visit to St. Louis sparked rumors that the American League was expanding to that city; an option that had been discussed but not overly pursued as of yet.

In 1901, Comiskey made a major change to the way he ran his ball club. Since taking over St. Paul, he split the duties of owner and manager but was ready to resign himself to the front office and allow his new superstar pick up, Clark Griffith, to handle the managerial duties on the field. Griffith, originally from Missouri, had played the last eight seasons for the Chicago Orphans and finished with a 14–13 record as a pitcher in 1900. He was a proven leader, a future Hall of Famer,[44] and the right kind of man to coexist with Dick Padden, last year's captain, in working toward another championship.

Padden was heavily scouted by National League teams after his outstanding season in Chicago. Prior to his year of redemption, pundits were calling him a "has been," but he was once again in their favor. Comiskey expected him to return, but Padden pulled a shocker by jumping ship for St. Louis, signing a $3,000 a year contract.[45]

The double cross was destabilizing to his team, and Comiskey told a reporter: "I don't mind losing Padden so much as the way he treated me after what I did for him last year. I have suspected all along that he was contemplating jumping, but he denied it all the time. Today, he sent me word he had signed with St. Louis. Well, I wish him good luck, but I'll bet he will wish he was back here before many weeks. Wait till some of those papers get to knocking him down there. And Padden will never have a chance to play in the American League again. When the National League lets him go it will be a case of minor league next time."[46]

Interestingly, Padden and Comiskey remained friends despite the initial vitriolic explosion, and in 1902, Padden would rejoin the American League as a member of the new St. Louis Browns.[47]

In addition to Griffith, Comiskey added several other impact players, among them being Billy Sullivan of Wisconsin, a talented catcher from the Boston National League club, and outfielder Fielder Jones.[48] Jones, signed for three years at $3,000 annually, had played with the National League champion Brooklyn Superbas in 1900, batting .310. Additionally, "Sandow" Mertes, who Comiskey recruited from California while in St. Paul, joined the club after playing for the Chicago Orphans, as did Jimmy Callahan, a coveted pitcher that President Hart didn't want to lose. Comiskey's $3,300 annual salary and the sales pitch of Griffith successfully earned Callahan's signature to a contract.

Paying competitive salaries, in addition to fixing up the South Side grounds, Comiskey was spending tens of thousands of dollars for the new season—as much as $32,000 for players alone.[49] The year before, no American League club had spent more than $20,000 on their entire roster and it was indicative of a significant upgrade in talent across the league.[50] As many as fifty National League players were said to be in the process of migrating to the American at one time or another, but only a couple dozen crossed over. Besides the pick ups by Comiskey, future Hall of Famers Cy Young,

John McGraw, Jimmy Collins, and Nap Lajoie debuted for the American League in 1901.

The White Stockings left Chicago on March 30, 1901, in a snowstorm headed for their training grounds in Missouri, while Comiskey remained home.[51] Thirteen players were in the bunch with more en route. An early mishap of the trip came when pitcher Jack Katoll dove headfirst into a shallow pool, apparently misjudging its depth, and cracked his head open on the concrete floor.[52] Luckily for him and the club, all he suffered was a wide cut and an aching neck.

Griffith immediately put the team to work, conditioning them on winding runs through the woods—during one of which two players got lost—and extensive base running and signal training. Batting was another crucial factor to improve upon, as even though they were pennant winners in 1900, they hit only .237 as a team and were last in the league.[53]

The weather didn't completely cooperate with the team during their stay in Excelsior Springs and instead of working on their fundamentals, players spent most of their time crowded around a slot machine at a neighborhood drug store.[54] Before returning home, a thief made off with a bunch of the players' gloves; the perfect send off. Comiskey had arranged for a number of exhibitions against collegiate and semi-professional teams back in the Chicago area, and during one of them, the high priced addition, Callahan, suffered a broken arm. The injury would cause him to miss the first month of the season.[55]

All the pomp and circumstance, extravagant decorations, and a band providing the soundtrack made Opening Day at the South Side Park on April 24, 1901 everything that could be imagined.[56] Comiskey was disappointed that Mayor Harrison didn't attend and throw out the first pitch, but otherwise, the event was tops all around. The white silk pennant with the words, "Chicago's Champions American League 1900" was hoisted up the flagpole as the 9,000 people in attendance cheered wildly. The White Stockings won over Cleveland, 8–2, and began the season on the right foot.

Across town, the Chicago Orphans, also nicknamed the Remnants, opened its season on April 26 before only 3,500 people, and the *Tribune* explained that the team was "not greeted with cheers as they came onto the field," and it was apparent which team held the public's favor. Comiskey and the White Stockings attended the game and saw the Orphans lose in 12 innings to the Cincinnati Reds, 8–7.[57]

Winning two of their first three, Comiskey's stadium was overwhelmed by a crowd of 15,000 on April 28.[58] People were standing all over the out-field—encroaching on the field of play—and police did their best to keep spectators away from the action . . . but it was impossible. Outfielders were unable to function, missing routine fly balls because of interference, and finding their ability to navigate the field extremely limited. Chicago took the victory with 13 runs to the one score for Cleveland, but for Comiskey, it was an eye-opener that he needed to further renovate his venue; something he worked on through most of the summer.

The team jelled very well under Griffith's management. Hitting was strong and the fielding of Isbell at first and Jones and Hoy in the outfield was stellar. Although his pitching was considered mediocre the year before, Griffith was finding his mark and fast becoming the most popular player on the team. Callahan, another talented pitcher, was going to pull double duty at second base before his injury, and Comiskey filled the hole with Dave Brain, an unproven infielder with some ability. But it wasn't until Mertes was moved to second from the outfield that the position was finally shored up. It didn't come naturally to "Sandow," but he was as enthusiastic about the job as everything else he tackled.

During the month of June, the White Stockings faced a lengthy road trip in the East and left Chicago in first place with a 25–12 record.[59] How-ever, at League Park in Boston, they ran into trouble, losing five in a row to Jimmy Collins' club, with Cy Young proving his mastery in the second game of a doubleheader on June 17, leading the Americans to a 10–4 victory.[60] The series and streak of losses briefly gave Boston first place and resulted in a five-day suspension for Griffith for unbecoming actions on the field.[61] More players, the press noted, were being put out of commission for sus-pensions under Ban Johnson's rule than by injuries.

Comiskey was frustrated by the abnormal fluctuations of his team and had a loud "conversation" with Griffith in front of an audience after one game that drew plenty of attention.[62] He also lectured the team after losses and told stories of his days with the Browns. The speeches helped their motivation, and by mid-August, the Stockings were in first place with Bos-ton still on their collective heels. A short time later, Comiskey took a pre-emptive step by reaching a deal with all of his unsigned players for 1902, locking up his entire roster.[63]

On August 14, 1901, Comiskey and Johnson went on a brief fishing trip to Northern Wisconsin, but the experience wasn't as calming as they expected.[64] At one point, their boat was jammed up against a rock in high rapids and both men considered a risky jump into the water in an attempt to swim to the shoreline. Luckily they escaped serious injury, but Comiskey suffered painful blistering on his feet from exposure and was bed ridden upon returning home. When he attempted to get around soon after, he developed a case of blood poisoning that kept him far from the supervision of his club. His presence was needed, as the standings were as close as ever and discipline among his players was slipping.

An incident on August 21 in Washington, D.C. was nothing short of a disgrace to everyone affiliated with the White Stockings.[65] Umpire Jack Haskell was in rare form that day, and his officiating, according to Chicago, was subpar right from the start. Haskell's irregular calls were first demonstrated in a game back in late June, and Griffith was thrown out of that affair. This time was different and tempers were flaring to the point of no return. Katoll, on the mound for Chicago, was getting pounded in the 4th inning. He threw a wild pitch that struck Haskell in the shoulder. Haskell, in turn, gave the base runner on third the score, claiming it was a passed ball that would've gotten away had he not been there. Blinded by rage, Katoll picked up the ball and hurled it at Haskell, striking him in the shin. He was immediately tossed from the game as other Chicago players rushed the umpire. Shortstop Shugart, who was not known for an outward display of fury, yelled at Haskell and within seconds, the two were engaged in a physical fight. One of Shugart's fists landed directly on the mouth of the official and the latter tried to use his mask to smash his opponent. Police broke the two up and both Shugart and Katoll were arrested and indefinitely suspended by the American League, with Shugart likely to be expelled from the organization.

Comiskey backed Johnson's decision whole heartedly and disapproved of Griffith's comments in the press that claimed if Shugart was blacklisted that all players were going to stage a walkout.[66] Johnson blasted Griffith back, blaming "inexperienced player-managers" for the increase in volatile situations across the league. In addition to the two suspended athletes, Chicago was without Griffith because of a broken finger and Callahan due to illness. Comiskey credited the outstanding work of pitcher Roy Patterson for keeping the handicapped club in first.[67] All four men were back in the lineup by September, and Comiskey, without question, used his ties to Johnson to get Katoll and Shugart reinstated.

Ironically, they dropped three straight at Boston and lost five in a row before winning their final game at Washington on September 27.

A doubleheader was planned for the 28th, but rain washed the games out. So with that, Chicago finished 83–53, four games ahead of Boston in the standings, and won their second straight pennant.[68] Comiskey and his team had achieved another honor, and it was well earned. But as the season ended, he was already in a different mode and focused on his next big project.

ENDNOTES

1 *Chicago Daily Tribune*, January 9, 1900, p. 4.
   Comiskey's funeral services were held at the Holy Family Church and he was buried at Calvary Cemetery. *Chicago Daily News*, January 10, 1900, p. 3.

2 *Boston Journal*, January 6, 1900, p. 3.

3 *Cincinnati Post*, January 18, 1900, p. 2.

4 *Chicago Daily Tribune*, February 25, 1900, p. 17.

5 *Chicago Daily Tribune*, March 3, 1900, p. 6.

6 *Chicago Daily Tribune*, March 15, 1900, p. 9.

7 *Chicago Daily Tribune*, March 18, 1900, p. 17.

8 *Chicago Daily News*, March 7, 1900, p. 6.
   The "White Stockings" term was literal for the socks the team wore. Ironically, the white socks became an issue when management realized it was nearly impossible to keep them clean. The *Tribune* explained that the stockings weren't as "serviceable" as other colors, but were an "essential" part of the uniform. They couldn't possibly be changed unless they were willing to alter the name of the team as well. *Chicago Daily Tribune*, February 26, 1902, p. 6. Modifying the club's name was considered, but Comiskey came up with a better idea. In 1903, when he updated the uniforms, he changed the colors of the stockings to navy blue, but to maintain the "White Stockings" custom, the blue socks had a four inch strip of white around the calves. *Chicago Daily Tribune*, April 8, 1903, p. 13. A few weeks later, it was reported that Comiskey had chosen not to change the "white stockings." *Chicago Daily Tribune*, May 2, 1903, p. 9.

9 *Chicago Daily Tribune*, March 9, 1900, p. 9.
   Hugh Fullerton, in 1942, said that Comiskey told him that he only had $30,000 when he made the move from St. Paul to Chicago. *Sporting News*, December 3, 1942, p. 6. Ban Johnson reportedly coordinated efforts with the Purdy Family, the landowners at Wentworth and 39th Street, and signed the lease because the Purdys were not acquainted with Comiskey. To turn the grounds into a suitable baseball venue, Comiskey needed to borrow money from Charles Somers of Cleveland and around $17,000 was initially invested in construction costs. *Chicago Daily Tribune*, March 10, 1929, p. A3. In time, further improvements to the stadium were made.

10 It was reported that Tony Mullane, who had known Comiskey since the early 1880s in St. Louis and had more recently been affiliated with the St. Paul club,

was going to manage the team in Comiskey's absence. *Cleveland Leader*, March 30, 1900, p. 6.

11 *Rockford Daily Register Gazette*, March 29, 1900, p. 3.

J. Louis Comiskey's health was in a delicate state of fluctuation for "nine days." *Chicago Daily News*, April 20, 1900, p. 6.

12 *Chicago Daily Tribune*, April 19, 1900, p. 4.

13 *Sporting News*, April 28, 1900, p. 5.

Around forty-four years of age, Patrick was the eldest Comiskey sibling. He was vital to his brother's baseball operations, working as treasurer of the St. Paul franchise and was expected to assume the same role for the White Stockings. Patrick was survived by a wife and two daughters. Amid the turmoil, Ted Sullivan was brought in to help on the administrative side of the new Chicago club.

14 The first game for Comiskey's White Stockings was to take place on Thursday, April 19, against Milwaukee, but bad weather caused him to push it back to Saturday. Comiskey went to St. Paul for the death of his brother and accompanied the body to Chicago on April 20. *Sporting News*, April 21 and April 28, 1900. There is some question whether or not Comiskey was able to attend his team's April 21 debut. The *Tribune* reported that April 23 was the "first time" he had been able to see his team play that year, and if that was true, he had missed the initial game. *Chicago Daily Tribune*, April 24, 1900, p. 4. Under the circumstances, Comiskey's absence, if true, was completely understandable as his family obligations were his first priority.

15 Just beyond right field of the stadium was a greenhouse and its operator complained about balls sailing over the fence and smashing his glass panes. He filed a claim against the team for his damaged property. *Chicago Daily Tribune*, April 25, 1900, p. 6.

16 *Chicago Daily Tribune*, April 27, 1900, p. 4.

17 *Chicago Daily Tribune*, April 30, 1900, p. 4.

18 *Chicago Daily Tribune*, June 8, 1900, p. 9.

19 The White Stockings, as of June 15, won eight games in a row and were closing in on first place. *Chicago Daily Tribune*, June 16, 1900, p. 6.

20 *Chicago Daily Tribune*, June 17, 1900, p. 18.

21 *Chicago Daily Tribune*, June 28, 1900, p. 6.

22 *Chicago Daily Tribune*, July 4, 1900, p. 6.

Heart disease was said to be the cause of Comiskey's death.

23 *Chicago Daily Tribune*, July 15, 1900, p. 17.

24 *Chicago Daily Tribune*, July 21, 1900, p. 7.

25 *Chicago Daily Tribune*, September 8, 1900, p. 6.

26 *Chicago Daily Tribune*, September 16, 1900, p. 18.

27 *Chicago Daily Tribune*, September 20, 1900, p. 8.

Later it was revealed that the club lost $9,681.94 on the 1900 season. *Chicago Daily Tribune*, December 4, 1908, p. 11.

28 *Chicago Daily Tribune*, August 25, 1900, p. 6.

29 *Chicago Daily Tribune*, September 21, 1900, p. 8.

30 The journey to Minnesota in September of 1900 was technically the first pilgrimage northward for Comiskey and Johnson in what would become the famous annual Camp Jerome (Woodland Bards) expeditions.

31 *Pawtucket Times*, October 15, 1900, p. 2.

32 *Cleveland Leader*, October 12, 1900, p. 6.
Also see: *Baltimore Sun*, October 13, 1900, p. 6.

33 *Baltimore Sun*, October 31, 1900, p. 6.

34 For Ban Johnson there was an ironic flavor in the ousting of Indianapolis, which was owned by John Brush. Several years before, Brush had tried to pull a coup in opposition to Johnson in the Western League and was outwardly antagonistic to the organization's president. Johnson survived the hostile maneuvers and was at the forefront of Brush's removal from the American League. *Chicago Daily Tribune*, November 4, 1900, p. 19.

35 *Cleveland Plain Dealer*, November 13, 1900, p. 6.

36 *Cleveland Leader*, December 1, 1900, p. 7.

37 American League owners were tired of making concessions to the National League, including turning over two athletes to James Hart in Chicago for the "right" to play ball on the South Side, and no longer needed any "protection." Thus, they refused to sign the old version of the "National Agreement." *Philadelphia Inquirer*, November 18, 1900, p. 13.

38 *Chicago Daily Tribune*, December 16, 1900, p. 18.

39 *Chicago Daily Tribune*, January 20, 1901, p. A17–A18.

40 *St. Marys Star*, January 10, 1901, p. 1.

41 *Chicago Daily Tribune*, January 4, 1901, p. 9.

42 *Chicago Daily Tribune*, February 9, 1901, p. 6.

43 *Chicago Daily Tribune*, February 22, 1901, p. 9.

44 Griffith was elected to the National Baseball Hall of Fame in 1946.

45 *Chicago Daily Tribune*, March 17, 1901, p. 19.

46 Ibid.

47 The Milwaukee Brewers moved to St. Louis after the 1901 season and became the Browns.

48 *Chicago Daily Tribune*, March 28, 1901, p. 6.

49 *Rockford Republic*, March 29, 1901, p. 6.

50 *Cleveland Plain Dealer*, March 6, 1901, p. 6.

51 *Chicago Daily Tribune*, March 31, 1901, p. 18.

52 *Chicago Daily Tribune*, April 4, 1901, p. 6.

53 *Washington, D.C. Evening Star*, February 15, 1901, p. 9.

54 *Chicago Daily Tribune*, April 13, 1901, p. 4.

55 *Chicago Daily Tribune*, April 16, 1901, p. 6.

56 *Chicago Daily Tribune*, April 25, 1901, p. 6.

57 *Chicago Daily Tribune*, April 27, 1901, p. 4.

58 *Chicago Daily Tribune*, April 29, 1901, p. 4.

59 *Chicago Daily Tribune*, June 7, 1901, p. 6.

60 *Chicago Daily Tribune*, June 18, 1901, p. 6., *Boston Journal*, June 18, 1901, p. 8.

61 *Chicago Daily Tribune,* June 20, 1901, p. 7.

62 *Chicago Daily Tribune,* July 21, 1901, p. 19.

63 *Chicago Daily Tribune,* August 14, 1901, p. 4.

64 *Chicago Daily Tribune,* August 20, 1901, p. 4.

65 *Chicago Daily Tribune,* August 22, 1901, p. 4. *Washington Post,* August 22, 1901, p. 8.

66 *Chicago Daily Tribune,* August 23, 1901, p. 4.

67 *Chicago Daily Tribune,* August 30, 1901, p. 7.

68 The club had receipts of over $71,000 in 1901 and made a profit for the first time. *Chicago Daily Tribune,* December 4, 1908, p. 11.

BRAWLS, SHOOTINGS, AND BASEBALL WAR

The refurbishment of his South Side ballpark was a financial investment that was quickly forgotten as Charles Comiskey watched thousands pack the grandstand and bleachers to see his White Stockings perform. Ticket vendors in the box office were collecting a pretty penny, and the vast Comiskey fortune was seeing no limits. During the off season, the park played host to many types of community events and athletics, but Comiskey realized there was an opportunity to expand his interests. A plan to turn baseball players into soccer stars was hatched a year before, and he was supportive of the concept. But by August of 1901, the idea had morphed into a straight soccer organization under the name: "National Association Football League."

All things considered, the endeavor wasn't a guaranteed moneymaker, but the promise of year-round, structured athletics at his stadium was an exciting prospect. The idea was conceived by Comiskey's old mentor, Ted Sullivan, a true sports entrepreneur and a man way ahead of his time.[1] Sullivan believed that with the right kind of leadership and orderliness, association football was going to be the next big thing. High railroad costs threw a snag into plans for a four-team circuit, but not before Comiskey fielded a talented squad captained by Scotsman Benjamin Govier. On October 20, 1901, the "Comiskeys" beat the Milwaukee "Brewers," 6–1 at home.[2]

In the post-monopolistic baseball world, the sport continued to change at a rapid pace. More and more National League players jumped sides in the league war. The years of abusing its power made the latter a shell of its former self, and in some towns, three-quarters of a club's roster was bailing for greener pastures. By the end of October of 1901, already two dozen players were switching sides and some pundits were predicting death for the National League. While the National League was dealing with serious issues, the American League was business as usual. And on December 3, 1901, approval was granted at the American League's meeting in Chicago to relocate the Milwaukee club to St. Louis under the management of Matt Killilea and Fred Gross.[3]

Right in the thick of things, Comiskey was benefitting greatly from the desire of National League players to abandon ship. His ambassador, Clark Griffith, went to New York City and promptly signed the backbone of the Giants, thirty-one-year-old shortstop George Davis, who had captained and managed the club for the previous two seasons.[4] He also brokered a deal with second baseman Tom Daly, the veteran of eleven seasons with Brooklyn. Daly, originally from Philadelphia, was in the twilight of his career but was still effective as an infielder and clubhouse leader. Adding Ed McFarland, a catcher from the Phillies, and outfielder Danny Green from the Remnants, Comiskey was building a superb team. In fact, some newspapers were claiming he already had an "All-Star" caliber squad.[5]

"I want no young bloods this year," Comiskey told a reporter, "but old and tried players, for it may be only a one year team, you can't tell in these war times. I don't care if they have gray beards, for I would know they got gray working for the men I took them away from. Why, I'd send nine Santa Clauses on the field if I thought they could make good."[6]

Michael O'Brien, shortly after the death of Comiskey's brother Patrick in 1900, was hired by the White Stockings owner to be his administrative assistant. O'Brien was a family friend, in keeping with Comiskey's tradition of welcoming only the most trusted people into the inner circle of his business. Living down the street from Comsikey's childhood home, where Charles's brother Edward still resided, O'Brien was a Chicago alderman and a clerk at city hall. He had also been involved in the Western League, working with Ban Johnson, and briefly operated the Omaha franchise.

On December 28, 1901, O'Brien passed away of tuberculosis at his Lytle Street home at the age of forty-two.[7] It was just another in a never-ending series of tragedies in the world of Charles Comiskey.

Another of Comiskey's valuable aides during this time was his nephew, Charles A. Fredericks, who was the son of his wife's sister. Fredericks was one of the original incorporators of the American League Base Ball Club of Chicago and the team's secretary-treasurer.[8] An amiable and smart businessman, he held the scorecard concession at Comiskey's stadium and was a regular on the assorted hunting trips taken by Comiskey and his pals.

At least three times in 1901, Comiskey and Johnson ventured into the great outdoors in pursuit of wild turkeys and other game. Their cordial friendship was seemingly as strong as ever, but one has to wonder whether or not the persistent remarks of sportswriters that Comiskey was the real force behind the American League was getting to Johnson. That belief was only accentuated when Comiskey, several days after Christmas in 1901, made public comments second-guessing a decision Johnson made regarding the National League and recommended that he return to Chicago for some "advice" on the matter.[9]

Egos were growing at a rapid pace and since both Comiskey and Johnson tended to take themselves too seriously on occasion, stray comments had the potential to start a quarrel. This time, however, there were no public indications of bad blood—but that's not to say there wasn't something brewing behind closed doors.

Over in the National League, things continued to spiral out of control. Comiskey's old boss, John T. Brush, was fighting for his life against a splinter segment of the league supporting the proposed presidency of A. G. Spalding, the former owner of the original White Stockings. Finding himself in a weakened political spot, Brush had little ammunition to fight Spalding's restructuring plans and sought help from across the great divide. He proposed to Johnson that the American League allow him and New York magnate Andrew Freedman to join the organization through the ownership of the Cleveland and Baltimore franchises, respectively.[10] Freedman would move the Baltimore club to New York, which would give the organization its desired Gotham franchise.

To Brush, this was the easiest route to harmony in baseball. Others disagreed, and for the time being, peace was on hold.

President Hart of the Chicago Remnants/Colts once again wanted to stage a head-to-head match-up against Comiskey's franchise for city honors. The two owners ran into each other in the Fisher Building, where both maintained offices, and engaged in an impromptu discussion about the idea. They agreed that a fifteen game series—to begin before the season started and conclude after it ended—would be a significant box office attraction for local fans and generate a lot of money for both franchises. While they made a verbal agreement, the series was never realized.

Intending to keep a better eye on their ball gloves, the White Stockings ventured back to Excelsior Springs, Missouri, for spring training. The players were met by snow, initially limiting their outdoor activities, but they settled into a routine of drills headed by Clark Griffith, who was returning as captain and manager for a second straight season. Comiskey remained in Chicago and focused on the further modifications to his stadium. A recent league wide raise in ticket prices saw grandstand seats increased from 25 cents to 75 cents, and Comiskey was improving all of his accommodations, fully expecting to have a successful season.[11]

Over the previous two seasons, sportswriters were taking a noteworthy liberty when reporting about Comiskey's franchise. The use of the name "White Sox" in coverage was considerably less prominent in 1900 than it was in 1901, and by 1902, it was quite common. Adding the abbreviated name to a headline saved space and editors made the most of it, actually becoming responsible for the general acceptance of the "White Sox" as the team's official name. Colorful writers, in their effort to be unique, called the team by a number of nicknames, including the "Pale Hose" or "South Siders."

Adding pitcher Virgil Garvin, late of the Milwaukee Brewers, and Sam Strang from the New York Giants to play third base, Comiskey felt his roster was complete to start the season. However, the exhibition work of the club was far from masterful as they were defeated by St. Joseph, a minor league team on April 10, and then were held to an 8–8 tie against Notre Dame a few days later.[12][13] They were also beaten by another minor league squad from Milwaukee at the South Side Park on April 20.[14] Although the team had experience, hitting, pitching, and speed, it was obvious that they needed additional time to blend their talent.

The 1902 playing season opened in Chicago on April 23, in the midst of a strong cold front, and 7,000 braved the weather to see their Stockings beat the Detroit Tigers, 12–2.[15] For the second straight season, a championship pennant was raised—this time, the dark blue honor with white lettering read: "Champions of the American League, 1900–1901."

Comiskey, who rarely attended away games, went to St. Louis on May 1, as the Browns tried to pay tribute to him with a special "Comiskey Day."[16] Joined by Johnson and Chris Von der Ahe, Comiskey was the man of the hour, but dismal weather conditions postponed the celebration. Later on in Cleveland, the team took four victories in a row, but the success was marred by the arrest of Jimmy Callahan for assaulting a bellboy at the Weddell

House.[17] He plead guilty, admitting that he'd lost his temper, and was fined by the local police court. Furious, Comiskey wired Griffith and demanded that the pitcher be sent home, but Griffith made a case for Callahan to stay with the team pending a further investigation of the facts.[18] Comiskey relented.

In the next stage of the war between leagues, the National League gained an important legal victory against all contract jumpers. On April 21, 1902, the Pennsylvania Supreme Court declared the "reserve clause" legal, and the basis gave owners solid traction to begin recalling contracted players who were already engaged in the American League season.[19] One step further, injunctions were sought to restrain the defectors, and the case of Nap Lajoie of the Philadelphia Athletics was the first real example of a player being prohibited from participating in American League games because of their previous contract in the National.

"I never heard such an un-American decision," Comiskey explained. "I have consulted several attorneys in Chicago and every one of them has stated that a contract which binds a man to a club for all of his life is unconstitutional, and that is just what the National League contract, such as Lajoie signed, does. For myself, I do not expect to lose a single player."[20]

The baseball war continued with Baltimore being the principal battleground for the next upheaval between the leagues in July, and on the surface, the maneuvering of National League owners was clever. Andy Freedman of New York Giants conspired to buy out the Baltimore franchise from the American League.[21] The purchase was unwelcomed by Johnson and his allies, but the situation swiftly worked to their favor when, because of a lack of players, there was no Baltimore team fielded for a scheduled game against St. Louis. That allowed Johnston to declare Freedman's stake in the league forfeited, while at the same time working with other American League owners to build a new Baltimore franchise from scratch.

"I think it is the cheapest play I ever saw pulled off in baseball," Comiskey said about the situation in Baltimore. "It's a poor play for the old league, I say. The American League had them all down and out last winter, and they know it. Both factions were trying to lean on us, and we could have killed the National League by saying the word. Now they will get 'cocky' because they think they have pulled off something. It has always been the good of the game with the American League, but it is always extermination and self-interest with the National. So long as we deliver the goods to the public, it will be with us."[22]

As for the White Stockings, they were playing abysmally. On the road, the team won only three of fourteen games, and displayed little enthusiasm to rebound from their slump.[23] The Sox dropped to third place and a stomach illness to Griffith and injuries to Billy Sullivan and Danny Green were costing them dearly. Plus an ugly rumor surfaced that Comiskey "smote" third baseman Sammy Strang after the latter's error cost the team a victory, and first place.[24] It was reported that Strang was bitter about the "blow" and didn't plan to return to the team next year.

The most demented off the field happening of the season occurred when Sox pitcher Virgil Garvin, a dental student during the off season with a history of violence, got drunk and went on a rampage in Chicago on the evening of August 28, 1902.[25] Garvin pistol whipped a police officer, then shot a bar owner in the left shoulder at Honore Street and Ogden Avenue. Garvin escaped capture, but ran into Comiskey the next day at the ball park and the latter told him: "You have shot yourself out of a job. I'm done with you. If I can't run a ball team without bad men, I'll quit."

Garvin's mayhem and resulting evasion cost him a grand total of $100, and he had a guaranteed job waiting for him next season with Brooklyn.

Redeeming himself for underachieving all season long, Callahan threw the American League's first ever no-hitter on September 20, in the initial game of a doubleheader against Detroit in Chicago.[26] The game was part of a special "Amateur Day" promotion and Comiskey and his wife were honored with gifts—the former receiving a new fishing outfit.

By season's end, the White Sox finished in fourth place behind Philadelphia, St. Louis, and Boston, concluding their campaign with record of 74–60, a stark disappointment considering the team's potential. It was a year to disremember and Comiskey made haste for a hunting vacation in Wisconsin to clear his mind.[27]

The deaths of three of his brothers within a year's span were mentioned in the press after a near fatal mishap to a fourth brother on October 24, 1902.[28] Edward Comiskey was almost killed when he was thrown from an electric streetcar and struck by a second car. The collective misfortunes added to the basis of an old family yarn and indicated Charles' superstitious nature.[29] Years before, he was playing catch in a lot on Chicago's West Side when an errant toss mistakenly hit an older woman.[30] The woman became irate and screamed, "May you live to see all your kith and kin die!"

Her words were horrifying and the strange deaths reminded Comiskey of that fateful day. The fact that Edward survived the accident may have eased his fear of any irrational "curse" haunting his family.[31]

Rumors were abounding throughout the offseason. While some had merit, one of the most laughable—to Comiskey, at least—was the fact that he was leaving Chicago and taking over the New York Highlanders, the American League's newest franchise.[32] Comiskey immediately dispelled the gossip, saying: "Why, I wouldn't trade Chicago for the other seven cities, including New York, with Jersey City and Weehawken thrown in. I wouldn't even go to New York except to attend a league meeting."[33]

Comiskey was also alleged to be moving his team from the South Side to the West Side, where he had an option on a new playing ground.[34] The idea was considered but seeing how much money he'd invested in fixing up his park, it was quickly nixed. The final rumor involved Griffith going to New York and becoming the leader of the Highlanders, with Comiskey returning to the dugout as the day-to-day manager. This was partially true. Griffith was released from his contract and went to New York, but Comiskey named Callahan the player-manager for the Sox.[35] [36]

Even though he wasn't returning to his old post, Comiskey was taking a renewed interest in his club during the off-season; different from previous years. For one, he planned to travel with the team to spring training in Mobile and was going to personally coach and monitor the growth of his players. He even donned the uniform for the first time in years on the afternoon of March 20, 1903, and played first base throughout a two-hour practice.[37]

Familiar faces Jimmy Callahan, Roy Patterson, Tom Daly, Frank Isbell, Ed McFarland, Fielder Jones, and Billy Sullivan were now supported by Lee Tannehill, "Cozy" Dolan, Pat Flaherty, Frank Owen, and "Georgetown" Doc White, who'd pitched two years with the Philadelphia Phillies. George Davis, making $4,000 a year for Comiskey, was expected to return and told the press that he had no plans to break his contract.[38] But he did exactly that. Having received more money from the New York Giants and John McGraw, Davis defected to the National League.

With no National Agreement, this sort of thing happened regularly. However, on January 10, 1903, in Cincinnati, the American and National Leagues ended the baseball war and established a new agreement that initiated a fellowship between the two organizations.[39] Comiskey, who acted as part of the American League's peace committee, was one of eight men to sign the treaty.

Davis was bound to the White Sox regardless of what was being reported and Comiskey was confident he had firm legal grounds protecting his interests. He told a reporter that "Davis will play with the Chicago Americans this year or retire from baseball."[40]

The truth of the matter was that Davis was bound to Chicago and the new informal credo for the American League was, "Once an American Leaguer, always an American Leaguer." Comiskey not only had a contract, but could utilize the reserve clause to keep Davis in perpetuity. He was angry about the situation and wasn't considering a trade or to sell Davis, even if it meant improving his ball club's chances in 1903. It was now a matter of principle.

On paper, on the field, and any other way considered, the White Sox were a subpar professional baseball squad going into the 1903 season. It was known that Comiskey had tried to buy a pennant the year before with a team full of stars and that methodology had failed. His new line of attack was an assortment of odds and ends, and when it was all said and done his philosophy was not a winning one. Comiskey himself refrained from boasting—as he was accustom to do prior to every year of play—but admitted he was content with his newcomers.[41]

After a pitiful spring training term in the south that saw the Sox hiding indoors from the rain more often than working out on the field, a number of men remained out of shape and unimpressive. Manager Callahan took advantage of a washout in Evansville on April 3, and called a team meeting.[42] He delivered a fiery sermon, lecturing the squad for "loafing" around the field and the inability of some of the new players to get into shape, including pitcher Edward "Davey" Dunkle, who was twenty pounds overweight. In addition, Comiskey had trouble getting much needed infielder Harry Gleason to report from Boston, and when the latter finally did in May, the two couldn't come to agreeable terms and Gleason ended up in the minors.

As the season opener approached, Comiskey's wife was battling a lingering cold and another ill-fated happenstance snuck up on his family a short distance from the South Side ballpark.[43] Comiskey's fourteen-year-old niece, Kate Comiskey, was crossing Wentworth Avenue and 37th Street on April 14, 1903, when she was struck by an electric car. She suffered a deep head wound and internal injuries but survived the accident.

Opening Day occurred at St. Louis on April 22, 1903, and the Sox stopped the Browns with 14 runs on 16 hits.[44] Left-hander Flaherty held their rivals to only four runs and there were many aspects of their teamwork to be proud of. In fact, the club surprised the entire league by taking first place and holding it for most of May. Over 26,000 saw the May 10 game against St. Louis at the South Side Park and Comiskey declared it the largest crowd ever to see a baseball game.[45] Following a 1–0 victory in Cleveland on May 27, Comiskey wired Callahan to buy every member of the Sox a new hat in a show of appreciation.[46] He took it a step further by offering players a $50 suit if they beat Cleveland again on May 29.[47]

And they did, 3–2. Just before an Eastern road trip a few days later, the entire team was measured for suits, and with the additional price for the promised hats, it cost Comiskey $1,000.[48]

As the season went on, popular catcher Billy Sullivan went out with an appendicitis that was nearly fatal, but it's said that Comiskey was by his side all though his operation at Mercy Hospital in Chicago.[49] In response, he picked up a recent release from Cleveland, Jack Slattery, to backup Ed McFarland behind the plate. Also, Comiskey made other roster moves, signing pitcher Nick Altrock, James "Ducky" Holmes, and trading Cozy Dolan and Tom Daly for George Magoon of the Cincinnati Reds. But the Sox were in heavy decline, winning only one game out of nine during their June road trip east, and were in fifth place . . . and the fall was not complete there. The club would soon settle into 7th place and remain there for the rest of the season.

If things couldn't get any worse—or stranger—outfielder Danny Green was attacked by umpire Jack Sheridan during a ballgame in New York on July 7.[50] A war of words prompted Sheridan to confront Green at the Sox's bench and they began to fight. Sheridan took his mask and slammed it down onto Green's head, cutting the player in three places. Green retaliated with several well placed punches to the umpire's face and ear. When the fracas ended, Sheridan was hauled off to jail, but Green refused to press charges.

Reports commonly said the Sox were outclassed on the field and there was a growing list of reasons why the team was performing so poorly. First off, it was impossible for the club to win away from home. In the month of July, the club won only five games on the road and lost the other fifteen. Sicknesses and injuries to Callahan, Patterson, Sullivan, Holmes, and others were a constant problem, and the politics surrounding George Davis was a cloud that hovered over the team the entire season. Younger players were lacking confidence and sportswriter "Sy" of the *Chicago Daily Tribune* remarked that Callahan was "not qualified" to be a major league manager.[51]

Altrock showed well in the team's last game at Boston, on September 22, pitching a four-hitter in a 7–0 victory.[52] Boston, incidentally, would become the 1903 American League champions. Six days later the White Sox finished the season with a 60–77 record. Green was the only regular player with a batting average over .300, and the hitting numbers for everyone else were way off the league average. Tannehill batted .225 and Isbell .242, while Flaherty only won 11 games and lost 25.

Although the season was over, baseball history was still made in the city of Chicago between October 1 and 15. Ever since Comiskey arrived in 1900, there was talk of a cross-town series between James Hart's National League squad and the Sox. The peace accord that settled the baseball war made it easier to discuss plans, and despite Hart's loud allegations that Comiskey was padding his attendance numbers by "50 to 100 per cent" earlier in the year, the series was going to be held beginning October 1 at the Cubs West Side Grounds.[53] For the first time ever, the two teams met on the field and the first club to win eight games in the fifteen game series was going to win the local championship.[54]

Starting off on the wrong foot, the White Sox lost the first three games of the series, scoring only one run and 10 hits. They returned to win the fourth and fifth games, and started to give the Cubs a run for their money. On October 11, Comiskey's squad won 2–0 at South Side Park before an overflow audience that nearly cost the Sox the game when they ran amok over the field before the game began. Lucky for the Sox, the umpire withheld a forfeit announcement because the crowd was generally peaceful in mood. The next day, controversial pitcher Rube Waddell sat on the Sox bench and helped coach the team to a 4–2 victory. It was now 6 games to 5 in favor of the Cubs.

On October 13, the Cubs won 5–1, and after the game, Comiskey told his team that he'd pay $2,500, to be shared amongst the players, if they won the next two games—which would tie the series.[55] The Sox accomplished the feat, winning 2–0 on October 14, and by the same score on the 15th behind the awesome pitching of Nick Altrock. Because Hart couldn't spare his players beyond October 15, the series ended in a stalemate.[56] Comiskey paid the bonus of $2,500 and said that the last win pleased him as much as any championship he'd ever enjoyed in his life.[57]

The ill will between Comiskey and Hart was at its height and the public was not yet aware that Hart was harboring a profound belief that his star pitcher, Jack Taylor, had thrown the three games he lost to the White Sox in the series; but that story was going to come out in due time.

With over thirty players on his roster, Comiskey was going to have to make big decisions before the beginning of the 1904 season. Among the new crop of athletes joining the team were Ed Walsh, a pitcher from the Eastern League, Claude Berry of Indiana who was recommended by Ted Sullivan, Jiggs Donahue, and rookie Charles Jones. Sullivan also steered Comiskey toward relocating his spring training to Marlin, Texas, known for its mineral baths.[58] He agreed, and as the team was prepping to leave for the "Lone Star State" in March, he went to New York for a league meeting and met with George Davis to work matters out.[59] Davis came to terms after a year's hiatus and told the press that the reason he wanted to play in New York was not due to Comiskey's management style but because it was his hometown.[60]

Accompanied by his wife and niece, Comiskey went to Texas and joined his team.[61] And Sullivan was completely right; Marlin was the perfect location for spring training as the weather was picturesque. The training the team received was the exact opposite of their inconsistent patterns of 1903, and the White Sox were already on their way to a much improved season.

On March 14, 1904, the thrill of being on the field was again too much to pass up and Comiskey briefly assumed control of the instruction from Callahan.[62] Since he had so many players to work with, Comiskey split the club into two teams for exhibitions, and he managed one while Callahan traveled with the other. The team reunited and toured from New Orleans to Des Moines through the first part of April. Comiskey returned to Chicago on April 5 and went to work making the annual repairs and upgrades to the South Side Park.[63] The park received four new turnstiles at the main entrance on 39th Street and got a fresh coat of paint.

Near-freezing temperatures and wetness put a halt to opening day festivities at the stadium on April 14, and the Sox lost to Cleveland 6–1 before just over 5,000 people.[64] A few days later, the last remaining holdout from the year before, Fielder Jones, signed a contract to play for Comiskey after initially trying to defect to New York and then to the California outlaw league.[65] Just like Davis, he was bound to the White Sox by the reserve clause and Comiskey didn't want to trade him. The *Tribune* noted that Comiskey offered Jones more money than New York had, and purposely did so to ensure there were no bad feelings.[66]

In contention from the start, Chicago stood in second place until the dreaded Eastern road trip in May, but pitchers Altrock, Walsh, White, Smith, and Owen were proving to be winners. Altrock gained a shutout at Boston on May 26 and hit a home run to support his cause in a 3–0 victory.[67] At Cleveland on May 28, backstop Billy Sullivan was beamed in the forehead by a fastball and knocked unconscious.[68] The heart of the team, Sullivan was able to walk off the field under his own power but suffered a deep cut over his left eye and missed some time. Ed McFarland, who was benched the season before for his outlandish behavior, was rehired by Comiskey and filled the catcher role admirably.

At the start of June, the Sox were lingering around fourth place. Callahan talked with Comiskey and decided that the club would be improved if he stepped aside as manager and let his longtime friend Fielder Jones take the helm.[69] Jones was a smart ballplayer, well liked, and respected by his teammates, the public, and sportswriters. Comiskey approved the switch and Jones embraced the decision. Even before the shift, Sox players were showing increasing confidence. They wanted to win and were doing the little things necessary to ensure they were in contention for every game, both at home and on the road.

But when Jones took over, the positive momentum was amplified. He shook up the batting order and his approach to the game was much different from his predecessor's. Fans were excited, packing South Side Park with a mass of 24,800 on June 19; and as of July 5, the Sox had won 20 of their last 31 games.[70] Injuries to McFarland and Holmes and the temporary departures from the lineup of Donahue, Green, and Walsh would have normally caused friction, but Jones found a way to keep his team strong. Back on the road in July, the Sox were beaten up by Philadelphia and lost four straight.[71]

Chicago rebounded magnificently, winning 14 of 21 games on the trip, and were within striking distance of first place.[72] Upon returning home,

Jones was presented with a floral piece at home plate on August 1, 1904, honoring his impressive work.[73] The team won four straight from Washington and took first place from Boston. On August 14, with Boston in town, over 30,000 baseball fans attended the game and watched the Sox lose 5–2.[74] Before the series was over, however, Chicago etched out a win over Cy Young, shutting Boston down in a 6–0 win.[75]

Comiskey again recognized the hard work of his players by buying them each $50 suits. They were doing very little wrong on the field, and Sy Sanborn of the *Chicago Daily Tribune* called the pennant race the "most sensational" in recent times.[76] In September, Chicago won four straight and then nine of ten, but couldn't bring down the two teams leading the league: Boston and New York. The season ended in that order, with Chicago's 89 wins and 65 losses in third place.

The real nuisance for the Sox was their inability to hit, and that was becoming a common theme. The team batting average was .242 and no player with over 70 games hit .300. Pitching was Comiskey's saving grace, as was Jones's leadership. If their hitting could somehow improve, they were certainly going to be a challenger for the championship in 1905. Incidentally, the integrity of the 1903 city series was called into question as the year was coming to a close. Chicago Cubs President James Hart expressed the notion that his pitcher, Jack Taylor, purposely lost games against the White Sox. It was a serious charge that Comiskey wanted investigated, sending a request to the National Commission to pursue the matter as soon as possible.[77] Hart seemed indifferent despite his allegations, and Comiskey responded by saying, "I am not through with the Taylor case, even if Hart is. He is the first person in my long connection with baseball to cast any reflection upon my honesty in the game and I shall go before that commission and demand a clearing up of the case."[78]

On the field and off, 1905 was certainly going to be a wild and wooly year for baseball, and Comiskey, as always, was right in the thick of things.

ENDNOTES

1 *Chicago Daily Tribune*, August 30, 1901, p. 7.
2 *Chicago Daily Tribune*, October 21, 1901, p. 8.
3 *Chicago Daily Tribune*, December 4, 1901, p. 6.
   Since Comiskey had widespread connections in St. Louis, he was put in charge of locating a ball field for the new franchise. He went to his old stomping

grounds and was successful, signing a lease for the Athletic Park, which was later transferred to the local owners.

4 *Chicago Daily Tribune*, December 19, 1901, p. 7.
There were rumors that Griffith, while in New York City, was acting on behalf of the American League in trying to land financial backers for a local franchise, a territory the owners were desperate to break into.

5 *Cleveland Plain Dealer*, October 25, 1901, p. 8.

6 *Chicago Daily Tribune*, December 4, 1901, p. 6.

7 *Chicago Daily Tribune*, December 29, 1901, p. 6.

8 The American League Base Ball Club of Chicago (the business name of the Chicago White Stockings) was incorporated in the State of Wisconsin on March 5, 1900, by Fredericks, William Lachenmaier, and George E. Heaney. The company had a capital stock of $30,000 or 300 shares at $100 each. Corporation documents for the American League Baseball Club of Chicago were reviewed. These materials were provided by the Wisconsin Historical Society in Madison, with the help of ARC-Circulation Coordinator Matt Tischer. At the time of incorporation in the Milwaukee offices of Henry J. Killilea, Comiskey was joined by his brother Patrick and nephew Fredericks. It was determined that the company's 300 shares were going to be divided three ways: 160 going to the Comiskey brothers, 80 to Heaney, and 60 to Henry and Matt Killilea. Heaney paid $4,000 for his shares. Comiskey would later buy out the Killileas and then pay Heaney $10,000 for all of his stock in 1903, becoming the sole shareholder.
Also see: *Chicago Daily Tribune*, December 4, 1908, p. 11, and the *Sporting Life*, January 23, 1909, p. 26. When Heaney sold out, there was talk that his shares were going to be taken over by Clark Griffith and Jimmy Callahan, but the duo was unable to come up with the money.

9 *Chicago Daily Tribune*, December 28, 1901, p. 6.

10 *Cleveland Leader*, January 21, 1902, p. 7.

11 *Chicago Daily Tribune*, March 6, 1902, p. 6.

12 *Chicago Daily Tribune*, April 11, 1902, p. 13.

13 *Chicago Daily Tribune*, April 15, 1902, p. 13.

14 *Chicago Daily Tribune*, April 21, 1902, p. 6.

15 *Chicago Daily Tribune*, April 24, 1902, p. 6.
Jimmy Callahan was on the mound, pitching a six hitter and the guys behind him were faultless in the field. The Tigers, on the other hand, committed six errors.

16 *Chicago Daily Tribune*, May 2, 1902, p. 13.

17 *Cleveland Plain Dealer*, May 8, 1902, p. 12.

18 *Chicago Daily Tribune*, May 9, 1902, p. 13.

19 *Philadelphia Inquirer*, April 22, 1902, p. 6.

20 *Chicago Daily Tribune*, May 1, 1902, p. 13.
At this juncture, American League owners, who were benefitting from contract jumpers on their teams, were against the reserve clause and the rule that players were restrained to a single franchise for the length of their careers. However, these same owners, Comiskey included, welcomed and utilized the reserve

clause once the baseball war ended. They realized just how advantageous the system was in the management and rule of their clubs.

21 *Philadelphia Inquirer*, July 17–18, 1902.
In support of the new Baltimore American League franchise, Comiskey sent Jack Katoll and Herm McFarland to join the squad.

22 *Chicago Daily Tribune*, July 18, 1902, p. 6.

23 *Chicago Daily Tribune*, July 31, 1902, p. 4.

24 *Salt Lake Telegram*, September 27, 1902, p. 7.

25 *Chicago Daily Tribune*, August 30, 1902, p. 3.

26 *Chicago Daily Tribune*, September 21, 1902, p. 9.

27 *Chicago Daily Tribune*, September 26, 1902, p. 6.

28 *Chicago Daily Tribune*, October 25, 1902, p. 5.

29 Comiskey was very much a superstitious man, much like most ballplayers. During his playing days, part of his routine was to blow his nose before going to the plate, of course, to ensure a successful hit. *St. Louis Post Dispatch*, June 4, 1887, p. 12. Another common myth was to wear the same, unwashed uniform during a winning streak. Any deviation would cause a prompt defeat.

30 *Elkhart Truth*, October 29, 1902, p. 2.

31 Edward Comiskey not only survived but lived another twenty-four years, passing away on January 11, 1927. *Chicago Daily Tribune*, January 12, 1927, p. 21.

32 *Philadelphia Inquirer*, December 20, 1902, p. 10.

33 *Chicago Daily Tribune*, December 20, 1902, p. 6.

34 *Chicago Daily Tribune*, October 15, 1902, p. 6.
Also see: *Chicago Daily Tribune*, November 25, 1902, p. 6.

35 *New York Times*, January 11, 1903, p. 10.
Comiskey was supportive of the franchise in New York and remained good friends with Griffith.

36 *Chicago Daily Tribune*, March 17, 1903, p. 6.

37 *Chicago Daily Tribune*, March 21, 1903, p. 8.

38 *Washington, D.C. Evening Star*, March 3, 1903, p. 9.
Davis was under contract to the White Sox for the 1903 season.

39 *New York Times*, January 11, 1903, p. 10.
The end of the war between leagues was one of the most important moments in baseball history. A report from a Boston newspaper claimed that Comiskey was the real mastermind behind the American League's defiant stance. It claimed that Comiskey was the "oddest genius baseball has ever had," and that he was "odd in his ways, in his speech, and in his actions." Nevertheless, his recommendations in the war were correct. *Boston Herald*, May 4, 1903, p. 8.

40 *Chicago Daily Tribune*, March 9, 1903, p. 6.

41 *Chicago Daily Tribune*, March 23, 1903, p. 6.

42 *Chicago Daily Tribune*, April 4, 1903, p. 8.

43 *Chicago Daily Tribune*, April 15, 1903, p. 6.

44 *Chicago Daily Tribune*, April 23, 1903, p. 6.

45 *Chicago Daily Tribune*, May 11, 1903, p. 6.

46 *Chicago Daily Tribune*, May 28, 1903, p. 8.

47 *Chicago Daily Tribune*, May 29, 1903, p. 6.

48 *Chicago Daily Tribune*, June 3, 1903, p. 6.

49 Ibid.

50 *Chicago Daily Tribune*, July 8, 1903, p. 8.

51 *Chicago Daily Tribune*, September 13, 1903, p. 11.

52 *Chicago Daily Tribune*, September 23, 1903, p. 6.

53 *Chicago Daily Tribune*, May 6, 1903, p. 6.
   While most sources call the National League team from Chicago the Cubs in 1903, the *Chicago Daily Tribune* always called them "Colts."

54 The games between the Cubs and White Sox were usually just called the city title or championship, and the newspapers called it the "City Series."

55 *Chicago Daily Tribune*, October 14, 1903, p. 6.

56 *Chicago Daily Tribune*, October 16, 1903, p. 8.

57 Ibid.

58 *Chicago Daily Tribune*, February 7, 1904, p. 10.

59 *Chicago Daily Tribune*, March 7, 1904, p. 8.

60 *Chicago Daily Tribune*, March 13, 1904, p. 11.

61 *Chicago Daily Tribune*, March 12, 1904, p. 8.

62 *Chicago Daily Tribune*, March 15, 1904, p. 8.

63 *Chicago Daily Tribune*, April 6, 1904, p. 6.

64 *Chicago Daily Tribune*, April 15, 1904, p. 8.

65 *Chicago Daily Tribune*, April 20, 1904, p. 6.

66 *Chicago Daily Tribune*, April 21, 1904, p. 9.

67 *Chicago Daily Tribune*, May 27, 1904, p. 4.

68 *Chicago Daily Tribune*, May 29, 1904, p. 9.

69 *Chicago Daily Tribune*, June 6, 1904, p. 8.

70 *Chicago Daily Tribune*, June 20, 1904, p. 10.

71 *Philadelphia Inquirer*, July 15, 1904, p. 6.

72 *Chicago Daily Tribune*, July 31, 1904, p. B2.

73 *Chicago Daily Tribune*, August 2, 1904, p. 6.

74 *Chicago Daily Tribune*, August 15, 1904, p. 8.

75 *Chicago Daily Tribune*, August 17, 1904, p. 6.

76 *Chicago Daily Tribune*, August 21, 1904, p. B2.

77 *Chicago Daily Tribune*, October 13, 1904, p. 8.

78 *Cleveland Plain Dealer*, December 22, 1904, p. 9.

9

THERE'S A FISH IN LEFT FIELD

Following every season, Charles Comiskey sought peace and quiet. The pennant chase and arduous politics of baseball was a harrowing experience, and each year new circumstances added to the stress levels of all major league owners. Comiskey's enduring refuge was the great outdoors; the vast sanctuary of hunters and fishermen. The calmness of the untamed world far from the hustle and bustle of big city living was addicting and he escaped as often as he could. Comiskey embraced the challenge of game hunting, proudly showing off his trophies as a marksman, and joshing his friends over an accomplishment in a half hearted, yet still competitive manner.

It is difficult to ascertain when Comiskey acquired the bug for the outdoors, but it is clear that he took advantage of his time while stationed in St. Paul as the owner of the Saints. Fishing regularly at Lake Sylvia and hunting around Duluth, he was away for weeks at a time and more often than not joined by Ban Johnson. Comiskey and Johnson were like peas in a pod, and accompanying them were fellow baseball magnates, railroad officials, sportswriters, and other dignitaries. Between 1898 and 1900, Comiskey and Johnson went on annual hunting trips in Minnesota and changed things up in the autumn of 1901, when they ventured into Northern Wisconsin.

The Flambeau River and surrounding area near Fifield was an ideal location and would become their principal getaway spot. Once in August and again in October of 1901, Comiskey and Johnson headed to the region to take advantage of the high quality recreation. The next year they went two additional times. In November of 1903, the pair was back in the territory, but this time they wanted to invest in a plot of land near Springstead, just south of Boot Lake, where they planned to build a cabin for regular use.[1] Reportedly purchasing the land from the government, they established it as the centerpiece location for their annual excursions.

The 1904 pilgrimage, held around October 10, was made by Comiskey, Johnson, Tom Loftus, and several others. Having busted in a final rush for the championship of the American League and facing a crisis that threatened his good name, Comiskey needed the vacation.

As was customarily done, Comiskey and Johnson shared their hunting and fishing prizes upon return, even sending a deer carcass to their mutual friend, Garry Herrmann, who was head of the National Commission.[2] It wasn't long before they were back in the complicated web of baseball politics, discussing a new salary system for players. Owners determined that the remarkable increase of annual wages brought on by the war between the leagues had gotten too far out of hand and a more reasonable scale was needed. The *Cleveland Leader* estimated that Comiskey's salaries for the upcoming season would run him at least $2,500 for each player.[3]

Any talk of a reduction in wages wasn't taken too lightly by the players. Sensing the backlash, Johnson responded with a categorical denial that the American League was going to cut salaries across the board. Subtle adjustments were made in both leagues, and owners managed to get away with the maneuver without serious repercussions. It was said that players understood that a more level scale was going to be implemented upon the peace accord between the leagues and expected only a slight decrease.

Comiskey was going to be paying as much as $45,000 in salary for his ball club in 1905.[4] Adding another $10,000 for traveling costs and $18,000 for "other expenses," it was estimated that he was fronting a total of $73,000, which was ranked fifth out of eight teams in the American League. On an annual basis, he was also pouring thousands into improvements and repairs to the rough around the edges South Side Park, a venue that, in spite of his efforts, was never going to be among the league's best. The location of the grounds was, notably, in a dilapidated part of the city, and the *Tribune* observed that Comiskey was "powerless to improve the locality" or "stir up desire for better appearances among property owners or tenants of the district."[5]

Rule changes were another concern of owners hoping to increase the offensive output of players, but Comiskey objected, stating: "Baseball was never more prosperous everywhere than last season. I didn't see any indication at my gates or in the returns from other cities where my club played that the public was sore on the rules or the game. I am in favor of letting the game alone as long as it pleases the people. Everybody wants more batting by the home team and less by the visiting team. The fans don't care if a visiting player never gets on a base so long as the home team gets there. My public didn't show me it was aching for a change."[6]

He continued to press for a full inquiry into the allegations made by James Hart about pitcher Jack Taylor and crooked games in the 1903 series against the Sox. "Charges of throwing games are too serious to be ignored," Comiskey told the *Tribune*, "and for the good of the game, I think the matter should be investigated."[7]

Hart seemed to have washed his hands of the situation and wasn't publicly expressing any sentiment about the circumstances. That brought an even more livid reaction from Comiskey: "The whole case is one of the biggest outrages I ever heard of. The National Leaguers have been talking about a player in their own league, calling him a crook and intimating all sorts of raw performances. I have filed charges against Hart, and demand that some sort of punishment be handed to him for injuring the reputation of my ball club and the game itself. I will push this case against Hart to the limit."[8]

"There can be no dishonesty in the game of baseball," Johnson added. "Since the days of Devlin, the game has enjoyed a high reputation for honesty. That reputation the national commission must safeguard under the provisions of the national agreement. We cater to the most intelligent class of citizens in America. They watch our every word and act. They are our best asset. One rash or thoughtless act may destroy all that it has taken a generation to build up."[9]

Inspired by Comiskey and Johnson, the National Commission decided to bring Hart and Taylor to trial to get to the bottom of the situation. Prior to giving formal testimony, Hart relayed the story as he knew it, explaining that Taylor was heard saying, "Why should I have won? I got $100 from Hart for winning, and I got $500 for losing."[10] Taylor said he wasn't guilty and "never" did anything crooked during his entire baseball career. Finally, on February 15, 1905, the pitcher was acquitted of the charge of dishonesty, but fined $300 for misbehavior.[11]

Even though Texas had proven to be a top quality spring training location, Comiskey elected to relocate the team to New Orleans in March of 1905, and went several days early with his wife and niece to enjoy the Mardi Gras festival.[12] The roster was made up of all the regulars, plus a recruit from the Cedar Rapids club, pitcher Louis Fiene. Some claimed utilityman Frank Isbell, part of the franchise since St. Paul, was never going to be on the chopping block because he'd demonstrated his loyalty to Comiskey long ago—and Comiskey valued the devotion to the club. Isbell told the press, "I've stuck to Comiskey quite a while, and he has treated me squarely, always. I've learned that I can't do better than to stick as long as he wants me."[13]

Similar to the previous year, Comiskey took a secondary squad through Texas and planned to venture from Galveston to Springfield, Missouri. He changed the itinerary, stopping off in Paris, Texas, to break the long monotony of the train ride, arriving on March 24.[14] That same train continued on and, two hours later, wrecked, injuring scores and killing a woman riding in the same car the Sox players were in. Comiskey was quoted as saying: "It was the luckiest escape [a ball team] ever had. If we had followed my original plan and remained on that train, there is no telling how many of us would be in the hospital now."

With all of his players under contract, a successful spring under their belt, and a lot of positivity surrounding the club, Comiskey was feeling good about the upcoming season. The threatened loss of second baseman Gus Dundon to appendicitis was worrisome, but he fortunately didn't require surgery and was able to play in the opener on April 14, a game which turned into a defeat at the hands of St. Louis, 2–1.[15] A brutal storm slammed Chicago and the Sox competed in snowy conditions two days later, beating the Browns 5–0.[16] Players, to keep warm, wore coats and sweaters in the field.

Devoid of much hitting, the Sox steadied themselves among the league's best and held the first place spot several different times in May. On May 30, 1905, the team dropped both games of a doubleheader to Detroit at home, losing by one run in each.[17] Keeping his players in check, then-manager Fielder Jones and Comiskey suspended Jimmy Callahan indefinitely because he was said to be out of condition.[18] Comiskey was steaming mad about Callahan's situation and vowed to never let him play for the Sox again. A serious injury to Danny Green's ankle, occurring when he slid into home, was another setback for the squad. Until Comiskey could make other arrangements to bring in a replacement, every player they had left was absolutely needed.

On Saturday, June 3, 1905 in Chicago, the Sox battled first place Cleveland.[19] Leftfielder "Ducky" Holmes left a bad impression on umpire "Silk" O'Loughlin when he griped about a questionable strike, and later after another call, a loud utterance of criticism boomed from Chicago's bench.

O'Loughlin didn't have to think twice and tossed Holmes from the game, which helped Cleveland go on to win, 5–4. On the surface, this was just another day in the world of pro baseball, but for the sport's history, it was a defining moment that will never be forgotten.

Before Sunday's game, President Johnson's secretary, Robert McRoy, appeared at the South Side Park bearing a gift and an important message for Comiskey.[20] The present was a string of fish caught on a recent outing, and it was a kind gesture from his friend. The message, however, was anything but kind and seemingly cancelled out Johnson's generosity. It said that Holmes was suspended for the language he used against umpire O'Loughlin.[21] Usually complaints of umpires and the resulting punishments took days to reach a conclusion, but in this matter, it was strikingly fast.

Unable to retrieve Callahan, who left moments earlier, Comiskey looked at the fish and sarcastically asked McRoy if Johnson "expected [him] to play the fish in left field."[22]

Comiskey was already reeling from the absence of Green and Callahan, and with Dundon sick, his roster was stretched to its limits. The Sunday contest ended up going sixteen innings, making matters even more intense in a high-profile game Comiskey desperately wanted to win.[23]

"It is the first time that play has been pulled off in this league, and I am the target," Comiskey told the *Tribune*. "Reports from umpires must be submitted in writing and notices of suspension sent by mail or wire. O'Loughlin must have broken into Johnson's house last night to get in his report. Whether he did or not, Johnson could have notified me by phone of his decision in plenty of time to enable me to use Callahan in the game. Or he could have started the suspension on Monday. Instead, he waited until afternoon and sent his secretary to notify me just before the game.

"With Holmes or Callahan in that game, we would have come pretty near winning it with another hit or two. Had I been given decent notice of the suspension, I could have used Callahan, for he was at the grounds until noon, and I fixed matters up with him to go east with the team. Then I let him go out to pitch for some semi-professional team, as he had agreed to do while suspended. I never imaged O'Loughlin could get such quick action from Johnson. It never happened before, and sometimes a decision has not been received until several days after the trouble occurred."[24]

This matter ignited the official feud between Comiskey and Johnson; two great friends who'd already done so much for baseball as a unified force. As noted earlier, there had already been instances of dispute and plenty of room for the clashing of egos. After all, Comiskey was often referred to and acknowledged as the real power behind the American League and credited by some as the man who personally ended the war between the leagues. Johnson, who was living and breathing the interests of the American League every day, was in an inferior position. Perhaps he needed to display his individuality and a separation between business and friendship by slamming Comiskey with a fierce and abrupt punishment.

But to Comiskey, it was interfering so harshly with his business, unreasonably in his mind, and clearly unfair in comparison to similar situations throughout the league. There was no forgiving Johnson's judgment and the press immediately knew it was the beginnings of a momentous rift. And it was. There was no doubting it.

Johnson's intentions were unlikely spiteful; after all, he sent a gift of fish—a longtime symbol of camaraderie. When asked about Comiskey's comments, he was subdued in the direct clarification of the status of their friendship and certainly couldn't backtrack in fear of looking biased.[25] He said: "As long as I have been at the head of the American League, I have insisted on clean baseball, and the language used by Holmes to O'Loughlin merited the punishment he received. I am only sorry I did not make the punishment more severe. Any magnate who stands for such actions is at liberty to withdraw from the league if he does not like the punishment imposed on his player. The American League is not run in the interest of one man, and will not be."

There, it was said: the league was not beholden to Comiskey and he was entitled to leave the organization if he felt the desire. Johnson demonstrated that he was impartial all through the ranks and that there was zero favoritism. Although there was room to meet in the middle, to compromise and shake hands as old friends, the two men decided to be utterly stubborn, and their bitterness festered as time went by.

Later that June, the Sox took three of four from the New York Highlanders during a more successful than usual Eastern road trip. However, Callahan caught up with some old friends while in the "Big Apple" and spent an inordinate amount of time socializing and drinking.[26] He showed up at the park "out of condition," and Jones initially tried to protect him by saying he was sick. But Callahan kept it up and was suspended once again. Sympathetic to their longtime pal, Comiskey and Jones decided to send him away on a temporary vacation into the country to "get right," and Callahan would rejoin the club after a short hiatus.

Despite the suspension to Ducky Holmes, sickness of Jiggs Donahue, the behavior of Jimmy Callahan, and the injuries to Frank Isbell, Danny Green, and Lee Tannehill, Jones led the team to a 10–4 record on the road, with one tie.[27] A rabid crowd of over 23,000 fans greeted them upon their triumphant return to the South Side Park on June 23, 1905.[28] The Sox won that game, 8–2, taking their fifth straight, and Cleveland was the only team above them in the standings. At St. Louis on July 1, Frank Owen pitched all 18 innings of a doubleheader—winning both games—and held the Browns to only seven hits in total.[29] The remarkable feat bumped Chicago into a tie for first place.

In July, the White Sox were knocked from the top spot, only to regain the position a few days later. Comiskey himself returned to the bench to help inspire his club in a game against New York on July 21, pushing his men to tie the ballgame in the bottom of the ninth and then win it in the twelfth, 2–1.[30] The team did itself no favors by breaking even during a home stand, going 8–9 with one tie, and as his squad went back on the road, Comiskey planned to enjoy a fishing trip in Wisconsin with his son.[31]

Just prior to leaving, he attended a lacrosse game at the South Side Park.[32] He'd been a sponsor of the sport, offering a special cup to the championship winner of a local series, but Comiskey was far from thrilled by what he saw on the afternoon of July 30. Players from the Chicago and Calumet teams decided to express their frustrations by fighting, and Comiskey was having none of it. He grabbed one of the major culprits and personally delivered him to a police officer. As the audience became more and more restless, Comiskey entered the grandstand to calm things down, of course, with additional police by his side, and prevented a potential riot.

President Johnson suspended Jiggs Donahue in August and Fielder Jones later in September for other umpire-related incidents, maintaining a level of consistency. The Sox dipped to third place, only to regain second before returning home on August 18. Over the span of three days, concluding on August 27, Chicago would take six victories from Boston.[33] The three doubleheader victories occurred within fifty-two consecutive hours, and the *Tribune* reported that it came pretty close to setting a new world record. Now a half game behind Connie Mack's first place Philadelphia Athletics, Comiskey took steps to draft and sign a handful of new players; backup athletes who would be used down the stretch if necessary.

And it was a good thing that Comiskey did so. During a practice session in Cleveland on September 2, 1905, Gus Dundon was accidentally knocked out by a flying bat and wouldn't play another game that season.[34] He suffered serious facial injuries and his presence on the bench was sorely missed. No matter the loss, the Sox visited Detroit, where the Tigers tried to repeat the feat of taking six wins in three days but were defeated in a doubleheader on September 6. In the second game, Frank Smith pitched a no hitter for the Sox, shutting Detroit out completely in a 15–0 rout.[35]

Of the four no-hitters in league history, Comiskey's pitchers had two of them, with Callahan notching the other in 1902.

A long road trip concluded the season, and Comiskey was following each inning closely by wire in Chicago. The Sox were victorious in doubleheaders at New York and at Boston, but it seemed for every hard fought win, Philadelphia kept pace. With five games left to play and the pennant in the American League not yet settled, the National Commission announced the dates for the upcoming World Series between the New York Giants and Philadelphia Athletics, completely discounting Chicago's chances to achieve the championship.[36]

Comiskey was livid, stating that it was unfair and would affect the mindset of his players. The commission denied any wrongdoing and didn't mean to impair his club in any way, claiming that just ten minutes were needed to implement a new schedule involving Chicago.[37]

The season was officially decided two days later, on October 6,[38] when St. Louis beat the White Sox, 6–2, and Philadelphia won the pennant.[39] Chicago finished the year in second place with a 92–60 record, two games behind the champions. To show the discrepancy between the second and third place clubs, Detroit, which placed right behind the Sox, was more than 15 games behind the Athletics in the standings. In a display of sportsmanship, Comiskey wired a message of congratulations to Philadelphia manager, Connie Mack.[40]

Throughout 1905, Comiskey haggled with Chicago Cubs owner James Hart over the details of a postseason competition. A best-of-seven series was mutually agreed upon, and on October 11, the Cubs won the initial game in what would be a clear cut display of one team's superiority over another. The Sox would win the second game by a score of 7–4, but the Cubs were simply a better team at this stage of the year, and won the third, fourth, and fifth games, capturing the series and the city championship.[41]

"They trimmed us good and square," Comiskey said after the defeat. "It is the worst trimming I ever have received, and I give the victors all the credit. They are a good ball team. I have been connected in some way with baseball since '76, and this is the worst defeat I ever got."[42]

For the first time since Comiskey implemented an annual postseason hunting and fishing excursion near Fifield, Wisconsin, Ban Johnson was not going along. His partners on the journey into the wilderness would be Tom Loftus, Charles Fredericks, John Agnew, and several others.[43] Johnson arranged his own trip into the tranquil Wisconsin woods, embarking a short time later, and set up shop along the Flambeau River.[44] The proximity of the two men, on the common ground they both scouted, didn't alleviate tension. Ironically, it may have heightened it.

Days after Comiskey returned, and to the shock of some people, he exposed Johnson as the newest threat to the future of the American League.[45] He elaborated by citing a plan by Johnson to merge the organization with the National into an eight or twelve club league. He said Johnson was working with National Commission chairman Garry Herrmann to formulate the consolidation and thought he was no longer acting on behalf of the league's best interests. In the same interview, Comiskey explained that he personally had always fought the National League and planned to continue doing so.

Johnson denied any such plot was underway and received a big boost of support at the annual American League meeting on November 23, 1905, when owners articulated their complete confidence in his leadership.[46] [47] A resolution was put forward blocking any form of merger with the National League, putting the issue to bed once and for all. Before heading back to what was really important—hunting and fishing—Comiskey candidly admitted that he never questioned Johnson's honesty.

That winter, Comiskey took refuge on a pristine 50-foot houseboat, specially customized for him by a company in Muskegon, Michigan.[48] Aptly named "White Sox," the boat featured a 24-horsepower engine and six rooms, and was stationed along the White River in Arkansas as Comiskey and his friends exploited a prime hunting region.[49]

An extensive spring training schedule was prepared for the White Sox in 1906. The team was first going to Jackson and Vicksburg, Mississippi, then fractured with one portion of the club headed to New Orleans and the other to Wichita. Comiskey figured out a way to continue reaping the rewards of his new toy, arranging to meet up with his houseboat at Rosedale, Mississippi,[50] and would venture back into Arkansas prior to joining the team at Wichita around March 23. Interestingly enough, Secretary Fredericks was in charge of the southern tour, while Louis Comiskey, the twenty-year-old son of Charles, was heading up the Wichita branch, with Frank Isbell as manager.

Contracts were received from all players except Jimmy Callahan, who decided to become an owner himself of an outlaw club in Chicago known as the Logan Squares. Ducky Holmes was released to manage in the minor leagues and Danny Green wasn't returning. Comiskey brought in recruits Bill "Tip" O'Neill to play right field, Frank Hemphill for left, and Ernest "Rube" Vinson as a backup outfielder. With George Davis ailing as the season began on April 17, player-manager Fielder Jones moved Lee Tannehill to short and put journeyman George Rohe in at third. Neither the second rate additions nor the injuries spelled a championship contender at the outset and the Sox were expected to quickly fall to the tail end of the standings.

Teams across the majors engaged in benefit games in the aftermath of the disastrous San Francisco earthquake and the Sox lost a dramatic 2–1 contest to the Detroit Tigers on April 30, with half of the gross receipts going to the relief fund.[51] The next day, Comiskey moved his offices out of the Fisher Building, which had been his primary headquarters since moving to Chicago from St. Paul.[52] It had previously made sense to share space with Ban Johnson, but times had changed and Comiskey was looking to create some distance. A new office was forged at 1423 Marquette Building and all of his famous wall mounts from hunting were once again proudly displayed.

One month into the season, the White Sox had dropped to seventh place and the outlook wasn't good. On May 25, 1906, Boston, destined for last place in the league, ended its twenty game losing streak by defeating the Sox 3–0 and holding the latter to only two hits.[53] As usual, offensive production was a weak spot and third baseman Tannehill was one of the most uninspired hitters. Even with a weak bat, his fielding made up for it and Jones kept him in the lineup. A 7–9 road trip in the East demonstrated the team's lack of strength, and as the club was returning home in early

June, a sly reporter painted a picture of discord and animosity within the ranks, citing an argument in Detroit between pitcher Frank Smith and Jones as evidence of the problems.[54]

Comiskey looked into the matter himself and was relieved that things weren't as bad as the press claimed.[55] The erroneous description of the club's lack of solidarity actually worked to further unite the players, inspiring motivation and even anger. Reborn, the White Sox began playing their best ball of the season, winning seven in a row from Philadelphia and Washington. Astutely, Comiskey hired former University of Chicago trainer Hiram B. Conibear to supervise the recovery of the injured and sick members of the team.[56] It was an impressive decision considering the number of ailing players, and Conibear quickly made an impact. His advice, healing strategies, and overall guidance were instrumental to the team's growing success.

For the first time in nearly a month, Chicago was back at .500 and in fourth place. On July 6, manager Jones visited Lancaster, Pennsylvania, to confer with Patsy Dougherty.[57] Dougherty was "owned" by Comiskey, having been purchased from the Highlanders, but he refused to join the Sox and insisted on playing for an independent club in Pittsburgh. Jones shared the same hometown as Dougherty (Bolivar, New York), and their friendliness off the field assisted the negotiations in a big way. By the end of the session, Dougherty enlisted in the Sox's 1906 campaign, and the team was greatly improved by his arrival.

Beginning on August 2, Chicago opened a record-breaking winning streak; one that would take them from fourth to first in remarkable fashion. The "Hitless Wonders," as the club was collectively known, did it through outstanding pitching, teamwork and a lack of serious injuries or distractions. Expert hurler Ed Walsh took a no hitter into the ninth inning versus Boston on August 3, but gave up a safe blooper to left—Boston's only hit— and Chicago finished with a 4–0 victory.[58] Walsh, known for his spitball, pitched a three-hitter on August 7 against the Athletics, outdueling Rube Waddell in another 4–0 win.[59] By August 11, the Sox had triumphed in ten straight games.

Just before leaving for Boston, Comiskey's squad tied New York in a scoreless effort on August 13, the only kink in what would ultimately be a run of 19 wins without a loss, which broke the American League record. While visiting the major metropolises of the Northeast, the team behaved responsibly—unaffected by the attractiveness of the nightlife—and unlike previous teams, was focused only on baseball. Conibear went along, helping players through the everyday bumps and bruises and assisting the injured. Twice during the summer, Comiskey escaped to the outdoors for brief mid-season vacations—once in July and the other in late August—only leaving town when his club was on the road.

While it seemed that the Sox were unbeatable and ready to close out their pennant victory in mid-August, their luck ran out. Dependable catcher Billy Sullivan was the recipient of a harsh foul tip to his thumb on September 2 at the South Side Park and was severely injured.[60] He was rushed to Mercy Hospital in Comiskey's automobile and there was doubt he'd be able to finish the season. More or less, Sullivan was the heart of the team and his replacements, Hub Hart, Jay Towne, and Ed McFarland, were unable to match his level of intensity. On September 21, 1906, the Sox were beaten twice by the Highlanders and fell to second place.[61]

Mammoth crowds turned out to see the final games of the season. Since the Chicago Cubs had already cemented their place as National League champions with a stunning 116–36 record, there was hope that the Sox would turn back the challenge of New York and engage in the first ever cross-town World Series. The numbers worked to the advantage of Comiskey, and by October 3, the pennant was decided in favor of the White Sox.[62 63]

"Chicago is the baseball center of the earth," Hugh S. Fullerton announced in the *Tribune*.[64] And it was true. All eyes were focused on Charles Comiskey and Charles Murphy, owner of the Cubs, as they anticipated the greatest baseball spectacle ever seen in the "Windy City." It was interesting, though, that the rivalry between the Sox and Cubs was all friendly in nature. There was the utmost respect between the ballplayers, managers, and owners, and this theme continued all through the series and its aftermath. Had James Hart, the recently retired owner of the Cubs, still been in charge, the atmosphere might have been different.

Even though the season was not quite over—but the pennants decided— the press had a field day reciting the spectacular come-from-behind achievement made by the Sox.[65] Credit was given to Comiskey and Jones, in large amounts, and the club's ability to prevail through almost insurmountable odds was unbelievable. Judging by the team's appalling team batting average (.230), it was amazing the Sox rose out of seventh place at all. In contrast, the pitching was stellar, and Comiskey's staff completed thirty-two shutouts during the course of the season. Altogether, every player on the team did their part, and it was a victory shared by twenty-five players—the total number of athletes to wear the White Sox uniform in 1906.

But there was still one accomplishment left: defeating the Cubs in the World Series. Under the direction of manager Frank Chance, the Cubs had arguably the best team in baseball. The New York Giants, in second place, were twenty games back when the season concluded. Behind the outstanding pitching of Mordecai Brown, Jack Pfiester, and Ed Reulbach, the Cubs were decidedly better than the Sox in direct comparisons. Still, it was hard to dismiss Comiskey's "Hitless Wonders," winners of 93 games; and the series promised to be one for the books.[66]

The jurisdiction of the World Series fell under the auspices of the National Baseball Commission and many rules and stipulations had to be implemented prior to the first game. One of the more pressing matters was a scheduled increase in ticket prices, an action Comiskey disagreed with.[67] He felt admission should be the same as the regular season, but was rebuffed in his argument. Box seats were going to sell for $2, while the 75 cent tickets were increased to $1.50. To comfortably accommodate the anticipated large crowds, Comiskey added extra seating at the South Side Park, and Murphy won the coin toss, which allowed his West Side Grounds to open the series.

Comiskey's men, Sullivan included, were in decent shape with only one serious absentee: George Davis at shortstop. In response, Jones used Tannehill at short and George Rohe at third. On the other side of the coin, the Cubs were missing Jimmy Slagle, who only batted .239 for the season but had proven to be a much needed force in the outfield. Betting was heavy in New York for the upcoming Series, but the *Tribune* stated that gambling in Chicago was somewhat quiet.[68]

On the morning of October 8, the White Sox reported to the South Side Park and listened to an impassioned speech by Comiskey.[69] The next day, the Sox and Cubs met in their first head-to-head contest for the 1906 World Series.[70]

Nick Altrock started for the Sox against Brown and both teams combined for eight hits (four each) over a competitive nine innings. The final result was a 2–1 victory for the Sox, and Rohe was acknowledged as the man of the hour, slamming a triple to left in the fifth and crossing home later in the inning on a fielder's choice. 12,693 fans attended the ballgame, which was less than expected but was about the same amount that witnessed game two at the South Side Park the next afternoon, October 10.[71] The Cubs rebounded to score three in the second inning on their way to a 7–1 win, with Reulbach holding the Sox to one hit after starting with six no-hit innings. The three errors committed by Comiskey's boys didn't help much either.

Game three saw the Sox win 3–0 in a pitcher's duel between Ed Walsh and Jack Pfiester, with both pitching complete games and striking out a total of 21 batters (12 for Pfiester and 9 for Walsh).[72] In the sixth inning, Rohe again came to the forefront by hitting a bases loaded triple to give his team a lead they wouldn't give up. On October 12, the Cubs tied the series at two games apiece with a 1–0 victory.[73] Mordecai Brown was dominant on the mound and the Sox only received base hits from Ed Hahn and Patsy Dougherty. The next day, Comiskey's men took a 3–2 series lead after an 8–6 victory.[74] Second baseman Frank Isbell committed two errors in the field (with the Sox making six total), but made up for it with four doubles before 23,257 people at the West Side Park. The flubs of Isbell and Rohe, who was also at fault for two errors, helped the Cubs score all six of its runs but the mistakes were not enough to cost the Sox the game.[75]

Comiskey's players were one game away from achieving the impossible. At home on October 14, 1906, the Sox beat the Cubs 8–3 and won its first World Series.[76] Having scored three runs in the first and four in the second, the Sox were in charge throughout the game. The climax came in the bottom of the ninth as most of the 19,249 people in attendance mobbed the field in excitement. The triumph was roundly endorsed across the sports world, and what the Sox had accomplished was truly amazing. They had the proper combination of players, personalities, and management to overcome constant hardship, and, in the end, fulfilling the ambitions of everybody associated with the club.

In terms of numbers, 99,845 fans watched the six games in Chicago and the total receipts added up to $106,550. The series was a complete success.

George Rohe with his .333 batting average was voted the offensive most valuable player, while Isbell also contributed eight hits. Once again, the pitching of Ed Walsh, Nick Altrock, and Doc White came through when the team needed them most, and their opponents, the talented Cubs staff, faltered at crunch time.

Moments after the game ended, in his private office at the stadium, Comiskey humbly accepted the hearty congratulations of President Murphy and others. His players, soon after dressing in their civilian attire, met their chief in a combined celebration of handshakes and smiles. With great pride, Comiskey presented Jones with a bonus check of $15,000 for their exceptional work, meant to be split up amongst the twenty-one players. That money, along with the regular winners' portion of the gate receipts, gave each Sox player a little over $1,900 apiece. In the other locker room, the Cubs received $100 bonus money from Murphy and were paid about $439 for the six games of work.

For the owners, their friends, and other dignitaries, the party moved over to the beautiful Pompeian Room at the Auditorium Annex where Comiskey freely expressed his happiness.[77] Carrying around a wad of cash and telling the press he planned to stay awake for the next twenty-four hours, he was living within the moment and enjoying the accomplishment of his team to the fullest. Elsewhere in the city, bonfires were set and a throng of fans traveled to the homes of Sox players as a demonstration of their joy.

In the days that followed, parades, dinners, dances, and other social events rejoiced in all things baseball and both teams were endlessly praised. Hugh Fullerton of the *Tribune* was acknowledged as the man who accurately predicted the outcome of the series, having run a column in the newspaper prior to the start by stating that the Sox would win in six.[78] Comiskey attended a handful of parties but dodged many others in his rush to get to his Wisconsin camp. For him, the best place to celebrate was in the restful serenity of the Northern woods.

ENDNOTES

1 *Chicago Daily Tribune*, November 25, 1903, p. 6.
  The camp was 30–35 miles north of Fifield, Wisconsin, near Springstead. Fifield was the nearest railroad station.
2 *Chicago Daily Tribune*, November 17, 1904, p. 6.
3 *Cleveland Leader*, December 31, 1904, p. 6.
  Manager Fielder Jones and George Davis were the highest paid players on the Sox and made more than $2,500 a year.
4 *Dallas Morning News*, June 4, 1905, p. 22.
5 *Chicago Daily Tribune*, August 9, 1903, p. 10.
6 *Chicago Daily Tribune*, August 9, 1903, p. 10.
7 *Chicago Daily Tribune*, December 20, 1904, p. 10.

8 *Chicago Daily Tribune*, February 17, 1905, p. 8.
9 *Chicago Daily Tribune*, January 11, 1905, p. 8.
10 *Chicago Daily Tribune*, January 18, 1905, p. 8.
11 *Sporting News*, February 25, 1905, p. 1.
12 *Chicago Daily Tribune*, March 1, 1905, p. 10.
13 *Chicago Daily Tribune*, March 12, 1905, p. A1.
14 *Chicago Daily Tribune*, March 26, 1905, p. A1.
15 *Chicago Daily Tribune*, April 15, 1905, p. 7.
16 *Chicago Daily Tribune*, April 17, 1905, p. 8.
17 *Chicago Daily Tribune*, May 31, 1905, p. 8.
18 Ibid.
19 *Chicago Daily Tribune*, June 4, 1905, p. A1.
20 *Chicago Daily Tribune*, November 26, 1905, p. A1.
   Hugh E. Keough explained "one of the trivial incidents" that instigated the Comiskey-Johnson feud, which happened to relate to Holmes' suspension and delivery of fish by McRoy. The "fish story" has been told and retold innumerable times and Keough may have been the first person to publicly relay the tale.
21 *Chicago Daily Tribune*, June 5, 1905, p. 8.
22 Ibid.
   Callahan had been reinstated by Comiskey, but for whatever reason, he left the stadium prior to the game and could not be recalled to play as a substitute for Holmes.
23 *Chicago Daily Tribune*, June 5, 1905, p. 8.
24 Ibid.
25 *Chicago Daily Tribune*, June 7, 1905, p. 8.
26 *Chicago Daily Tribune*, June 21, 1905, p. 10.
27 *Chicago Daily Tribune*, June 25, 1905, p. A2.
28 *Chicago Daily Tribune*, June 26, 1905, p. 8.
29 *Chicago Daily Tribune*, July 2, 1905, p. A1.
30 *Chicago Daily Tribune*, July 22, 1905, p. 8.
31 *Chicago Daily Tribune*, July 30, 1905, p. A2.
   Also joining them on the trip were John Agnew and sportswriter Gus Axelson.
32 *Chicago Daily Tribune*, July 31, 1905, p. 8.
33 *Chicago Daily Tribune*, August 28, 1905, p. 8.
   Also see: *Boston Journal*, August 28, 1905, p. 4.
34 *Chicago Daily Tribune*, September 3, 1905, p. A1.
35 *Chicago Daily Tribune*, September 7, 1905, p. 6.
36 *Chicago Daily Tribune*, October 5, 1905, p. 6.
   In his anger, Comiskey announced that if his team won the pennant, he'd decline a World Series opportunity and face the Chicago Cubs instead.
37 *Chicago Daily Tribune*, October 6, 1905, p. 10.
38 Away from the field, on October 8, 1905, at the corner of Thirtieth and State Streets, Comiskey's chauffeur Charles Anderson ran over a twenty-two-year-old pedestrian named William Welch, seriously injuring him (*Chicago Daily Tribune*, October 9, 1905, p. 3.). Comiskey himself wasn't in the automobile, but his son

Louis was. Anderson was arrested on the scene, pending Welch's prognosis at a local hospital. The resulting condition of Welch and further particulars about this situation could not be located.

39 *Chicago Daily Tribune*, October 7, 1905, p. 6.

40 *Chicago Daily Tribune*, October 9, 1905, p. 10.

41 *Chicago Daily Tribune*, October 16, 1905, p. 3.

The Cubs were led by Frank Chance, who, years later, would be named manager of the White Sox—but never actively serve because of illness.

42 Ibid.

43 *Chicago Daily Tribune*, November 1, 1905, p. 10.

44 *Chicago Daily Tribune*, October 22, 1905, p. A1.

45 *Chicago Daily Tribune*, November 21, 1905, p. 10. The next day, Comiskey claimed he had been misquoted.

46 *Chicago Daily Tribune*, November 22, 1905, p. 10.

47 *Chicago Daily Tribune*, November 24, 1905, p. 10.

48 *Muskegon Daily Chronicle*, October 25, 1905, p. 2.

A photo of his boat was printed in the *Chicago Daily Tribune*, September 2, 1906, p. D5.

49 *Chicago Daily Tribune*, December 19, 1905, p. 12.

Comiskey said it was the "best hunting region" he'd ever "struck."

50 *Chicago Daily Tribune*, March 15, 1906, p. 10.

51 *Chicago Daily Tribune*, May 1, 1906, p. 10.

52 *Chicago Daily Tribune*, May 2, 1906, p. 10.

53 *Boston Herald*, May 26, 1906, p. 1.

54 *Chicago Daily Tribune*, June 1, 1906, p. 10.

55 *Chicago Daily Tribune*, June 2, 1906, p. 6.

56 *Chicago Daily Tribune*, June 16, 1906, p. 10.

57 *Chicago Daily Tribune*, July 7, 1906, p. 10.

58 *Chicago Daily Tribune*, August 4, 1906, p. 10.

59 *Chicago Daily Tribune*, August 8, 1906, p. 8.

60 *Chicago Daily Tribune*, September 3, 1906, p. 10.

61 *Chicago Daily Tribune*, September 22, 1906, p. 10.

62 *Chicago Daily Tribune*, October 4, 1906, p. 1.

63 Not only did the 1906 Cubs have the best record in baseball, but their 116 wins are still the most in franchise history. It was also the first time they'd even won over 100 games. They have only reached that feat four times since: 1907 (107), 1909 and 1910 (104), and 1935 (100).

64 *Chicago Daily Tribune*, October 4, 1906, p. 1.

65 *Chicago Daily Tribune*, October 7, 1906, p. B1-B2.

66 The nickname "Hitless Wonders" for the 1906 White Sox was indeed well suited. They are the only team in baseball history to have the lowest team batting average for their league and still win the World Series. The only two teams that came close to this record were the 1974 Oakland Athletics (lowest average in AL West, second lowest in AL) and the 1995 Atlanta Braves (lowest average in NL East, second lowest in NL).

67 *Chicago Daily Tribune,* October 5, 1906, p. 10.

68 *Chicago Daily Tribune,* October 8, 1906, p. 10.

69 *Chicago Daily Tribune,* October 9, 1906, p. 2.

70 *Chicago Daily Tribune,* October 10, 1906, p. 1.

71 *Chicago Daily Tribune,* October 11, 1906, p. 1.
Before Fielder Jones' first at bat, he was presented with a beautiful silverware set from his teammates and Comiskey in honor of his excellent work as manager. His wife was given a gift as well.

72 *Chicago Daily Tribune,* October 12, 1906, p. 1.

73 *Chicago Daily Tribune,* October 13, 1906, p. 1.

74 *Chicago Daily Tribune,* October 14, 1906, p. 1.

75 Through the first five games of the 1906 World Series, the home team had lost each game.

76 *Chicago Daily Tribune,* October 15, 1906, p. 1.
Full coverage of the Series was also presented in the *Sporting News,* October 20, 1906.

77 *Chicago Daily Tribune,* October 15, 1906, p. 3.

78 *Chicago Daily Tribune,* October 15, 1906, p. 4.
Predicting the winner of the World Series was a gimmick Fullerton became famous for. His inside baseball "Dope" was observed by fellow pundits, executives, players, and enthusiasts and his methodical system of breaking down each position was revolutionary. Some fellow writers, however, seemed to take joy when Fullerton got a prediction wrong; but when at Fullerton's level, there was bound to be jealousy. In 1906, Fullerton worked for the *Tribune,* but he'd later move over to the *Chicago Herald and Examiner.* His work was also syndicated to other papers around the country. His accurate prediction of the 1906 Series added great credibility to his annual prophecies.

10

SEVEN YEARS OF BAD LUCK

The exhilaration of the championship conquest surrounded the members of the White Sox for weeks—if not months—after the World Series of 1906 concluded. Some members of the squad took advantage of financial opportunities by playing exhibition games and garnered a little extra cash on the road. Lavish galas were staged in the hometowns of players who triumphantly returned, and they were treated like celebrities in the city of Chicago. Charles Comiskey was personally honored by a banquet at Mangler's famous restaurant on La Salle Street and again by friends in St. Louis at the Southern Hotel on November 26, 1906.[1][2] Of course, while along the Mississippi River, Comiskey took advantage of an opportunity to meet up with his houseboat for another stimulating excursion into the wilds of Arkansas.[3]

His presence was required at the annual American League meeting in Chicago on December 12 to discuss the matters of the day.[4] Since June of 1905, the entire landscape of major league baseball was hindered to some degree by the overarching affects of the feud between Comiskey and Ban Johnson. The quarrel continued as the two men ignored each other like schoolchildren, and only occasionally did one of them refer to the other, but usually in passing.

Former Sox manager Jimmy Callahan said he was altogether surprised that Comiskey was able to win the World Series with Johnson working against him.[5] According to the abundance of stories printed on December 13, and the days following, Comiskey and Johnson came together at the league meeting and cordially ended their dispute. Sportswriters were thrilled by the reunion, although talk of a "perfect harmony" existing was an overstatement.[6] They were on speaking terms again, which was a tremendous first step that once seemed impossible, but the ground they stood on was extremely fragile; brittle enough that even a stray sneer had the possibility of triggering a collapse.

As a display of his graciousness, Comiskey furnished a complete banquet for his American League comrades and newspapermen in the English room of the Annex that evening. Along with Johnson, he recited many stories from their escapades in the outdoors, and the gathering shared in the "mellowing influence of the bubbles," according to the *Tribune*.[7]

In early January of 1907, Comiskey battled a slight illness while beginning to collect contracts from players for the approaching season.[8] With the annexation of the World Series, several members of the Sox expected a raise, and Comiskey was more than accommodating. Pitchers Nick Altrock and Ed Walsh were among those to receive a salary boost and player-manager Fielder Jones was also financially rewarded for his leadership. Repeatedly, Comiskey said that he planned to keep his team mostly intact and test out a few new recruits like Mike Welday, Lee Quillin, Lawrence Chaney, and Buck Freeman.

The White Sox owner was in the midst of organizing a grand schedule for spring training, forging a path into Mexico and becoming the first major league team to prepare for an upcoming season outside the United States.[9] Sending the original trailblazer, Ted Sullivan, to do the advance work, Comiskey finalized details with the Illinois Central Railroad and "chaperone" Robert Carmichael. President Johnson was originally slated to join the party but cancelled at the last minute due to illness. On March 5, 1907, the "White Sox Special" departed Chicago for the South, packed with twenty-five players, various family members, and a group of eager press writers.[10]

Just before debarkation, Comiskey embraced the excitement of the moment by announcing that he was again offering a $15,000 bonus to the team if they repeated as champions.[11] Spirits were high, and the enthusiasm seen by people along the train route was inspirational. The double locomotives and decorated cars were hard to ignore—bordering on ostentatious—but appropriate for baseball's kings in their maiden journey as champs. Regrettably, the trip was haunted by regular mechanical difficulties while en route, putting the team far behind schedule.[12] The Sox found themselves having to forfeit two games, and Comiskey even debated cancelling the trip altogether.

A strange episode occurred at San Antonio, while players were sightseeing and taking in historic locations like the Alamo.[13] Pitcher Frank Owen was putting on a show of his own, reciting the story of his accidental self-inflicted gunshot wound to his thigh that occurred back in January. For effect, he even displayed his trusty revolver, a big error in judgment to make in Texas. A local policeman swooped in and arrested Owen for carrying a concealed weapon, but the athlete was released after several hours behind bars. He submitted bond and promised to return for a court date after the Mexican trip.

Once in Mexico, the Sox played each other in exhibitions, defeated local teams, and performed before small audiences. The exhaustive journey, altitude, and dry climate had a terrible effect on the physical health of certain players, Jones, in particular, and several men came down with painful sore throats. Fans in certain instances gave the champions a hard time when it came to errors in the field, but it wasn't anything more than the regular spring hiccups.[14] One evening, a woman's terrifying shrieks at the team's hotel got their collective hearts pumping and players banded together to search for a purported robber.[15] The reporter on hand noticed that Owen, of course, was brandishing his infamous revolver, however no one was shot or arrested.

In terms of spreading interest in baseball and general sightseeing, the tour was a major success. Financially, it wasn't a considerable achievement. Comiskey sent a box of cigars to the Mexican president as a gesture of goodwill and gratitude, and the White Sox returned to the U.S. to finish their training. One half of the club went directly to New Orleans, run by Jones, and the other half traveled up through Texas, managed by Lou Comiskey.

The season opened on April 11 in St. Louis, and Comiskey attended the festivities to see old friends, but watched his team lose 1–0.[16] During the initial series, Lee Tannehill was spiked in the leg and seriously injured. He'd develop a bad case of blood poisoning and miss several months of action. George Davis was also battling a back injury, causing Jones to put Quillin at third and Rohe at short. Relying on two relatively inexperienced players to substitute for veterans was a major hindrance for the early going of the 1907 season. Comiskey, himself, returned to Chicago a few days later, intending to supervise additional improvements at the South Side Park. Among the changes he was actively considering was the implementation of an electronic scoreboard and batting cages.

The raising of the American League flag during the home opener on April 18 occurred without incident . . .the same cannot be said for the hoisting of the World Series pennant, which coincided with an even bigger celebration at the South Side Park on May 14. [17][18] A massive automobile parade to the stadium was followed by a presentation of the pennant to Chicago Mayor Fred Busse. Members of the White Sox began to pull the banner up along the tall pine flag staff behind the centerfield bleachers as an estimated 15,000 fans watched on. The pennant wasn't even halfway up when the pole broke in the center, sending the banner crashing to the ground. Superstitious people immediately called for seven years bad luck to the Sox, a premonition Comiskey disregarded. To top it off, the game was then rained out. Incidentally, a couple weeks later, the groundskeeper of the park, John Reuther, raised the pennant on a new flagpole without any fanfare.

On May 4, 1907 in Detroit, the Sox achieved a rare triple play, but Ed Walsh was a victim of the third out when he was steamrolled at the plate by a base runner.[19] With neck and shoulder injuries, he was going to be out of commission for weeks. Additionally, manager Jones was briefly suspended by Ban Johnson for a comment he made to an umpire in Cleveland.[20] By this time, it was pretty well known that the Comiskey-Johnson rivalry was rekindled.[21] Comiskey was angry that Johnson broke a pledge to support the Topeka franchise's shift to the Western League. Other factors fueled the bitterness as well, and it was amazing that the "reunion" survived as long as it did before fracturing.

The White Sox were a first place team for all of June and July, steadily holding back Philadelphia, Cleveland, and Detroit. Comiskey, trying to strengthen his club even more, outbid his competition for the rights to Washington's former manager, Jake Stahl . . . but Stahl resisted as his heart was set on playing for Boston.[22]

Demonstrating the relationship between Comiskey and the local media, the Chicago Press Club staged a banquet for him on June 24, and on July 4, in what would later become a tradition at Chicago's American League park, a fireworks show was presented.[23] [24] A portrait in fire was created in the likeness of Comiskey as well as Jones, during the revelry.

At St. Louis, in a benefit for the local newsboys' home, Comiskey returned to the field for the first time in years on July 25.[25] He played first base for the Chicago team of "Fat Men," guys weighing north of 200 pounds, and lost to the St. Louis "heifers," 14–7.

Overtaken in the standings by the Tigers and Athletics, the Sox were struggling at bat and didn't have the positive momentum of the year before.

When the season finally concluded on October 6, Chicago finished in third place, 5.5 games behind the Tigers with an 87–64 record. The Tigers would go on to play the National League champion Chicago Cubs, but lose four straight after the opener ended in a 3–3 tie, giving the Cubs their first World Series championship.

Fatigued by the continuous stress of the season, Comiskey endured a scary moment during dinner at his home when he collapsed on the evening of October 10, 1907.[26] Placed under the care of a doctor, he retired to his property at McHenry, Illinois, and the *Tribune* initially reported his condition as "nervous exhaustion," but later stated that it was just "a bad cold." Nevertheless, he was back on the job within days, and finalized a trade with Boston for shortstop Fred Parent.[27] In exchange, Comiskey liberated holdout Jake Stahl and Stahl ended up in New York in the final stage of a three-team swap.

More than ever, Comiskey's postseason ventures into the wilderness were seen as a measure of status amongst the hierarchy of baseball. Ban Johnson led one troupe into the Wisconsin woods, going to Hayward, followed by Comiskey's twenty-person faction the next day. Rather than go to the camp near Springstead, Comiskey switched things up and moved a little more north to the Mercer area, on Trude Lake.[28] He affiliated himself with the Jerome Hunting and Fishing Club, which became the headquarters for his annual expedition.

Among Comiskey's party were his son Lou, Tom Loftus, Charles Spink, and Gus Axelson. Also included was an array of die-hard fans, many of whom would become official members of the White Sox Rooters' Association.[29] Incorporated by Robert E. Cantwell, the association was comprised of affluent, ultra-loyal followers; individuals who attended every home game and some on the road. They expressed their support with unabashed enthusiasm, and, at times, carried megaphones to not only cheer on the Sox, but pester rivaling squads.

The acceptance of organized rooting as a respected entity by Comiskey was controversial, especially since the extreme actions of rooters were considered somewhat detrimental to the sport. He helped legitimize the concept in Chicago, and similar organizations were active in other parts of the country, including the Royal Rooters in Boston. The sycophantic rooters were becoming increasingly influential and they cherished their inside tract to Comiskey himself. They were, after all, hanging out socially with the boss.

In the span of two days—December 5–6, 1907—Comiskey was sued twice over two very different issues. On December 5, he was named the defendant in a $10,000 damage suit in response to a September car accident when his chauffeur struck and injured a seven-year-old child.[30] The next day he was named in a Federal suit when George E. Heaney, an original incorporator of the American League Base Ball Club of Chicago, complained that despite being a shareholder, he never received any dividends from the company prior to selling out.[31] The victim of the first suit ended with a $2,000 victory. Heaney's effort was remanded to Milwaukee Circuit Court and remained an active case through 1910.

Comiskey, for the first time since becoming an owner, began to seriously stockpile players, building an immense forty-eight-man roster. Most of the athletes were young potentials and he was searching for a diamond—or two—in the rough. He spent over $15,000 on new players from all over the Western League, American Association, and other organizations, including the semi-professional ranks.[32] Most of the time he received good advice and stellar financial deals on up-and-comers from fellow magnates and managers he was friends with.

For instance, Comiskey bought the rights to Jake Stahl from the Washington Senators when many other teams were looking for his services. And just who was the manager of the Senators? Joe Cantillon, a longtime pal and regular on the annual hunting trips. Cantillon's brother Mike ran the Minneapolis club and there too was another connection for scouting information. Frank Isbell stepped into an ownership role in Wichita after the 1907 season and also offered Comiskey a number of players. Another hunting buddy and "rooter," John F. Higgins bought the Des Moines club of the Western League and did the same thing.[33]

But Comiskey never forgot his true allies, and when it came time to disperse of his extra talent, he sent players to Des Moines, Dubuque, Minneapolis, and to Jimmy Ryan's Montgomery club. In some instances, he maintained an option to recall them in the case that one of his regulars was injured or out of commission for whatever reason.

Preliminary talks to return to Mexico and venture to the Yucatan peninsula for spring training in 1908 were replaced with an extravagant journey to California instead. With Western League President Norris "Tip" O'Neill as his advance scout to Los Angeles, Comiskey went to work arranging nonstop train service to the West Coast, avoiding all the troubles of the previous year.[34] An offer to take the White Sox to Honolulu surfaced, but such a long tour needed plenty of forethought.[35] Comiskey planned to consider it for 1909 if an optimal timeline could be arranged.

The persuasion and influence of Comiskey was displayed during the December 1907 annual meeting of the American League in Chicago.[36] Of the eight clubs in the organization, seven of the owners were in favor of expanding the World Series to nine games and agreed with the upsurge supporting the idea in the National League. Comiskey was the only owner against it. He argued the matter, convinced his peers, and like Juror #8 (Henry Fonda) in *12 Angry Men*, the entire body voted against the expansion of the series. His major assertion was that the National League was always going to be better rested for a long postseason, while the winner of the more competitive American were going to be handicapped by exhaustion. Thus, the expanded series benefitted the Nationals.

During the off season, Fielder Jones turned down a lucrative offer to enter the timber business in Oregon to manage the White Sox for a fifth season.[37] Among the newcomers into camp were outfielder John Anderson of the Senators, catcher Al "Lou" Shaw, catcher Arthur Weaver, third baseman Billy Purtell, and pitcher Moxie Manuel. Others on the spring training roster included Fred Olmstead, Champ Osteen, Frank Lange, Sheldon Lejeune, and Frank Dick. Three long affiliated players were gone from the team: Ed McFarland was traded to Boston, Isbell remained in Wichita with his varied business interests, and Roy Patterson retired to Minnesota. Comiskey also released George Rohe, the hero of the 1906 World Series, and Gus Dundon.

Pitcher Nick Altrock's 7–13 record in 1907, and the factors that were suspected in contributing to the disappointing numbers, earned him a special condition clause in his 1908 contract.[38] The anti-booze stipulation allotted a bonus of $900 if he could stay sober throughout the season. Altrock signed the contract, with hesitancy, and Comiskey hoped he'd return to his previous form.

The Sox were booked in as many as 75 exhibition games for the spring training season; beginning in Los Angeles and continuing by two separate squads, one in the South and the other through the Midwest. Tied up with the last minute details, Comiskey skipped out on the American League's schedule meeting in New York, but found time to attend a banquet staged by the White Sox Rooters' Association at Brooke's Casino.[39] The Association, under President Joe Farrell, demonstrated the merits of an organized rooting operation, and threw a memorable party for all who attended.[40]

On February 29, over seventy people packed the "White Sox Limited" headed for California. Comiskey was joined by his wife Nan, son Lou, nephew Charles Fredericks, niece Mabel, and her two children.[41] Other friends and rooters joined along as well. When the train stopped in Kansas, hundreds of people greeted the team, and Comiskey spent time shaking hands with those in the crowd in what a newspaper dubbed, "political campaign style."[42]

In terms of time, the Sox fared much better going to the West Coast than they did to Mexico, and immediately went to work upon arrival. Audiences as large as 6,000 people watched Chicago play Los Angeles, and the local team took advantage of the travel-weary club, beating them 6–3.[43] Comiskey went to San Francisco with one half of the club, while Jones and his "regulars" finished off dates in Southern California, then depared for New Orleans.

Games were played from San Diego to Evansville, Indiana, and nearly everywhere in between. A measure of teamwork and camaraderie was achieved—no question about it—but the Sox were exhausted by the volume of games and extent of their travels. Comiskey made his first Chicago appearance in a month on March 30 and boasted about the success of the trip, reporting that the team was $7,000 ahead.[44] He was confident in their playing ability and began to finalize his roster for the launch of another championship season.

As could be expected, more and more distance was being created between Comiskey and his players on a yearly basis. The days of his overwhelming presence being felt on the bench and hovering over the shoulder of his manager were long passed. He mingled in the company of his players during the train ride to California and was among them for the initial stages of spring training, but freely admitted that he hadn't seen any of his athletes in the weeks prior to the beginning of the season on April 14, 1908.[45] He was kept abreast of their condition via wire and heeded the recommendations of his manager and Fredericks, accompanying the first team, and his son Lou, who was leading the secondary squad.

Despite the spectacular efforts of Tyrus Raymond "Ty" Cobb, the White Sox overcame the fierce challenge of the American League champion Detroit Tigers on opening day, winning 15–8.[46] Cobb had three hits—including a home run—and was outstanding in the field. The Sox proved better on this occasion, and the huge crowd supported their every move. It was going to be a long season, however, as the Tigers were still the hands on favorite to repeat as champs.

On May 5, 1908, the fifth place Sox were on tap to battle Cleveland at the South Side Park in a special "Comiskey Day" salute. The Mayors of Milwaukee, Cleveland, and Dubuque were to join Mayor Busse of Chicago in an awesome automobile parade, culminating in a huge celebration at the park. Everything humanly possible was done to arrange all aspects of the party, but a deluge of rain caused the event to be postponed.

With every win came a defeat and Chicago was still playing .500 ball by the end of May.[47] John Anderson was hitting well and Ed Walsh was redefining what it meant to be the ace of a pitching staff, but the rest of the team was struggling to get out of sixth place. They soon figured it out. Between June 4 and June 16, the Sox managed to win thirteen games in a row; a blitz that took the club right to the top of the standings.[48] Immediately in reverse, the Sox continued to streak, losing seven in a row between June 22 and June 28, falling behind St. Louis and Cleveland with a 35–28 record.

Frank Smith, usually reliable on the mound, rebelled and went home to Pittsburgh after what was said to be an argument with Comiskey.[49] He denied breaking any team rules and refused to return, demanding to be traded or sold. Fredericks resolved the difficulties and Smith rejoined the club before the end of July.

Comiskey's focus during the summer was on player acquisitions, social and charitable functions, and an odd legal entanglement involving the White Sox Rooters' Association. He recalled Frank Isbell and signed two prospects, Walter Mattick and Art Bader. Comiskey, in honoring his former team, its owner and players, held a special "Cincinnati Day" at the South Side Park on June 16, and a benefit for renowned billiard player Jake Schaefer on July 14.[50] A short time later, he was able to return the favor for the team's superb spring training session in Los Angeles by chaperoning the mayor of the latter city around Chicago.[51]

Politics within the rooters' association and a division of members caused a significant break in the unit's harmony. Claims that its treasury had been stolen and incessant backstabbing contributed to the plight of the group, but an even more damaging legal matter gripped the heart of the organization in 1908 that shot all the way up—right to Comiskey.

In June, a good number of rooters—plus Comiskey and his son Louis—were all called by the State of Illinois to testify in a murder case. Their statements, it was believed, were going to directly contradict the sworn testimony of a man who claimed to have witnessed a murder. According to prosecutors, the individual was not in Chicago at the time and couldn't have seen the killing take place because he was on a train headed for Wisconsin for Comiskey's annual hunting trip the October before.

The supposed witness was H. H. Stridiron, and his attorney Robert Cantwell were both incorporators for the Association. Cantwell was defending the three men on trial, and it was alleged by the prosecution that he had personally partaken in a conspiracy to prevent the truth from becoming known. He reportedly knew that the witness was on the train to Wisconsin but was not forthright in admitting it. Cantwell denied any wrongdoing. Several weeks later, Comiskey and others testified before a Cook County Grand Jury and Cantwell was indicted for perjury. When it was all said and done, not only were the three men acquitted in the murder trial, Cantwell himself was acquitted in his perjury case, which was finalized on March 2, 1911.

The actions of Cantwell were going to make headlines again in 1908, this time a little closer to the diamond and would effectively taint the good intentions and destroy the reputation of the White Sox Rooters' Association forever.

In a lesser incarnation of the rained out "Comiskey Day," an event was held at the South Side Park on August 15, 1908, honoring the Sox owner.[52] The festive atmosphere was heightened by a benefit for Chicago's Working Boys' home, and featured a ball game between the Aldermen of Chicago against the Aldermen of St. Louis. An estimated 6,000 people were in attendance and $20,000 was collected for the charity. Sox players Nick Altrock and Jiggs Donahue were the umpires for St. Louis's massacre of Chicago; a defeat by the score of 18–0.[53]

As the season was nearing a conclusion, the pennant race in the American League was shockingly close. On August 31, Detroit was in first and St. Louis second, with Chicago not far behind in third and Cleveland on their tail. The four-way battle was captivating and the teams were separated by mere points in the standings. Six straight wins from September 17 to 23 carried the Sox into second place with an 81–61 record, but they fell back to third later that month. Considering all the variables that could have flushed one of the teams from contention, all four stayed within range of the championship for the last month of the season.

There was plenty of excitement left. Unfortunately, on September 28, 1908, the negative kind of excitement reared its head at the South Side Park.[54] Umpire John Kerin called an end to a game between Chicago and Boston because of darkness, with the score tied 2–2 in the 10th inning. Fans at the stadium were not thrilled by Kerin's work, particularly a call in the seventh that could have given the Sox the lead, but only one fan sought vengeance. This spectator turned criminal waited for Kerin and then sucker punched him in the nose, knocking the umpire out cold. Although he ran off before being apprehended, he was identified as attorney Robert Cantwell.[55]

Rooters were already chided for their overblown attitudes and excessive actions, and now a member had physically attacked an umpire. It was a public relations disaster for the White Sox Rooters' Association, which had made great strides, and reflected badly upon Comiskey for giving credence to the organization. Cantwell was later found guilty of assault and fined.[56]

Comiskey's most valuable player of the 1908 season was unquestionably Ed Walsh. On October 2, 1908, Walsh pitched in one of the greatest pitching duels in Major League Baseball history.[57] The game, at Cleveland, saw Walsh strike out 15 batters over the course of eight innings, giving up only a single run. Addie Joss did one better, pitching a masterful effort and throwing only the second perfect game since 1900. Four days later, the Tigers beat the Sox 7–0 to end the season. The standings stood with Detroit at the top, Cleveland in second, and Chicago in third with an 88–64 record—only 1.5 games back.

The *Tribune* called it the "greatest of American League pennant races," and Comiskey remarked about the loss to Detroit, saying: "That game meant more to me than any game I ever saw."[58]

Comiskey added: "I feel doubly sorry for Walsh, after all his grand work," and that he planned to take off for the wilderness of Wisconsin, "where I shall try to forget baseball worries."

Walsh would finish the season with a 40–15 record, 1.42 ERA, and pitched in 66 games for a total of 464 innings. It was a remarkable performance, filling the voids left by Altrock and Smith during the apex of the season. Patsy Dougherty led the team in batting with a .278 average, while Fred Parent, Fielder Jones, and Billy Sullivan all underachieved. A little more offensive power in the right spots would've pushed them over the top, but it was not to be. Major changes were in store for the club going into the 1909 season, and Comiskey was eyeing a new project that was literally going to change the landscape of professional baseball in Chicago.

A more subdued reunion occurred in 1908; one that was considered less meaningful than the time prior, and it was between Comiskey and Ban Johnson.[59] Their stubborn behavior in the "war," considering all of the time they spent not talking to each other, was at an elementary level. Frankly, it didn't speak highly of either man to continue such an immature grudge seeing how close they were prior to their initial break. But it was almost impossible for them to be both friends and business associates. There was just too much baggage and too strong of egos.

Nevertheless, on September 15, a mediation party of mutual acquaintances brought Comiskey and Johnson together at the South Side Park, and once again, peace was made. For the first time since 1904, Johnson was joining Comiskey in his annual hunting trip to Mercer, Wisconsin.[60] On October 17, a group of eighteen left Chicago, and faithful friends Tom Loftus, Charles Spink, John Agnew, and James Mullin were a part of the crew, as expected. Considering all the trouble the White Sox Rooters' Association had created, it was obvious Comiskey needed to be a little more careful about selecting his hunting companions. He still welcomed Joe Farrell and a handful of trusted pals, and two weeks of frivolity in the wilderness was enjoyed.

The benefits of escapism were optimal for the likeminded souls, but the combined perks of the quiet northern forests couldn't halt bad news from arriving on Comiskey's doorstep. His dependable groundskeeper at the South Side Park, "Old John" Reuther, passed away following an operation on October 22.[61] German born Reuther had been with Comiskey since St. Paul, and had postponed cancer treatment to fulfill his duties for the 1908 season. Deeply appreciative of his devoted employees, the Sox owner considered postponing his trip to observe Reuther's recovery, but there were few positive expectations for improvement. Thus, the news wasn't shocking, but still immensely painful.

Despite his emphatic declarations to dislike New York because the big city made him feel lonely, Comiskey was again rumored to be trading in his ownership of the Sox for that of the Highlanders.[62] It was undoubtedly the prevailing gossip of recent years, and as always, held no significance. He was not in the mood for reckless baseball chitchat, and within days of returning from Wisconsin, he was already on the move for a quail hunt in the Cedar Rapids area.

Ironically, instead of "Eight Men Out," nine Sox players were temporarily banned from Organized Baseball by the National Commission on November 5, 1908 for playing an outlaw team.[63] The suspended included Frank Smith, "Doc" White, and Jiggs Donahue, and all were eventually reinstated after paying a fine.

Comiskey's distractive hobby took precedence, and he spent additional time at his Wisconsin sanctuary and then ventured into Canada during the Thanksgiving holiday. Things took a turn for the worse when he was nearly stranded by a freak storm and spent a few aimless hours in a Minnesota forest after his guides got lost.[64] Once he made it back to Chicago, he had an arsenal of stories to tell and a stash of game to share with friends.

Going into the 1909 season, there were two major facets of discussion. The first was the self-imposed retirement of player-manager Fielder Jones, a maneuver Comiskey flatly refused to believe.[65] Jones indicated his intentions months before and was ready to stick by his guns. The only condition that would get him to return was for Comiskey to offer him a stake in the White Sox, and that was because he wanted to shore up his earning potential after his playing days were over. The other issue concerned Ed Walsh, the outstanding pitcher of 1908, who desired a significant raise in salary from $3,500 to upwards of $7,500. He too wanted to maximize his income after a dazzling year on the mound.

These were stressful times, especially since Comiskey was about to announce the construction of a modern baseball stadium on the South Side. With a $150,000 land purchase, he was going forward with a plan he'd been thinking about for years.[66] He'd finally be able to abandon his ramshackle venue and accommodate all of his patrons with an upscale facility that rated amongst the best in the world. Blasted by a heavy spell of rheumatism in early February 1909, Comiskey was stuck in bed for several days, only to rebound with the use of a cane.[67] His morale remained strong and he expected everything to fall into place.

Many upstarts were longing for a spot on the roster, and instead of Ed Walsh, Comiskey added Martin Walsh, the sibling of the 40-game winner. Martin was also a pitcher and in possession of a good fastball, but lacked the discipline and control that his brother exhibited. Other imports of note were Davey Altizer from Cleveland and Gavvy Cravath of Boston.

On February 26, 1909, the train known as the "White Sox Special" commenced for spring training in California, and more than seventy people were onboard.[68]

Comiskey was utterly convinced that Jones was going to return to the Sox, but after the latter failed to show up as expected, he decided to go up to Portland and speak with him in person. In the meantime, catcher Billy Sullivan was the manager of the first squad, while George Davis performed similar duties for the second.[69] After Comiskey's plea to Jones at Portland failed, there was considerable disappointment amongst team members, and although Sullivan understood the honor of being manager, he knew the difficulty ahead of balancing his role as catcher with the job of supervising the club.[70]

Hugh E. Keough, in his *Tribune* column, wrote that Comiskey's jaunt to Portland in effort to sign Jones was "almost pathetic."[71] Comiskey simply refused to take no for an answer. In contrast for the case of Walsh, he was willing to say "I'm through with him," but he was not yet ready to give up on Jones. It wasn't until April 12 that Sullivan was officially backed as the Sox manager, and Comiskey expressed complete confidence in his veteran's leadership. Two days later, the regular season began at Detroit.

The distractions over the managerial position and Walsh contributed to a slow start for the Sox, including a spell in last place. Comiskey's anxieties multiplied following a game at the South Side Park on April 25, 1909, when a fire broke out in the "50 cent section," and ruined a 250-foot area of the park.[72] Diligent firefighters, including volunteers, put out the inferno before it destroyed the grandstand, but not before an estimated $10,000 in damages were sustained. Comiskey expressed his deepest gratitude to the fire department and promised season tickets to all those who aided in extinguishing the blaze.

All things considered, the situation could have been much worse. Comiskey previously discussed the possibility of losing his park to a fire with Cubs President Charles Murphy, and the two agreed that if that ever happened, the displaced team would play their home games in the other's ballpark. The necessity wasn't there in this instance, and Comiskey planned to rebuild the damaged sections.

The first season with Sullivan at the helm was underway, and while things weren't going exactly as hoped, there was still plenty of optimism on the South Side of Chicago.

ENDNOTES

1 *Chicago Daily Tribune*, November 9, 1906, p. 10.
2 *Chicago Daily Tribune*, November 27, 1906, p. 10.
   During the St. Louis dinner, Comiskey was presented with a diamond pin by former St. Louis Browns secretary and old friend, George Munson.
3 Going along on the trip were Herman Schaefer of the Detroit Tigers, Joe Cantillon, and Charles Spink of the *Sporting News*. *Chicago Daily Tribune*, November 27, 1906, p. 10.
4 *Chicago Daily Tribune*, December 13, 1906, p. 12.
   The conference was staged at the Auditorium Annex.
5 *Chicago Daily Tribune*, November 5, 1906, p. 6.
6 In contrast to the articles claiming "harmony" and renewed friendship, there were reports that Comiskey reluctantly agreed to end the "war." According to the *Philadelphia Record*, Comiskey delivered an anti-Johnson speech during the league meeting, and then walked out. He was convinced to return and bury the hatchet, and for the sake of business, he agreed. The newspaper claimed they were "still bitter enemies." *Baltimore Sun*, January 8, 1907, p. 8.
7 *Chicago Daily Tribune*, December 14, 1906, p. 12.
   Also see: *Sporting News*, December 22, 1906, p. 1.
8 *Chicago Daily Tribune*, January 4, 1907, p. 10.
9 *Chicago Daily Tribune*, January 11, 1907, p. 10.
10 *Chicago Daily Tribune*, March 6, 1907, p. 10.
   The "White Sox Special" was formerly known as the "Cuban Special."
11 Ibid.
12 *Chicago Daily Tribune*, March 8, 1907, p. 10.
13 *Chicago Daily Tribune*, March 9, 1907, p. 10.
   Owen's injury occurred in his hometown of Ypsilanti, Michigan on January 19, 1907.
14 *Chicago Daily Tribune*, March 14, 1907, p. 12.
15 *Chicago Daily Tribune*, March 16, 1907, p. 10.
16 *Chicago Daily Tribune*, April 12, 1907, p. 11.
17 *Chicago Daily Tribune*, April 19, 1907, p. 10.
18 *Chicago Daily Tribune*, May 15, 1907, p. 1.
   A ferocious gust of wind was blamed on the breakage of the flag pole. Another gloomy result of that fateful afternoon was the invitation extended to Chicago's building commissioner by Mayor Busse. Instead of watching the game, the building commissioner spent his time inspecting the park, and later sent Comiskey a list of changes the latter needed to make because of safety infractions.
19 *Chicago Daily Tribune*, May 5, 1907, p. A1.
20 *Washington, D.C. Evening Star*, April 28, 1907, p. 62.
21 *Chicago Daily Tribune*, May 1, 1907, p. 12.
22 *Boston Journal*, May 11, 1907, p. 4.

Comiskey reportedly paid $4,000 for the rights to Stahl. In June, Stahl bought a semi-professional ball team in Chicago.

23 *Chicago Daily Tribune,* June 25, 1907, p. 9.

Among those in attendance for the "tribute" to Comiskey were Cap Anson and James A. Hart.

24 *Chicago Daily Tribune,* July 4, 1907, p. 6.

25 *Chicago Daily Tribune,* July 26, 1907, p. 2.

26 *Chicago Daily Tribune,* October 11, 1907, p. 2.

27 *Philadelphia Inquirer,* October 14, 1907, p. 10.

28 After taking a train to Mercer from Chicago, the various individuals heading to the camp endured a twelve-mile additional ride along a logging road. In the past, the retreat was much less extravagant compared to what it would become, especially after Comiskey, and later Ban Johnson, poured money into the area to build comfortable cabins and recreational areas. A chef was on hand to prepare meals, and all guests were treated in the most generous manner. From their Trude Lake location, the sportsmen were able to explore the vast wilderness. There was plenty of hunting and fishing, canoe rides, and hiking up to Norway Point and along the Butternut Trail. It was a refreshing experience, providing all the beautiful sights and sounds of rural America. More details about Camp Jerome can be found in an article by Malcolm MacLean, *Sporting News,* November 2, 1916, p. 3.

29 The White Sox Rooters' Association was formally incorporated in Illinois on May 12, 1908, by Robert E. Cantwell, H. H. Stridiron, and John S. Moisand. There were thirty-seven directors affiliated with the organization, including Hugh E. Keough, Gus Axelson, John Burns, Joe Farrell, and Edward Heeman. The Dugan Club, with Bill Dorgan as president, was another popular Sox rooter group with an origin in Chicago taverns.

30 *Chicago Daily Tribune,* December 6, 1907, p. 4.

31 *Chicago Daily Tribune,* December 7, 1907, p. 6.

The reason why Heaney didn't see dividends on his investment from 1900–03 was because of the club's heavy expenses in fixing up the stadium and signing players. Basically, there were no profits left over to split. Court documents for Heaney's case were unavailable from the Milwaukee County Historical Society and the resolution of the matter is unknown.

32 *Chicago Daily Tribune,* December 11, 1907, p. 12.

33 Higgins was a printer in Chicago, and through his friendship with Comiskey and Western League President "Tip" O'Neill, he entered the baseball business. In August 1911, he sold out to O'Neill and Comiskey was reported to have been heavily involved in the financing of the deal. *Chicago Daily Tribune,* October 23, 1911, p. 12. It was claimed that Comiskey paid as much as $18,000 for the franchise. Des Moines, Wichita (later moved to Pueblo), and Minneapolis were considered "farms" for the White Sox, and Comiskey was believed to have monetary interest in each of the clubs. In many instances, he was able to get one of his insiders, a former player or friend, to manage the team, thus securing prime scouting reports. It could be said that Comiskey's alliance with

O'Neill, and the latter's powerful position in the Western League, was a significant asset to the Sox. Some people were not thrilled by the Comiskey-O'Neill connection and the apparent ethical questions that were brought up by a major league owner having such an influence of a minor organization. *Idaho Statesman*, August 30, 1911, p. 7. These same complaints were levied at John T. Brush in 1895. The only difference was that Comiskey wasn't using his position in the American League to hurt the Western. If anything, he was raising the organization's notability by sending players with major league experience to Western teams.

34 *Chicago Daily Tribune*, November 30, 1907, p. 10.

35 *Chicago Daily Tribune*, December 15, 1907, p. C2.

36 *Chicago Daily Tribune*, December 14, 1907, p. 12.

37 *Chicago Daily Tribune*, January 3, 1908, p. 12.

38 *Chicago Daily Tribune*, February 13, 1908, p. 6.

39 *Chicago Daily Tribune*, February 28, 1908, p. 2.

The event was staged on February 27, 1908.

40 Joseph Chesterfield Farrell was a magnetic personality and lyricist for over 200 published songs.

41 *Chicago Daily Tribune*, March 1, 1908, p. B1.

42 *Chicago Daily Tribune*, March 2, 1908, p. 12.

43 *San Diego Union*, March 7, 1908, p. 3.

44 *Chicago Daily Tribune*, March 31, 1908, p. 8.

45 *Chicago Daily Tribune*, April 14, 1908, p. 12

46 *Chicago Daily Tribune*, April 15, 1908, p. 10.

47 Through the first 38 games of the season, the White Sox only had back-to-back wins twice—on April 25 and 27 (both against St. Louis) and May 19 and 21 (against Washington and New York).

48 *Chicago Daily Tribune*, June 17, 1908, p. 18.

49 *Daily Illinois State Register*, June 22, 1908, p. 2.

50 *Chicago Daily Tribune*, July 15, 1908, p. 12.

51 *Chicago Daily Tribune*, July 21, 1908, p. 6.

52 *Chicago Daily Tribune*, August 16, 1908, p. 4.

53 *Chicago Daily Tribune*, August 13, 1908, p. 6.

While the rest of the White Sox were in Washington for a game, Altrock and Donahue stayed behind to umpire the charity exhibition.

54 *Chicago Daily Tribune*, September 29, 1908, p. 8

55 *Chicago Daily Tribune*, September 29, 1908, p. 1.

56 *Chicago Daily Tribune*, October 13, 1908, p. 3.

57 *Cleveland Plain Dealer*, October 3, 1908, p. 1.

58 *Chicago Daily Tribune*, October 7, 1908, p. 12.

59 *Chicago Daily Tribune*, September 16, 1908, p. 12.

60 *Chicago Daily Tribune*, October 18, 1908, p. B1.

61 *Chicago Daily Tribune*, October 23, 1908, p. 10.

62 *Chicago Daily Tribune*, December 6, 1908, p. B1.

63 *Chicago Daily Tribune*, November 6, 1908, p. 10.

The outlaw team the Sox players engaged was the Logan Squares of Chicago, which took place during a barnstorming tour.

64 *Chicago Daily Tribune*, November 28–29, 1908.

65 *Chicago Daily Tribune*, December 21, 1908, p. 12.

66 *Chicago Daily Tribune*, January 3, 1909, p. A3.

A subsequent report cited the purchase amount as being $100,000. *Chicago Daily Tribune*, January 24, 1909, p. H18.

67 *Chicago Daily Tribune*, February 3, 1909, p. 12.

68 *Chicago Daily Tribune*, February 27, 1909, p. 7.

69 After dividing the team into two squads, Comiskey earned about $15,000 profit for exhibitions during spring training. *Wilkes-Barre Times*, April 2, 1909, p. 13.

70 *Chicago Daily Tribune*, March 26, 1909, p. 8.

Comiskey offered Jones a $15,000 salary to return. Jones said he'd agree to $10,000 plus a percentage ownership of the franchise, but Comiskey wouldn't budge on that issue.

71 *Chicago Daily Tribune*, March 28, 1909, p. C1.

Keough, known as "HEK," author of the entertaining "In the Wake of the News" column in the *Tribune*, was a close friend of Comiskey and socialized with his wife many times. His death on June 9, 1912, was a stunning blow to the Chicago sports community. Hugh S. Fullerton assumed the job as writer of the column until replaced by Ring Lardner in June 1913.

72 *Chicago Daily Tribune*, April 26, 1909, p. 1.

11

BASEBALL PALACE OF THE WORLD

Years of baseball prosperity in both the American and National Leagues encouraged owners to improve their local stadiums to accommodate larger audiences in reinforced concrete and steel structures. At the forefront of this trend were officials in Philadelphia, St. Louis, and Pittsburgh, and new venues began opening during the 1909 season. Owners touted their buildings—claiming to have the best in the world—and the upgrade was a symbol that demonstrated baseball's growth into a thriving multi-million dollar industry. Charles Comiskey didn't want to be left behind. He long dreamed of having an admirable stadium, and the recent fire of the wooden stands at the South Side Park was a reminder of the changes that needed to be made.

The ideal stadium differed from owner to owner, and the aesthetic design was restricted by monetary limitations behind the project. While putting together the cash to finance the plan, Comiskey searched for the right kind of inspiration for a park. He joined well-known Chicago architect Irving Kane Pond as a judge in a contest for architecture students in 1907 to see who could draw the ideal grounds.[1] Having personally supervised the parks at St. Paul and Chicago and visited nearly every major stadium in North America—both as a player and magnate—Comiskey had a good vision for what would ultimately become the home of the White Sox.

Step one was finding suitable land, and Comiskey was a man who treasured tradition and familiarity. That being said, he initially discussed terms with the owner of the current South Side Park at 39th Street and Wentworth Avenue to buy or lease the land for twenty years. A mutually satisfactory agreement could not be reached, so Comiskey moved on. He looked four blocks north to the plot of territory that once catered to baseball audiences during the Brotherhood era. The area included West 35th Street north to West 34th Street and Shields Avenue on the west to Wentworth Avenue in the east.

Comiskey inquired about the land and found a receptive seller. As a whole, the territory encompassed a little more than 12 acres and was owned by Mrs. Roxanna Atwater Wentworth Bowen, the only surviving child of former Chicago Mayor "Long" John Wentworth.[2] The property had been in her family for decades and served many functions, more recently as the staging area for a sizable wrecking company.[3]

Much work still had to be done before the first brick could be laid. Comiskey needed to find an architect and consent to a design first and foremost, and he planned to give the wrecking company time to relocate.

Meanwhile, "Big" Ed Walsh continued his holdout.[4] He hired a lawyer and was threatening to petition the National Commission to be declared a free agent based on a sketchy complaint over the timing of his contract's arrival. He also grumbled about Comiskey's treatment with regard to "money matters." That belief disregarded the fact that Comiskey gave Walsh a $3,500 bonus for winning 40 games the previous season.

Comiskey had an innate affection for loyalty and searched for the quality in his players. During the course of his career as an owner, few athletes held out for larger salaries and most of the time, contract negotiations were swift and painless. If the issue of a raise came up, it was considered on a case-by-case basis, and Comiskey had shown willingness to compromise. Tact was important and discussions of pay were in-house; not for public consumption. In no shape or form was Comiskey going to be bullied into paying an increased salary, and it didn't matter that it was his superstar pitcher who was holding out. Years before, George Davis sat out an entire season hoping to be traded or sold, but Comiskey wouldn't acquiesce.

There was no flexibility when being pressed, and Comiskey would rather see Walsh retire than come to terms by coercion. The reserve clause bound the pitcher to the Sox and if he chose not to sign his contract, he was effectively banished from Organized Baseball.

Interestingly, Walsh's brother, Martin, who was recently released to the Western League, had a different overall impression of the owner:

"I'd rather be canned by Mr. Comiskey than by any other man in the baseball business," he explained to the *Tribune*. "He is the nicest man I ever met in my life."

Before the end of April, Walsh realized his holdout strategy was going nowhere and ventured to Chicago to meet with the boss.[5] He arrived on April 29, and spoke with Comiskey at the park, but their initial meeting ended without a contract being signed. Over the next twenty- four hours, Comiskey was the busiest man in baseball, always unavailable for another conference as Walsh stewed on the sidelines, watching his teammates practice. It was undoubtedly a mind game that Comiskey was playing, and Walsh finally gave in. Sullivan produced a contract, the pitcher signed, and everyone was satisfied.

The 1909 season was ugly from the start. Players were underperforming, and the Sox quickly dropped to sixth place. Comiskey felt obligated to make some changes, and on May 16, he picked up a rebellious spirit in Bill Burns, trading veterans Jiggs Donahue and Nick Altrock, plus Gavvy Cravath to Washington to obtain the 6'2" southpaw.[6] Burns had a little trouble with management while with the Senators and pundits felt a fresh start would do wonders for the twenty-nine-year-old pitcher.

For Sox faithful, losing two heroes of the 1906 championship campaign in Altrock and Donahue was upsetting, but neither player had returned to their former stride. Pitcher Frank Owen, another World Series vet, was also sold to Toledo.

In a sidebar to the season's progression, Comiskey invited former heavyweight boxing champion James J. Jeffries to visit the South Side Park and workout with the team. The pugilist agreed, and on May 17, 1909, he made an early morning appearance at the park with his sparring partner Sam Berger and was greeted by Comiskey.[7] Humorously, he signed a two week contract with the Sox and was given a uniform. Jeffries joined the men on the field, initially as a pitcher, and then as a first baseman. Players deliberately gave him a hard time while at first, throwing the ball wild to make Jeffries work. After three hours on the diamond, he was said to be bruised but appreciative of the challenging exercise.

Later, representative of the respect Comiskey had throughout the universal sports world, Jeffries and reigning boxing champion Jack Johnson wanted him to be the stakeholder for their future fight, which took place in Reno on July 4, 1910, and was won by Johnson.

Still suffering from bouts of rheumatism, Comiskey cancelled a trip to Philadelphia to see the newly constructed Shibe Park and instead went fishing with Ban Johnson on Rainy Lake, Minnesota.[8] The duo spent time overlooking land for a potential hunting preserve, including talk of purchasing an entire island in that region. While Comiskey was out of contact, Sullivan was confronted by the first distressing actions of the recently acquired Bill Burns.[9] Burns refused to join the club at the team hotel (The Arlington) in Washington, D.C., and then demanded that Secretary Fredericks pay his bill for his stay at the Dewey Hotel. Fredericks refused and, in response, Burns threatened to defect to the California outlaw league.

It was a petty squabble and forgotten within a couple days. Relentless rain washed out game after game at Washington, but a highlight for players was their brief meeting with President William Howard Taft on June 9.[10]

The Sox were off balance and it was turning out to be an unremarkable season. In terms of talent, Sullivan was able to mix and match his lineup while searching for the perfect combination. He was also capable of making easy substitutions in the case of injury. The outfield core was a combination of Eddie Hahn, Patsy Dougherty, pitcher "Doc" White, and Dave Altizer, with Freddie Parent and Mike Welday able to fill in and perform respectably. In the infield, Lee Tannehill and Freddie Parent switched off at shortstop, and Tannehill did the same at third with Billy Purtell. Frank Isbell was the steady first baseman but was occasionally swapped out for George Davis. And when Sullivan was out of the lineup, Frank "Yip" Owens and Fred Payne were behind the plate. On the mound, Frank Smith was the most reliable. Otherwise, Sullivan's staff consisted of Walsh, White, Burns, Jim Scott, Lou Fiene, and Harry Sutor.

Having accepted the dim fate of his team, Comiskey coordinated with Ted Sullivan and other scouts to begin signing players for next season. Among the first was Arnold "Chick" Gandil, a Pacific Coast Leaguer from the Sacramento club.[11] Said to be a power hitter, Gandil was intersecting with the White Sox and Comiskey for the first time in what would become a long and controversial association.

The team then paid $6,500 cash plus four players, to Providence for Russell "Lena" Blackburne, one of the most highly touted youngsters in recent years.[12] Additionally, the team signed Roland Barrows, Charles "Bob" Messenger, Fred Olmstead, Rollie Zeider, Willis Cole, and John "Shano" Collins, all part of a massive batch of new prospects. It was later estimated

Young Charles Comiskey led the
St. Louis Browns to four-straight
American Association (AA) titles
and a world championship in the
1880s. *Image courtesy of the National
Baseball Hall of Fame Library, Cooperstown, NY*

Card of Charles Comiskey from
an 1888 pack of Old Judge
Cigarettes. *Image courtesy of the
Metropolitan Museum of Art*

Card of Charles Comiskey from
an 1887 pack of Allen & Ginter's
Cigarettes. *Image courtesy of the
Library of Congress*

The likeness of Charles Comiskey
as a member of the St. Louis
Browns in 1888, captured on a
Goodwin and Company tobacco
trading card. *Image courtesy of the
National Baseball Hall of Fame
Library, Cooperstown, NY*

Team portrait of the 1888 St. Louis Browns. Comiskey is right
in the middle. *Image courtesy of the Library of Congress*

Individual portraits of the 1902 Chicago White Sox.
Image courtesy of the Boston Public Library

Portrait of Charles Comiskey, circa 1910. *Image courtesy of the California Digital Library*

From 1900 to 1927, Ban Johnson served as the President of the American League and was, without question, a complete and utter credit to the sport. *Image courtesy of the National Baseball Hall of Fame Library, Cooperstown, NY*

Charles Comiskey (left) shared many of the same qualities as his longtime pal Ban Johnson (right), but their similarities also prevented reconciliation after their friendship turned sour. When Johnson died in 1931, they still had yet to make peace. Comiskey died seven months later. *Image courtesy of the National Baseball Hall of Fame Library, Cooperstown, NY*

Photographic montage with a portrait of American League President and Founder Ban Johnson, in center, surrounded by the individual portraits of the eight American League teams. *Image courtesy of the Boston Public Library*

Photographic montage from 1902 of each American
League team, with League President Ban Johnson in the
center. *Image courtesy of the Boston Public Library*

Hardnosed Billy Sullivan Sr. was the Sox backstop from 1901 to 1914, and although he only had a career .213 batting average, he was a legend in Chicago. *Image courtesy of the National Baseball Hall of Fame Library, Cooperstown, NY*

Fielder Jones managed the White Sox from 1904 to 1908, and led Chicago to its first World Series title in 1906. *Image courtesy of the National Baseball Hall of Fame Library, Cooperstown, NY*

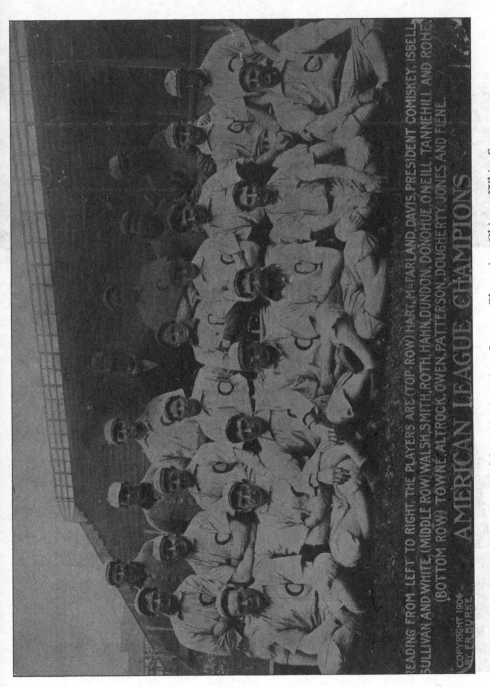

READING FROM LEFT TO RIGHT. THE PLAYERS ARE (TOP ROW) HART, McFARLAND DAVIS, PRESIDENT COMISKEY. ISBELL SULLIVAN AND WHITE. (MIDDLE ROW) WALSH, SMITH, ROTH, HAHN, DUNDON, DONOHUE O'NEILL TANNEHILL AND ROHE. (BOTTOM ROW) TOWNE, ALTROCK, OWEN, PATTERSON, DOUGHERTY, JONES AND FIENE.

AMERICAN LEAGUE CHAMPIONS

COPYRIGHT 1906
BY F.R BURKE.

Team portrait of the 1906 American League Champion Chicago White Sox. Comiskey is the only one wearing a suit. *Image courtesy of the Boston Public Library*

Panoramic view of a game at the South Side Park between the Chicago White Sox and New York Highlanders on September 23, 1906. The White Sox are in the field. *Image courtesy of the Boston Public Library*

A two-man team operated the old scoreboard at the South Side Park in Chicago, where the White Sox played from 1900 to 1910. *Image courtesy of the National Baseball Hall of Library, Cooperstown, NY*

An image of the West Side Grounds during the 1906 World
Series between the Chicago White Sox (away) and Chicago Cubs
(home). Here the White Sox are at bat with the bases loaded and
the ball in play. *Image courtesy of the Boston Public Library*

A scene outside South Side Park before Game 6 of the 1906 World
Series. The Sox were victorious by a score of 8–3, and won the Series, 4
games to 2. *Image courtesy of the Boston Public Library*

FIFTH GAME
WORLD'S CHAMPIONSHIP SERIES
CUBS vs WHITE SOX.
National League Grounds Saturday October 13th 1906

Panoramic photo, in two sections, of the West Side Grounds during Game 5 of the 1906 World Series. The Chicago White Sox won the game 8–6 to take a 3–2 lead in the series. *Image courtesy of the Boston Public Library*

Hall of Fame catcher Ray Schalk played 17 years for Comiskey and was the heart and soul of the White Sox. *Image courtesy of the National Baseball Hall of Fame Library, Cooperstown, NY*

Versatile Shano Collins played 16 Major League seasons—11 with the White Sox—and finished up his career with the Boston Red Sox in 1925. *Image courtesy of the National Baseball Hall of Fame Library, Cooperstown, NY*

Comiskey waited his entire career as an owner for a team of hitters, and by 1917 he was stocked with a lineup of sluggers including (from left to right): Joe Jackson, Shano Collins, Happy Felsch, Eddie Murphy, and Nemo Leibold. *Image courtesy of the National Baseball Hall of Fame Library, Cooperstown, NY*

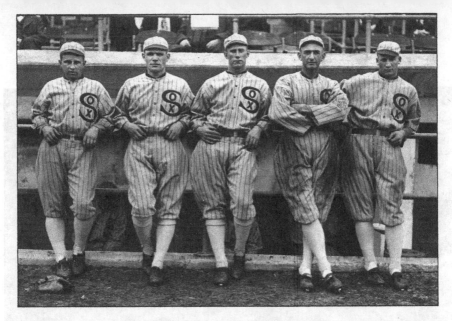

Members of the 1917 White Sox relax for a group portrait prior to a big game (from left to right): Nemo Leibold, Eddie Murphy, Shano Collins, Joe Jackson, and Happy Felsch. *Image courtesy of the National Baseball Hall of Fame Library, Cooperstown, NY*

Eddie Cicotte, winner of 209 games in his 14-year career, was the ace of the White Sox staff until being banned from baseball in 1920. *Image courtesy of the National Baseball Hall of Fame Library, Cooperstown, NY*

"Shoeless Joe" Jackson is regarded as an American icon by a segment of the baseball public. His career statistics, including a lifetime .356 batting average, would have made him a strong candidate for the National Baseball Hall of Fame had he not agreed to participate in the throwing of the 1919 World Series. *Image courtesy of the National Baseball Hall of Fame Library, Cooperstown, NY*

Hall of Fame thrower Ed Walsh (right) won 40 games for the White Sox in 1908. More than a decade later, he joined Sox manager Kid Gleason (left) as a coach, mentoring many up-and-comers in the finer points of pitching. Gleason managed the Sox from 1919 to 1923, and finished with a career record of 392–364. *Image courtesy of the National Baseball Hall of Fame Library, Cooperstown, NY*

An article run in the *Sporting News* on October 7, 1920, after the "Black Sox" scandal, telling readers to "Fix these faces in your memory." *Image acquired from The Chicago Black Sox Trial: A Primary Sources Account by Wayne Anderson*

Cartoon by Ted Brown of the *Chicago Daily News*, stating that when the "Black Sox" players were acquitted, baseball Commissioner Kenesaw Landis was still unimpressed. *Image acquired from the Literary Digest (08/20/1921)*

The "Old Roman" Charles Comiskey was a fixture in baseball for more than 50 years. His passion and commitment to the Chicago White Sox never diminished despite health problems and the embarrassment of the "Black Sox" scandal. He loved Chicago, his fans, and, of course, everything about baseball.
Image courtesy of the National Baseball Hall of Fame Library, Cooperstown, NY

that Comiskey paid as much as $100,000 for talent, but he shied away from confirming the price of any signees, telling the *Tribune*, "Concerning the terms, I do not like to talk. I believe in keeping the money end of the game in the background."[13][14]

By the end of August, the White Sox were hovering around .500 and in fifth place.[15] Small improvements were visible, and although Chicago was batting last in the league, it was first in fielding. On September 25, 1909, the club won both games of a doubleheader against Washington and shored up a fourth place position in the standings behind Detroit, Philadelphia, and Boston.[16] A short time later, the Sox took four of five at Philadelphia, which helped the Tigers secure the pennant.

Comiskey arranged a postseason series with President Charles Murphy of the Cubs, which finished second in the National League behind Pittsburgh. The Cubs were a much better team and squashed the Sox, winning four of five games between October 8 and October 15 to capture the city championship.[17] The final game was a one-hit shutout by Mordecai "Three Finger" Brown. Over 74,000 people watched the series and Sox players took home around $455 each as the losers' share.

Forward steps in the development of Comiskey's new stadium were being made almost weekly. After a long debate and a shuffling of designers, Comiskey hired Zachary Taylor Davis, a thirty-seven-year-old architect, to map out the specifications and layout. Davis was well regarded in his field and owned plenty of experience working on high dollar, large scale packing plants and buildings.

Completely familiar with all the modern amenities, he helped Comiskey fashion a beautiful blueprint with a preliminary drawing of the proposed park printed in Chicago newspapers on September 5, 1909.[18] Changes still needed to be made, as an early drawing included a grandstand configuration in the likeness of the Roman Colosseum. Davis also toured the new stadiums in St. Louis, Philadelphia, and Pittsburgh in effort to improve on those designs.[19]

Comiskey was confident the stadium would be ready by the opening of the 1910 season. Haggling with contractors delayed things considerably, and he was engaged in negotiations with several different firms for the construction project. Assisted by longtime friend, John P. Agnew, a contractor himself, Comiskey wanted more realistic figures; essentially meaning that the high estimates had to be brought down to a more manageable level.[20] In personal conference, he was told that the price could be lowered significantly, as much as a few hundred thousand dollars, while maintaining the artistic value that was initially proposed.

The double decked structure that Davis imagined was likely going to run more than $500,000. It was eventually concluded that the Roman column façade and total usage of the cantilever construction style that provided an unobstructed view of the field from anywhere in the grandstand were cut from the budget. Although he was wealthy, Comiskey was certainly no Rockefeller and was always mindful of expenses. He was paying cash out of his own pocket for the park and felt the burden of the costs, especially when combined with his regular immense overhead. That was the downside of having no business partners, a fact he usually reveled in. Shrewd decisions had to be made and he was responsible for making the final call.

Financially, Comiskey was a self-made man. He wasn't the recipient of any grand family fortune and made every nickel and dime himself. When he was starting out back in the late 1870s and early '80s, guys like Ted Sullivan mentored him in the discipline of living cheap through a baseball season and spending thriftily to save the bulk of his income. In doing what he loved for a living, Comiskey also developed a fear as a young man that baseball was going to lose its luster in the public's eye and no longer provide the earning capabilities to sustain a family. If that internal anxiety were to ever become fact, he needed to be prepared and sock away as much money as possible. Perhaps this phobia was spawned by his father's constant reminder that a trade was more valuable to a man than playing first base.

Years had passed and Comiskey's fortune grew to the point that some pundits were calling him the richest man in the sport. But Comiskey still harbored memories of life thirty years before, in a post-Civil War society, when baseball as a full-time industry wasn't guaranteed for the future. He resigned himself to the regular cost of doing business, spending exorbitant amounts of money on talent, and was often in possession of one of the highest salary lists in the league. To a certain degree in his personal life, he embraced his wealth, buying property, a houseboat, and several automobiles, including a a luxuty model Rainier complete with a chauffeur. But throughout, he retained his modesty and was eternally respectful of money.

Not a naïve man or the type of individual to be sold on something of importance the first time around, Comiskey consulted heavily with Agnew and waited patiently for a contractor to present the right numbers for the new stadium. Like Davis, Comiskey toured the new parks in St. Louis and Pittsburgh and felt the last minute changes were acceptable. It was becoming apparent, however, that the new venue wasn't going to be completed by the opening of the next baseball season.

On the managerial front, Sullivan indicated midway through the 1909 campaign that he didn't want to repeat in the role next year. Comiskey heeded the information, and only a few weeks after the season's conclusion, he met with future Hall of Famer Hugh Duffy and secretly discussed the vacant position. Duffy was co-owner of a team in Providence, incidentally the same club that produced Comiskey's biggest "find," Lena Blackburne. During his distinguished career, he played for Cap Anson in Chicago but became a legend in Boston.

Their conference on October 18, 1909, was productive and Duffy was soon announced as the first bench manager for the Chicago White Sox.[21] With that major issue out of the way, Comiskey ventured to the Mercer, Wisconsin, area for his annual hunting trip, and spent time on his houseboat with friends a few weeks later.[22]

Twenty-four-year-old Louis Comiskey was a faithful observer of his father's passionate work attitude and ethic and had been engaged in the happenings of the Sox for many years. Baseball was also in his blood and he wanted to make a career as an owner himself. In early December 1909, negotiations for Louis to purchase the Denver franchise of the Western League were in full motion.[23] Charles Fredericks, the go-to man for transactions such as these, went to Denver to discuss terms, but found that only half of the Denver club was for sale—this was unsatisfactory to Louis and the deal was voided.

With at least eight trips together between October 1909 and January 1910, Charles Comiskey and Ban Johnson were almost inseparable. For business, they ventured to St. Louis, New York, Pittsburgh, and then spent about ten days recuperating in Excelsior Springs, Missouri. Additionally, Comiskey moved his office back into the Fisher Building where Johnson still maintained his office on the fifth floor. Things couldn't have been better between the two.[24]

Positive news on the ballpark finally arrived and made headlines on January 30, 1910.[25] The day before, Comiskey had reached an agreement with the Wells Brothers contracting firm of Chicago to build the fences, bleachers, pavilions, and grandstand. Providing the structural steel and iron was the George W. Jackson Company. James Clarkson of the *Chicago Examiner* noted that a conservative estimate for construction was going to run "between $325,000 and $350,000." The grandstand itself would rest in the corner of 35th Street and Shields Avenue. It would face northeast at about the same angle of the current stadium.

Excavation was to begin almost immediately, and although they were hampered by snow, the contractors believed they could be finished for a memorable, July 1, 1910, grand opening.

With the stadium questions finally solved, Comiskey, Agnew, and Johnson traveled south to rendezvous with the houseboat for a trip along the White River. Outside Fulton, Kentucky, they were involved in a train accident, but all walked away from the wreck without major injury —and continued their vacation.[26]

Of the fifty-seven players initially on the reserve roster, Comiskey arduously cut it down to about thirty-eight for the third annual spring training tour of California. For the 2,000-plus mile journey aboard the "White Sox Special," Comiskey, his family, Johnson, and Ted Sullivan were among the contingent departing Chicago on February 25, 1910.[27] Finally realizing that the exhausting training trips were mostly unsuccessful in getting his men into the proper shape, mentally and physically, Comiskey promised this was the final trip to the coast.

A train wreck and flooding stranded the Sox as they made their way west, and the team spent extra days in Utah and Idaho before finally reaching their destination. To make matters worse, ex-manager Billy Sullivan stepped on a rusty nail in Los Angeles on March 12, and developed blood poisoning in his leg.[28] He underwent two operations and was not only under the threat of amputation, but his life was in danger. Sullivan remained in Southern California after the team departed and slowly recovered, but his future on the field was questionable to say the least.

Back in Chicago, the first brick—green in color—was laid at the new ballpark by architect Davis at a special celebration on March 17, 1910.[29] Comiskey remained in California, but other news was taking center stage in his mind. He was recently notified that his best friend, Tom Loftus, was suffering from inoperable throat cancer, and his condition was dire.[30] He remained in close contact with the Loftus family before venturing to see him in Dubuque late in March.

Hugh Duffy and Comiskey managed to work the Sox roster down to twenty-six players, and on April 14, 1910, the new season kicked off without the usual fanfare seen in recent years.[31] Veterans Fred Parent, Patsy Dough-

erty, and Ed Hahn were supported by shortstop Lena Blackburne, first baseman Chick Gandil, and the recently announced field captain Rollie Zeider
at second base. Before nearly 20,000 spectators, the Sox won the initial
game against St. Louis by a score of 13–0 behind Frank Smith's one hitter.
Two days later, Loftus passed away in Dubuque at the age of fifty-three.[32]

About forty structural iron and steel workers laboring at the new stadium, along with 860 of their brethren working on other projects throughout Chicago, went on strike early in May.[33] Demanding higher wages, their
issue wasn't directly tied to Comiskey, but the timing of his construction
effort unfortunately coincided with their planned walkout. Without continued work by that segment of the operation, everything suffered; even progress on the diamond and field couldn't proceed because of the unused steel
lying all over the place.

The strike lasted for five weeks, coming to an end with concessions
favoring the workers. Instead of 62.5 cents an hour, they were to receive 65,
five less than what they originally wanted. But the agreement put them back
to work and allowed Comiskey to breathe a little better. The July 1 deadline
was only a short time off.

On the field, the White Sox were painful to watch. During their first East
Coast trip, they went 3–9, and by June 1, fifteen games had been postponed
due to weather.[34] A lack of veteran field leadership, scarce hitting, and inju-
ries were costly. The *Tribune* reported that Comiskey went out to the South
Side Park to see the team with paychecks for "the preceding half month."[35]
He wasn't greeted by men sorrowful for their lack of winning effort, and
Comiskey was quoted as saying, "Every last man of them stepped right up
and took his salary with an air of having earned it." He wasn't pleased by the
direction of the team and shortly thereafter, sold pitchers Bill Burns and
Harry Suter, with more changes expected.

With little offensive firepower and relying mostly on the shoulders of
Ed Walsh and "Doc" White, there was minor improvement as weeks
passed. Comiskey got rid of outfielders Hahn and Willis Cole and signed
Charles French, George Browne, Albert "Red" Kelly, and Paul "Molly"
Meloan. In a blockbuster trade, slumping pitcher Frank Smith (4–9) and
Billy Purtell (.223 batting average) were sent to the Red Sox for third
baseman Harry Lord and second baseman Amby McConnell.[36] Lord was
an established star in the league and his hitting ability was exactly what
Chicago needed. The "kids" of the team had heart, but not yet the skill
and were far below expectations.

Final preparations for the park were being made on the eve of July 1, 1910.[37] Thousands of opera-style seats lined the grandstand, ready to be occupied.[38] The strike delayed full completion of the park and temporary chairs were erected on the second deck because the concrete didn't set in time to install permanent seating. Within the grandstand, every 33 feet a steel pillar had been placed about halfway between the front and rear of the structure to support the second deck.[39] Views were slightly hampered from behind the uprights, but fans, in time, adjusted to the issue as they enthusiastically embraced the park.

Total seating capacity was upwards of 30,000 and there was room for about 37,000 counting standing room occupants. Fourteen turnstiles were available at the main entrance to the grandstand with availability to box seats and the 50 cent pavilion. The bleachers, which cost 25 cents, had access at the corner of 34th Street and Shields Avenue. One notable feature missing from the new park was a drinking concession underneath the grandstand, which was a popular hangout at the old grounds. Hearing the disapproving remarks of patrons about the seedy nature of the establishment, Comiskey did away with it, even though it was a guaranteed money-maker.

A huge electric scoreboard was implemented that would keep the audience abreast of the score and the press were situated at the front of the second deck, right behind the catcher. In the final days, electricians and painters were the most active and work continued hours before the gates opened at 1 p.m. on July 1.

Unfortunately, in the last minute haste, a fifty-one-year-old cement worker named Frank McDermed lost his balance while working at the top of the grandstand and fell to the ground below.[40] Suffering internal injuries, he died later in the day, leaving his wife and eight children. It was a gloomy beginning to Comiskey Park's legacy but the gates swung wide on time and the first fans streamed into the park as one of the five instrumental bands on hand entertained them with music.

Dignitaries from all over baseball, from Garry Herrmann to Cap Anson, turned out for the auspicious event.[41] The total attendance was somewhere between 28,000 and 30,000 people and before the game, Comiskey was honored at home plate by his friends as the crowd roared in approval. As part of the festivities, a squad of soldiers, representing a huge contingent of military members in the audience, hoisted an American flag as the national anthem was performed.

Comiskey beamed from ear to ear, shaking hands and greeting people like a proud father. His contentment remained even after the 2–0 loss to St. Louis. Following the game, he hosted a reception in his upstairs office and then a banquet at the Chicago Automobile Club for 150 people. In all, it was a landmark affair, and without question, the most memorable occasion of the 1910 baseball season for the Sox.

Another road trip was unsuccessful in July, and Chicago won only 5 out of 21 games played.[42] They were in seventh place with a 35–55 record. Duffy continued to shuffle the lineup and got some exciting moments out of Meloan at the plate. He appeared to be a "wonder" initially but his batting slowly tapered off. Night games of lacrosse, soccer, and semi-professional baseball were played at Comiskey's stadium in August of 1910, testing the feasibility of contests staged under arc lighting.[43] The experiments went well but there was an ingrained belief that baseball was an afternoon sport and that fans wouldn't have it any other way.

Teasing a hold on fifth place several times, the Sox finished the season in sixth with a 68–85 record. The American League champion Philadelphia Athletics went on to beat the Chicago Cubs in the World Series, 4 games to 1. For the Sox, Walsh went 18–20 (1.27 ERA), while White was 15–13 (2.66 ERA) and Olmstead 10–12 (1.95 ERA). The team batting average, representative of the problems throughout the year, was a stunning .212, which was last in the league. Patsy Dougherty, usually a reliable hitter (a career .284 hitter), slumped with a .248 average, and Harry Lord, Comiskey's big pickup, led the team in batting with a .297 average. Team fielding also dipped to .954, tied for sixth among the eight American League clubs.

The Sox were a disappointment, but Comiskey cared much more about the health of his nephew, team secretary Charles Fredericks, who became ill mid season. Fredericks needed to rest and took six weeks to convalesce at Hot Springs, Arkansas, along with Lou Comiskey. The heavy demands of baseball were taking its toll on all members of the Sox management.

As expected, Comiskey headed to the Wisconsin woods to unwind after a nerve-racking season, and accompanying him on the annual trip were Ban Johnson, Charles Spink, and many others.[44] At the same time, his wife Nan and Jennie Johnson, spouse of the American League president, vacationed in Excelsior Springs, Missouri.[45] [46] On October 30, 1910, a fire broke out at the New Elms Hotel, where the two women were staying, and Comiskey was the first one out. She realized that Johnson was not behind her as she expected and quickly told firefighters. Several men rushed in to save Johnson before she was completely overcome by smoke, narrowly escaping death.

Up north in the Wisconsin wilderness, their husbands were completely unaware of their harrowing experience. At the time, Comiskey and Johnson were concentraing on much more innocuous happenings, like the establishment of a new club: the Woodland Bards. Headed up by the gregarious Joe Farrell, the Bards quickly turned into the hot ticket social group for sportswriters and pundits. A few weeks after formation, the Bards pitched in to decorate Comiskey's new offices at the park and held an "informal banquet" in his honor at the Chicago Automobile Club.[47]

Comiskey originally intended to fashion what the *Tribune* reported to be a "lounging and reading room" under the grandstand.[48] Instead, he turned the idea into the lavishly constructed "Bards' Room," a comfortable recreational area for members of the club. While he usually met up with friends in his executive offices before and after games, Comiskey provided food and beverages in the Bards' Room for his guests.[49] The hilarious anecdotes of Farrell and his pals, war stories from hunting trips, and commentary on recent baseball episodes were boundless within those walls.

In November of 1910, Comiskey's stadium—billed as the "Baseball Palace of the World"—received two Boston visitors, Hugh McBreen, treasurer of the Red Sox, and architect James E. McLaughlin.[50] They were in town to garner ideas for the construction of their new field, Fenway Park, which would open in 1912. Notably, John Agnew, Comiskey's assistant in the building of his grounds, was hired by Garry Herrmann to supervise the erection of Redland Field (later to be known as Crosley Field), a stadium for the National League's franchise in Cincinnati.

Only a couple weeks after mingling with Comiskey and the baseball elite in Chicago at a special dinner honoring sportswriter Ring Lardner, Chief James J. Horan, the city's fire marshal, was killed in a stockyard blaze along with twenty-one other firemen on December 22, 1910.[51] Horan had been a die-hard baseball lover and a member of the fire department for nearly thirty years. Following the accident, Comiskey talked about Horan, saying, "He was the most fearless man I ever knew and the squarest as well as the bravest. To me, it is like losing a member of my own family."

Despite his innumerable efforts to regain his health, Fredericks continued to ail, which deeply distressed Comiskey. Fredericks was such a major
asset to the franchise and his demise was a crushing one. Harry Mitchell
Grabiner stepped into the prominent position and became acting secretary
for the Sox.[52] A young man in his early twenties, Grabiner worked his way up
from selling scorecards as a teenager, to the ticket counter, and finally into
the front office, where he gained Comiskey's complete confidence. He
learned directly from the boss and was a natural organizer, capable of admin-
istering any number of tasks to include the supervision of annual contracts.

Training camp was established at Mineral Springs, Texas, and there were
some old faces in camp, like ex-manager Jimmy Callahan and Jiggs Donahue, as well as new additions Frank "Ping" Bodie and Matty McIntyre. The
latter, recently of the Detroit Tigers, ingratiated himself by cleaning out the
clubhouse in a staged break-in one night, only to reveal the prank moments
later.[53] While Donahue didn't return to the team, Callahan did, and along
with new captain, Harry Lord, the Sox were infused with a striking new
confidence that the previous season lacked. "Chick" Gandil, Fred Parent,
Charles French, and "Molly" Meloan were released, and the high-priced
Lena Blackburne, who was perpetually injured, was absent from the club as
the season began.

By the end of April 1911, Comiskey was ecstatic that his team was showing a real hitting ability led by Lord, Callahan, McIntyre, and Bodie. First
baseman Shano Collins was improving and the Sox were finally competing
for a spot in the first division. On May 10 at Comiskey Park, they hit safely
19 times and 20 the next day, winning both games against the Washington
Senators.[54] [55] Chicago was briefly in second place, but spent more time
between fourth and fifth in a competitive race for the third spot behind
Detroit and Philadelphia.

When a potential pitching superstar named Marty O'Toole of the St.
Paul minor league club went on the market, Comiskey demonstrated his
willingness to spend money.[56] He bid $20,000, which would have been the
highest price ever paid for a player. However, Pittsburgh owner Barney
Dreyfuss topped him, purchasing O'Toole for $22,500.

As was his custom, Comiskey raided the various leagues, recalling eight
of his farmed out recruits and owned over two dozen minor leaguers in

total. One of his young hopefuls was George "Buck" Weaver of Pennsylvania, an infielder scouted by Ted Sullivan and sent to the San Francisco Seals of the Pacific Coast League to mature.[57] With plenty of obvious talent, Weaver had many teams looking his way and Comiskey spent $2,500 to reacquire him.

Down the stretch, the Sox needed a boost, and Ed Walsh once again proved his value to the team. He scored a one-hitter against the Tigers on August 14, but was still unsatisfied by the result.[58] So when he went out against the Red Sox two weeks later, he made sure to be satisfied and pitched a no-hitter.[59] That summer, it was also belatedly realized that Billy Sullivan had been the first catcher to play 1,000 major league games behind the plate, and then he caught his 1,100th soon thereafter.

Another incident, on a more comedic note, happened during a charitable function for the House of the Good Shepherd on September 9, 1911.[60] Comiskey turned out for the festivities, and when he walked up to the front gates, expecting to pass right through, a girl working the counter asked him for his ticket. Comiskey grinned and explained who he was and that it was his stadium, but the girl was steadfast and got him to pay anyway. The press loved it—Comiskey paid admission to his own field!

The season came to an end with the White Sox winning 77 and losing 74, finishing in fourth place by a fraction over Boston.[61] As a team, the club batted .269, much better than in 1910, and both Matty McIntyre and Harry Lord had over 175 hits on the year.[62] In fact, it was unusual for the "hitless wonders" to possess two players in the regular lineup with better than a .300 average. Despite the progression, the Sox were considered the underdogs in the city championship series against the second place Cubs.

Game one began on October 13, 1911 and the White Sox were victorious by the score of 4–3 behind Walsh's excellent work.[63] In the ninth, Hugh Duffy's men rallied for three runs in the ninth to win the game, and eight Cubs players were fined by the umpire for criticizing calls in a wild afternoon of baseball. The next day, the Sox won again, 8–7, in a closely contested battle. In the bottom of the ninth, second baseman Amby McConnell caught a fierce liner and tagged the base to make an unassisted double play that ended the game.

On October 15, "Doc" White, before over 36,000 fans at Comiskey Park, shut the National Leaguers down, and the Sox won their third straight over the Cubs, 4–2. Because of weather conditions, the final game was held three days later, and Walsh heroically returned to the mound to close out the series with a 7–2 win.[64] The South Siders had swept the Cubs in what was said to be the first time that a major league postseason championship was decided in four straight games. Nearly 100,000 people saw the series and the Sox surprisingly batted over .340 compared to the Cubs' .221.

As another baseball year was in the books, Comiskey had several things on his mind.[65] For one, the condition of Charles Fredericks showed no signs of improving. Additionally, his son Louis, who was overweight, was struggling to maintain his health and needed to scale back his commitment to the White Sox. Their suffering was an endless cause of grief for Comiskey because not only were they beloved family members, but they were his right and left arm in guiding the franchise. Comiskey had wanted to delegate even more responsibilities to Louis and Fredericks, but with both men trying to get well, Comiskey needed to lay the job at the feet of young Harry Grabiner—or someone else for that matter.

The other topic of concentration was a proposed trip around the world by the Sox. If anyone in baseball had the ability to make such an extravagant plan possible, it was Charles Comiskey. Only time would tell whether he'd make this dream a reality.

ENDNOTES

1 *Boston Herald*, February 7, 1907, p. 10.
The contest took place at the Chicago School of Architecture.
2 *Chicago Daily Tribune*, January 24, 1909, p. H18.
3 At one time, part of the grounds was a cabbage patch. *Chicago Daily Tribune*, May 30, 1921, p. 15. Signor Scavado operated a truck garden on the location, according to sportswriter Edward Burns, and he affirmed that the park was not built on a garbage dump, despite rumors. *Chicago Daily Tribune*, September 5, 1937, p. A2.
4 *Chicago Daily Tribune*, April 16, 1909, p. 13.
5 *Chicago Daily Tribune*, April 29, 1909, p. 8.
Once the contract was signed, it was noted that the salary was less than Walsh wanted, but more than likely "an advance" over his 1908 wages. The amount, however, was a "profound secret." *Chicago Daily Tribune*, May 2, 1909, p. B1.
6 *Chicago Daily Tribune*, May 17, 1909, p. 12.
Cravath was the real loss in the trade. In a few years, he would become one of the top hitters in the National League, batting .341 for the Philadelphia Phillies in 1913 and leading the NL in home runs six times (1913 & 1914: 19; 1915: 24; 1917: 12; 1918: 8; 1919: 12).
7 *Chicago Daily Tribune*, May 18, 1909, p. 9.
The uniform the Sox gave Jeffries didn't fit but that didn't hinder his enthusiasm to practice with the team.

8 *Chicago Daily Tribune,* June 1, 1909, p. 8.
Comiskey wanted to examine and get tips for his own stadium by looking over Shibe Park.

9 *Chicago Daily Tribune,* June 9, 1909, p. 12.

10 *Chicago Daily Tribune,* June 10, 1909, p. 8.

11 *Chicago Daily Tribune,* July 7, 1909, p. 8.

12 *Chicago Daily Tribune,* July 9, 1909, p. 6.
The price paid by Comiskey for Blackburne was said to be the "greatest ever paid" for a minor leaguer. *Sporting Life,* July 17, 1909, p. 11. A few weeks later, Blackburne suffered a broken fibula in a game at Montreal, an injury that would prevent him from reaching his full potential in the majors. *Sporting Life,* August 14, 1909, p. 15.

13 *San Diego Union,* September 4, 1909, p. 7.
Another report claimed that Comiskey spent $44,300 for players and another $11,300 for draftees, adding up to $55,600. *Sporting Life,* November 27, 1909, p. 2.

14 *Chicago Daily Tribune,* August 18, 1909, p. 8.

15 *Chicago Daily Tribune,* August 28, 1909, p. 6.

16 *Chicago Daily Tribune,* September 26, 1909, p. C1.
The Sox finished the season with a 78–74 record and a .221 batting average.

17 *Chicago Daily Tribune,* October 16, 1909, p. 1.

18 *Chicago Sunday Examiner,* September 5, 1909, p. S3.

19 Many stories claim that Ed Walsh either traveled with Davis or added his input on the design of the new stadium, aiding in the creation of a "pitcher's ballpark," with long fences and plenty of space.

20 *Chicago Daily Tribune,* November 2, 1909, p. 8.

21 *Sporting Life,* October 30, 1909, p. 5.

22 *Chicago Daily Tribune,* October 21, 1909, p. 8.

23 *Chicago Daily Tribune,* December 7, 1909, p. 16.

24 *Chicago Daily Tribune,* January 1, 1910, p. 14.
The move was temporary, as Comiskey soon settled into his permanent headquarters at the new Sox stadium upon completion of the structure. Norris "Tip" O'Neill, President of the Western League, who'd been sharing office space with Comiskey for years, would continue to do so at Comiskey Park.

25 *Chicago Examiner,* January 30, 1910, p. S1.
All through the construction process, Comiskey's stadium continued to share proximity with the wrecking company of Sebastian Krug, whose operation had resided on the eastern portion of the grounds long before Comiskey purchased the land. On April 1, a fire broke out in a lumber pile in Krug's work area, about 100 feet from the new grandstand. High winds sent potentially dangerous embers toward the structure, and it was moments away from catching ablaze. Adroit firefighters rushed to the scene and put out the fire before any damage could be done. *Chicago Daily Tribune,* April 2, 1910, p. 11.

26 *Chicago Daily Tribune,* February 2, 1910, p. 12.
Johnson was said to have been bruised up by the accident. It was during this hunting trip that two live American Eagles, including one Bald, were captured

and shipped to Chicago. At one point, it was considered putting them on display at the new park. It isn't known if they ever were, but Comiskey Park did house a number of animals through the years, including hunting and guard dogs and a moose.

27 *Chicago Daily Tribune*, February 26, 1910, p. 14.

28 *Chicago Daily Tribune*, March 17-27, 1910.

29 *Chicago Daily Tribune*, March 18, 1910, p. 18.

The brick measured 2 × 4 × 8 and was green in color to commemorate St. Patrick's Day.

30 *Chicago Daily Tribune*, April 1, 1910, p. 14.

31 *Chicago Daily Tribune*, April 15, 1910, p. 13.

32 *Sporting Life*, April 23, 1910, p. 4.

33 *Chicago Daily Tribune*, May 3, 1910, p. 12.

34 *Chicago Daily Tribune*, June 1, 1910, p. 14.

35 *Chicago Daily Tribune*, June 2, 1910, p. 12.

36 *Chicago Daily Tribune*, August 12, 1910, p. 10.

37 Comiskey, having learned from experience, knew it was vital to harmonize his stadium project with adjacent landowners and tenants to prevent future complications. He didn't want a surge of complaints later on about the noise or the volumes of traffic brought to the area for games. One of the preventative measures he took was to personally buy much of the surrounding property. He also encouraged friends to do likewise. *Chicago Daily Tribune*, January 21, 1914, p. 10. In other circumstances, he paid off the mortgages for area residents, building a fellowship that allowed Comiskey Park to thrive.

38 *Chicago Daily Tribune*, February 24, 1910, p. 12.

The seats were imported from the Heywood Bros. and Wakefield Company.

39 *Chicago Examiner*, January 30, 1910, p. S1.

40 *Chicago Daily Tribune*, July 2, 1910, p. 10.

Historian David J. Fletcher of the Chicago Baseball Museum explained that Comiskey originally wanted to postpone opening day to avoid being held on a Friday, which was considered unlucky and a "bad omen." chicagobaseballmuseum.org/chicago-baseball-museum-Comisky-Park.php.

41 Chicago Mayor Busse and National Commission chairman Herrmann paid tribute to Comiskey at home plate and a large banner was unveiled with the words, "Chicago Congratulates Comiskey." Catcher Billy Sullivan made his return on that celebrated day, and wore one of the brand new uniforms specially tailored by "Doc" White's company. Ironically, the only Sox member not to be decked out in a fresh "suit," and standing out like a sore thumb in the old gear, was outfielder Charley French. For whatever reason, his uniform wasn't available. The old stadium was torn down by early October. *Chicago Daily Tribune*, October 3, 1910, p. 21.

42 *Chicago Daily Tribune*, July 27, 1910, p. 10.

43 *Chicago Daily Tribune*, August 26-28, 1910.

44 *Chicago Daily Tribune*, October 26, 1910, p. 10.

45 *Chicago Daily Tribune*, October 31, 1910, p. 1.

46 Born Sarah Jane Laymon, she was known as "Jennie," and wed Ban Johnson on December 24, 1893. The couple had homes in Chicago and Spencer, Indiana.

47 *Chicago Daily Tribune*, November 27, 1910, p. C2.

48 The reading room was for Sox officials, players, and friends, and was intended to keep the athletes out of "mischief" during down time, as well as "improve" their minds. *Chicago Daily Tribune*, April 13, 1911, p. 21.

49 Comiskey, early on in his Sox ownership, took it upon himself to provide food and beverages for sportswriters in between double headers at his home grounds. No doubt, it was a gesture of goodwill as it allowed the scribes to remain at the stadium rather than having to leave for lunch, and Comiskey was lauded for his hospitality. The banquets were initially held in his offices and then moved to the beautiful Bards' room. The *Tribune* commonly mentioned these luncheons and always seemed to reiterate that "Admiral" John Agnew "poured." It seems that Agnew, in addition to being a distinguished contractor who helped in the construction of several major league parks, was the official bartender for the Bards. Also see: *Chicago Daily Tribune*, June 13, 1916, p. 15 and July 30, 1916, p. B2.

50 *Chicago Daily Tribune*, November 29, 1910, p. 10.

51 *Chicago Daily Tribune*, December 23, 1910, p. 2.

52 Grabiner was the son of Samuel and Hannah Grabiner, born on December 26, 1887 in Chicago. U.S. World War I Draft Registration Cards, Ancestry.com. Grabiner's passport application for 1924 stated that he was born in 1889. U.S. Passport Applications, Ancestry.com. In 1911, he also became the club's business manager on the road, working alongside John Conahan. A biography of Grabiner appeared in the *Sporting News*, July 27, 1939, p. 2.

53 *Chicago Daily Tribune*, March 18, 1911, p. 17.

54 *Chicago Daily Tribune*, May 11, 1911, p. 10.

55 On May 10, 1911, the White Sox defeated the Washington Senators 9–6 and would win again on May 11 by a score of 20–6.

56 *Chicago Daily Tribune*, July 23, 1911, p. C1.
   O'Toole spent five seasons in the majors and underachieved, ending up with a 27–36 record.

57 *Chicago Daily Tribune*, August 24, 1911, p. 10.

58 *Chicago Daily Tribune*, August 15, 1911, p. 10.

59 *Boston Herald*, August 28, 1911, p. 1.

60 *Chicago Daily Tribune*, September 10, 1911, p. 3.

61 *Chicago Daily Tribune*, October 9, 1911, p. 11.
   Both Chicago and Boston ended the season with a .510 win-loss percentage. Most sources list Boston as having attained fourth place in 1911 with the White Sox in fifth.

62 Harry Lord finished the 1911 season with 180 hits and Matty McIntyre finished the season with 184.

63 *Chicago Daily Tribune*, October 14, 1911, p. 1.

64 *Chicago Daily Tribune*, October 19, 1911, p. 1.

65 It was reported that he sometimes yearned to walk away from the day-to-day operations of the Sox. *Chicago Daily Tribune*, March 26, 1909, p. 8.

12

CIRCLING THE GLOBE

The resounding economic success of the White Sox changed the life of Charles Comiskey. His admirable wealth turned to opulence and he advanced into another realm of aristocrats within the Chicago elite. It was a fortune he never thought imaginable in the vocation he loved. Only twelve years earlier, he entered the market at the head of a rickety squad in a confrontational clash against the establishment, the National League, and was relentless in his fight. Success was far from guaranteed, but he made the most of it and his club survived the ordeal. In the process, the Sox gained tens of thousands of loyal supporters throughout the region and he personally and financially flourished.

Comiskey paid off associates he had borrowed money from, early investors, and continued to benefit from smart financial maneuverings. He also lent money to friends like James McAleer, a former manager in St. Louis and Washington and member of the Woodland Bards. McAleer needed $70,000 to purchase an interest in the Boston Red Sox in September 1911, and Comiskey obliged by giving him the full amount.[1]

Comiskey took great pride in his organization and the way it was run and constantly turned away potential partners trying to buy into the franchise. He loved his new ballpark and, in a way, it was an extension of himself. He spent a lot of time working on its visual appeal and ensuring that the on-field play was as smooth as possible. Negative elements such as gamblers and scalpers were always hanging around and he fought them tooth and nail because he didn't want his park to gain a bad reputation as a haven for either.

The comfort of fans was a top priority. By January of 1912, he was already discussing a $100,000 extension of the grandstand's second deck down the first and third baselines, which would increase the attendance by nearly 6,000 seats.[2] The overflowing demand shown in 1911 demonstrated that the additions were a necessary.

Garnering mainstream attention for his commitment to sportsmanship, his gentlemanly behavior, and civic contributions, Comiskey was acknowledged as a brainy diplomat, regardless of the crowd he entertained. He possessed many of his father's finest qualities, and it was only natural that some people believed there was a more suitable path for Comiskey than baseball—politics. Over the previous fourteen years, he'd been confronted numerous times by an upsurge of encouragement into that realm. From a position as alderman in St. Paul in 1898 to Cook County Sheriff in 1906 and support for U.S. Senator in 1909, Comiskey's name had been attached to many political titles . . . none of which he desired.[3][4][5]

The Democratic powers that be decided in early 1912 that Comiskey was the right candidate for Illinois Governor. Edmund M. Allen, who was the current mayor of Joliet, Illinois, was empowered by his political brethren to visit Comiskey in Chicago to discuss the opportunity.[6] Before the meeting, Allen spoke to the press about the Sox owner, saying: "Comiskey is a man who has come from the bottom and made a name and a fortune for himself. Everywhere he is known as a square man. He's been successful and we believe he's fitted today to take the responsibility of handling the affairs of the state.

"He has no factions behind him and he has no enemies. To me, he stands out as a big man, and he has won his place on his merits. He would make a good governor for the same reason that he made himself a good baseball leader—he was square with everybody."

Humbled and honored by the endorsement, Comiskey wasn't going to entertain the idea; not even for a moment.[7] Baseball was his love and his business, and the temptations of full-time civic duty was nowhere in his field of vision.

In recent years, he was shying away from public speeches and toned back his relentless promise for a championship pennant. It was almost as if all the recent poor finishes had put a strain on his confidence. On an annual basis, rooters packed the train depot to see the team off for spring training, and Comiskey was usually the center attraction. He was quick to say a few words about the upcoming season and easily inspired the crowd. But lately, he was much more subdued and his wife Nan gave a rousing speech at the 1911 celebration.[8] At one recent banquet, he was so overcome by emotion, he was unable saying anything but "thanks," and a recurring cold seemed to follow and overcome him at the most undesirable moments.

In an effort to solve one pending crisis, Comiskey named Jimmy Callahan to replace Hugh Duffy as the Sox manager.[9] Callahan led Chicago in disappointing fashion in 1903 and half of the '04 season (an 83–97 record) and lacked the administrative experience to be a successful manager at that time. Since leaving the majors, he owned the Logan Squares, a semi-professional club, and received a first-class education in management. He was an old-school athlete, hustling for every base, and Comiskey appreciated his energy on the field. In addition to being a player-manager, Comiskey wanted Callahan to take an active interest in scouting and signing talent, planning for spring training, and other business affairs.

Callahan lived in Chicago and he could easily assume office duties throughout the winter, especially while Comiskey was on vacation. Quickly jumping into the thick of things, he talked trades with his peers at the meetings in New York in December but found most teams wanted Ed Walsh or Rollie Zeider.[10] While neither man was on the market, he instead made one of the most important acquisitions in franchise history in William J. "Kid" Gleason, who was a forty-five-year-old veteran of five major league clubs over a span of two decades. Originally from Camden, New Jersey, he was the third of nine children and first became a member of the Philadelphia Quakers (later becoming the Phillies) in 1888.

Owning a brilliant eye for baseball, Gleason was astute in all facets of the game. He was small in size (5'7") but a giant at second base in his heyday and tough to the core. His relatable personality and wise perspective made him a natural assistant manager for Chicago. Callahan wanted him to inspire the team with his aggressive spirit and mentor the younger talent. Out of the New York conferences, the signing of Gleason was the best thing that happened to the Sox.

With Callahan and acting secretary Harry Grabiner collecting contracts and preparing for spring training in Waco, Comiskey spent three weeks deep sea fishing off Florida with Ban Johnson in January of 1912.[11] Having released Amby McConnell to Toronto and facing the retirement of Patsy Dougherty, the Sox were missing two experienced players. Matty McIntyre spent time in Cuba and missed training altogether, but returned in April, denying that he was a holdout and upset about his contract. He'd later be sent to the minors and retired soon thereafter.

The popular Billy Sullivan was yet another veteran planning to end his career and a serious injury to his collarbone early in the season diminished his role.

Walt "Red" Kuhn, a catcher, second baseman Morris Rath, and Jack Fournier, a first baseman discovered by Ted Sullivan in Calgary, were among the new blood. Agile Buck Weaver, twenty-one years of age, was said to be the "most promising recruit" obtained in years.[12] He lived up to all expectations and earned the starting shortstop position.

The White Sox started the 1912 season in prime fashion and appeared to be a world championship caliber team. Callahan's men advanced to first place on April 24 and escaped the normally tough eastern road trip from May 7 to 23 with 11 victories in 14 games and a 25–8 record.[13] Although pitcher Jim Scott was out of action because of rheumatism, the team had thrived through the first part of June.

Things quickly turned around, and the Sox lost 12 of 17 games at home from June 1 to 18. In response, Callahan shuffled the lineup and moved Harry Lord from third to the outfield, also installing Babe Borton at first. For an eastern swing, Comiskey ventured with the team for the first time in years, and with Callahan, agreed to sign Edward Cicotte on July 10, 1912.[14] Cicotte was 52–46 in five years with the Red Sox and displayed signs of greatness. But as of late, he was failing to produce.[15] His problems with Boston's management compounded things and was placed on waivers midseason. Picked up by Chicago, he initially protested and threatened to go home to Michigan. Within a day, however, he was in Philadelphia meeting with Callahan, fully accepting of his new team.[16]

It was clear at the time that the Sox were taking a chance on Cicotte. He was reported to have a "lame arm" and his last few starts in Boston were painfully rough. If he bounced back, he had the potential to one day replace Walsh as the ace of the pitching staff.[17]

Around this same time, the Sox made another major acquisition that would have lasting consequences. Hugh Duffy, who went on to manage Milwaukee of the American Association, recommended Ray Schalk to Comiskey, calling him, "the best catcher in the country."[18] Originally from Harvel, Illinois, Schalk was twenty years of age when he was signed by Chicago for as much as $15,000, plus Lena Blackburne and Jimmy Block. Similar to Cicotte, Schalk had potential to be a superstar and maybe even the heart of the team behind the plate. He had a lot to prove and filling the shoes of Billy Sullivan was going to be tough.

The Sox dropped below .500 in August and fought hard to remain afloat. Stunningly, they beat the Tigers in four straight games at Detroit to close out the season on October 6, 1912.[19] Chicago finished fourth in the American League with a 78–76 record. The hitting of Shano Collins and Ping Bodie were highlights for the club, and they had a team average of .254. Walsh was the only positive on the pitching staff, finishing the season with a 27–17 record and 2.15 ERA.

In defense of the city championship, the White Sox met the Cubs in a best-of-seven series. The two initial games ended in draws; one because of rain and the other for darkness. Shortstop Buck Weaver was an early casualty of the "Civil War" when he collided with Harry Lord while going for a fly ball.[20] Weaver was carried from the field and displayed lasting effects of what was believed to be a serious concussion.

Finally, on October 12, the Cubs were victorious before over 30,000 fans at Comiskey Park, winning 5–4 in what I. E. Sanborn of the *Tribune* called a "remarkable" contest.[21] The Cubs also won the fourth and fifth games, and were on their way to a sweep when Walsh fought back for a Game Six victory on October 15 in eleven innings.

In the eighth inning of Game Seven with the Cubs leading the series 3–1, the Sox rallied with four runs in the eighth inning to take the lead and won 7–5. The next day, on October 17, Walter Mattick hit a bases loaded triple in the ninth to give Comiskey's team the advantage, and the game ended by the score of 8–5. The returning Weaver, who also proved to be a hero, hustled for a home run after a long blast earlier in the afternoon. The White Sox had tied the series in unbelievable fashion. The finale was held on October 18 at Comiskey Park, and the Sox were through participating in dramatic contests.[22] Apparently, they wanted to end it with a bang, and after 16 unanswered runs were scored, the South Siders were victorious in winning their second straight city title.

Comiskey was as proud as ever, and told the *Tribune:* "It looks as if we have the start of a great team now, and they ought to cut some figure in the American League next year."[23]

In St. Louis, his old boss, Chris Von der Ahe, was in his last stages of life, and Comiskey was personally distressed. Their relationship was a storied and cherished one. Having met for the first time thirty years earlier, they enjoyed the many great achievements in baseball, including four straight pennants and a world championship in 1886. They'd contributed to each other's financial growth and prosperity, but as Comiskey developed his fortune, Von der Ahe was in decline. He had lost the St. Louis Browns when he went bankrupt and became borderline destitute. Towards the end of his life, Von der Ahe relied on the goodwill of Comiskey, who sent regular checks to help, and prepared for his own death by erecting a monument at Bellefontaine Cemetery.

On February 17, 1913, Comiskey made a trip to see Von der Ahe.[24] Emotionally on edge, Von der Ahe cried and said it was the "proudest moment" of his life that Comiskey made a special journey to visit. Comiskey was also affected by the poignant scene and it was a final goodbye of sorts. Four months later, on June 5, Von der Ahe passed away at the age of sixty-one.[25] Among his pallbearers were Comiskey, the Gleason brothers, and Charles Spink.

Future Hall of Famer John J. McGraw, manager of the National League's New York Giants, shared many traits with Comiskey. They both excelled on the diamond as players, were gifted leaders, and were true visionaries of the sport. In 1912, McGraw was in the planning stages of a trip around the world, akin to the Albert G. Spalding-Cap Anson tour of 1888; a massive undertaking that combined baseball, sightseeing, and spreading the influence of America's national pastime abroad. McGraw's scheme fell through, but he wasn't giving up on the idea.

Comiskey was also an adventurer. He took his White Sox to Mexico in 1907 and expressed an interest in trips to the Yucatan Peninsula, Honolulu, and Australia. Even more pertinent was the fact that since 1888, he yearned to take a ball club around the world, just like Spalding.[26] Twenty-five years had passed since, but he hadn't given up on the concept. When McGraw and Comiskey converged in January of 1913 during a meeting in Chicago, they were equal in their aspirations to undertake the endeavor, and served to be exactly what the other needed to accomplish the feat.[27]

Spring training in 1913 saw a return to California to Paso Robles, an enjoyable small resort community northwest of Los Angeles. Despite a change in surroundings and climate, the Sox were in significant disarray, and timely hitting was their number one problem. To gain much needed experience, veteran Davy Jones of the Detroit Tigers was purchased for

$2,500.[28] Additionally, Joe Berger of the Pacific Coast League was the talk of camp and expected to replace Buck Weaver at short.[29] Weaver, however, worked overtime to bat left and hoped the change would improve his offense.[30]

As a token of appreciation, the Sox delegation, to include sportswriters and friends, chipped in to purchase Nan Comiskey an Abalone blister pearl dinner ring for her generosity in coordinating the venture of the Sox trip to the west coast.[31] Before leaving California, the Comiskeys spent time in the Los Angeles area and then hopped on an east bound train.[32] They took in the sights at the Grand Canyon before returning to Chicago on March 25.

Callahan implemented his own style of training techniques to put the team through the ringer and figured out the best lineup he could manage. Harry Lord was moved back to third, Buck Weaver was named the primary shortstop, and the outfield was made up of Walter Mattick, Ping Bodie, and Shano Collins. The team had three primary catchers, Ray Schalk, Ted Easterly, and Walt Kuhn, and a fairly strong pitching staff, but nobody would have thought that twenty-four-year-old Ewell Albert "Reb" Russell, a fresh recruit from the Texas League, was going to be the team's most reliable arm. Russell would led the team in games pitched (52), innings (316.2), and victories (22).

Old faithful Ed Walsh was not himself in 1913 and missed a great portion of the season to arm trouble. The lack of hitting power remained a major weakness, and Callahan changed the game day roster innumerable times. Davy Jones was sold before the end of May because of his failure to make an impact and outfielder Walter Schaller didn't live up to expectations. On June 1, 1913, Callahan arranged to trade Rollie Zeider and Babe Borton to the Yankees for first baseman Hal Chase.[33]

Chase had been with New York since 1905 and was a stellar athlete, but the downside was that he was perhaps the most controversial man in baseball. For years, he had terrorized the management of the Yankees with his behavior, and his outstanding fielding was often overshadowed by his keen ability to disrupt team balance. His arrival in Chicago was a dangerous move, but it had the potential to pay off if Chase abided by the rules.

Plain and simple, it was yet another year of rebuilding for the Sox. Comiskey began loading up on prospects like Buck O'Brien, Henry "Hi" Jasper, Tom Daly, and Edd Roush, as well as spending $18,000 in cash and players for Larry Chappell of McClosky, Illinois.[34] Chappell was a star in

Milwaukee for the American Association and was highly sought after by a number of major league clubs. In his never-ending quest to land a good outfielder, Comiskey outbid his counterparts to secure his rights. With Walsh out of the rotation and Billy Sullivan no longer behind the plate, the Sox were going through some brutal growing pains and the standings reflected their plight.

At the end of the season, Callahan's warriors were in fifth place with a 78–74 record. The pitching of "Reb" Russell, Jim Scott, and Eddie Cicotte, who finished with a 1.58 ERA and an 18–11 record, were among the positives. Buck Weaver, with his new left-handed swing, improved almost 50 points from 1912, and finished with a .272 average.[35] [36] Hal Chase batted .286, Ping Bodie batted .264, and as a team, the Sox were last in the league; sporting a dismal mark of .236.[37]

Johnny Evers' Cubs faired a bit better, landing in third place in the National League with a record of 88 wins and 65 losses. The annual city series, according to the prediction of Sam Weller of the *Tribune*, was favoring the Cubs, expecting them to end their rival's winning streak.[38]

The Sox were as game as ever, and took the first contest on October 8, 1913, behind the work of Russell and Scott, but lost the second when Cicotte collapsed under the pressure.[39] The Cubs pummeled Scott and earned the 8–0 win before nearly 18,000 people in game three at their West Side park. Cicotte helped the Sox tie the series on October 11, with a 5–2 victory, and it seemed as if the ineffectiveness of Comiskey's offense was only a rumor. Game five was also won by the White Sox, led by Shano Collins' four hits and the spitball work of Joe Benz.

Weller's prophecy, based on the inability of Ed Walsh to perform, was flawed. In game six at Comiskey Park, the Sox prevailed 5–2 and won their third straight city championship.[40] The players each received $807 for the series and Ring Lardner wrote an amusing article in the *Tribune* recommending to Comiskey that he offer a financial incentive to the team every season in an effort to get them to perform better.[41] He continued that the Sox played against the Cubs like "men possessed" and had Comiskey made the right kind of financial proposition beforehand, the team would likely have won the World Series.

The world tour loomed over much of everything for Comiskey that year. Arrangements were in constant flux and adjustments to the itinerary were made on the fly. Callahan met with government officials while in Washington, D.C. to discuss their journey, and embassies from around the world were notified by the U.S. Secretary of State to support the tour as much as possible. Ted Sullivan, who was always on the move, served as an advance agent, and Albert Spalding met with Comiskey to give him advice based on his experiences.[42] Before setting sail from Vancouver on November 19, a full exhibition schedule was arranged by Acting Secretary Harry Grabiner and John McGraw.

All things considered, the scope of the expedition was the biggest undertaking ever attempted by Organized Baseball. It encompassed 38,000 miles, eleven countries, and four months of travel.[43] While the basis for the trip was to share America's pastime abroad, it was also an opportunity to experience other cultures. For Comiskey, the journey was the realization of a personal goal and it meant a lot to his wife and family. He was fronting a considerable amount of money, as much as $100,000, including $1,500 per person, and was so adamant about the tour that he was willing to take a financial loss to see that it went forward.[44]

Only several of the White Sox regulars went along (Joe Benz, Jim Scott, and Buck Weaver) and because Jimmy Callahan was such an instrumental part of the journey, Comiskey and McGraw made him an equal partner. Promising pitcher Urban Clarence "Red" Faber of Cascade, Iowa, who was recently signed by Comiskey in August of 1913, joined the pitching staff but was later turned over to the Giants for the duration of the tour. Additionally, Sam Crawford of Detroit, Herman Schaefer from Washington, and Walter Leverenz of St. Louis were members of the American League contingent.

Premier athlete Jim Thorpe, recognized around the world for his Olympic conquests in 1912, played for the Giants and added to the box office allure of the journey.

The *Empress of Japan* disembarked Victoria, British Columbia, as scheduled with thirteen players from the Sox, ten from the Giants, and thirty-eight others.[45] Terrible ocean conditions delayed the vessel and hexed the passengers by way of an unavoidable seasickness.[46] Once they arrived in the Far East, the teams performed for enthusiastic audiences in the Philippines, China, and Japan. The journey proceeded to Australia, Egypt, and then Italy and the tourists were graciously received at every port by rooters and royalty, government officials, and even old friends.

On February 9, 1914, en route to Rome from Naples, Comiskey fell ill on the train and his quick deterioration worried his family a great deal.[47] It was initially assumed that his symptoms were in tune with a heart affliction, but a doctor diagnosed him as having acute indigestion. Early reports in Chicago stated that his condition had already improved and the news eased a lot of concerned minds back home. A specialist in Rome put Comiskey through an exhaustive series of tests, and a couple days later, although still not recovered, he mustered the strength to visit the Vatican and meet Pope Pius X in one of the highlights of the tour.[48]

Comiskey missed other events of the trip because of his condition and remained in bed for days. Over 4,200 miles away in New Haven, Connecticut, his stepmother, Rose, passed away at the home of relatives.[49] She was seventy years old.

In fragile shape, as his only method of sustenance was goat milk, Comiskey wasn't yet out of danger.[50] His stomach problems persisted and he saw another doctor in Paris before rejoining the expedition in England. On February 26, a massive crowd of over 30,000 spectators at Stamford Bridge, the football stadium in London for Chelsea of the English First Division, watched the Sox beat the Giants, 5–4, in eleven innings.[51] In attendance for the glorious affair was King George, who witnessed his first ever baseball game and took time to greet and shake hands with Comiskey and others in the touring party. The torrent of excitement in London not only served as a topper for the entire journey, but inspired the powers that be to discuss a potential return trip to Europe later in 1914–15.

That plan was cancelled by the onset of World War I during the summer of 1914.

Professional baseball in the United States was experiencing a war of its own, and the magnitude of the conflict grew while Comiskey and his cohorts were overseas. The prominent businessmen behind the upstart Federal League, an outlaw group, were engaged in a swift and hard-hitting scheme to strengthen the eight teams within its organization. At the same time, officials yearned to diminish the American and National Leagues by signing away its top athletes. Everyone from Ty Cobb to Joe Jackson was offered huge financial rewards for breaking away from their existing contracts and jumping to the new organization.

In Chicago, Charles Weeghman was in charge of the local outfit, the Chi-Feds, and hired former Cubs star Joe Tinker to serve as manager. He also initiated the building of a new stadium on the north side of the city, at a vacant lot on the corner of Addison and Clark Streets.

The rapidity in which the Federals were making progress was stunning. Charles Murphy, president of the Cubs, was desperately trying to combat Weeghman and admitted that he was working to protect Comiskey's interest as well as his own.[52] Efforts to block the Addison Street venue were unsuccessful, and to this day, Weeghman Park remains the home of the Cubs; now known as Wrigley Field.

The Federal League was empowered by jumpers, and the White Sox players were relentlessly tempted by offers. Kid Gleason, Eddie Cicotte, and numerous others were promised significant raises.[53] And with Comiskey and Callahan out of the country, the team was vulnerable to a full-fledged raid. However, the Sox were lucky enough that only catcher Ted Easterly abandoned the team when he joined the Kansas City Packers, and in many instances, it was a sign of loyalty to the club and Comiskey that they remained.

On March 6, 1914, the world tour officially came to an end in New York when the *Lusitania* arrived in port.[54] Thousands of people greeted the travelers, including a massive delegation from Chicago. Comiskey, his color gone and walking with a cane, looked like a completely different person from the man who left in November. The accounts of his failing health were absolutely true, and although he was in good spirits, he "did not look like a well man when he landed," according to the *Tribune*. The next night, he was honored with an ovation lasting nearly five minutes at a special banquet, but refused to make a speech because of his weakened state.

Comiskey was emotionally affected by the welcome of an estimated 2,000 people when his train arrived back in Chicago, and he expressed a genuine happiness to be home.[55] He felt good enough to deliver a speech at a second dinner celebrating the expedition, and soon thereafter, ventured into the Wisconsin woods for a thorough rest in his most relaxing environment. Over the next few weeks, he spent a lot of time away from the public eye, trying to recover his lost strength.

For spring training, the Sox worked out in Paso Robles under the guidance of Kid Gleason. There were many questions about the competitiveness of the club in 1914, but one of the biggest unresolved topics was that pertaining to the future of Ed Walsh. His arm had yet to improve from the injuries he'd sustained the season before, and he was facing another possible year on the bench. He was an invaluable asset as a coach and mentor, and if he couldn't pitch, he would be used in other capacities. But as soon as he was ready, Callahan wanted him back in the game.

At the end of spring training, a failure to properly supervise the return trip from California left the Sox players on an old, unsteady train in shoddy conditions.[56] The dismal ride was a poor reflection on Comiskey and his assistants, and likely left some of the men with a bad impression of their leader. However, Comiskey hadn't spent a moment planning for the training jaunt and was in Wisconsin when the train fiasco occurred. I. E. Sanborn of the *Tribune* blamed it on the railroads and said that Comiskey was not getting the kind of comfortable service he paid for.

Larry Chappell, the $18,000 man, suffered a foot wound during spring training that developed into blood poisoning, which kept him off the opening day roster. Lena Blackburne, who had been reacquired after a year in the minors with Milwaukee, was at second base, Buck Weaver at short, Harry Lord on third, and Hal Chase, originally a holdout, signed and returned to first base. While the outfield was supposed to be made up of Ping Bodie, Shano Collins, and Jack Fournier—although the latter was out with an ankle injury—alternate outfielders were slipped into the game-day roster, but none were overly effective. In fact, the Sox didn't appear much different than they had in 1913.

"Red" Faber, the 6'2" giant, was impressive during the world tour, and made his major league debut for Comiskey in April of 1914. He'd eventually throw over 180 innings in 40 games that season, and repeatedly displayed cunning and science on the mound; often showing off the perfection of his spitball. Youngsters Mel Wolfgang and Bill Lathrop were supporting pitchers, backing up the top four of Chicago: Russell, Ed Cicotte, Joe Benz, and Scott, all of whom finished 1914 with a losing record.[57]

Scott, on May 14 against Washington, tossed a no hitter through nine innings in a scoreless game, but gave up two in the 10th and lost the game, 1–0. Benz, on the final day of May, repeated Scott's feat, but was victorious against Cleveland. Walsh ended up missing most of the season and only participating in eight games, one of which included a complete game shutout against the New York Yankees on July 13.[58] It was a masterpiece, and the New York crowd rewarded his excellence with a prolonged applause.

The acquisition of Ray Demmitt, an experienced outfielder from Tigers, was a big plus for the team, but they continued to suffer both on offense and defense. Captain Lord was so depressed by his own play that he abruptly quit the team on May 12.[59] In response, Callahan named Weaver captain, but the team was devastated by the loss of such a veteran hand. A few weeks later, Lord asked Comiskey for his unconditional release, but Comiskey turned him down, telling the player that it would be virtually impossible to secure waivers from the rest of the league. Another significant blow to the team occurred on June 15, when first baseman Hal Chase, a guy many of the young players looked up to, announced that he was leaving the Sox to jump to the Federal League.[60] He gave ten days notice, and then reneged on it by playing for the Buffalo Buffeds on June 21.

The barely existing stability of the White Sox was now completely gone, and they were guaranteed to end the season with a losing record. Comiskey filed an injunction to prevent Chase from playing for Buffalo and a temporary block was obtained, though was vacated by a judge in July.

Scotty Alcock, Jim Breton, and Howard Baker were tried out in the infield, and Blackburne's lowly batting average was not fulfilling his promise when he was first signed.[61] A number of other recruits were given an opportunity, and Comiskey's scout Jack Doyle was urgently looking to sign any minor league player who showed any ability to hit. On August 8, 1914, Comiskey publicized that Oscar Felsch, a twenty-two-year-old prospect from Milwaukee of the American Association had been purchased for $11,750 in players and cash.[62] Nicknamed "Happy," Felsch was a good natured outfielder with plenty of talent, but Comiskey wanted hitters, and Felsch reportedly had 16 home runs that year, according to the *Tribune.*

The season ended without much fanfare, and for good reason. The White Sox finished in sixth place with a 70–84 record and a .239 (.241) batting average,[63] which was second to last in the league behind the New York Yankees (.229). Redemption, to a degree, was right around the corner; at least in Chicago baseball circles. With three straight city championships, the Sox always seemed to buck up against the Cubs, and this year was no different.

On October 7, 1914, the Cubs won the initial game of the series, but the Sox tied it up the next afternoon at the West Side Grounds, winning 5–2. The Cubs took the next two, and had a decisive advantage with a 3 games to 1 lead. In game five, Comiskey's players showed immense heart, taking the win by the score of 3–1, with big defensive plays by Ray Demmitt and Shano Collins. On October 13, the White Sox beat the Cubs to tie the series, and two days later, before nearly 15,000 fans, they won again to clinch their fourth straight Chicago title.[64]

Year after year, the offense of the White Sox disappointed Comiskey, his manager, and fans. Their sub-par hitting was like clockwork, and although they could beat the Cubs, they were a perennial second division squad in the American League, finishing fourth or lower six years straight. The lack of pure hitters was an unsolvable crisis, and Ed Walsh was quoted in the August 4, 1914 edition of *Baseball Magazine* as saying: "Nobody can be a great batter and wear a White Sox uniform. I don't know why it is, but that's the truth. Put my 'sox' on Ty Cobb and let him wear my uniform or some other club uniform that would fit him, and he wouldn't hit three hundred."

In no way could the Sox compete with Connie Mack's Philadelphia Athletics, the unstoppable winners of 99 games and the pennant; their fourth in five years, including three World Series wins. But ironically, the Athletics were in major turmoil. Financial strife made it necessary to break up Mack's championship team, especially after losing the 1914 World Series in four straight games to the Boston Braves. To eliminate high expenses, Mack sold superstar Eddie Collins to Comiskey for $50,000 in cash, which was announced on December 8, 1914.[65] It was the biggest transaction in baseball history to date and gave the White Sox one of the greatest athletes ever to play the game.[66]

Finally, Comiskey had a natural hitter on his roster. Collins was a fine second baseman, a better-than-.300 hitter, and a true leader. His arrival, plus the development of young stars like Buck Weaver, Ray Schalk, and Red Faber, as well as the progress of Ed Cicotte, was bolstering the White Sox for a serious run at the pennant. In fact, with a few crucial additions, it was the makings of a potential dynasty.

ENDNOTES

1 *Sporting Life*, October 12, 1912, p. 15.

2 *Chicago Daily Tribune*, January 10, 1912, p. 6.

3 *St. Paul Globe*, March 16, 1898, p. 1.

4 *Chicago Daily Tribune*, June 26, 1906, p. 4.

5 *Chicago Daily Tribune*, April 8, 1909, p. 10.

6 *Chicago Daily Tribune*, February 8, 1912, p. 6.

7 *Chicago Daily Tribune*, February 9, 1912, p. 12.

8 *Chicago Daily Tribune*, February 28, 1911, p. 8.

9 *Chicago Daily Tribune*, October 24, 1911, p. 13.

10 *Chicago Daily Tribune*, December 13, 1911, p. 16.

11 *Chicago Daily Tribune*, January 13, 1912, p. 10.

12 *Chicago Daily Tribune*, March 15, 1912, p. 7.
Weaver, during spring training, was forced to cope with the recent passing of his mother, and proved to be a courageous young man. His attitude was exactly what Callahan and Gleason wanted from their recruits.

13 *Chicago Daily Tribune*, April 25, 1912, p. 11.

14 *Chicago Daily Tribune*, July 11, 1912, p. 13.

15 In four years with the Red Sox (1908–11), Cicotte had a record of 51–43, with a 2.53 ERA. While he had been quite successful in 1909 (14–5) and 1910 (15–11), he struggled in 1911 and finished the season under .500 (11–15).

16 *Philadelphia Inquirer*, July 11, 1912, p. 10.

17 In nine appearances (six starts), Cicotte was 1–3 with a 5.67 ERA for the 1912 Red Sox.

18 *Cleveland Plain Dealer*, July 15, 1912, p. 6.

19 *Chicago Daily Tribune*, October 7, 1912, p. 24.

20 *Chicago Daily Tribune*, October 12, 1912, p. 21.

21 *Chicago Daily Tribune*, October 13, 1912, p. C1.

22 *Chicago Daily Tribune*, October 19, 1912, p. 23.

23 *Chicago Daily Tribune*, October 19, 1912, p. 24.

24 *Chicago Daily Tribune*, February 18, 1913, p. 11.
They met in the latter's home at 3613 St. Louis Avenue, the same residence where they had first met decades earlier.

25 *Sporting News*, June 12, 1913, p. 4.
Incidentally, the November before, John T. Brush, another of Comiskey's ex-bosses, passed away. *Philadelphia Inquirer*, November 27, 1912, p. 12. Despite a rocky relationship, especially after Comiskey became an owner, the latter refused to remain bitter. In the 1918 book *Commy*, he said that Brush was one of the "best men" he ever worked for. Axelson, Gustave W., *Commy: The Life Story of Charles A. Comiskey*, p. 124. He attended Brush's funeral, along with Ban Johnson.

26 When Spalding was looking to put together a superior team to journey abroad in 1888, representatives of his outfit went to St. Louis to discuss the possibilities of Comiskey joining them. Comiskey was interested in the idea. However, the financial side was lacking. He said: "I might have gone had Spalding offered anything like a fair inducement. Only think of it. His figures were $50 for the trip and expenses. Why that would not have been cigar money." *Sporting News*, September 22, 1888, p. 6.

27 *Chicago Daily Tribune*, January 24, 1913, p. 10.

28 *Ann Arbor News*, January 16, 1913, p. 1.

29 *Chicago Daily Tribune*, February 23, 1913, p. C1.

30 *Chicago Daily Tribune*, February 28, 1913, p. 13.

31 Ibid.

32 *Chicago Daily Tribune*, March 21, 1913, p. 15.

33 *Chicago Daily Tribune*, June 2, 1913, p. 13.

34 *Chicago Daily Tribune*, July 15, 1913, p. 13.

A biography of Chappell appeared in the *Chicago Daily Tribune*, August 17, 1913, p. C2.

35 *Chicago Daily Tribune*, November 24, 1913, p. 17.

36 Buck Weaver had a batting average of .224 in 1912, which would be the lowest of his nine-year career.

37 From the inception of the American League, the White Sox hitting was historically bad. Not only did they have the AL's lowest team batting average in 1913, but from 1901–13, Chicago never was better than fifth (out of eight teams) in batting average and were dead last four times (1906, .230, 1909, .221, 1910, .211, and 1913, .236).

38 *Chicago Daily Tribune*, October 6, 1913, p. 23.

39 *Chicago Daily Tribune*, October 9, 1913, p. 23.

40 *Chicago Daily Tribune*, October 14, 1913, p. 13.

41 Ibid.

42 *Chicago Daily Tribune*, October 2, 1913, p. 13.

43 *Chicago Daily Tribune*, March 7, 1914, p. 14.

44 *Chicago Daily Tribune*, September 28, 1913, p. C2.

45 *Washington Post*, November 20, 1913, p. 8.

46 *Chicago Daily Tribune*, December 27, 1913, p. 4.

47 *Chicago Daily Tribune*, February 10, 1914, p. 14.

48 *Chicago Daily Tribune*, February 12, 1914, p. 10.

49 *Chicago Daily Tribune*, February 14, 1914, p. 14.

50 *Chicago Daily Tribune*, February 15, 1914, p. B1.

51 *New York Times*, February 27, 1914, p. 1.

52 *Chicago Daily Tribune*, February 14, 1914, p. 14.

53 Cicotte initially refused his tendered Sox contract and was a holdout. *Chicago Daily Tribune*, December 28, 1913, p. B1. There was speculation whether he was using the advances of the Federal League as leverage to get more money out of Chicago. With both Comiskey and Callahan overseas, Kid Gleason negotiated with Cicotte and got him to sign "at one of the largest salaries paid a pitcher in the American League," according to widespread press reports. *Watertown Daily Times*, March 11, 1914, p. 8.

54 *Chicago Daily Tribune*, March 7, 1914, p. 14.

55 *Chicago Daily Tribune*, March 10, 1914, p. 16.

The newspaper reported that the "cheers of the fans brought tears" from Comiskey. He said: "There's no place like home," upon arrival in Chicago.

56 *Chicago Daily Tribune*, April 7, 1914, p. 15.

57 At the conclusion of the 1914 season, four of the five main pitchers for the Sox finished with losing records: Reb Russell (8–12), Ed Cicotte (11–16), Joe Benz (15–19), and Jim Scott (14–18).

58 *Chicago Daily Tribune*, July 14, 1914, p. 11.

59 *Chicago Daily Tribune*, May 14, 1914, p. 15.

60 *Chicago Daily Tribune,* June 16, 1914, p. 17.
Chase complained that his wages had been cut $2,000 by the Sox, which Comiskey denied. He received a financial offer he apparently couldn't refuse from Buffalo, and jumped to the outlaws.

61 Lena Blackburne finished the 1914 season with a .222 batting average.

62 *Chicago Daily Tribune,* August 9, 1914, p. B1.

63 We have listed the batting average as .239, but the official American League report issued after the season concluded states that the average was .241. Because of this discrepancy, we have put the American League report's average in parenthesis. *Sporting Life,* October 10, 1914, p. 10. The Sox ended the season in sixth place with a record of 70–84, tied with New York.

64 *Chicago Daily Tribune,* October 16, 1914, p. 13.

65 Collins signed a five-year contract with the White Sox for the 1915–19 seasons. It was reported that Comiskey paid $50,000 in cash to Connie Mack of the Philadelphia Athletics and agreed to pay Collins $10,000 a year. *Chicago Daily Tribune,* December 9, 1914, p. 18. Later, it was revealed that Collins' annual salary was $15,000. The *Sporting News* noted that Comiskey's "keen insight into the future and his experience with recalcitrant and unappreciative players" spurred the concept of signing his athletes to contracts longer than one year. *Sporting News,* December 2, 1915, pg. 1.

66 In twenty-five seasons, Eddie Collins would amass over 3,300 hits (with 2,643 of them being singles, which is currently 3rd all-time), 512 sacrifice hits (best all-time), over 700 stolen bases, a .333 batting average, most assists by a second baseman (7,630), win the 1914 AL MVP, and be elected to the National Baseball Hall of Fame in 1939.

13

NO LONGER THE "HITLESS WONDERS"

The high-octane baseball war continued and neither side was giving an inch. With seemingly unlimited funds, the ambitious moneymen of the Federal League remained relentless in their pursuit of big named superstars. Ty Cobb, Joe Jackson, Sam Crawford, Tris Speaker, and Eddie Collins were among those approached by agents offering outrageous salaried contracts that, in most cases, dwarfed what the owners of their current clubs were paying them. Mammoth multi-year deals were enticing, and officials in both the American and National Leagues were scrambling to protect their players by any means necessary.

In the case of Collins, only five months before he inked a deal with Charles Comiskey, he was actually re-signed by Philadelphia A's manager Connie Mack in a preemptive type move to head off any jump to the Federals.[1] When the negotiations to have Collins switch allegiance to the White Sox began, Collins made it clear that he wanted to stay in the east, where he had a home outside Philadelphia. But Comiskey was not only willing to pay Mack $50,000 in cash for the player, but give Collins $15,000 in upfront bonus money, plus as much as $15,000 a year for five years. President Ban Johnson, eager to keep Collins in the American League, was so enthusiastic about the transaction that he wrote the bonus check himself, only to be reimbursed by Comiskey later.[2]

A cunning move by the Federal League precipitated Comiskey's feverous actions, and, according to the *Sporting News*, encouraged the latter to spend big bucks to land Collins.[3]

Walter Johnson, the brilliant right-handed pitcher for the Washington Senators, was at the top of the Feds' list of potential acquisitions, and for months rumors circulated about his coming defection. Finally, in early

December, it was announced that Johnson had been secured by Joe Tinker of the Chicago Whales of the Federal League (previously known as the Chi-Feds) for an estimated $20,000 annually. The news rippled across the national sporting community and American Leaguers were devastated.

Johnson, who'd won 28 games in 1914 and was considered the "greatest baseball pitcher of the age" according to the *Baltimore Sun*, was so valuable to the Senators that a $100,000 insurance policy was taken out on him by management. He was a considerable draw for fans and could single-handedly boost attendance for the Federal League around its circuit, but especially in Chicago, at the probable expense of Comiskey's Sox. Comiskey was in full war-time mode and was unwilling to be overshadowed in any way. Within days, the record deal for Collins was made public.

Johnson, a short time later, was persuaded to remain loyal to the Senators and, ironically, never did defect. But Comiskey's feat in signing Collins was lauded, and he was thoroughly happy with the deal. He was admittedly fatigued by buying unproven minor leaguers at significant cost, only to have them fail time after time. Landing Collins was the chance of a lifetime to bring aboard one of the league's most valuable players, and Comiskey made the most of it.

Newspaper writers were more often commenting on Comiskey's disappointment in the performance of the White Sox. His frustrations and overbearing stress played havoc with his health, and he suffered throughout the winter with stomach problems. When he was feeling strong, he made time to enjoy Camp Jerome with Ban Johnson and friends and had two separate rousing affairs with the Woodland Bards at hotels in Chicago. The lively parties kept his spirits in good shape just prior to another bombshell announcement that startled his fans and had many seriously worried.

On December 17, 1914, a man with no major league experience—as a player or in any other regard—was named to replace Jimmy Callahan as manager of the White Sox. Clarence Henry Rowland, a thirty-five-year-old with plenty of minor league credentials, was assigned to the spot, and his appointment was met with little fanfare. Originally from Wisconsin, "Pants" Rowland grew up in Dubuque and impressed Comiskey years before with his passion for baseball, intellect, and ability to judge talent. The hiring of what many unimpressed people called a "bush leaguer"

displayed a distinct change in philosophy for Comiskey, but he was confident in the maneuver.

Rowland was as energetic as they came.[4] He was an unyielding fighter for his team on the field, but, at the same time, had considerable expectations from his men in terms of discipline and performance. With a lot to prove, he planned on implementing his own system of beliefs and values, and wanted to discard any dead weight. Considering Rowland's greenness, it was rumored that Comiskey was closer to the actual management of the club than at any point in recent years and was simply using Rowland as a mouthpiece for unpopular decisions. However, Rowland was given a great deal of autonomy and the go-ahead by Comiskey to turn his Sox into a winner.

Some of Rowland's early decisions were controversial. He eradicated the coaching position and the influential Kid Gleason was unconditionally released from his duties on the team. Also, he decided that Collins, surprisingly, would not serve as the on-field captain; that such a position was unneeded. The well-liked Ping Bodie was sold to San Francisco and Billy Sullivan, the loyal catcher with more than a decade of service to Comiskey, was released without warning, which drew much criticism.

During spring training in Paso Robles, Rowland put his team through a rigorous conditioning routine—including five mile walks—and laid down the law about the kind of behavior he wanted on the field and off. He especially wanted his players to take the game more seriously and to cut out the in-game joking around that only served as a distraction. He indicated to the press that some of his players were drawing paychecks and couldn't play ball, while others failed to adhere to orders. In Rowland's eye, players Reb Russell and Larry Chappell were overweight and also on the chopping block.

As expected, Collins's impressive playing ability brought out the best in his teammates, and the Sox were brimming with self-assurance as the season began in April of 1915. The Boston Red Sox were predicted to win the pennant, but seeing that Comiskey's men were so much improved, they were surefire contenders. Rowland initially used Bunny Brief at first base, one of his weakest spots, and Thomas Quinlan in right field. Third base consisted of Lena Blackburne, Jim Breton, and Bobby "Braggo" Roth at different times, and the combination of Collins and Buck Weaver at second and shortstop respectively, was on par with any top rated duo in the big leagues.

After the Sox won their seventh straight victory on April 28, 1915 (after previously losing six in a row), James Crusinberry of the *Chicago Daily*

Tribune remarked: "The old days of the hitless wonders have passed." Indeed hitting like champions at certain points, the club definitely experienced intermittent growing pains. Comiskey liked what he was seeing but still wasn't satisfied. He continued to improve his roster, acquiring outfielders Nemo Leibold on waivers and John Edward "Eddie" Murphy for $11,500 from the A's, and offered $15,000 and four players for superstar Ray Chapman of Cleveland. Rowland participated in a couple secret meetings with Cleveland owner Charles Somers, an old friend of Comiskey, and some sort of arrangement was discussed, but nothing finalized.

Veteran Ed Walsh was honored by a special "Ed Walsh Day" at Comiskey Park on July 16 and an estimated 28,000 fans watched him throw a complete game in a 6–2 victory. It was reminiscent of the old days and Walsh was carried off the field by fans as part of the post game celebration.

Behind Boston and Detroit in the standings, the White Sox were 20 games over .500 by the last week of July. Even with his team's success, Comiskey wasn't content and lambasted American League umpiring and blamed them for several losses that he thought should have been wins.[5] This outburst drew Ban Johnson out in defense of his officials, but luckily, this difference in opinion didn't leave any lasting friction. In the midst of their championship run, Boston acquired premier shortstop Jack Barry of the Athletics, a player Comiskey also had his eye on. The *Tribune* noted on August 9, 1915, that Comiskey was willing to make a higher bid for Barry than Boston had, but because of a timing issue, the deal was concluded before his offer reached Connie Mack.[6][7]

There were two other significant pick ups for the White Sox in August of 1915; one of them being left-handed pitcher Claude "Lefty" Williams, a successful thrower for the Salt Lake City franchise of the Pacific Coast League. Williams had proven to be a winner in the minor leagues and, given a shot in a Sox uniform, was expected to earn a regular berth on the staff.

The other acquisition was none other than Joseph Jefferson Jackson, the sensational batting expert from Cleveland. Jackson, known as "Shoeless Joe," was having a troubling 1915. Early in the season, the Cleveland press got on his case for being out of shape, and fans let him hear their loud squawks during home games. He was shifted from the outfield to first base and battled an injury in June that sidelined him for a short time. The *Cleveland Plain Dealer* reported that his offense had slipped since shifting positions, and on July 7, he received cuts and bruises after an accident involving his automobile with a horse and wagon.

In mid-August, Joe Tinker, the man who sought Walter Johnson for the Federal League in Chicago, had dinner with Jackson in Cleveland, trying to tempt the latter to jump sides. He offered a three year deal at $10,000 annually, but Jackson refused. Comiskey swooped in, worked out a deal with Cleveland owner Charles Somers, and acquired Jackson on August 20. The exact cost was unknown, but the *Plain Dealer* thought the deal was around $25,000 in cash, plus three players, while the *Tribune* figured it was more like $15,000 and a trio of athletes. Other sources placed the total price, including the players, to as much as $65,000.

Somers blamed a "bad financial year" for having to let the star go, as Cleveland was facing one of its worst attendance years ever, and the Cleveland press noted that Jackson no longer possessed the drawing power he once had. After the deal, Jackson expressed contentment that he was helping Somers in some way, and told the *Plain Dealer:* "I stand a chance of getting into some sweet World's Series money," now that he was with a real contender.

I. E. Sanborn of the *Tribune,* on August 20, explained that Comiskey had obtained Eddie Collins, Eddie Murphy, Nemo Leibold, and now "Shoeless Joe" Jackson to win the American League pennant, and it was obvious to all baseball aficionados that anything less would be a major disappointment.

Jack Fournier, a leading batter for the Sox, went out with an arm injury around that same time, and Rowland moved Shano Collins to first base and used Murphy, Jackson, and "Happy" Felsch in the outfield. Before August was through, Comiskey acquired prospect Fred McMullin from Los Angeles, who was a skillful third baseman.

Despite his spending, Comiskey's team faltered, and the excitement slowly evaporated. Boston and Detroit were far out of reach for a championship bid and it would remain that way when the season ended.[8] The Chicago city series against the Cubs followed soon thereafter, and once again, the Sox won four of five games and took the title. Solid pitching, clutch hitting, and teamwork were responsible for the wins, and contributions came from everyone.

At the conclusion of the series, players were peeved at Comiskey because they weren't entitled to part of a $21,000-plus gate for game five, which took place on a Sunday at Comiskey Park. The stipulations for the series only gave them a cut of the first four games, and the athletes had wanted the games on Thursday and Friday to be postponed because of poor weather, thus giving them part of the big weekend income. On October 11, 1915, the

Tribune quoted an unnamed Sox player as saying: "Leave it to the big bosses to cop all the dough."

An unnamed Cubs player in that same article said: "They always told me Comiskey was a friend of the ball player. I understand he was responsible for our playing on the two cold days. Consequently, he gets the big money from the big Sunday crowd," and that the players got the smaller amount collected on the cold days.

Across the major leagues, a wider and wider divide grew between players and club owners. Considering the larger paydays offered to the upper echelon of stars and the extreme salaries being pushed by the Federal League, a disproportionate view of salary figures existed in the minds of the athletes and magnates. Gone were the days when players were involved with the sport for love of the game; now, it was all business.[9] Players were looking after their own interests with closer scrutiny and were willing to buck magnates over figures time after time. Their ideas over money amounts were not always realistic, yet most times, owners agreed or compromised at the least.

The financial health and stability of clubs throughout the majors demanded shrewd leaders meticulously wise to business.[10] Operating expenses were costly, and as salaries rose, owners were forced to make tough decisions that were unsatisfactory to players. More retraction in wages was expected, and the animosity of players was on the rise.

Comiskey was, despite all his substantial investments, going to wear the same badge his fellow owners wore: being labeled a penny-pincher and cheap. It was hard to imagine anyone calling Comiskey excessively frugal, as his freewheeling style of buying players, both from the majors and minors, was highly known. But in all, owners were tagged as being greedy, and Comiskey was lumped into the pile regardless of his proven record.

With regard to the recent hostilities in baseball, the *Sporting News* credited Comiskey as being the "best fighter" in the war against the Federal League, having "paid more money to keep star players" from the outlaw organization than any other magnate.[11]

The season's finish was demoralizing to Comiskey, especially since he'd paid so much money for proven stars, and he expressed his honest feelings when saying he was disappointed in the outcome. Even though the finish was not what he expected, Comiskey still praised his team and hoped for better results in 1916. Indicative of his divided mindset, the *Chicago Examiner* reported that Comiskey "thought more" about the capture of his prized moose, which had escaped his Wisconsin retreat, "than he did about the city championship."[12]

Following nearly two weeks of festivities at Camp Jerome, Comiskey returned to normalcy and tended to team operations. At the forefront of his mind was strengthening his club, and Ray Chapman of the Indians was at the top of a short list of big names he wanted to acquire. Frank "Home Run" Baker was also being sought after to fill the third base slot, and rumors were rampant that he was close to being purchased from the Philadelphia Athletics. Another proposition had Joe Jackson being traded to the New York Yankees for Fritz Maisel, and Clark Griffith of Washington wanted to unload Chick Gandil in a trade to the Sox for Jack Fournier.[13] None of these deals were made while Comiskey was in New York in December of 1915, but what was accomplished was a peaceful resolution to the Federal League war. Charles Weeghman, owner of the Federal League's Chicago franchise (the Whales), worked a deal to purchase the Chicago Cubs, thus moving the club from its residence on the West Side to his new stadium on the North Side at Addison and Clark Streets. Comiskey was all smiles. Even though his team outdrew both the Cubs and the Whales combined and he'd gained several noted stars during the course of the war, he was exceedingly happy that the conflict was over. It was believed that the Cubs' move northward was going to boost the popularity of Comiskey's club, as west-side fans turned their attention to the striking play of Buck Weaver, Ray Schalk, and the Sox.[14]

The ambiance at Comiskey Park remained electric through seasons of disappointment, injuries, weak batting, and utter failure. The longstanding popularity of the White Sox was uncanny, practically unrivaled anywhere in the majors. In 1915, the team drew an estimated 660,000-plus people at home, which led both leagues, and another 350,000 on the road.[15] Comiskey was renowned for creating the special atmosphere at his stadium, and the warm decorations, loud rooters, and bands combined to a memorable experience that kept people coming back day after day.

In response to his fans loyalty, Comiskey desperately wanted to reward them with a pennant. It was something he personally desired as well, as he was branded a "tough loser." Entering 1916, it was another year of promise, and after a decade of letdowns, the Sox needed to break the spell and produce a legitimate championship run.

The importance of baseball, however, took a backseat to the death of Charles Fredericks on January 11, 1916, at the age of thirty-eight. Immensely intelligent, Fredericks was the go-to business manager for the Sox from its inception through 1910, when illness thwarted his ability to perform full-time duties for the team. His value to Comiskey was limitless. Fredericks had toured with the Sox extensively as a road agent, made many friends with players and executives, and after being incapacitated by sickness, Comiskey announced that the Sox would never have another secretary as long as Fredericks lived.

Comiskey kept his word. Unfortunately, he was out of town when his nephew passed away but returned as quickly as possible to handle the funeral services.

In advance of the 1916 season, Rowland invoked a little psychological warfare with Joe Jackson, telling the press that Jackson might be coming off the bench to give more playing time to another outfielder.[16] Stunned by the news, Jackson rushed to Chicago and met with Rowland and Comiskey, affirming his commitment to the team and expressed his motivation to "out-hit Ty Cobb." To back his word, he planned to begin his training early to ensure he was in top flight condition once the team gathered in the spring.

Comiskey's frustrations over the previous season waned and he was feeling physically stronger after vacationing at a resort in Excelsior Springs, Missouri. He took comfort in the fact that his team was laced with offensive talent and that there were three batters with career averages over .300: Collins, Fournier, and Jackson. "It looks like the best hitting club I ever had in Chicago," he told the *Sporting News* in its February 17, 1916, edition, and with "some great pitching and catching, the boys ought to go out and win a lot of games." While Comiskey wasn't planning to raise the championship banner just yet, he was highly optimistic and expected his club to be in the race from the start.

Rowland's fresh perspective, plus Comiskey's awareness about the various explanations of why the Sox were underachieving, prompted an important new philosophy toward spring training. For years, the team left Chicago in late February and experienced long trips from either California or Texas with well over sixty exhibition games played by two squads. Sportswriters were often critical of the grueling schedule, blaming it on the club's inability to maintain its strength in the heart of a race. Rowland and Comiskey decided that this year, the trip was to begin on March 12, and the team was going to play half the exhibitions it usually did.

The formula had its pros and cons, but no one could say that the team's management wasn't actively trying to come up with novel ways to inspire winning baseball.

One of the major happenings of the American League in early 1916 was the financial catastrophe facing owner Charles W. Somers of the Cleveland Indians. In fact, his situation was so gloomy that bankers had confiscated his stock and were selling the club for $560,000.[17] Ban Johnson took a heightened interest in the struggles of Somers because the latter had been such a big part of the American League's growth as well as being a close personal friend of both Johnson and Comiskey. A wealthy businessman in the early 1900s, Somers' vast fortune aided a number of different clubs during the early days of the organization, including the White Sox, and now that the tables were turned, Johnson and Comiskey were ready to repay the favor.

There was little hesitation in helping Somers, and Johnson formed a Chicago-based syndicate to purchase the Indians. At the head of the group was James C. Dunn, an eminent contractor in Chicago, who'd assume the presidency of the Cleveland club. Dunn, as well as minority shareholder, John Valentine Burns, were members of the Woodland Bards, the pro-Comiskey outfit. Burns even went as far back as being an original director of the White Sox Rooters' Association in 1908 and spent a lot of time shoulder-to-shoulder with Comiskey at Camp Jerome, fishing and hunting.

Even more remarkable, the exit of Somers made it possible for both Johnson and Comiskey to become shareholders in the Cleveland franchise at the cost of $100,000 each. Their investment was really just a loan to Dunn with stock being handed over as collateral. Comiskey later admitted that he invested in the Indians "for the purpose of relieving a tense situation" and that he "never held onto the stock with any idea of profiteering" from it.[18] Their ownership was kept secret from the public, although the *Sporting News* did indicate that there were silent partners in the new syndicate.[19]

Neither Comiskey nor Rowland were successful in making any substantial additions to the club prior to spring training, and the extravagant "White Sox Special" departed Chicago with over sixty travelers, including nearly two dozen players.[20] As part of the send-off party at the train station, 3,000 faithful displayed their support and optimism was the prevailing sentiment amongst fans going into the new season. Comiskey, joined by members of his family, went south with the club, mixing business with pleasure, but made a point to return to Chicago in plenty of time to visit Camp Jerome once more before the season began.

When camp opened, rookie Zeb Terry from Stanford University was named the starting shortstop after impressing Rowland during spring exhibitions, and Buck Weaver was moved to third. Native Chicagoan Jack Ness was another touted prospect for the Sox in camp. He was a veteran of the minors and batted over .300 for Oakland of the Pacific Coast League. If for any reason Fournier fell apart at first base, Ness was waiting on deck.[21]

In preparation for the home opener, Comiskey made a wide number of improvements at his stadium; from a new scoreboard to colorful decorations everywhere imaginable. The infield was completely reworked and seats were given a new coat of green paint. When Opening Day finally arrived on April 12, 1916, a good number of the 31,000 fans at the park found traces of still wet paint on their clothes when they stood up, a dismal bonus to a losing game, as starter Reb Russell was pummeled in a 4–0 loss to Detroit. That night, at the Chicago Automobile Club, the Woodland Bards hosted a banquet for a group of Dubuque rooters, and Comiskey made a potent statement: "Clarence Rowland will be manager of the White Sox as long as I am owner and president of the club."[22] No doubt everyone at the event was in a festive mood and Comiskey's declaration, popular with the guests from Dubuque, was going to be contingent on Rowland's production of at least several pennant victories.

But it was quickly apparent that the 1916 team wasn't on the right track, and by early May, the team was playing .500 ball and in sixth place. Four straight losses to Cleveland later in the month was discomforting and somewhat of a jolt to those expecting much more from the South-Siders. The Indians, under Dunn and his partners, were making great headway in the American League and sitting atop the standings. The most likely reason for their hot start was the superior play of Tris Speaker, who had been purchased from the Boston Red Sox before the start of the season.[23]

The press jumped on the rumor that Rowland was going to be fired for the club's erratic behavior on the field, but Comiskey shrugged it off as being irresponsible blabber.[24] It was only a slump, and Rowland just needed time to figure things out. But amidst the gossip was the possibility that in addition to the dismissal of the manager, players were going to be traded or sold. The fact was that Comiskey was not getting a return on the high salaries he was paying his athletes and a breaking point was approaching. On May 24, the Sox were in last place with a 13–19 record and, as James Crusinberry of the *Tribune* noted, the team couldn't "be playing any worse."

The members of the White Sox were said to be depressed and lacking the will to win. On the last day of a road trip in Washington, the team held a players only meeting and impassioned speakers roused the spirit of the dejected. The session was intended to inspire—and it worked. On May 28, the club won both games of a doubleheader against Cleveland before an audience of 30,000. Taking on the challenge of getting back to .500, the Sox were in a different mode, and the massive offensive power of the team was being displayed more and more. Finally, they achieved the goal, resting at 28–28 on June 24, but they were still in sixth with plenty of room to gain ground in the standings.

Claude "Lefty" Williams was steadily improving and was a key member of the pitching staff. His contributions helped the Sox into third place and a 50–40 record. During the latter part of July, Comiskey exercised an option on Charles "Swede" Risberg, an infielder in the Pacific Coast League.[25] A few weeks later, another signing was made, but this individual was much more recognizable. William "Kid" Gleason, released prior to the 1915 season, was brought back to aid Rowland in the management of the team.[26] Where he was once deemed disposable, Gleason's value was now recognized in terms of coaching, influence, and connecting to the players. His return was applauded by the Sox roster, and all reports that he was going to replace Rowland were promptly denied.

The evolution of abilities of Williams, Risberg, and the rest were going to be highly impacted by the return of Gleason, and the Sox were a little closer to making history with his reappearance. Amazingly, even before "Kid" rejoined the team, the Sox demonstrated their grit by taking hold of first place in the American League to start the month of August. It was a brief stretch, as the Boston Red Sox were determined to reign supreme and assume the lead. Slumping again in August, Chicago nosedived back into third, but the race remained competitive well into September. When the season ended, they were alone in second place behind Boston, possessing a respectable 89–65 record.

Respectable, yes, but it still was not a pennant. The White Sox were not in the World Series, and Comiskey was, once again, highly disappointed.

It is hard to pacify an ultra-competitive spirit and impossible to do so by always finishing in a position other than first. Comiskey yearned for a winner and it was becoming harder and harder to maintain his positive attitude. For the money he was paying, he felt he was owed it and his players were failing him. From his regular seat at the rear of the grandstand, he was

glued to the action of every home game, reacting emotionally and anima-
tedly to close plays, feeling the all too familiar pain of being let down. The
failure to achieve a championship was reflective of his ownership ability and
decision making, which, incidentally, he redirected toward the players
themselves since their on-field actions were responsible. "I might have gone
out on first base myself last year and maybe we would have won the pennant," Comiskey told the *Tribune*.[27]

The annual Chicago city series was a formality at this point, and the
White Sox were in dominant shape on the mound, in the field, and behind
the bat.[28] At Comiskey Park on October 4, 1916, the series began and the Sox
were victorious by the score of 8–2 before 17,250 fans. James Crusinberry of
the *Tribune* explained that the game lacked the old passion displayed by the
crowd and summed it up by saying that the time honored rivalry between
the clubs was gone.[29] The Sox were unstoppable against the Cubs and ended
up winning four straight and capturing their sixth consecutive city title. If an
MVP of the series had to be selected, it was hard to dismiss the outstanding
play of Joe Jackson, whose offensive production was off the charts. He batted
.500 (7–14) and smashed a trio of doubles in the third game.

Less impressed with a local pennant, Comiskey vacated the city for his
Wisconsin camp. While en route along the Manitowish River, his party was
caught in a cold rainstorm and the Sox owner caught a serious cold, bordering on pneumonia.[30] While he made sure his guests were afforded all
the luxuries of the camp, he stayed mostly bedridden. His recuperation was
to continue at Excelsior Springs, but he felt well enough to visit relatives at
Notre Dame, and then traveled to Cody, Wyoming with Ban Johnson and
Indians co-owner John Burns to hunt and view some property.[31]

Comiskey was mum on the status of Clarence Rowland and the managerial position. Lots of rumors were floating around in the press; even talk
that John McGraw of the New York Giants was Rowland's replacement.[32]
Apparently, Comiskey wanted to make it known that no jobs were safe, and
that by prolonging an announcement, he was giving his manager time to
think and rethink his strategy for 1917. It was time to make good, as his job
was in jeopardy. Shortly before Christmas, Comiskey declared Rowland
would be back for his third year at the helm of the Sox.

Before the start of the 1917 season, the friendship of Comiskey and
Johnson was never stronger. The latter gave Comiskey a set of golf clubs
and the two planned to learn the sport during a late December trip to
Excelsior Springs with their wives.[33] Similar in so many ways, the friends

were almost like brothers, but just around the corner was a life altering disagreement fixed within the structure of baseball—one that would tear them apart forever.

ENDNOTES

1 Eddie Collins signed a three year contract to remain a member of the Philadelphia Athletics for the 1915–17 seasons, on July 21, 1914. At the time, he received a significant pay increase from a reported $6,000 a year to upwards of $14,000 annually. *Philadelphia Inquirer*, July 22, 1914, p. 10.

2 *Sporting News*, January 9, 1936, p. 5.

3 *Sporting News*, December 16, 1915, p. 1.

4 Rowland was a fighter in every sense of the word, both in terms of arguing with umpires over calls and in literal fisticuffs. During one particularly high tension game against the Cleveland Indians on June 25, 1916, at Comiskey Park, Buck Weaver got into an on field scrap with Ivan Howard, clearing both benches. Rowland was in the thick of the battle and reportedly gained a "vice grip" on one unfortunate member of Cleveland. *Chicago Daily Tribune*, June 26, 1916, p. 11.

5 Comiskey complained about the American League umpiring, saying it was the worst he'd ever seen. *Chicago Daily Tribune*, July 22, 1915, p. 11.

6 Due to the July 4 holiday in 1915, Comiskey didn't receive information from Connie Mack of the Philadelphia Athletics that Jack Barry was on the market. By the time he placed a bid, Barry was already sold to the Boston Red Sox. *Chicago Daily Tribune*, August 9, 1915, p. 9.

7 The *Sporting News*, on October 28, 1915, indicated that if Comiskey would have signed Jack Barry, his team would have likely captured the American League pennant. Barry, in turn, helped the Red Sox win not only the pennant, but also the World Series. Reports claimed that if Comiskey landed Barry, Buck Weaver would have been moved to third base.

8 The White Sox finished the 1915 campaign in third place with a 93–61 record. Boston and Detroit snagged 101 and 100 wins, respectively, and the Red Sox captured the World Series title with a 4 games to 1 victory over the Philadelphia Phillies.

9 Owner of the Pittsburgh Pirates, Barney Dreyfuss was quoted as saying that, "years ago, we had men of our clubs who played baseball because they loved the game," and that they rarely "had differences over salary." He explained that now, the sport had "financiers in their places," and that money was "uppermost" in players' minds. *Sporting News*, March 18, 1920, p. 8.

10 It was estimated that magnates were investing $1 million or more to finance their teams and it was a necessity that they were "businessmen first and sportsmen afterward." *Chicago Daily Tribune*, December 3, 1916, p. A4.

11 *Sporting News*, December 30, 1915, p. 1.

12 Camp Jerome, Comiskey's Wisconsin retreat, had been the home of his pet moose "Big Bill" since it was a calf. Bill escaped by trampling through a fence

and Comiskey offered a $300 reward. Some weeks later, an Indian named Jim Cowboy located the moose in Brule, Wisconsin, more than 100 miles away. *Chicago Examiner*, October 12, 1915 and *Chicago Daily Tribune*, October 12, 1915.

13 Washington Senators manager Clark Griffith and first baseman Chick Gandil were at odds despite the latter's powerful batting and solid fielding. Griffith made it known that he wanted to trade Gandil and the latter was on the market throughout the latter part of 1915 and into early 1916. It was reported that Griffith parted ways with Gandil because the latter smoked cigarettes.

Also see: *Sporting News*, March 23, 1916, p. 6 and *Sporting News*, March 30, 1916, p. 4. An earlier "response" from Chicago regarding the proposed Gandil for Jack Fournier trade stated that Fournier wouldn't be sent to Washington "for a half dozen Gandils." *Sporting News*, November 25, 1915, p. 7.

14 *Sporting News*, December 30, 1915, p. 7.

15 Official attendance numbers at Comiskey Park were rarely given out as club policy. Estimates were offered for all major league teams in 1915. Boston was the second biggest draw and Cleveland was worst, drawing 211,100 at home. *Sporting News*, January 6, 1916, p. 3.

16 *Chicago Daily Tribune*, January 15, 1916, p. 10.

Also see: *Sporting News*, January 27, 1916, p. 4.

A few weeks later, George S. Robbins of the *Sporting News* advocated the trade of Joe Jackson for Fritz Maisel of the New York Yankees. Another article asserted that Comiskey had wasted large amounts of money on Larry Chappell and Lena Blackburne but that his failures didn't stop him from "overpaying for Jackson." In February 1916, Chappell was sent to the Cleveland Indians as the third player in the Jackson trade. *Sporting News*, February 24, 1916, p. 1, 4. Chappell turned up overweight at spring training and was later released by Cleveland to Columbus of the American Association.

17 *Sporting Life*, February 26, 1916.

The article stated that the purchase price may have been $50,000 less than Cleveland bankers originally asked, putting the amount at $510,000. Other publications estimated the price to be as low as $450,000.

18 *New York Tribune*, February 10, 1920, p. 12.

19 *Sporting News*, March 2, 1916, p. 1.

20 Comiskey always ensured his athletes trekked to spring training in style. For well over a decade, he spent considerable sums to furnish a high-class train for his entire outfit. Prior to the 1916 journey, it was announced that management had arranged for a special bowling alley on one of the train cars, as well as a putting green in another. The press mentioned that a rivalry existed between Comiskey and Charles Weeghman, owner of the Cubs, regarding the various luxuries their train offered—as if they were one upping each other to provide a better quality ride. *Boston Journal*, February 28, 1916, p. 9.

21 Fournier's production as a hitter fell off considerably in 1916 and Jack Ness did assume the first baseman's role. Ness ended up batting .267 and Fournier .240. Fournier, it was said, was an unnatural first baseman, and that contributed to his

unimpressive numbers. He'd rather play right field. *Sporting News*, December 21, 1916, p. 4.

22 *Chicago Daily Tribune*, April 13, 1916, p. 14.

23 Ed Bang of *Sporting Life* indicated that James Dunn's willingness to spend "coin" for players rivaled that of Comiskey. Dunn reportedly claimed that Speaker cost more than Eddie Collins or Joe Jackson and might have been $60,000 cash. *Sporting Life*, April 15, 1916, p. 8. Comiskey had nothing but compliments about Speaker. *Chicago Daily Tribune*, May 21, 1916, p. B2.

24 *Chicago Daily Tribune*, May 23, 1916, p. 15.

25 *Chicago Daily Tribune*, July 27, 1916, p. 11.

26 *Chicago Daily Tribune*, August 20, 1916, p. B1.

27 *Chicago Daily Tribune*, December 20, 1916, p. 15.

28 The 1916 city series ended in a four straight game victory for the White Sox, played between Wednesday, October 4, and Saturday, October 7. Prior to game four, there was considerable talk about what a game five would mean to the owners, upwards of $18,000 in gate money, and how all of that big-time Sunday money would be lost if the Sox won. Gamblers, reportedly, were also in on the hype, betting that the Cubs were going to win because the series was definitely going to play out through Sunday. But it didn't, and James Crusinberry of the *Tribune* denoted that the series "scored one for the honesty of baseball." Also see: *Chicago Daily Tribune*, October 7, 1916, p. 13 and October 8, 1916, p. B1.

29 *Chicago Daily Tribune*, October 5, 1916, p. 6.

30 *Chicago Daily Tribune*, October 23, 1916, p. 14.

31 Comiskey and Johnson were contemplating buying a huge tract of land in Wyoming. Along with Joe Ray and Ray Ketcham, they were looking at purchasing 8,000 acres and then leasing 12,000 more with the intent of entering the beef manufacturing business. *Chicago Daily Tribune*, November 24, 1916, p. 14.

32 *Chicago Daily Tribune*, October 5, 1916, p. 11.
Another piece of gossip had George Stovall, who had managed the St. Louis Browns and Kansas City Packers, replacing Rowland.

33 Johnson bought two sets of golf clubs, giving one to Comiskey, and keeping the other for himself. He also gave Comiskey a wristwatch, which had yet to become completely socially popular. Comiskey shied away from the watch and I.E. Sanborn of *Sporting Life* explained that Comiskey felt the item was "too faddish for him." *Chicago Daily Tribune*, December 20, 1916, p. 15 and *Sporting Life*, January 6, 1917, p. 5. Public accounts of Johnson's thoughtfulness toward Comiskey sporadically show up in historical records. In 1913, Johnson commissioned a special painting of Comiskey in his outdoor gear and holding a knife, standing toe-to-toe with a large bear. The painting was representative of "The Trapper," Comiskey's nickname in the wooded environment. It was presented to him at a surprise Chicago Automobile Club banquet. *Chicago Daily Tribune*, November 5, 1913, p. 17.

14

THE HAPPIEST MAN IN CHICAGO

The successful end of the Federal League war was a mammoth achievement for Organized Baseball and renewed popularity in 1916 seemed to allow many people to breathe a sigh of relief. After all, the sport was on the upswing. But the positivity and good feelings were met by a continued ground swell from within the ranks of the players. Lawyer David L. Fultz, a graduate of Brown University and member of four major league clubs between 1898 and 1905, was the driving force for a union known as the Baseball Players' Fraternity. The union, formed initially in 1912, worked to ensure a level of fairness in contracts and salaries, and gave the athletes a unified voice when going up against owners.

Magnates were on the record throughout the 1915 and '16 seasons, adamantly declaring that there was going to be a reduction in salary figures. Wartime contracts, which were used by owners to protect their players from jumping to the Federal League, were expiring, and the decline in monetary amounts was a demoralizing thought to Fultz and the athletes he represented. As things were coming to a climax, Fultz issued a list of four demands and an ultimatum, threatening a strike by as many as 700 players if the requests were not heeded.[1]

Notably, the proposed decrease in wages were not publically mentioned as one of the complaints by the union, but owners and sportswriters saw through the haze and put two and two together. Owner Barney Dreyfuss of the Pittsburgh Pirates said Fultz's tactic was nothing more than an "organized holdout," and the strike threat was an attempt to dissuade owners from following through with their promise.[2] Ban Johnson was fearless in his approach to the Fraternity, warning players that their actions might have long term consequences affecting their future standing in the American League.

The always bold Joe Vila, a New York based correspondent for the *Sporting News*, explained that, "the players as a whole have done so much harm to the national pastime that the public will relish a complete victory for the magnates which would result in a reduction of inflated craniums and a new spirit of sportsmanship on the diamond."[3] He added that "greedy players" were attempting to gain a stranglehold on owners by "hogging the money" that the public was expected to pay, and fans had "no use for the overpaid players who wear jewelry and drive expensive motorcars." Sportswriters estimated that $1.5 million was paid for players' salaries in 1916.[4]

Brooklyn owner Charles H. Ebbets, coming off a pennant winning season in the National League, was at the forefront of trying to shrink his payroll, and faced dire consequences. Ten of his players were unhappy with the new terms and holding out for more money. The *Sporting News* indicated that if the members of the Brooklyn club showed "as much energy" in the World Series against Boston as they were "in protesting against the cuts in pay," the games "might have been more interesting."[5] Brooklyn was defeated by the Red Sox, 4–1.

The magnates were far from faultless. In fact, Francis Richter of the *Philadelphia Press* declared that owners were responsible for a "large share of blame for the attitude of the players" and the general spike in commercialism.[6] Their "willingness to exploit both the game and the players were promptly seized by the players as a means of financial aggrandizement—for which they can hardly be blamed, as they were out to get the largest reward possible for their services, just as the magnates were out to secure the largest possible patronage for the game."

Owners and players alike were awarded with stereotypical and sordid reputations based on the behavior of the most press worthy. The same sort of greed that magnates displayed was matched by an annual list of holdouts; the men who were dead set on remaining on the sidelines until their employers paid up. Both sides of the complicated matter were settled into the customary routine that sparked up when contract talks came around, and altogether, it wasn't a sound representation of gentlemanly sportsmanship and a collective working for the betterment of baseball.

Interestingly enough, members of the same team could have starkly different opinions of their boss depending on whether or not they were happy with their salaries. Each athlete unquestionably envisioned dollar signs in a personal way, figuring they were worth at least a certain amount. If they were satisfied at contract time, their boss was considered financially liberal and perhaps even generous. If not, the owner was nothing more than a tightwad, eternally greedy, and failing to see the true value of his players. This same disgruntled athlete was liable to voice complaints to fellow teammates and maybe sportswriters, spreading a singular perception of the owner that perpetuated these stereotypes.

When it came time to negotiate contracts, Charles Comiskey had to minimize memories of his own personal experiences as a ball player. The days of playing when a love for the game superseded any desire to become wealthy on the diamond were long gone. Baseball was a business, and at contract time, he was faced with the challenges of any other owner. He had to try and accommodate and pacify the members of his team.

Comiskey and his secretary Harry Grabiner had a system of preparing contracts that assessed the individual player's contributions for the previous season. To a lesser degree, it took into consideration one's potential in the future, hopes, and promises, but most importantly, it was how they performed day in and day out in the thick of the recent pennant chase.

In the instance of Eddie Collins, Comiskey agreed to a set salary that wasn't contingent on his substantiating his worth on the field, and that was extremely rare. Had Collins been tendered a contract for 1917 based on a story going around that Comiskey was unpleased with the second baseman's play, he likely would have seen a salary offer lower than his reported $15,000 a year.[7]

The foundation for Comiskey and Grabiner in drawing up contracts for the Sox was that simple—it was based on proven value. A slumping player had opportunities to break out of their funk, but a man out of shape and collecting a sizable paycheck for doing very little was a sincere detriment. And owners had to be weary of players sitting back and cashing checks. Washington Senators manager and part-owner Clark Griffith decided not to offer any contracts for longer than a year to avoid such situations and used a bonus system to reward players for verifiable results.[8] Griffith managed the Sox in 1901–02, and was mentored by Comiskey, who had used bonuses back to his days in St. Paul, perhaps even earlier.

Following an evaluation by Comiskey and Grabiner, contracts were mailed out and the numbers weren't always attractive to the recipients.[9] Players felt they deserved more time and again, regardless of the owner, the team, or the financial circumstances. But once the initial contract was mailed out and returned unsigned, it didn't mean there wasn't room to negotiate. Comiskey, throughout his tenure as an owner, showed his willingness to compromise, and if it meant he needed to bend a little more, so be it.

James Crusinberry of the *Chicago Daily Tribune* detailed Comiskey's proficient ability to sign his men to contracts in the face of financial disagreements in a column on January 21, 1917.[10] Owing to his considerable experience, plus the advantage of being on his home turf in the confines of his executive office—likely with Grabiner looking on—Comiskey was expertly persuasive. He began by asking the player what salary he wanted, then, after being told, wanted to know why the player deserved that amount. Once the player offered his reasoning, mostly promises for next season, Comiskey focused on the year previous, pinpointing specific moments of fault on the field.

In the article, Crusinberry explained that after Comiskey finished elaborating on all of the flawed play, the athlete's "idea of his own worth probably . . . shrunk about $2,000 a year." Conversely, it was added that if a player was giving his all throughout the season, "he generally [found] a substantial increase in his pay without the asking."

Several books have reiterated the same callous "take it or leave it" declaration by either Comiskey or Grabiner when confronted by a disgruntled player.[11] The repeated statement paints Comiskey to be completely inflexible in his contractual discussions, which is again refuted by over two decades of team ownership and player management. In a moment of fury or stubbornness, it is easily possible to see Comiskey make such a proclamation. But since he had such a substantial investment in the members of his team, it would prove costly to let any of his superstars walk off the job for any length of time. Through a mixture of compromise and persuasion, Comiskey figured out a way to settle amicably.

"The only time I couldn't reason with my players," Comiskey explained in Crusinberry's article, "was during war times, such as while the Federal League was going. Several times, players came to me asking for more money. When I asked them why they wanted it and they answered because they could get it from the other fellows, I had no argument to make. All I could do was to thank them for giving me the chance to meet it or refuse it."

When Comiskey was faced with the prospect of losing his players to a rival league, he made the necessary financial concessions to keep them happy. It wasn't a matter of "taking it or leaving it," but coming to a peaceful resolution. Going in 1917, there wasn't a third major league striving to sign away talent, but Comiskey was still not in a place to discard his athletes over pay squabbles. There were salary decreases on the Sox, but only minor ones. First baseman Jack Ness became a holdout over a $500 reduction and was released. Red Faber was also a holdout, but signed just prior to the team's journey to Mineral Wells, Texas, for spring training.[12]

Despite all of the contentions that Comiskey was highly economical and that his men were so vastly underpaid, the White Sox payroll was one of the highest in the major leagues. According to an estimate by the *New York Times*, Comiskey paid a salary list of about $130,000 in 1916 and the amounts were not expected to change much in 1917.[13] Only one team, the New York Giants—including the salary of manager John McGraw—was higher.[14]

Altogether, Comiskey paid his men more than the world champion Boston Red Sox, New York Yankees, Cleveland Indians, and Detroit Tigers; and outside the Giants, every team in the National League.

Considering that fact, it wasn't hard to believe that Comiskey's men displayed loyalty in the baseball difficulties of early 1917.[15] Eddie Cicotte, Joe Benz, Ray Schalk, and Lefty Williams were reportedly members of the union but were completely against going on strike. The argument of the Players' Fraternity slowly fizzled out in February, and the strike that once seemed intimidating, evaporated into thin air.[16]

The festive members of the Woodland Bards were always looking for a reason to celebrate, and over the course of two days, January 13–14, 1917, they ate, drank, and were merry in dedication of the new Bards' trophy room at Comiskey Park.[17] Trophies, in this sense, were the stuffed heads and birds from their hunting expeditions, which went hand-in-hand with the array of delicacies they enjoyed, from venison to quail. Each animal represented a different and unique story and the Bards were all too ready to recite the tales in the most humorous fashion.

Comiskey was called away from the second evening of festivities for the Christening of his first grandchild. Dorothy Elizabeth was born to Lou and Grace Comiskey on December 26, 1916, and a party was held at the latter's home on Ingleside Avenue. After the familial event concluded, Comiskey raced back to the park to rejoin his friends in all their outrageousness.

Another deeply personal situation arose in 1917 that needed to be addressed. Ed Walsh, the heart and soul of the Sox pitching rotation for years, had attempted numerous comebacks and was given nothing but time to try to regain his lost ability. Stories that he was unconditionally released surfaced and it wasn't until the team was departing for spring training that it was apparent that Walsh's days as a member of the Sox were over.[18] Comiskey cared for Walsh and wanted him to make good in his post-baseball life, offering to finance a business endeavor for him in any city he wanted. However, Walsh didn't give up trying to return, briefly pitching for the Boston Braves, Milwaukee Brewers, and Bridgeport Americans before retiring for good in 1920. He was also a manager in the minors, and in the early 1920s, returned to the Sox as a coach.

Prior to heading to Mineral Wells for spring training, Comiskey and Rowland needed to address the longstanding first base problem. Cleveland was having a similar difficulty with their veteran, Arnold "Chick" Gandil, and considering their options.[19] Gandil, originally from Minnesota, was the son of a gardener and spent time in his youth living in Seattle, Washington and Oakland, California.[20] It was from the latter home that he broke out onto his own as a teenager, living all over the Southwest part of the U.S., playing baseball and boxing. He used his height (6'1") and great strength to earn a living in either athletics or at hard labor and earned a reputation as a tough guy.

It didn't take long for Gandil to earn that same repute on the diamond. He was the type of player who could take a beating, including being injured, and remain in the game; fighting for every play. At first base, he was well above average, being able to snag off-line throws in all directions and was even known for catching with both hands. On offense, he was streaky, and when he was on fire, he was a true asset. But when he originally joined the White Sox in 1909, he couldn't hit a curve ball and was bounced from the team without much notice in September of 1910. Gandil's memory was strong, and in 1915, when Washington wanted to trade him to the Sox for Jack Fournier, he protested feverously.[21]

Times had changed, and in light of his unfavorable popularity in Cleveland and poor showing, a new start was desirable. On February 25, 1917, Comiskey purchased Gandil from the Indians for at least $5,000, according to the *Tribune*, and writer John Alcock was convinced that the Sox were headed for the pennant now that first base had been sufficiently strengthened. [22]

Briefly considered a "holdout" before meeting Comiskey in Texas and signing a contract, Gandil was seemingly unbothered by the fact that he was going to be playing next to one of his biggest on-field adversaries, second baseman Eddie Collins. The rivalry between Gandil and Collins went back nearly five years when Gandil was with Washington and Collins was with Philadelphia. During a game in June of 1912, Collins lifted his knee and smashed

Gandil in the face when the latter was attempting to steal a base.[23] It was called deliberate, and although he suffered a broken nose, injured cheek, and a black eye, Gandil remained in the game. Two weeks later, Gandil retaliated by trying to spike Collins in Washington.[24] Both were professionals and had a job to do for Comiskey, so any personal feelings had to be repressed.

With the entrance into World War I expected, magnates and managers decided to coordinate an effort to train their players in the ways of military drill. Prompted by New York Yankees' part owner Captain T. L'H. Huston, the idea was immediately embraced by Comiskey, Ban Johnson, and other owners. Comiskey hurriedly lined up a young sergeant named Walter Smiley of Pennsylvania, who was working as a recruiter in the "Windy City." Smiley was no stranger to baseball, having coached several army teams, and was a capable disciplinarian. He accompanied the club to Mineral Wells and taught marching, physical training, and company drill. Players used their bats as rifles and the Sox took to the daily regimen fairly easy.

It was a matter of pride for Comiskey to see his team adhering to a military-type structure. Regardless if the players knew it or not at the time, their actions were strengthening the club's teamwork, as well as sharpening their minds and improving their physical condition. Pro-Chicago sportswriters were expressing their confidence in the Sox, touting the slugging of Joe Jackson, Swede Risberg at shortstop, and Happy Felsch in the outfield. Of all players, pitcher Eddie Cicotte probably benefited the most from the military training.

Admittedly, Cicotte didn't take baseball seriously enough, and skidded by on pure talent without putting in the extra effort to train.[25] Motivated by Sergeant Smiley and personally rejuvenated, he really "worked"; putting in the added time to get in shape. The *Sporting News* noted that Cicotte gave up drinking beer and that drinking had prevented him from becoming the stellar hurler he had morphed into. On April 14, 1917, shortly after the season began, Cicotte pitched a no-hitter at St. Louis, defeating the Browns by the score of 11–0.[26] It was a remarkable achievement and indicated his early state of readiness when it usually took more time for him to round into shape.

Rowland led his team into first place early in the season, yet the snide comments by detractors still continued.[27] Some people just couldn't be convinced that he was a big league leader and the kind of manager who could inspire victories. The competition in the American League was thick and the path to the championship was not going to be an easy endeavor.

Tension across the major leagues increased when Congress declared war on Germany, officially entering the Great War. No one was quite sure how it was going to impact baseball and those involved.

For the home opener at Comiskey Park on April 19, the members of the Sox marched onto the field in army uniforms and holding rifles, putting on a motivational show for patrons. The military drilling of baseball players was credited with stimulating high-levels of patriotism. Comiskey himself was inspired. He vowed to donate 10 percent of all receipts from home games during the 1917 season to the American Red Cross, and was the only major league owner to do so.[28] He routinely invited soldiers and sailors from the various installations around the Chicago area to be his guests at Comiskey Park, including the Seventh Regiment stationed right near the ball grounds on Wentworth Avenue. Teamed with the Woodland Bards, he donated hundreds, perhaps thousands, of baseball uniforms to the military. And in July, the Sox and Philadelphia Athletics played a morning exhibition game for the soldiers at Fort Sheridan. In addition, if the military ever needed use of his stadium, it was available to them free of cost. U.S. Army Adjutant General Henry McCain was a close friend of Comiskey and appreciated all of his efforts as well of that of Ban Johnson and Captain Huston.[29]

The excessive hype about Chicago's chances wore off when the Sox fell to third place.

Joe Jackson, Eddie Collins, and Buck Weaver were underperforming on offense and no member of the team was batting .300.[30] Cicotte, at times, appeared to be carrying the team on his back, and behind Rowland's ingenuity, the Sox won eight in a row from May 12 to 19 against the Yankees, Athletics, and Red Sox. The focus was on Cicotte and his unhittable style of pitching, and throughout the season, managers and players griped about his alleged use of an illegal "shineball."[31] They claimed he was doctoring the ball in some way and halted action numerous times to examine the balls he threw.[32] Some were even forwarded to Ban Johnson, but the latter found no evidence.

Fast becoming the most efficient pitcher in the league, Cicotte was proving his smarts by invoking a psychological element into his repertoire.[33] With so much being talked about his unique style, many batters were already mentally defeated when they stepped into the box to face him. They were fearful of his reputed shineball, thus making his fastball or knuckler so much more potent. Every move he made was watched, and managers like Lee Fohl of the Indians and Clark Griffith of the Senators were waiting to catch him in the wicked act of altering the ball . . . but they never did.

Taking 19 out of 23 games from mid-May to mid-June, Chicago fought their way back into first place, edging out the ever competitive Red Sox. But during a road trip into Boston, things took a turn for the strange. For years, "Beantown" was one of the most notorious gambling centers in all of baseball. At both American and National League parks, betting was flaunted out in the open, and most of the time, very little was done to curb the actions of gamblers. On Saturday, June 16, the White Sox were leading when rain halted the game in the top of the fifth inning. Hooligans proceeded to rush the field, physically interfering with Chicago players in the hope that it would be called—reportedly because gamblers were big losers in the series and couldn't bear another loss.

In the melee, Buck Weaver and Fred McMullin were arrested and charged with assault and battery.[34] Oddly, they were the ones being attacked by the riotous crowd and were simply defending themselves. The game was resumed and Chicago ended up winning 7–2 when Cicotte outpitched Babe Ruth.

Watching his team play impressively, then lose embarrassingly—like a five error game against Cleveland on June 30 in an 11–1 loss—Comiskey planned a quiet getaway with his wife, niece Mabel Bernoudy, and her children Marie and Albert to Yellowstone Park. The trip was custom-timed to coordinate with a July road trip, as Comiskey liked to be home when his team was. Shortly before he left town, Ruth was suspended for ten games after a run-in with an umpire, severely hindering Boston's chances to challenge for the pennant.

The Sox improved in batting as a team, advancing to third in the league (their highest ranking as a franchise), and individually, as Weaver, Felsch, Jackson, and Collins improved their numbers. Weaver, a vital member of the squad, suffered a broken index finger on his left hand in a collision with Ed Ainsmith of Washington on August 10.[35] The loss of such a big on-field presence and fan favorite was bad news to Comiskey, and, in response, he sent an inquiry to veteran infielder Bobby Byrne, recently of the Phillies, and signed him. However, Byrne didn't pan out, only participating in one game, and was released in September. Rowland sent McMullin to fill the third base vacancy and he did so well that once Weaver came back, he was temporarily moved to shortstop to keep McMullin in the game.[36]

Going into the stretch, a serious push in the standings gave the Sox momentum, which was done with a combined effort of clutch hitting, dazzling pitching, and exceptional leadership by Rowland and Kid Gleason. Even with a lead of more than five games over Boston, the team didn't let up, practicing extensively and playing exhibitions on off days to keep in form. Red Sox owner Harry Frazee wanted to derail Chicago's drive, offering a $1,000 bonus to each of his players if they could top the White Sox at the end of the season.

Unfortunately for Frazee, the financial incentive was too little too late, and although it was practically determined that Chicago was headed to the World Series, Comiskey remained low key. On the afternoon of September 21, he closely monitored a telegraph machine imparting information from a game at Fenway Park in Boston. Frustrated by the sluggish arrival of news on the "ticker," he turned to the telephone and waited out a dramatic ten-inning victory, 2–1, led by Red Faber and Shano Collins. The win officially secured an American League pennant for Chicago.

Comiskey was wrought with emotion. John Alcock of the *Tribune* noted that his hand was visibly shaking and about the first thing Comiskey did was turn to his son Lou, telling him to call his mother and share the news.[37] His nerves were almost wracked to the point in which he was unable to speak and needed time to regain his equilibrium. Shortly thereafter, he wired congratulations to Rowland and his team, telling the manager to buy them "as fine a dinner as you can with my compliments," and according to the *Tribune*, he stopped just short of telling Rowland to "Buy 'em Boston if you can get it."

Players were treated to a victory party that night at a downtown tavern, and the club reportedly "spared no money to get the best Boston had."[38] The *Tribune* reported that the "lid was off for the evening so the boys could make merry."[39]

Comiskey's eleven years of frustration were over. He chased and chased the elusive championship of his league, buying players with reckless abandon and trying to build a respectable contender for his fans. Finally, he'd done so with a mixture of proven stars and developed talent. Their final record was 100 wins and 54 losses; exemplary in every way. For the team's manager, Clarence Rowland, he was given his due as a legitimate and credible leader, and Comiskey's decision to hire him was vindicated. But there was still one series to go, and John McGraw's New York Giants were no pushover.

Winning the coin toss, Comiskey elected his home park as the venue for the first two games, which were going to be the first World Series at Comiskey Park. He went into full preparation mode, working fourteen-hour days to stomp out the crooked work of scalpers and handling the applications for reservations. Thousands of requests poured into his office, and Comiskey was faced with having to turn down many of his loyal enthusiasts once the reserved seating limits were reached. In turn, he received letters of anger, which caused him much anguish. The last thing he wanted to do was disappoint his faithful supporters. The *Tribune* estimated that there were as many as 283,000 disheartened fans from throughout the region.

Before political and military dignitaries, over 300 media correspondents, and a crowd of 32,000 spectators at Comiskey Park, game one of the World's Series was played on October 6, 1917. The Sox came on strong, as Happy Felsch hammered out a home run and Joe Jackson made an incredible diving catch in an impressive 2–1 victory.[40] All facets of the event, on the field and throughout the stadium, were primed and conducted with the utmost professionalism by Comiskey's staff.[41] In the Bards' room, food and beverages were served on a continuous flow, earning the Sox owner nothing but praise for the way he treated visiting notables. Comiskey was a generous host and the ease and attractiveness of his stadium left guests with pleasant thoughts. Afterwards, Comiskey told the *Tribune*: "I don't know why I shouldn't be the happiest man in Chicago." He went on to add that he was proud of his club "individually and as a team when it was over."[42]

Chicago rooters were even more ecstatic following game two after the Sox beat New York 7–2 behind Red Faber's pitching. During the first part of the game, Comiskey wasn't smugly lounging back feeling like a king . . . anything but that. He was wound very tightly and decided to stand on the steps of the grandstand and watched nervously rather than sit comfortably in his box with his wife. When the Sox went on to score five runs in the bottom of the fourth to break the 2–2 tie, he retired to the quietness of his office to calm his overflowing anxiety.

Revealing his sentiments about the occasion, he said: "I want to thank the people of Chicago for their patronage. I want them to know that I did everything possible to take care of them and am glad I have given them a team that looks like a world's champion."[43]

The Series shifted to New York City, and in addition to the White Sox players, Comiskey and his wife, and other club officials, more than 400 enthusiasts traveled via the special train arranged by the Woodland Bards. The Bards were living the high life. They gravitated to hot spots throughout Manhattan and were welcomed by George M. Cohan and Sam Harris at the Friars Club, where Comiskey and friends spent a couple hours on October 8.[44] Hotel lobbies were full of celebrities, including the rich and famous and sports heroes from all walks of life.

Perhaps distracted by the glitz and glamour of New York, the Sox were blanked by Rube Benton in game three, losing 2–0.[45] On offense, Chicago landed five hits, but committed three errors, with two by Shano Collins and the other by Ed Cicotte. New York fans were loud in their reactions to Sox players, booing them around every turn, which was said to be retribution for the unfriendly reception Giants third baseman Heinie Zimmerman had received in Chicago.

The Sox were held scoreless again in game four; a real surprise to fans and pundits. James Crusinberry of the *Tribune*, commenting on the vacant seats at the stadium, wrote that if there had been $5,000 to $8,000 more to add to the players' receipts, "the Sox probably would have gone out and knocked the Giants flat."[46] It was yet another reflection upon Chicago's perceived fascination with greenbacks and that they were strictly a "money team." He added that the "White Sox love money, at least some of them do."

Of course it was going to take much more than two losses and a tied up series to knock the positivity out of the perpetually hopeful Woodland Bards. On the special train back to Chicago, Comiskey and his allies shared space and consorted with former World Featherweight boxing champion, Abe Attell.[47] Attell's friendliness with Sox insiders was not out of the ordinary, as he was always hanging around looking for inside tips to feed his gambling interests. No doubt, he was enjoying the comforts provided by the Bards and utilized whatever information he gathered for game five.

Back in Chicago, the Sox won game five, 8–5, in a uniquely physical contest that displayed the enthusiasm and passion of the players involved. With that, the spotlight went back to New York for a make-or-break game for the Giants. On October 15, 1917, at the Polo Grounds, the White Sox defeated the Giants 4–2 and won their first World Series championship since 1906. Red Faber, Joe Jackson, Buck Weaver, Chick Gandil, and Eddie

Collins were among the heroes of the Series, and manager Rowland was praised by some of the same people who had previously criticized him.

Comiskey, who sat near the Sox dugout for the first two losses in New York, altered his routine and moved to a box in the upper deck. Maybe having the boss out of viewing range helped the Sox perform. Nonetheless, Comiskey expressed his joy by saying "No one in America can be as happy now as I am. It always has been my wish to play New York for the championship of the world, and now that we have played it and won, I feel as if my life in baseball is completed."[48]

The outrageously festive clubhouse party at the stadium continued at the Ansonia Hotel, where the players were staying, and branched out to various locations in Manhattan. Comiskey, however, was not in the center of that celebration. He instead went to his room at the Biltmore Hotel and displayed his merriment for less than an hour before departing New York for Chicago on the Lake Shore Limited. He wasn't going to wait for the special train, the Bards, and players; he wanted to get home—and probably out to his sanctuary in Wisconsin as soon as humanly possible. Excited fans awaited his arrival at the LaSalle Street station, but he debarked at Englewood to avoid any fuss. Although the Series victory was a great accomplishment for the club and for himself personally, the wear and tear on his being had taken its toll.

The 1917 season was a memorable one for the Chicago White Sox and Charles Comiskey, and if achieving a World Series victory was exhausting for the Sox leader, 1918 and all of its pitfalls were going to be a living nightmare.

ENDNOTES

1 *Trenton Evening Times,* January 21, 1917, p. 17.
2 *Sporting News,* January 25, 1917, p. 2.
    On this same page, there are additional comments by sportswriter W. A. Phelon relating to the strike threat, and a column about the top rate treatment players received, particularly while traveling. "No profession is so well taken care of as the ball player," the article noted, "but the very best is none too good for the athlete of present day."
3 *Sporting News,* January 25, 1917, p. 1.
4 *New York Times,* February 25, 1917, p. 74.
    Dreyfuss of Pittsburgh said that the cost of salaries was closer to $2 million. *Sporting News,* January 25, 1917, p. 2.
5 *Sporting News,* February 1, 1917, p. 6.

6 *Sporting News*, October 17, 1918, p. 2.

7 *Sporting News*, February 22, 1917, p. 4.

8 *Sporting News*, January 11, 1917, p. 7.

9 Asinof, Eliot, *Eight Men Out*, p. 21.
   Asinof noted that players stared "glumly" at the contract terms offered by Comiskey.

10 *Chicago Daily Tribune*, January 21, 1917, p. A2.
   The column was reprinted in the *Sporting News*, February 1, 1917, p. 8. Additionally, it is entirely feasible, albeit speculative, that Comiskey considered extenuating circumstances and factors when making his evaluations prior to sending out contracts. That includes, and is not limited to, previous injuries, personality conflicts, and whether or not the player was respectfully handling his contract negotiations or playing hardball. Comiskey was easily offended at times and would not succumb to being bullied. There was, notably, a lot of psychological warfare mixed into the negotiations, and, in a way, it was used to inspire the player to do even better on the field for next season. And this became even more fruitful if a bonus was mentioned as a possibility for good work.

11 Asinof, Eliot, *Eight Men Out*, p. 21.

12 *Sporting News*, March 8, 1917, p. 1.

13 *New York Times*, February 25, 1917, p. 74.

14 McGraw's salary was $30,000 a year, reportedly, and the Giants total salary list was said to be $150,000.

15 *Sporting News*, January 25, 1917, p. 1.

16 *New York Times*, articles between February 14 and February 18, 1917.

17 *Chicago Daily Tribune*, January 14, 1917, p. A4.

18 *Sporting News*, January 4, 1917, p. 1., *Chicago Daily Tribune*, March 4, 1917, p. A1.
   Later in 1917, Ed Walsh signed with the Boston Braves in another attempt at a comeback. He pitched at the North Side park in Chicago against the Cubs on August 2, and held the latter scoreless for five innings.

19 *Sporting News*, January 25, 1917, p. 6.
   Gandil played the "poorest" ball of his career for Cleveland in 1916, according to the article, and a contract hadn't yet been sent to him for 1917. He said that he had quit smoking cigarettes and his health was improved. Incidentally, when Washington sent Gandil to Cleveland in 1916, Clark Griffith, manager of the Senators, admitted that he got rid of Gandil because he was a smoker. *Sporting News*, March 23, 1916, p. 6.

20 1900 & 1910 United States Federal Census Records, Ancestry.com. In most genealogical databases, including the California Death Index, Social Security Death Index, and World War I Draft Registration records, Gandil was listed as "Arnold Gandil," and not "Charles Arnold Gandil," his reported "full name."

21 *Sporting News*, November 18, 1915, p. 6.
   When Gandil was released from the White Sox in 1910, he was called a lemon, and sent to Montreal of the Eastern League along with Charles French. Gandil "never has forgotten the insult."

22 Both *The Baseball Encyclopedia* and Baseball Reference list Gandil's purchase cost
   at $3,500.

23 *Richmond Times Dispatch,* June 22, 1912, p. 6.

24 *Washington, D.C. Evening Star,* July 8, 1912, p. 10.

25 *Sporting News,* October 25, 1917, p. 2.

26 *Chicago Daily Tribune,* April 15, 1917, p. A1.
   Cicotte's no-hitter was pitched on the fourth day of the 1917 season and was one
   of the earliest on record for any season.

27 There were constant rumors about potential replacements for Rowland as manager, including John McGraw and Bill Carrigan. Comiskey appeared to dismiss
   the word of critics, and probably did, but it was the complaints of his players that
   he'd ultimately listen to.

28 The complete amount raised for the Red Cross and donated by Comiskey for
   the 1917 season was $17,113, according to the *Chicago Daily Tribune.* Comiskey
   donated another $5,000 in 1918.

29 *Sporting News,* August 2, 1917, p. 1.

30 *Sporting News,* June 7, 1917, p. 5.
   The White Sox were last in the American League in team batting with a .227
   average. Jackson, Weaver, Leibold, Felsch, and Shano Collins were listed among
   the league batting leaders, but none were over .275, and Eddie Collins was surprisingly absent.

31 *Sporting News,* August 23, 1917, pgs. 1,2.
   White Sox pitcher Dave Danforth was regarded as the man who introduced the
   "shineball" to the American League. He taught Cicotte, and Cicotte was fast
   becoming the master of the pitch. On August 14, Cleveland superstar Tris Speaker
   was nearly killed by Danforth when a pitched ball hit him above the right temple.
   After the incident, Speaker talked about Danfroth and his contributions to the
   shineball fad. He felt that if Ban Johnson outlawed rubber-lined pockets in uniforms, the White Sox would be considerably lower in the standings.

32 *Chicago Daily Tribune,* August 31, 1917, p. 11.
   Comiskey was angry following a game on August 30, in which he said it took
   fifty-five minutes to play an inning because of the constant interruptions by
   rivals to the pitching of White Sox hurlers. It was damaging to his fans, he
   explained, and the next time his team played Washington, he planned to have
   his pitchers wear skirts so that there would be no question that they weren't
   rubbing the ball on their pants.

33 Eddie Cicotte would end the season with 28 victories versus 12 losses, according
   to baseball-reference.com. The *Sporting News,* on September 27, 1917, indicated
   that Cicotte lost his chances to earn 30 victories when he was defeated on September 19 by the Athletics. He played straight through until the end of the season, winning his final game on September 29, at New York.

34 *Sporting News,* September 27, 1917, p. 1.
   Both players were cleared of all charges when the case was dismissed after the
   complainant failed to show to court.

35 *Sporting News,* August 9, 1917, p. 1.
   Weaver was said to be leading the team in hitting, better than Jackson, Felsch, and Collins.
36 *Sporting News,* September 20, 1917, p. 6.
   McMullin was acknowledged as somewhat of a "mascot," proving to be a positive influence on the team. There was an organized effort by players to convince Rowland to keep McMullin in the game after Weaver's finger healed. Rowland consented, moving Weaver to shortstop and benching "Swede" Risberg.
37 *Chicago Daily Tribune,* September 22, 1917, p. 13.
   Multiple sources have referred to a pennant-winning bonus from Comiskey to his players as being a case of flat champagne. The White Sox won the pennant in Boston in 1917 and were banqueted in that city as a token of Comiskey's appreciation. Additionally, before the Sox went on their final road trip, they were given an initial celebratory dinner by Comiskey's friend John P. Harding, owner of the Hotel Planters and treasurer of the Woodland Bards. Once they returned from the east, the team was again honored at a gala at the Edgewater Beach Hotel. If a case of flat champagne was sent to the Sox at any point, it was likely unintentional, and more the fault of the supplier than that of any one person. However, Comiskey obviously honored his team in other ways—either first hand or by the work of his friends. However, no primary source was located to substantiate the champagne tale. It may have been pure fiction in attempt to run down the reputation of Comiskey. The book *Eight Men Out* depicts the scenario as happening in 1919.
38 *Chicago Daily Tribune,* September 23, 1917, p. A1.
39 *Chicago Daily Tribune,* October 2, 1917, p. 13.
40 Happy Felsch won a $50 Liberty Bond for his home run in game one, provided by actor Al Jolson, who promised the gift to any player who hit one out of the park during the World Series. Interestingly, Jolson, and other New York visitors, were upset during the Chicago games that they didn't receive "choice" seating by White Sox management.
41 Comiskey assembled a large contingent of police to oversee the event, including 190 in uniform, 70 more that were mounted, and 50 detectives. In case of emergencies, there were two ambulances, doctors in the crowd, and uniformed firemen. *Chicago Daily Tribune,* October 8, 1917, p. 13.
42 *Chicago Daily Tribune,* October 7, 1917, p. A3.
43 *Chicago Daily Tribune,* October 8, 1917, p. 13.
44 *Chicago Daily Tribune,* October 10, 1917, p. 19.
   George M. Cohan, a well-known entertainer, was a called a "natural rooter" for the White Sox. He reportedly had a prestigious "gold pass" to Comiskey Park, which could be used for free entry any time he wanted. Another report stated that Cohan "holds one of the three gold passes for Comiskey Park." *Chicago Examiner,* October 16, 1917, p 7. The other two were held by Sir Thomas Lipton and John L. Sullivan. Cohan was a big-time baseball gambler and won over $20,000 on the 1917 Series. *Chicago Daily Tribune,* October 16, 1917, p. 17. Notably, a fourth "gold engraved life pass" was given to sportswriter Ring Lardner on

August 13, 1919, at a special dinner honoring him in the Woodland Bards' room at the stadium. *Chicago Daily Tribune,* August 14, 1919, p. 13.

45 *Chicago Daily Tribune,* October 12, 1917, p. 17.

The New York Giants beat the Chicago White Sox, 5–0, in game four.

46 *Chicago Daily Tribune,* October 12, 1917, p. 17.

An estimated 5,000 fewer people attended the fourth game of the World's Series at the Polo Grounds in New York. The players' share of the Series covered only the first four games and the amounts added up to $152,888.52. Upon winning the World Series, Sox players earned a little more than $3,669 apiece. Sox pitcher Jim Scott, who volunteered for the U.S. Army Officers' Reserve during the season, was given a share of the World Series cut.

47 *Chicago Daily Tribune,* October 13, 1917, p. 15, *Chicago Examiner,* October 13, 1917, p. 8.

During the ride, Abe Attell reportedly sparred with Woodland Bards President Joe Farrell. Notably, the Woodland Bards called itself, "The Most Exclusive Organization in the World."

48 *Chicago Daily Tribune,* October 16, 1917, p. 17.

15

BASEBALL'S MONEY PLAYERS

Many sportswriters across the baseball landscape were caught up in a sort of hero worship for Charles Comiskey, and relentlessly called him the high and mighty "Old Roman" as a display of esteem. In their praise, they seemed to overlook one important fact about the White Sox owner: he was just a human being. He was a mere mortal and far from a perfect man. For years, scribes portrayed him as the all knowing veteran leader of the American League. They saw his decision-making as not only being constructive for his interests in Chicago, but for his peers in other cities as well. The way he carried himself with dignity, used common sense, and treated his fellow man with respect earned the utmost admiration throughout the sports world. His business acumen was always on target and the way he knew players and their faults helped churn out high caliber teams one after another.

But all the compliments almost became propaganda. Comiskey knew where he stood in baseball's hierarchy and surely utilized his knowledge at league meetings, but no man was infallible. Age and sickness combined with the constant illnesses of his wife and son, were demoralizing to his heart. His passion for baseball and a deep seeded longing to win was obsessive, but not in any sort of negative way. It was his business, and the years of disappointments created a nervousness that he yearned to squash. Equally, he wanted to provide a winner for his South Side contingent.

Comiskey, physically, was slowly burning out. It was a a slow fizzle that seemed to ebb a little more at his health and inner soul every year. After staking almost his whole being on his chances in 1917, the Sox defeated the New York Giants and his dream was realized. He said: "The White Sox once more are champions of the world and I feel as if nothing in baseball matters from now on."[1] Maybe he really believed that to a certain extent. Even so, baseball was his life and outside his family, the Sox were his everything. Although he said that nothing in baseball mattered anymore, he also declared his desire to win one more time before he got too old.

And it was a realistic point of view. Over the years, he increasingly relinquished power to his subordinates, and more often avoided interactions with fans and reporters when he used to naturally savor those moments. No question about it, the Comiskey of 1917 and '18 was a much different man than he was a decade earlier. By personal choice, he withdrew from a spot amongst the leaders of baseball striving for the sport's forward movement. But it might not have been a conscience decision, nor did sportswriters immediately recognize what was happening.

The weather at Camp Jerome was rougher than usual for the members of the Woodland Bards in late October of 1917, but the sustained celebration for the Sox victory continued anyway. Comiskey, Ban Johnson, and dozens of friends enjoyed the tranquility of the region and briefly forgot the horrifying war in Europe and the tumultuous world of baseball politics that they left behind.

Snapping back to reality upon his return to Chicago, Comiskey answered letters of congratulations and worked with Harry Grabiner to figure out plans for spring training.[2] Johnson went in another direction and made it known that he'd be willing to step away from baseball to support the military effort as part of the War Department. The longtime friends planned to travel to Dover Hall, Georgia, with their wives for some additional rest and relaxation, but Comiskey's wife Nan took sick and they were unable to make the trip.[3] Instead, the Comiskey's went to Excelsior Springs, a familiar resort area that had proven valuable in the past.

Charles enjoyed his Thanksgiving in Wisconsin, and before he left, had some parting words for Johnson: "Well, Ban, I'll only be out of the city for a few days, but please don't close my ball park before I return."[4]

The joking statement by Comiskey referenced Johnson's somewhat hasty actions to alter the conventional system of major league baseball to not only appease government officials, but to secure the sport's footing during a time of war.[5] Johnson was basically walking a tightrope between owners and Washington, D.C., trying to make bold recommendations to pacify all. One of his innovative concepts was to ask the government flat out to exempt eighteen players from every American League team from military service to ensure baseball would be sustained in 1918. Some owners were supportive, but others, like Comiskey, hated the idea with a passion. He felt that the war effort came first and didn't want to ask an exemption for any reason.

Johnson was also in favor of reducing the season's schedule from 154 games to 140, and again, he garnered some likeminded allies.[6] Comiskey again opposed. He felt the current structure was popular and each owner had flourished, so why make any changes? This was a fine example of Comiskey's "stand pat" attitude that seemed to crop up many times during the war and its aftermath, particularly when reacting to Johnson's novel ideas. Baseball's future was in sincere doubt and the political marksmanship among magnates was much more intense than usual.

Both Comiskey and Johnson had logical reasoning for their views and, in these two instances, Comiskey's positions won out over the American League president. It wasn't a direct confrontation between the two friends, but it was known that Comiskey had enough influence to sway the tides. Comiskey, in the last year, had two other complaints involving Johnson: the incompetency of league umpires and the constant harassment of his pitching staff regarding the elusive shineball. Any approved government interference in baseball and additional war measures that altered the game as they knew it—according to Comiskey—was absolutely out of the question.[7]

In light of the uncertain season ahead, owners discussed ways to reduce expenses at the annual meeting of the American League in December of 1917. Comiskey was awarded the pennant of the organization and was reelected vice president.[8]

One of the major issues for any team in the aftermath of a world championship victory was the maneuvering of players seeking higher salaries as a reward for their contributions. Contrary to this regularity, Comiskey didn't have much of a problem lining up his men for the 1918 season. Eddie Cicotte, Lefty Williams, Chick Gandil, and all the rest signed without incident, which was slightly odd because if they wanted an opportunity to pressure Comiskey for a raise, this was the time. The war likely was responsible for keeping any excessive greed in check. With most of the team agreeing to their new deals, there were two notable holdouts, Reb Russell and coach William "Kid" Gleason, who was substantially important during the previous season.[9] While Russell eventually came around and signed, Gleason remained on the sidelines for the entire year.

The Sox regulars were practically unaffected by the National Army draft, and it was assumed that because most members of the club were married, the team would remain intact. Red Faber, who was unmarried, was expected to be lost, and his departure was going to be a major blow to the pitching staff.[10] With the remainder of the club in place and considering the substantial losses to rivaling teams, it was predicted that the White Sox were in line to repeat as American League champions.

Just prior to the beginning of the pennant race, another Ban Johnson suggestion was met with discord from the Chicago camp.[11] Johnson wanted to use the new Daylight Savings Bill passed by Congress to shift the start time of baseball games from 3:00 to 4:00 in the afternoon. Comiskey was again appalled by the thought of change and forced the issue to be amended to being the prerogative of each individual owner rather than a league-wide edict.

With a shortened spring training leaving his pitchers out of shape and missing the team's mediator in Gleason, the season began on April 16, 1918, with a 6–1 loss at home to the St. Louis Browns. Four hurlers tried to salvage the game, but Cicotte, Danforth, Faber, and Russell came up empty in the defeat. As a sign of the times, the stadium was the victim of an increased amount of vandalism on off days, at night, and when the team was out of town.[12] Comiskey's answer was to buy additional St. Bernard dogs to patrol the venue. He felt canines were the "only real protection for property" in Chicago.

As the season progressed, the luck of the White Sox had obviously run out and nothing but ugliness surrounded pretty much all aspects of Comiskey's club. Very quickly, the thought of winning back-to-back pennants seemed a surefire impossibility. Captain Eddie Collins was in tip-top shape, and early in the season, became the official "Ironman" for the major leagues when he established a new record for consecutive games played with 473, passing Sam Crawford.[13] His health was touted in the *Sporting News* and it was predicted that he'd set a pretty high new benchmark. But within days, Collins was spiked by Cleveland's Bobby Roth and knocked out of the game, ending his streak. Other injuries to Eddie Cicotte, Ray Schalk, and backup catcher Byrd Lynn, plus the ptomaine poisoning suffered by Chick Gandil, weakened the team considerably.

Then another blow occurred in May of 1918, when Joe Jackson ran out on his White Sox contract to join the Harlan and Hollingsworth shipbuilding company of Wilmington, Delaware.[14] Jackson, concerned that his status change to Class 1A meant he was headed for war, felt he was being discriminated against and that he had the legal right to take up essential employment to provide for his family. Nevertheless, Comiskey felt betrayed and used his reactionary anger to lash out at Jackson in the press. Jackson was not only painting ships for a steady paycheck, but playing ball in the "Steel League," which was considered to be a shady hideout for athletes trying to evade military service.

Jackson's reputation was severely hurt by the jump and Comiskey did him no favors. Even the insinuation of disloyalty was seen as a personal attack by Comiskey, and he wasn't letting anyone who so boldly walked out on him get away with it.

Almost a month later, Jackson's buddy Lefty Williams and Byrd Lynn followed suit, jumping from the Sox to the shipbuilding organization.[15] Whereas the two players planned to give Comiskey a couple days notice, the Sox owner basically told them not to bother, immediately suspending both, and declaring: "I don't consider them fit to play on my ball club." The *Sporting News* routinely called the acts of these jumpers "desertions," while others referred to the players simply as "slackers."

Comiskey explained: "I would be willing to give up every ball player on my squad if they wanted to do their duty by their country, but can't bear to see any of my men going to the ship yards, where they do a little work and draw a lot of money."

The service flag for the Chicago White Sox ended up with nineteen stars, plus one gold star after recruit Leo Constantineau, serving in the navy, died of influenza on October 1, 1918.[16] [17] Severely handicapped by the losses of Jackson, Williams, and Lynn, as well as lackluster play for the remainder of the team, saw the Sox fall to fifth place by the end of June. The team relied greatly on the work of Cicotte, and he didn't win his first game of the season until May 31. However, the club's inability to support him with any offensive production was a major fault, and frustrations were growing. As a consequence of the rising uneasiness on the Sox and the tension amongst players about the war, Happy Felsch suddenly quit on July 1, 1918, and returned to his home in Milwaukee.[18]

Comiskey's animosity was mounting at a rapid pace. Felsch walked away when the team needed him most, and again, the coveted characteristic of loyalty turned into betrayal. Sportswriters were aware of the fact that Comiskey vocalized his anger after Jackson left the team, but when Felsch quit, he was largely silent. Any internalized resentment was not advantageous to his already shaky health. George S. Robbins of the *Chicago Daily News* and a regular reporter for the *Sporting News* was as close to Comiskey as any other scribe in the business. He revealed that the Sox owner was "sick and weary," and completely "disheartened" by the negative cluster of happenings in recent months.[19]

The War Department announced mid-season that a new "work or fight" rule would apply across the board and that there was no exemptions for ballplayers. Starting September 1, players of age had to be engaged in essential employment or enlisted. Ban Johnson responded by proposing August 20 as a date to end the season and allow for a World Series to be played prior to the first of September. American League representatives met in Cleveland while Comiskey was at his Wisconsin refuge, but from the message he sent, it appeared that he was in favor of ending the season early.[20] Before the end of the month, though, Comiskey had changed his mind, and was against the August 20 end date.

Baseball politics and tensions were elevated to their highest point in years. Owners were lining up on different sides of the field of battle, and a hearty fight was expected for a second league meeting in Cleveland.[21] Comiskey was rejuvenated enough by his mini-vacation to attend the conference and try to persuade his comrades to continue baseball through Labor Day. His influential nature, and that of Clark Griffith of the Washington Senators, steered the ship out from under the power of Johnson to score a victory. The World Series was going to be played after September 1, regardless if it complied with the War Department or not.

Once again, Comiskey's opinion won out over Ban Johnson, and altogether the situation added a lot of friction to the American League. The hostilities behind closed doors were kept private, but after the meeting, a public statement demonstrated the apparent real feelings of three owners toward Johnson.[22] Bold criticisms and a desire for change in league leadership confirmed that the difficulties weren't skin deep and not easily going away.

Harry Frazee of Boston, an ardent anti-Johnson guy, Charles Comiskey, and Clark Griffith were the trio of dissenters. In their proclamation, they stated that in no way were they out to purposefully defy the government by wanting to continue after September 1. They were unhappy with the way Johnson was running the league and wanted to take a more active part in controlling things from that point on. Days later, interestingly enough, Comiskey denied he had any part in the statement criticizing Johnson, and affirmed that he said everything he wanted to during the meeting in Cleveland.[23]

Before the season was finally put out of its misery, Swede Risberg and Fred McMullin departed for their homes in California, planning to join the wartime efforts there, and Eddie Collins enlisted in the Marines. Comiskey was proud of the men for doing their duty for the nation, saying: "I am delighted that the White Sox club was fortunate enough to include men of this caliber."[24] Stepping into vital roles on the team were rookie infielder Babe Pinelli and veteran outfielder Wilbur Good. Thirty-five-year-old Jack Quinn, recently out of a job after the closing of the Pacific Coast League, was a passed over right hander and essentially forgotten about.

Quinn joined the White Sox and pitched like a superstar, going 5–1 with a 2.29 ERA. He represented a winner on a team of despondent players, and was one of the very few bright spots of the entire year. The season ended on September 2, 1918, with the Sox losing both games of a doubleheader in Detroit, and finishing with a 57–67 record.

For years it seemed that the drawing power of Comiskey's White Sox was unchallengeable, and that it was a foregone conclusion that Chicago would be among the league leaders at the box office. But that wasn't the case in 1918. Fewer than 200,000 fans attended games at Comiskey Park, and on some occasions, the crowds were less than 1,000 a game.[25] The dramatic drop off in attendance caused a very real anxiety in Sox management about the instability of the marketplace. Since the war was still going on, thoughts about the 1919 season were a little less optimistic than they were in previous years.

Seeing that he had a better structure in place to handle large crowds, Comiskey's venue was picked as the site for the home games of the Cubs in the World Series against the Boston Red Sox. All the Cubs could muster were two wins against the American League powerhouse, and lost the series in six games. Charles Weeghman, President of the Cubs, sent a letter to Comiskey afterwards to thank him, and stated that his efforts added to his "nationwide reputation for good sportsmanship and to our admiration for you."[26]

Throughout the year, the National Commission of baseball was called upon innumerable times to settle various forms of controversy. In two cases,

Comiskey received favorable decisions. Claude Williams, the shipyard jumper, felt he was due money from the Sox, but the commission denied him on the grounds that he broke his contract. Jack Fournier, another former Chicago player, was affirmed by the commission as still being tied to the Sox despite claims otherwise. A third dispute involved pitcher Jack Quinn, as the New York Yankees asserted they had bought him outright from the Vernon Tigers.[27] The commission evaluated the evidence and agreed.

Comiskey was battling more health issues in 1918, according to George S. Robbins of the *Sporting News*, and was generally "downcast."[28] The logical place for him to rest was Camp Jerome. On September 19, Comiskey and Johnson both departed for their favorite outdoor recreational spot, but remarkably, they didn't travel together like they had in the past.[29] Johnson went by train, while Comiskey elected to go by car. The strife in baseball and personally in Comiskey's life caused their friendship to suffer, and emotions were running high. Outbursts in meetings were customary from time-to-time, but this latest round of complications hurt a little more than usual. Comiskey, especially, was sensitive to the actions of Johnson as it related to how it impacted his club.

At different times, they were brothers and enemies, and their similarities caused them to quarrel very easily. Although Johnson was more passive in the face of aggression, particularly while being loudly lambasted at league meetings, he was just as stubborn as Comiskey. If they weren't careful, their mulishness was going to prevent reconciliation.

Many stars of the baseball ranks (Ty Cobb, Grover Alexander, Eddie Collins, Tris Speaker, and others) were serving in the war, and the progress of the A. E. F. overseas was on the minds of all. The semi-professional baseball league in Chicago was filling up with weekend warriors; guys who were working in factories and playing ball on Saturday and Sunday. Among them were Ray Schalk and Buck Weaver. Comiskey Park filled up with football fans and military service squads for games in late 1918, and no one was quite sure if major league baseball was going to return to the stadium the following spring.[30] [31] But when the Armistice came on November 11, 1918, effectively ending World War I, optimism was renewed.

That is, to a certain degree. American League magnates supported the shortening of the 1919 season to 140 games, as they were unconfident about future ticket sales.[32] The keyword was "retrenchment" for owners, and a general reduction in expenses was desired. One option was salary cuts, perhaps to as low as $1,200 per player for the season. The National

League discussed a $55,000 a year salary limit for each team that would have made the numbers impossible to figure out, especially in the American League and for Comiskey.[33] The *Sporting News* denoted that only five of his players made up $41,000 worth of salary, and he'd have to split the remaining $14,000 among at least fifteen other players.

The reservation list of the Chicago White Sox included four notables who were deemed ineligible for the 1919 playing season.[34] They were Joe Jackson, Lefty Williams, Byrd Lynn, and Happy Felsch, while Kid Gleason, Red Faber, Joe Jenkins, and Jim Scott were among the voluntarily retired—the last three being in the service. The American League, as a body, decided it would withhold a sweeping judgment on the shipyard jumpers and allow each individual owner to decide whether or not to allow the players back into their fold or not. Many sportswriters had already either forgiven or defended the rights of Jackson and similar athletes to do what they did and the furor that was in place during the summer had fizzled almost completely out.

Some reports had Jackson on the open trade market and rumors circulated that Yankees manager, Miller Huggins, was interested because he needed an outfielder.[35] There was also news that Eddie Collins was contemplating retirement. Comiskey was mum on both topics.[36] His silence was deafening to writers and fans as they waited for him to comment on the future of Jackson and Collins and address the gossip that Clarence Rowland wasn't going to manage the Sox in 1919. Comiskey, as he was preparing to leave for Florida with his wife on December 31, 1918, surprised the press and followers when he announced that Rowland was out and that Gleason was returning to lead the White Sox.

Relations between Comiskey and Gleason were considered estranged, which brought about most of the bewilderment, but the shock was accompanied by some anger from sportswriters. George S. Robbins in the *Sporting News* explained that Comiskey was "more sharply criticized" for his decision than at any time during his tenure as boss in Chicago.[37] The fervor had nothing to do with the choice of Gleason, but more about the way in which the popular Rowland was being treated. It was assumed that since Comiskey waited so long to make a decision, it was far too late for the manager to secure suitable employment elsewhere. Comiskey didn't have time for that argument, and may have planned the announcement to coincide with his going out of town to avoid any trouble.

The ouster of Rowland was not personal, nor did Comiskey purposely try to injure his future prospects in baseball. In fact, they remained friends after parting ways. The maneuver was in response to the inner turmoil brewing from within the ball club and the perception that Rowland had lost his grip on the somewhat unmanageable bunch of temperamental athletes. Comiskey acknowledged the complaints of Eddie Collins, maybe others, and the choice of Gleason was also rumored to have been based on the suggestion of Collins.

For Gleason, it was his first opportunity to manage after decades of big league service. His appointment was lauded, and he was seen as the best man for the job. Owning the right kind of personality, he was an affable yet an inflexible disciplinarian who cowered to no man. He brought out the best in players, taught rookies—and even veterans—tricks that made them household names, and was credited with the wisdom that launched Buck Weaver's ascension to superstardom. His toughness was indisputable, and when Sox players joked about his age during the 1917 season, the 5'7", fifty-year-old proceeded to topple his critics in impromptu wrestling matches, one after another.

All in all, Gleason was flat out respected, and with him at the helm, the Sox were going to be forcibly united into a cohesive faction—whether they consciously agreed or not. The 1919 season was certainly going to be a year to remember for the Chicago franchise, although many things still had to happen before opening day. First and foremost was the reintegration of the shipyard jumpers, a move that Gleason wanted to implement from the start of his campaign. Comiskey's promise to forever bar Jackson, Williams, and Lynn from playing again was overridden by Gleason's motivation to rebuild the team. Gleason went out to the Chester shipyards in Pennsylvania and spoke with Williams personally, agreeing to settle the pitcher's dispute over back pay to get him to return.

Comiskey spent most of January in South Florida with Nan, whose ailing health continued. It had been a little over a year since her condition worsened, and in late 1917, she declined so rapidly that doctors wondered if she'd be able to fight her way back. Nan was confined to a bed for a time at Mercy Hospital in Chicago and indisposed for months. Finally, she recovered enough to travel, but her illness persisted. They both hoped that the sunshine of Florida would help her physical and mental state. It did.

In the meantime at meetings in New York, both leagues adopted a conservative 140-game schedule as a measure of financial prudence, expecting salaries to be adjusted for a five-and-a-half month term instead of six, and the American League took up the issue of a team salary limit. A maximum

$10,000 or so limitation would help the lesser successful teams, but was acknowledged as creating nothing but hardships on the players. In a day and age when athletes wanted more money, any talk of scaling back was particularly detrimental to morale, and no action was taken in that regard.

After settling the shipyard complexities, Gleason focused on his pitching staff—a resounding problem—and worked several angles to secure a trade, ultimately coming up empty. Losing hurler Jack Quinn to the Yankees was substantial, and the Sox unsuccessfully appealed to the National Commission over his rights. Other players were signing their 1919 Sox contracts at a normal pace, and with another opportunity to holdout in effort to garner more cash, guys like Jackson, Williams, Felsch, and Cicotte remitted their documents without as much as a peep.

Chick Gandil was another story. The thirty-one-year-old was one of the hardest working men in baseball, but his return to the majors was not yet guaranteed.[38] His wife, Laurel Fay (which she usually spelled Faye), was desirous to remain on the West Coast because she didn't like the east, and Gandil certainly had to take that into consideration. He probed other options by writing letters to club owners and found an opportunity with the San Francisco Seals of the Pacific Coast League. Between a minor league salary and a day job, it was possible to make somewhere near his income with the Sox, but Comiskey wasn't going to give up his talented first baseman and approve his release. Another option was to holdout for more money, but Gandil didn't. He affixed his signature and reported for spring training in March.

Two others, Swede Risberg and Buck Weaver, also wanted more money. Of the two, Risberg fell into line without much trouble, but Weaver felt he was worth more, and in many ways, his salary dispute helped mold a more accepted perception that Comiskey was underpaying his talent. Robbins of the *Sporting News* declared Weaver the "greatest" box office draw on the White Sox, and it was impossible not to compare him to Eddie Collins, the highest paid athlete on the club. There was an unreal level of competition among the two infielders—mostly on Weaver's part—and his recognition of Collins' $15,000 a year salary was more than fleeting.

To take that another step, Collins' impressive annual wages was a cloud over the entire White Sox team. It established an unrealistic sky-high ceiling that all other salaries in the sport were compared to and created tension where it might otherwise been avoided. John B. Sheridan, who wrote an insightful column in the *Sporting News*, gave his opinion that $3,500 should be the standard salary for a regular major league player, and that $7,500 was exclusive for upper echelon athletes like Ty Cobb.[39] He couldn't even imagine someone being paid more than $7,500—and that included Cobb.

Collins' $15,000 per annum was unbelievably staggering, especially since he wasn't the guaranteed .300 hitter he'd been earlier in his career. In 1918, Weaver led the team in batting with a .300 average, and that was evidence enough to him that he deserved a more Collins-like paycheck.[40] Robbins guessed that Weaver was getting about $4,000 a year and that he was asking for $2,000 more—in addition to a three year contract.[41] Comiskey reportedly answered the request by giving the customary league-wide response that the uncertainty of baseball was forcing a more moderate approach to contracts.

Yes, the war was over and attendance was expected to rise, but from a business approach, management still had to be a little tentative. Weaver had some leverage against Comiskey's retort, and that was continued employment with the Fairbanks-Morse Company out of Beloit, Wisconsin. It seemed that factory work, plus playing for the company's baseball team, was going to earn him more than his current Sox salary. Always colorful and smiling, Weaver was a natural for the big leagues, and any chance of his stepping out of the limelight was completely harmful to the game. Fans rejoiced seeing him giving his all, and in this instance, Comiskey needed to compromise.

Usually, Comiskey didn't bend to holdouts. Pressure for more pay turned his stomach inside out, and literally, during this stretch, he was battling abdomen difficulties to the point in which he was unable to eat. Doctors were worried that he had little strength and had lost weight. His problems were only multiplied by his wife's sustained health trouble, and they made a hasty retreat for Hot Springs, Arkansas. Just before he departed, Weaver popped into town to discuss terms. Gleason worked on him, and within thirty minutes, he signed a three-year deal reportedly worth $7,250 a year.

Rain at Mineral Wells, Texas, put a damper on the early days of spring training in late March of 1919, but the team rounded into condition under the guidance of Gleason. In preparing his infield, Gleason moved Weaver to third base and awarded the impressive Risberg the starting shortstop position. The Sox manager also found a diamond in his assemblage of rookie pitchers at camp. The standout was Richard "Dickey" Kerr, a left-hander originally from St. Louis, but now making his home in Paris, Texas. Kerr stood only 5'7", and Gleason knew that he didn't physically measure up to the typical pitching star. But that typecast was superseded by Kerr's abnormal poise on the mound, and Gleason went to great lengths to help adjust his throwing style.

Red Faber was discharged from the service and his place in the rotation was assured, pundits believed, but the confidential "dope" indicated that he was still far from himself. His pitching speed and strength had been sapped by his time in the military and he needed time to recover. Without Faber in his regular form and Kerr yet unproven, the Sox only had two first-class pitchers in the fold: Eddie Cicotte and Lefty Williams. For the long haul, that presented a definite problem, but without a trade or purchase of an established name, that was the way the season was going to begin.

The hard-hitting Sox started with a bang, excelling in all areas and secured first place early in the championship crusade. Over their first twelve games, the team batted over .300 and Cicotte won four consecutive appearances. Bookmakers were unimpressed by the quick start of Chicago, and predicted that the Red Sox were going to win the pennant, followed by the Yankees.[42] However, Boston was underachieving, and after Cicotte outpitched Carl Mays in a 1–0 pitchers duel on May 14 at Comiskey Park, the "Red Hose" were 7–5, while the White Sox were 13–4. Gleason initially used Kerr out of the bullpen as he tried to get quality work from another starter besides Cicotte, Williams, and Faber. Dave Danforth and young Frank Shellenback were not fulfilling the need, and Comiskey added to his staff by picking up 6'4" right-hander Grover Lowdermilk via waivers.

More times than not, the Sox defense came to the aid of a bruised pitcher, and if they were behind, the lineup of big bats supplied enough runs to overcome the deficit. Reversing the fortunes of a sour game was the trademark of the White Sox in 1919, and late inning rallies were commonplace; a system that all players participated in—even the pitchers. The Collins boys, Weaver, Jackson, and Gandil were running the bases hard, hitting to the gaps, and making sacrifices to score any way possible. It was smart baseball with an unparalleled competitive spirit, making it somewhat easy to consistently surmount the pitching quandary.

With Chicago on a five game winning streak going into the final day of May, emotions were running high against the Indians, and both teams were displaying signs of aggressiveness on the field. In the eighth inning of their game on May 31, Gandil took offense to a slide by Cleveland outfielder Tris Speaker, and after the side was retired, the former instigated a fight.[43] The two brawled unmercifully and earned indefinite suspensions. The Sox lost their next game, and the three following at Detroit. On June 10 in Boston, Cicotte and his mates handed Babe Ruth his first loss of the season with a victory at Fenway Park, 5–3. Cicotte was 11–1 on the mound with only 12 earned runs.

In late June, the Sox were knocked down to third place behind New York and Cleveland in the midst of heavy competition. Gleason addressed the slump by changing the batting order, shifting Eddie Collins from third to second in the lineup and moving Weaver to third.[44] In response, the team started July by winning 10 of 12 and regained the lead on July 10, 1919.[45] The day before, Red Faber demonstrated that 50 percent of his normal ability was much better than nothing at all.[46] He relieved a game started by Kerr against Philadelphia and earned a win. Later that afternoon, in the second of a doubleheader, he returned to the mound and pitched a complete game, winning again.

An estimated 30,000 excited fans witnessed a remarkable game winning home run by Joe Jackson into the right field bleachers at Comiskey Park on July 20, 1919. The drive ended a heated ten-inning contest against the Yankees, ending by a score of 2–1. In a demonstration of club unity, as Jackson rounded third, his teammates ran with him along the baseline to home plate, ready to celebrate the dramatic conclusion. Everything was starting to go right for the White Sox, and their momentum continued to gain steam.

Comiskey missed some mid-season action at the home grounds, which was unusual for him, and tended to the fishing holes of Wisconsin. But when Carl Mays, a controversial but talented pitcher suddenly fell out of favor at Boston, he was fully prepared to make Red Sox owner Harry Frazee a cash offer of more than $25,000—perhaps as much as $40,000.[47] Frazee instead wanted players, and Comiskey wasn't looking to break up any part of his outfit for a trade.

Mays was a firecracker ready to explode and had he joined the Sox, his uneasy behavior might have caused the club to combust in terms of team chemistry. On the other hand, he might have added the pitching strength they needed to overcome any potential hurdles. Mays was traded to the Yankees, and he was, shortly thereafter, suspended by President Ban Johnson for breaking his Boston contract by refusing to play for the Red Sox prior to being sent to New York. Johnson felt he was acting on behalf of owners in his decision, but his opponents believed otherwise. They perceived his actions to be a coordinated effort to weaken the Yankees to help the Indians, a team that Johnson was financially involved in.

Surprisingly, and outside of his standard nature, Comiskey gravitated toward the Mays situation, which was nothing more than a contentious political conflict that rested far outside the direct sphere of the Sox. He joined with Frazee of Boston and Yankees owners Captain T. L'H. Huston and Jacob Ruppert in a formal alliance against President Johnson, using the Mays case as a launching pad for a movement to oust Johnson from his post. Comiskey's concern in the matter was curious but he was fully engaged and prepared to go the distance.

Rather than hash the grievance out in a private meeting of the American League, the Yankees took it to the courts and obtained a temporary injunction that restrained Johnson from preventing the use of Mays.[48] The result was a Civil War within the organization, with Comiskey and his allies on one side and the five other clubs supporting Johnson. Ironically, Comiskey, Huston/Ruppert, and Frazee happened to constitute a majority of the four-club American League board of directors; a directorate that rotated on a yearly basis. The other position was held by James Dunn of Cleveland, and Johnson, as league president, would serve as the chairman of the board.

The rebellious trio planned to use their leverage as members of the board to accomplish their solitary goal: to expel Johnson from big league baseball.

For maybe the first time in his career, Comiskey was on the outside of popular opinion when it came to the sportswriters covering the skirmish.[49] He was also severely straining relations with friends James Dunn and Frank Navin, owners of Cleveland and Detroit respectively. The entire feud was going to present potentially damaging consequences to the league and distracted from the retooling baseball as a whole was trying to accomplish post-war. Sports scribes, generally considered Johnson to be a crucial element in baseball's success. Any conspiracy to overthrow his regime was met with fury by pundits, and they redirected the venom back onto the mutineers. Comiskey was in the cross hairs, and his cloak of invincibility that once shielded him from condemnation was shredded.

Additionally, Comiskey's anti-Johnson stance might have affected an important business transaction with the Philadelphia Athletics that unquestionably would have impacted things later on in the year. Manager Connie Mack was shopping right-handed pitcher Scott Perry around and Chicago wanted him to the tune of $25,000, plus shortstop Swede Risberg.[50] Listening to the rhetoric surrounding Mays, Mack pulled the deal from the table because he was aligned with Johnson.

So there were two questions that begged to be answered: Why did Comiskey join a clique of owners fighting over the troublesome Carl Mays? And why was he risking his own reputation by involving himself in a pointless argument that did nothing for his club?

The only explainable solution was that Comiskey's fierce stubbornness came into play to such a degree that his mind was made up that Johnson had to go and there was no changing it. He was seemingly fed up with what he believed to be the continuously harmful actions of his power-hungry former crony. He'd disagreed with nearly all of Johnson's recommendations over the past two years, and his animosity climaxed with the ruling that sent Jack Quinn to New York.

Any more reconciliation between the two old friends was not to be, much to the detriment of both men, their wives, and the sport itself. Mays, the other owners, and whatever else was happening at the time, meant very little when compared to the bottom line reasoning for Comiskey's involvement. He simply wanted Johnson gone.

Gleason's warriors were indifferent to the politics and continued to chase the pennant. With their confidence riding high, some of the Sox players spent time assessing the financial aspects of the approaching World Series; specifically trying to figure out what the players' split would mean to them individually.[51] The fact that it was early August, two months before the Series was to be staged, didn't matter. The specific divide of money was still unclear, and Buck Weaver expressed his frustrations. "What I would like to know is what are we going to get out of this Series? The players don't know. It doesn't look as if anybody else does."[52]

Another anonymous Sox member apparently was under the belief that players were going to be receiving a flat $2,100 payment for participating in the Series, which was not acceptable in any regard.[53] He declared that he "would not play" for that sum, and he guessed "that half of the other fellows on the Sox wouldn't." Harry Neily of the *Chicago American* recorded the statement, adding that the man's comments were made in the presence of one-third of the players, and that he was "one of the hardest working" athletes on the team. A general anxiety about the fairness of the Series payout was visible among a certain segment of the club, and the sentiment of money was a focal point.

Throughout all the internal issues, Eddie Cicotte was having a remarkable season. The turnaround from 1918, when he won 12 games and lost 19, was extraordinary, and, at thirty-five years of age, the veteran remained one of the best pitchers in the majors.[54] As the year progressed, pundits wondered how much more of the constant work his arm could take, and by September, there was talk that he was burned out. A few days after winning his 28th victory at home on September 5, he joined his teammates for an eastern road trip, starting in Washington on September 9. En route, Cicotte took sick, and simple exhaustion may have figured into his condition.[55] Gleason, who was ever in touch with the needs of his athletes, gave Cicotte a break, and rested him a full thirteen days.[56]

Being the most heavily relied upon pitcher in a Sox uniform and with the anxiety of having to lead the team into the upcoming World Series, Cicotte was a burdened man. In fact, his personal life was just as stressful. His wife was seven months pregnant with their third child and he'd recently purchased a $4,000 farm and assumed a mortgage. He was also involved in a garage business in Delray, just southwest of Detroit. So it was completely understandable that, between his life outside the game and responsibilities in it, he had the weight of the world on his mind.

Comiskey traversed back and forth between Chicago and New York several times in the process of dealing with the league war. On his sixtieth birthday, he watched his club take an eleven-inning thriller from Boston in a come-from-behind showing. The attitude of the players, at least on the field, remained constantly strong; probably thanks to Gleason's efforts. They finalized their championship run on September 24, when they beat St. Louis, 6–5, behind the pitching of Cicotte and Kerr. It was Chicago's second American League pennant in three years and symbolized the power of the White Sox—and ultimately the potential to be a prominent dynasty in the annals of baseball history.

Immense coverage of the pending World Series began almost immediately, and every sportswriter had an opinion, prediction, and lots of conjecture to add to the excitement. Gamblers were out in full force, rooters were confident and touting their teams, and owners were making final arrangements to accommodate huge throngs of enthusiasts. This time around, the White Sox were facing a solid competitor, the National League champion Cincinnati Reds. The Reds were owned by Garry Herrmann; an old friend of Comiskey and a member of the Woodland Bards. Herrmann was also, significantly, the chairman of the National Commission.

In a move considered suspect, Herrmann roundly supported a late-season push to adopt a best of nine format for the World Series. He received a majority of votes approving the measure from both leagues, and the concept was accepted. Comiskey disliked the idea for the reason that it broke the standard and accepted tradition of the event. Some writers panned him for trying to keep the Series short because of his lack of solid pitchers, while Herrmann was charged with purposely lengthening it for that same reason.

The play on the field would dictate who'd become world champions, and none of the pre-game speculation was going to turn the tides. The fact was that Chicago did only have two surefire pitchers: Cicotte and Williams. Kerr, the rookie, was the X factor. But unfortunately for Sox fans, Faber, the hero of the 1917 Series, was unlikely to factor into the result. If for any reason Cicotte or Williams failed to produce, it was going to be a protracted nightmare for Comiskey and his club. The championship hinged on their performance.

George S. Robbins, in sizing up Comiskey's players going into the Series, made a striking comment in the August 28, 1919, edition of the *Sporting News*: "The Sox are great money players. Show that gang a bunch of coin and they'll do almost anything except commit murder."[57]

ENDNOTES

1 *Chicago Daily Tribune*, October 16, 1917, p. 17.
2 *Sporting News*, November 8, 1917, p. 5.
  Comiskey reportedly received more than 2,000 telegrams and letters after the Sox won the championship. He took the time to respond to each. There was talk of the White Sox shifting their spring training from Mineral Wells, Texas to Palm Beach, Florida.
3 *Chicago Examiner*, November 6, 1917, p. 10.
  The hunting and fishing grounds of Dover Hall was near Brunswick, Georgia, and was said to be quite similar to Camp Jerome in Wisconsin.
4 *Chicago Examiner*, November 28, 1917, p. 8.
  According to the article, Johnson laughed at Comiskey's comment, and "ordered another round."
5 *Chicago Examiner*, November 23, 1917, p. 10.
6 *Chicago Daily Tribune*, November 2, 1917, p. 13.

It was reported that Comiskey and Johnson had a "friendly argument" about limiting the schedule to 140 games. Comiskey believed that, to meet all expenses, clubs had to play a full 154-game schedule.

7 Ban Johnson, in his eagerness to work out an amicable deal with the government regarding baseball, suggested allowing Washington, D.C. officials to take over control and operate all American League teams in 1918. It was seen as a drastic measure that Comiskey opposed.

8 *Chicago Daily Tribune*, December 13, 1917, p. 21.

Comiskey was initially elected vice president of the American League on December 14, 1916. He assumed the position vacated by Charles Somers, who sold out of Cleveland and retired from major league baseball.

9 Sportswriters hedged their comments on the reason why Kid Gleason didn't return to the White Sox in 1918. The ever professional Gleason refused to hash any grievances out in the press, and simply stated that his faltering Philadelphia pool room business demanded his full attention. The real reason was said to be a bonus that Gleason was due, that he hadn't been paid. Comiskey disagreed, saying that Gleason "received everything due him from the White Sox," *Chicago Daily Tribune*, January 1, 1919, p. 21. Gleason later told the press to "forget" any previous squabble after being hired as manager, noting that "Commy is the best man in the world personally, and as a baseball man, he is second to none," *Sporting News*, January 9, 1919, p. 1.

10 Faber joined the U.S. Navy and was stationed at the Great Lakes Naval Training Center near Waukegan, Illinois, north of Chicago.

11 *Chicago Daily Tribune*, April 1-2, 1918, p. 13.

12 *Chicago Daily Tribune*, April 24, 1918, p. 13.

13 *Sporting News*, May 2, 1918, p. 2.

Collins' consecutive game playing streak ended at 478.

14 *Chicago Daily Tribune*, May 14, 1918, p. 15.

Following a 6–4 loss at Philadelphia, Jackson parted ways with the White Sox to join a shipbuilding company based in Wilmington, Delaware.

15 *Chicago Daily Tribune*, June 12, 1918, p. 11.

Also see: *Sporting News*, June 20, 1918, p. 1. The latter source said it was manager Clarence Rowland who told Williams and Lynn to immediately leave the ballpark, and not Comiskey. It was believed that because Jackson and Williams were such good friends, called "inseparable companions," Jackson influenced the Sox pitcher to leave the Sox for the shipyards. Williams was also close with Lynn, having both ascended to the majors from a club in Salt Lake City. More insight into the friendship between Jackson and Williams can be found in the *Sporting News* from March 13, 1919.

16 *Sporting News*, November 7, 1918, p. 3.

Four members of the team became officers, including Alfred Von Kolnitz, who rose to the rank of major, the highest ranking player from the majors. Pitcher Jim Scott became a captain. Most of the Sox players to join the military were rookies, and the two most prominent were Eddie Collins (marines) and Red

Faber (navy). Comiskey's nephew Albert Bernoudy and chauffeur Walter Gear also enlisted for service.

17 *Boston Herald,* October 4, 1918, p. 6.

The $18,000 minor leaguer that Comiskey bought back in 1913, Larry Chappell, also died of influenza while serving in the Army. He was twenty-eight years of age.

18 *Chicago Daily Tribune,* July 2, 1918, p. 9.

Also see: *Sporting News,* July 4, 1918, p. 1. There were several rumors floating around about why Felsch really walked away from the White Sox. The initial report was that he was going to work for a gas company in his hometown for essential war employment. Other gossip said he was running for the shipbuilding yards as soon as the smoke cleared. But there may have been other factors. Earlier in the season, Felsch took a few days to rush to the aid of his brother, Charles, who was seriously injured in an army accident in Texas. Upon his return, there were some complaints that his getaway included time in Milwaukee instead of returning straight back to the team, and he may have been docked pay. Needless to say, Felsch came away from the situation with bad feelings. His on-the-field play was not up to his usual standard, and it appeared as if his mind was elsewhere. Another story claimed Felsch had bad blood, perhaps even a literal fight, with someone on the team, rumored to be Eddie Collins. The final version was that Felsch was upset with Comiskey because he didn't get a bonus that the latter offered if Felsch didn't drink during the season. Comiskey claimed that he violated the agreement, and thus didn't deserve it, but that he received it anyway.

19 *Sporting News,* August 1, 1918, p. 1.

Robbins was surprised that Comiskey disregarded the important Cleveland meeting of the American League and didn't use his influence to help straighten the situation out. Comiskey's indifference was becoming more and more apparent.

20 *Chicago Daily Tribune,* July 22, 1918, p. 9.

Harry Grabiner attended the Cleveland meeting on Comiskey's behalf.

21 *Chicago Daily Tribune,* August 4, 1918, p. A1.

American League owners met again in Cleveland on August 3 to discuss the future of the 1918 season. Ban Johnson felt going into the conference that he had enough votes to end on August 20. But Comiskey teamed up with magnates in Boston, Washington, and an unnamed third club (unconfirmed to be New York), and had the support of the entire National League to gain a triumph. The season would be closed out on September 2.

22 *Chicago Daily Tribune,* August 4, 1918, p. A1.

Ban Johnson was the first to make a statement following the meeting in Cleveland. He reiterated the wishes of the War Department and said that if the owners wanted to defy the government, "that is their business." To that, Frazee, Comiskey, and Griffith issued a rebuttal.

23 *Chicago Daily Tribune,* August 11, 1918, p. A1.

Even though Comiskey denied his participation in the statement, his signature was at the bottom along with Frazee and Griffith.

24 *Chicago Daily Tribune*, August 11, 1918, p. A1.

25 *Chicago Daily Tribune*, August 6, 1918, p. 14.
For a game against Philadelphia at Comiskey Park, "not more than 600" people were present, according to James Crusinberry. It was "about the smallest crowd on record" for the stadium. In addition to being a hot day, there was an insufferable smell blowing into the grounds from Chicago's world-famous stockyards. Those few fans in the right bleachers suffered the most. According to baseball-reference.com, the Sox drew 195,081 in 1918 and were fifth in the American League in attendance.

26 *Chicago Daily Tribune*, September 15, 1918, p. A5.
Weeghman also thanked the Woodland Bards for their contributions to the entertainment, something the members knew really well.

27 *Sporting News*, August 29, 1918, p. 1.
Quinn attended the American League meeting in December and admitted that he'd rather play with Chicago than New York. *Chicago Daily Tribune*, December 13, 1918, p. 15.

28 *Sporting News*, September 5, 1918, p. 1.
Both Comiskey and his wife also fought off influenza in October 1918. *Sporting News*, October 24, 1918, p. 1.

29 *Chicago Daily Tribune*, September 20, 1918, p. 18.
Also see: *New York Tribune*, October 3, 1918, p. 13, noted that Comiskey and Johnson were hunting together in Wisconsin in spite of their recent problems. Only a few friends joined them, as the annual Woodland Bards outing was postponed because of the war.

30 *Chicago Daily Tribune*, October 17, 1918, p. 14, November 28, 1918, p. 23.
Initially, officials from Camp Grant wanted to use Grant Park, but found they were going to have to invest as much as $10,000 to provide seating. Comiskey allowed them to stage these events free of cost.

31 *Sporting News*, October 31, 1918, p. 4.
Ban Johnson wanted to completely cancel the 1919 season. He was labeled a "pessimist," where John Heydler of the National League, Comiskey, Frazee, and Griffith were much more upbeat about baseball's return. *Sporting News*, November 14, 1918, p. 2. Johnson quickly changed his tune when there was an uprising of support favoring baseball's return. It should be mentioned that while Comiskey was becoming less and less of a lieutenant for Johnson, Phil Ball of the St. Louis Browns was turning into one of Johnson's biggest allies in the league.

32 *Chicago Daily Tribune*, December 13, 1918, p. 15.
Comiskey was reelected American League vice president at the organization meeting in Chicago.

33 *Sporting News*, January 23, 1919, p. 2.
Collins, Schalk, Jackson, Faber, and Cicotte were five players on the White Sox whose combined salaries amounted to $41,000. Ban Johnson said using a salary limit system was impractical. Baseball historian Bob Hoie notes that Weaver would have to be substituted for Faber to get a combined five-player salary of $41,000.

34 *Sporting News*, November 21, 1918, p. 6.

35 *Sporting News*, December 26, 1918, p. 8.
   Huggins denied he had any interest in Jackson, but it was known that he wanted an outfielder who could produce at the plate.

36 *Sporting News*, January 2, 1919, p. 1.
   When asked about the various issues pertaining to the White Sox, Comiskey replied that he wasn't talking baseball at that time and that there was plenty of time to discuss things later.

37 *Sporting News*, January 9, 1919, p. 1.
   The following week, in the same publication, Robbins commented that many of Rowland's friends vowed to never again attend games at Comiskey Park because of the unfair way Rowland was treated. Behind the scenes, though, it was believed that Comiskey helped broker Rowland's purchase of the Milwaukee club of the American Association with Sox rooter Hugh Brennan in February 1919. Comiskey also sent a number of his rookies to Milwaukee for development, including Johnny Mostil,

38 *Salt Lake Telegram*, January 29, 1919, p. 9.
   Sporting News, February 6, 1919, p. 2.

39 *Sporting News*, November 21, 1918, p. 6.

40 *Sporting News*, March 13, 1919, p. 1.
   Weaver was quoted in 1918 as saying that he had, "the best season of [his] life," and that he "outbatted and outplayed Eddie Collins."

41 Robbins' estimate of Weaver's salary was incorrect, as Weaver was already making $6,000 a year at the time.

42 *Sporting News*, May 15, 1919, p. 5.

43 *Sporting News*, June 5, 1919, p. 2.

44 *Chicago American*, June 27, 1919, p. 7.

45 *Chicago Daily Tribune*, July 10, 1919, p. 16.
   After the games on July 9, 1919, New York remained in first place with a record of 40–23 (.635) and the Sox were 43–25 (.632). The Sox took first place on July 10.

46 *Chicago Daily Tribune*, July 10, 1919, p. 16.

47 *Chicago Daily Tribune*, July 21, 1919, p. 15.
   It was said that as many as six clubs in the American League were after Mays.

48 *New York Times*, August 7, 1919, p. 16.
   Also see: *Chicago Daily Tribune*, August 9, 1919, p. 9. Comiskey went to New York for a meeting of the board of directors on August 14 and acted as chairman as the three anti-Johnson members voted to reinstate Mays. *Chicago American*, August 15, 1919, p. 6.

49 *Sporting News*, August 7, 1919, p. 1.
   One of the most candid writers about the Mays case was Joe Vila, who was firmly in the corner of Johnson.

50 *Chicago American*, August 7, 1919, p. 7. Despite the public rumors that Scott Perry was on the market in 1919, there are beliefs to the contrary. Ultimately, he was never traded or sold and finished his career in a Philadelphia Athletics uniform in 1921.

51 *Sporting News*, August 7, 1919, p. 4.
    Matt Foley of the *Chicago Herald and Examiner* was the original source, according
    to the article. Foley wrote that the Sox "already have divided their World's Series
    money."

52 *Chicago American*, August 30, 1919, p. 7.

53 Ibid.

54 *Sporting News*, June 5, 1919, p. 1.
    George S. Robbins explained that the Sox barely supported Cicotte with runs
    the year prior, including a stretch in which only a single run was scored in 51
    innings.

55 *Chicago American*, September 15, 1919, p. 7.
    It was said that Cicotte had suffered from a "severe cold." Manager Gleason also
    noted that Cicotte had gained weight during the season, but that it meant he
    was in good shape rather than the opposite. After his September 19 appearance
    in Boston, Cicotte was given permission to venture away from the team to spend
    time with family in Detroit. *Chicago Daily Tribune*, September 20, 1919, p. 15.

56 For a detailed explanation of the $10,000 supposedly promised Cicotte for win-
    ning 30 games, see Chapter Twenty.

57 *Sporting News*, August 28, 1919, p. 1.
    Robbins also stated, "Probably not in the history of baseball has there been a
    greater money team than the White Sox."

16

AN UNFORGIVEABLE BETRAYAL

Many factors in the baseball universe and on the fringe of the sport were coming together in customary fashion to celebrate the annual World Series. Hotels were filling up with avid supporters and the enthusiasm of sportswriters was at a fever pitch. The science of the match-up, the head-to-head player comparisons, and all other analysis was being nitpicked to exhaustion by hordes of reporters. The always dedicated Hugh Fullerton was leading the way with his exclusive "dope" and his predications were as good as any.[1]

In his wisdom, Manager Kid Gleason allowed the White Sox to let down their guard a bit at the latter stages of the 1919 regular season, believing that the reduced intensity would allow players to regain any lost strength. George Phair of the *Chicago Herald and Examiner* noted after a 3–1 loss to the St. Louis Browns on September 25, that the "Sox did not play a regular big league game of ball."[2] The next day, it was more of the same with second-string pitcher John "Lefty" Sullivan throwing for a full nine innings and being hit 19 times for 10 runs in another defeat.[3] In all, the Sox lost their final four games of the season. Regardless, Gleason's peers, Tris Speaker, Jimmy Burke, and Miller Huggins, having seen the Sox all year, predicted that they would still prevail over the Cincinnati Reds.

Charles Comiskey was subdued in terms of his public visibility and sent his son Louis and Harry Grabiner to Cincinnati for the coin toss to determine where the first two games of the Series would be held. Garry Herrmann of the Reds was victorious and secured the rights to games one and two for Redland Field, which, incidentally, had been built with help from one of Comiskey's longtime friends, John Agnew. The fact that Comiskey had managed previously in Cincinnati was not lost in the storyline either, and added to the emotion of the Series.

Much like the decision that expanded the Series from a best of seven to a best of nine, Comiskey disagreed with the National Commission's ruling that boosted ticket prices for the big event.[4] Box seats were going to cost $5.50, while the bleacher seating at Sox Park, which was regularly 25 cents, was $1.10, including tax. He felt the same way about ticket prices before the 1906 World Series and hated to see his loyal rooters forced to pay more money at the gate. In spite of the increase, the demand remained high in both cities, but a question lingered whether the interest would be sustained if the Series went the full nine games.

Little did anyone know at the time, but this was going to be the last hurrah for the Woodland Bards, for the most part. President Joe Farrell arranged a special train for more than 220 people that left Chicago for Cincinnati on the evening of September 30, 1919. Comiskey was joined by friends John Burns, James Mullin, Sam Pass, actor George M. Cohan, attorney Clarence Darrow, and dozens of others.[5] Conspicuous on the journey were members of the Tennes Family, real estate brokers in the Chicago area, including brothers William and Charles. Another sibling, Mont Tennes, a Sox booster and infamous gambler, was likely also aboard with his son Ray.

Comiskey missed out on the final game of the season because his son Lou, recently returned from Cincinnati himself, had fallen seriously ill with appendicitis.[6] Lou was to have been on the festive Bards train, but was bedridden, and his father unquestionably had a heavy heart when he left Chicago.

The National League champion Reds were the sentimental favorites and underdogs, according to the majority of pundits scouting the game. A professional club for thirty-eight years, Cincinnati had only captured one championship, and that was the 1882 American Association pennant. Led by Pat Moran, the team was stocked with a number of talented athletes, including several former Chicago players. Comiskey's squad in previous years had discarded Eddie Roush, Morris Rath, and Hod Eller when they were early in their careers. Roush was a top hitting outfielder, batting .321 in 1919 and hurler Eller went 19–9. The Reds were strong in the pitching department with six men having 10 or more victories, including Slim Sallee, a 21-game winner, who met defeat at the hands of the Sox in 1917 when he was playing for New York.

Critics combated talk of the Reds' excellent pitching staff by observing that the White Sox were the best hitting team in the American League. They'd demonstrated a heart to win and ability to offensively strike without remorse. The twenty-three members of the Sox team arrived in Cincinnati on the morning of Tuesday, September 30, 1919, and staged a practice at Redland Field. Their base of operations were out of the Hotel Sinton and the lobby of that establishment, as well as the Gibson Hotel, were the primary centers for baseball enthusiasts, reporters, and players. They were also infested by an eager contingent of gamblers who'd made their way in from all parts of the country.

Unlike contemporary newspapers, the periodicals of this era commonly quoted gambling odds of high-profile baseball events in sports pages. The night before game one, the Sox were favored at 6/5 odds.[7] But one *Herald and Examiner* writer noticed that there was "not much betting" in Cincinnati because the locals wanted to utilize the established odds, while Sox betters refused to offer them.[8] However, there was plenty of Chicago money in town, especially when counting the members of the Woodland Bards, Chicago Board of Trade, and a tribe of rich Texas oilmen led by Jack Art of Wichita Falls—who were solidly behind the Sox.

Ed Heeman, a member of the Bards and employed at the Board of Trade, closed a $10,000 bet with an out-of-town broker before even leaving Chicago.[9] Upon arriving in Cincinnati, his group sought to bet another $25,000 at even money, but all they could find were Reds supporters asking for 8/5 odds.[10] The Board of Trade baseball troupe, as a whole, reportedly put up $50,000 in wagers with a reputed bookmaker named Louis Katz in Cincinnati.[11] Bard Tom Reed, on his own, bet $2,000 on the Sox, and, later, sports promoter John "Doc" Krone did likewise. Art's faction were said to have, over the course of the first two games, gambled as much as $50,000.[12] Of course, Cohan and Tennes were heavily involved in the betting, and their combined wagers were over $100,000.

The opening game began on the afternoon of October 1, 1919, at Redland Field with just over 30,500 spectators on hand.[13] Comiskey lingered quietly in the midst of the background noise as the Sox took the field, and his expectations were probably just for a continuation of the success his team garnered during the regular season. At times, winning appeared so naturally for Gleason's men, and with Eddie Cicotte on the mound, he was assured of an all-around good showing. The regularly enthusiastic Bards were charged up prior to the game, but were quickly hushed by the unsatisfactory performance of the Sox. Cicotte, who hit the first batter he faced, was pulled in the fourth inning after six earned runs, and the Reds won 9–1.

One loss was somewhat demoralizing, but not enough to knock Chicago out. Comiskey was searching for any kind of positivity going into the second game, and after a restless night, he received a strange early morning phone call.[14] It was about 6 a.m. when he spoke with Mont Tennes, the Chicagoan who was well-tied into the gambling underworld, and was told that he had some important information to discuss. Comiskey wasted little time, asking his faithful ally Norris "Tip" O'Neill to meet with Tennes and report back. The news was altogether disheartening: Several members of the White Sox were crooked; playing to lose instead of to win and working in cahoots with a gambling syndicate.[15]

Previous to the Tennes phone call, Comiskey likely heard the usual rumors, but was experienced enough in baseball to know that gossip such as players throwing a game and being in the pocket of gamblers was somewhat common in the annual Series. But Tennes' insight was information from an acquaintance purportedly on the inside, to a certain degree. It had to be acknowledged.

Comiskey received the frightful news and was compelled to act. "I immediately told John Heydler, President of the National League," Comiskey later explained.[16] What he didn't do was directly inform American League President Ban Johnson, specifically because he "had no faith in him."

More to the point, Comiskey would never have belittled his club in front of Johnson based on gossip, regardless where it came from. Even the rumors of a fix was embarrassing to a club owner, especially the closer it got to home. Additionally, the power struggle in the league continued as well, and Comiskey was clear in his position. The comments of Tennes, little did Comiskey know at the time, had absolute truth to them, and several members of his ball team had turned traitor. He was being double crossed to such an extent that no one in baseball history had ever encountered anything similar before.

Going back a little in time to the inception of the plot, it is clear that there are a number of inconsistencies surrounding its origin. There is enough evidence to support more than one theory; particularly the supposition that the initiative for the fix may have been independently discussed by opportunist gamblers and several members of the Sox before coming together to merge their crooked interests.

During the summer of 1919, a 6'2" former ball player from Texas did some traveling on business. He mingled with old pals in St. Louis, wearing a "rusty brown suit," and was the kind of guy players enjoyed associating with.[17] He was full of stories, personable, and, most importantly, trusted. Players knew when they talked to William "Sleepy Bill" Burns that they were getting the genuine article. He also talked money, proving to be a successful businessman after retiring from baseball, and athletes wanted to benefit from his knowledge.

Burns spent $500 for an oil lease that morphed into $16,000.[18] He invested further, turning his profits into holdings that were said to be worth an estimated $60,000 in 1919. Seeking to cash in by selling his oil property, he planned to meet up with potential buyers in New York City and Montreal, but while in the former locale, he met up with a bunch of old friends and found the experience invigorating. It was reminiscent of old times with Rube Benton and Jean Dubuc, longtime friends and current members of the New York Giants. Burns was a barnacle on the team for a stretch, also hanging out with unruly characters Hal Chase, Heinie Zimmerman, and Benny Kauff. The combination of Burns, Benton, Kauff, Chase, and Zimmerman was rowdy to say the least, and their likely conversations would've turned the stomachs of baseball purists.

Giants' manager John McGraw admitted that Burns even tried to sell him an oil lease around this time.[19] McGraw came to the realization that his team had several "undesirables" during the 1919 pennant fight, and only weeks before the Sox-Reds series began, he suspended Zimmerman after he caught wind of his alleged attempts to bribe fellow teammates. Additionally, McGraw felt that Chase's "dishonest" play and a faked injury contributed to four crucial losses against Cincinnati in August, helping knock the Giants out of the championship campaign. In sum, he believed that Chase and Burns were directly responsible for the Giants second place finish—and the Reds ascension to the Series.

The brainchild of what was amounting to be the "Black Sox" scandal has, throughout the years, been credited to various people.[20] The *Washington Post*, on October 23, 1920, indicated that Hal Chase was the initial component of the fix.[21] Chase, who played for the White Sox from 1913–14 before jumping to the Federal League, was at the center of his own gambling and bribery scandal in 1918 while with Cincinnati, and his unsavory nature was well established. If the *Post* article is accurate, it is not improbable that Chase first broached the idea with Burns while Burns was hanging around the Giants in New York. Chase knew that Burns' friendliness with Sox players gave him an inside avenue to discuss potential options with guys he thought might be receptive.

There is no way to absolutely verify Chase was the singular mastermind for the concept, but the idea may have cultivated in the environment constructed by Chase, Burns, and others in that New York contingent.[22] Envisioning the scenario for a moment, one could see a lot of half-hearted conversations, joking, and an accumulation of alcoholic beverages being consumed. Then, a corner was turned, when thoughts of fixing the Series became less complicated and more possible, especially when it was realized that there were accessible players on the White Sox. Additionally, the overall atmosphere in baseball was extremely ripe for a major gambling heist.[23]

Burns could see the dollar signs on the wall and was completely stimulated to pursue this course of action. In need of some backup, he called on his trustworthy friend, William Joseph "Billy" Maharg of Philadelphia. Maharg's playing career was exceptionally brief—only playing in two games—but he was more known for his time in the ring as a professional fighter in the lightweight class.

Maharg rushed to New York exactly when the White Sox were in town to play the Yankees, and on September 16, 1919, after a rainout at the Polo Grounds, the duo conveniently found their way to the team hotel, the Ansonia on Broadway, and met up with members of Comiskey's club.[24] Under the cover of planning a hunting trip to New Mexico with Sox pitcher Bill James, Burns pulled Eddie Cicotte aside and briefly discussed a fruitful opportunity, albeit it was unspecified at that time.

Cicotte and Chick Gandil, interestingly, had already spoken to each other in confidence about fixing the World Series.[25] Their discussion may have taken place as early as September 8, and might have involved others on a train headed for an Eastern road trip. They agreed in theory that if the money was right, they'd possibly participate in such a scheme. With the taboo topic already broached in private, Cicotte and Gandil were open to what Burns had to say, and participated in a second meeting two days later. That's when the question was posed: Could the 1919 World Series be thrown for potentially tens, if not hundreds of thousands of dollars?

Gandil was immensely street-smart and the talk of a huge payday outside of his regular Series income was the opportunity he needed to walk away from the majors. He'd had a bruising year, and not counting his regular knee problem, he faced a serious stomach ailment and a threat of appendicitis during the season. The latter problem caused him to lose fourteen pounds and took a serious toll on his mind and body.[26]

His fight with Tris Speaker was another reminder of the kind of personal spirit he employed on the diamond. He was an incredible athlete, but was prepared to give up his Sox uniform to manage in the minors on the west coast. The wishes of his wife to remain in California were heavy in his mind. What he needed most was a chunk of cash, and Burns' scheme hit the mark. Of all the Sox players to hear about the scam, he was the most enthusiastic.

Gandil and Cicotte believed in Burns. They saw him as a winner, having made a good fortune outside of baseball, and his word was always his bond. Gandil was briefly teammates with Burns during his first stint with the Sox in 1910, and Burns was an impressionable figure. So when it came time to discuss the terms for their participation, Gandil and Cicotte asked for $100,000, an amount they felt was both suitable and attainable by Burns and his contacts. The money would be evenly split up among five key members of the team. Burns agreed to work on the financing, and the meeting broke up. With that, officially, the fix was in motion.

By this time, the plot was known by at least four members of the White Sox. Gandil self-appointed himself the conveyor of the message, first reaching out to his personal clique on the team: his California brethren Swede Risberg and Fred McMullin.[27] On the field, the Sox were a compatible unit, but off, they were probably the most dysfunctional outfit in the big leagues. Gandil already knew which teammates would consider such an operation and which would quickly blow the lid off the plot by informing management. Risberg and McMullin were dependable, Gandil knew that for sure, and counted on them to help rope several others into the web.

At twenty-four years of age, Risberg would be the youngest player involved in the scandal. Born in San Francisco, he was the son of a Swedish longshoreman and ended his formal education in grade school.[28] Risberg's baseball skills were developed in the Pacific Coast League, and he transitioned from being a pitcher to the infield where he displayed talent at not only shortstop and third, but at first for the Sox, covering for Gandil when he was out. His arm and range proved to be gold for Gleason in the 1919

campaign, and his iron nerve was known throughout the league. His toughness was an asset to Gandil in the plot, but his temper was also known to get
him into trouble.

While in California working for a shipbuilding company in late 1918,
Risberg played on the company's ball team to earn a little extra money. A
close play started an argument with an official that quickly got out of hand,
and he ended up knocking umpire Jakey Baumgardner out with a single
punch.[29] His actions earned him an indefinite suspension, but it didn't matter because within a few months, he was back with Chicago—and all was
forgotten. However, the incident added to Risberg's reputation, and to this
day is often recited as an example of his fierce attitude and physicality.

Risberg's value as a player in the majors wasn't more than $3,500 a year,
and his offensive production was a handicap. A married man, his wife was
expecting their second child shortly after the World Series in October, and
like Gandil and McMullin, Risberg desired to remain on the California
coast rather than play for Chicago.[30] In August 1919, Risberg's name came
up in a possible trade to Philadelphia, which would have sent him even
further east, no doubt a disconcerting notion. Gandil's proposition opened
up new options that were never going to be available again, and the way the
veteran sold the idea made it sound much too easy.

Utility infield Fred McMullin was three years older than Risberg and in
his fifth year in the majors, also having been a product of the Pacific Coast
League. Originally from Kansas, his family relocated to the Los Angeles
area when he was a teenager, where his father labored as a carpenter.[31] He
joined the Sox in 1916, and offered the team glimpses of a truly great third
baseman. Early in 1919, McMullin was a holdout for more money. This
issue soon passed, but he rode the bench, and midseason, one writer particularly noted that he was a tradable player because of his reduced status.[32]
Gleason thought enough about McMullin to send him to Cincinnati prior
to the close of the National League season to spy on the Reds.[33]

Next, Gandil targeted pitcher Claude Williams. He approached "Lefty"
even before the Sox left New York for their final tour in Boston, outside the
Ansonia Hotel.[34] Williams was told that the Series was going to be fixed, and
Gandil "wanted to know what [he] would do about it." Williams, it can be
assumed, was taken aback by the exposure of a plot, and explained he
needed some time to think about it.

The twenty-six-year-old was the second best pitcher on the White Sox
staff behind Cicotte, and put up 23 victories in 1919. In 297 innings, Wil-

liams had an ERA of 2.64 and was continuing to improve each year.[35] Originally from Missouri, he advanced as far as his freshman year in high school and demonstrated an aptitude for the diamond which carried him to the Salt Lake City franchise of the Pacific Coast League in 1915.[36] He joined the Sox the next season and was on the path to greater things when he walked away from Chicago during the war, in what was dubbed a full-blown "desertion." The move put him on the wrong side of Charles Comiskey, and was a huge impediment in any bargaining power for a salary raise he might have normally had going into 1919. Williams didn't protest the contract he was offered, even though it was well within his rights to do so, and joined the team when called to report.

A married man with no children, Williams came face-to-face with mortality during a game against St. Louis on July 25, 1919, when a batted ball by Hank Severeid came within an inch or two of smashing against his temple on the side of his head.[37] Knocked to the ground in what was probably the scariest three minutes of his life, he was thankful his reflexes were enough to put his hand up to protect himself.

A $20,000 offer by Gandil looked real good to Williams on that September day. But was it worth throwing away his integrity, his pride, and potentially everything he'd ever worked for?

That's when Gandil pulled his greatest trick of persuasion, used multiple times throughout his quest to build the coalition of crooked men. Gandil told him: "Whether or not [Williams] took any action, the games would be fixed," Williams later admitted.[38] With it being framed in such a way, Williams felt that "if it was going to be done anyway, [I] may as well get what [I] could" out of it. The fifth, and one of the most important men, was onboard.

The White Sox went to Boston following their September 18, 1919, loss at New York. Over the next two days, Joseph "Sport" Sullivan, a forty-eight-year-old broker, accepted a formal role in the fix. Sullivan was a man who lived a duel existence. On one side, he was married and a father of three living peacefully in suburban Sharon.[39] On the other, he was one of the most prominent gamblers in Boston, living the high life with untold riches and a chauffeur. He hung around Clark's Hotel on Washington Street and his familiar countenance was seen anywhere there was action, from horse races and pool halls to Fenway Park. In his line of business, he became friends with people from all walks of life, including ball players.

One of Sullivan's comrades was none other than Chick Gandil. The *Washington Post* article of October 23, 1920, made mention that Hal Chase was the first to call Sullivan, telling him of the concept, which allowed Sullivan to coordinate his effort with the arrival of the Sox in Boston. It is impossible to know whether Chase made that phone call or if Gandil reached out to him on his own accord once in Boston.[40] Eliot Asinof's bestselling book, *Eight Men Out*, reported that "exactly three weeks" prior to the 1919 Series, Sullivan was prompted by Gandil to join him for a meeting at the team hotel in Boston.[41] However, the Sox were not in Boston "exactly three weeks" before the Series. They didn't arrive until September 18 or the morning of the 19.

As for a possible August meeting, the White Sox, depending on their arrival, were in Boston between August 1 and 4. But due to appendicitis, Gandil missed the whole series because he was back in Chicago recovering.[42]

Regardless, Gandil and Sullivan met and arranged an $80,000 deal, entirely separate from the Burns agreement. The *Boston American* newspaper, over a year later, reported that Gandil, Sullivan, and Cicotte discussed the fix at the Hotel Lenox.[43] The addition of Sullivan added a second benefactor and rewarded the traitors with even more money for their crooked actions.

Back in New York, Burns and Maharg sought to escalate their presence in the gambling hierarchy by reaching out to the man at the top of the food chain: Arnold Rothstein.[44] If anyone in the country had the means and possible interest in such a scheme as to throw the World Series for $100,000, it was Rothstein. Comparable lightweights in the gambling world, Burns and Maharg went looking for financing among their own circles, but the kind of money involved made it a big league operation, one that only a guy like Rothstein could pull off. They quickly realized that all roads lead to the New York based millionaire, and tried to gain access to him at the Aqueduct Racetrack in Queens, but were unsuccessful.[45]

Another attempt to induce Rothstein to join their scheme was made with Benny Kauff of the Giants, although the Rothstein conference in a restaurant at the Hotel Astor was exceptionally brief.[46] Rothstein immediately notified all at the table that he "wouldn't listen to anything in which that man is concerned," pointing at Kauff. Once Kauff was out of the picture, Rothstein may have entertained a second meeting, but the gist was all the same. He refused to participate in what he perceived to be an unmanageable mixture of characters running amok. Rothstein liked schemes that he could control, and the demonstration by Burns and Maharg didn't inspire confidence.

Enter thirty-six-year-old Abe Attell. The smallish former world-class boxing champion picked up on the sensational plot and was eager to be involved. With tentacles all over the sports map, including among the Woodland Bards, he was willing to take the gambling risks that Rothstein normally would avoid.

On September 29, 1919, Attell, joined by a Des Moines theatrical man named David Zelcer posing as "Bennett," and Chase met Burns at the Ansonia Hotel in New York.[47] His purpose was to con Burns into believing that Rothstein had changed his mind and wanted him to act as a go-between for their gambling outfit and the Sox players. Attell wanted Burns to go to Cincinnati to ensure the crooked athletes were informed that the fix was a go, and that they were to receive the full $100,000 amount discussed with Cicotte and Gandil. "Bennett," it was explained, was there as Rothstein's representative. Rothstein, in reality, hadn't changed his mind about working with Burns, and Zelcer as "Bennett" was not representing his interests in the slightest.

With Attel on their side, the reborn Burns and Maharg were off to Cincinnati to meet with the tainted Sox players. After initially being disheartened that their plot was never going to get off the ground, things completely reversed—and there they were, steaming forward, spirits high, thinking about all the money they were going to make.

In Chicago, on that same date, the Sullivan branch of the fix was being ushered forward as well. Unbeknownst to Burns, Sullivan's shrewd manipulations had taken him to the same location Burns' had: at the doorstep of Arnold Rothstein.[48] To Rothstein, Sullivan was a professional gambler and a guy whose reputation preceded him. Sullivan coveted the same kind of secrecy and concealment that he did. Sullivan was also a leading baseball expert.[49] It was said that he knew more facts and figures than many major league managers.

Sullivan and his confederate, Nat Evans, using the alias "Brown," appeared at the Warner Hotel to smooth over any remaining questions with White Sox players. According to Cicotte's confession, "eight" members of the club were in on the fix by that point, including Joe Jackson, Happy Felsch, and Buck Weaver, with all eight in on the summit that day.[50] Williams remembered the meeting differently. He claimed that only himself, Cicotte, Gandil, Felsch, and Weaver were present, along with the two eastern syndicate gamblers.[51] The players might have thought they were getting the entire $80,000 in one lump sum on that occasion, but they had another thing coming.

A partial payment of $40,000 had been turned over to Sullivan, but he pocketed $30,000 of it to gamble on the Series. The other $10,000 went to Cicotte, carefully placed under his pillow to ensure he was onboard for that game one effort—or lack thereof. The other players would have to wait to see a dime.

Southwest of the Warner Hotel, a short distance away, quietly rested the baseball stadium bearing the name of the man these players were conspiring to double cross: Comiskey Park. It was an unimaginable concept to naïve sports lovers, and for the men who'd worked so hard to achieve a spot on a major league roster, they were throwing their future away. But at the time, they didn't know it. They were so short sighted in a grab for money that whatever repercussions might ultimately lie ahead, were blatantly ignored.

Each player had their own individual motivations. The chance for thousands of dollars, basically free money at the loss of their integrity, was worth it. And it seemed that they could potentially walk away scot-free. Whether their salaries were too low or they had pressing family obligations and bills, the athletes must have confronted themselves in the mirror at one time or another and still decided to participate. To them, it was a necessary risk.

All of the gamblers ventured to Cincinnati for game one. Burns and Maharg arrived on September 30, and conversed with Attell. They saw that the latter had quite a large crew of Midwestern associates on hand to make bets and collect money. In effort to bring things full circle, for their side of the plot at least, Burns and Attell agreed they'd see the players together, and Burns went up to the seventh floor at the Sinton Hotel to make arrangements. A short time later, Attell and "Bennett" joined seven of the crooked Sox, as Jackson was the only absentee.[52] Attell confirmed that he had $100,000 ready to be paid for the throwing of the Series, to be paid in $20,000 installments after each of five expected losses.

The players had little choice, and agreed. They were also given assurances that Rothstein was behind the financing and their money was guaranteed. Burns in his 1921 court testimony recited a memorable line from the Sinton Hotel meeting said by Cicotte.[53] The pitcher told the group he'd "throw the first game if he had to throw the baseball clear out of the Cincinnati Park."

With the plans for the fix agreeable on all sides, the conspirators were content. And, the next day, the Cincinnati Reds were victorious in game one, which was exactly according to plan. Even the hit batsman by Cicotte to start the contest was reported to be a signal to gamblers that the deal was going forward as scheduled.

Charles Comiskey and his manager Kid Gleason were wholly unaware of the unscrupulous actions going on in secret around them. Gleason, in particular, who'd felt he was on the same wavelength of his players all season long, was stunned by the news when told by Comiskey on the morning of the second game in Cincinnati. Like everyone else, he'd heard the gossip but brushed the nonsense off his shoulders and carried his head high. He knew his men were on the level, but the reality of Comiskey addressing such mischief was a definite eye-opener. Gleason still felt he had control of the situation and that the Sox were going to win the Series regardless of what was being said.

Gambling odds reacted to the Sox loss and the best that could be found was even money. Gleason, who was enjoying the Latonia Racetrack just over the Ohio River in Kentucky while in Cincinnati, gave an impassioned speech in the Sox clubhouse before the second game on October 2, 1919, and tried to motivate his team the best he could.[54] He heeded Comiskey's word of warning, and the fact that he was told to watch the players closely—with full authorization to substitute out anyone he suspected of crookedness.

Gleason talked about underestimating the skill of the Reds, and that quickly became the byline of the entire Series in the press. The Sox had entered the fracas with an impression of invincibility, had ended their season on a less-than-stellar note, and miscalculated the abilities of Cincinnati on the field. Directly opposite of that, the Reds won their last three of four games in the regular season, finishing with a sense of unity and fight that carried into the battle with Chicago. Behind pitcher Dutch Ruether, Slim Sallee, Ray Fisher, Jimmy Ring, and Hod Eller, the Cincinnati players were starved to win over the illustrious White Sox and to demonstrate that they were not just filler competition for the best in the business.

Lefty Williams, a reliable force all season for Gleason, went to the mound in game two. He fared well until the fourth inning, when things completely fell apart. Williams walked three batters and gave up three runs on two hits.[55] His wildness, which reappeared in the sixth, accounted for six base-on-balls, and led the Sox to defeat, 4–2. The Sox faithful were dropping bundles of money, and newspapers mentioned some of the big losers to be members of Woodland Bards, Jack Art's Texas oil men contingent, and George M. Cohan.

The Series shifted to Chicago and Comiskey Park was adorned with hundreds of large American flags in the front of the stands as a display of the festiveness.[56] The colorful decorations were not met by an enthusiastic crowd. In fact, the two defeats were a dark cloud over the stadium. The animated rooters were passive, or missing, as many empty seats could be seen from the field. Gleason picked Dick Kerr to start game three, and the underdog hurler accomplished what neither Cicotte nor Williams could by defeating the Reds, 3–0.[57] The shutout was invigorating to the White Sox universe, and Comiskey must have let out a sigh of relief. Chicago was finally showing signs of life.

About five thousand more fans appeared for the fourth game at Comiskey Park than the third, and the anticipation was great. Using his years of baseball experience, Gleason chose Cicotte to pitch, knowing that it was improbable that an athlete of his caliber was to have two bad games in a row . . . but Gleason didn't know that the rumors of the fix were true, and that Cicotte, unlike Kerr, was playing to lose. The $10,000 Cicotte had already been paid was tucked away in a safe location, and now, once again, he had to "produce" on the mound.

Cicotte wasn't afraid to manufacture a losing effort, that's for sure. Incidentally, the *Chicago Herald and Examiner*, the day after the October 4, 1919, loss, explained that he had pitched "masterly" ball, but that "tough luck" or "over-anxiety" caused him to make two bad throws in one inning.[58] Cicotte himself admitted that he was a "bundle of nerves," which went to show he had vaudevillian prospects after his baseball career was over. Unless he was stressed that he was unable to throw gently enough for the Reds to make contact. When the game was over, Cincinnati had won, 2–0, and Cicotte was tagged with two errors.

The Reds had a 3–1 lead in the Series and Comiskey was unavailable for comment. Rain postponed the next game, which was scheduled for Sunday—an important box office day for home baseball teams, and Kid Gleason was caught in the clubhouse that afternoon with two players enraptured by the card game, Canfield.[59] He was willing to talk, saying that he didn't know what was wrong with his ballclub. He was asked if Williams was going to pitch the next game, and he told the reporter, "No, I think I'll go in myself."

Some of the Sox players were upset at their own failure to live up to expectations. After leading the American League with a team batting average of .287 during the season, the club was hitting under .200, and guys like

Eddie Collins and Happy Felsch were shadows of their former selves at the plate. And outfielder Nemo Leibold hadn't been able to make contact.

There was another terrible result for Chicago fans on October 6, 1919, at Comiskey Park before over 34,000 people. Of course Lefty Williams was tied into the conspiracy, but writer Hugh Fullerton felt that the blame could not be placed on him.[60] It was his support that "cracked," delivering three hits and also three errors in a 5–0 defeat. Later that night, Comiskey, Joe Farrell, and other Woodland Bards shuttled back to Cincinnati for a do or die game six. Everything was on the line with Kerr back in the saddle, and since he was the only winning Sox pitcher this series, there was still some hope.

Ten innings were necessary for the White Sox to win their second game of the Series on October 7, and Kerr went the distance.[61] Buck Weaver provided an offensive spark by launching rallies in the sixth and tenth innings with leadoff doubles and was the hero of the day. While the Sox would come out victorious by a score of 5–4, the Reds still held their overall advantage with a 4 games to 2 lead. Cicotte pitched the next game, held the following afternoon, and came up a winner for the first time, 4–1, at Redland Field.[62] Writers lauded his work and both Shano and Eddie Collins were superior at bat, the former making three hits and the latter two. Jackson and Felsch also had successful days at bat, with two RBI each.

The Sox were one game away from tying the Series and forcing a dramatic game nine. Gamblers who'd bet on the Reds to win the championship watched the momentum shift with dismay and were pained by the turn of events. A commitment was a commitment, though, and to the members of the scheming Sox, there was only one satisfactory conclusion. Williams pitched the last game of the Series on October 9 at Comiskey Park, and in the first inning, he was mutilated beyond recognition.[63] The *Herald and Examiner* indicated that none of Williams' three appearances were "up to within 20 percent of his American League standard."[64] Jackson created a ruckus with his third inning homer (the only of the Series for either team), but it just wasn't enough. Chicago lost game eight by the score of 10–5, and the Reds were World Series champions.

The next day, Fullerton renewed the spirit of his "dope" after his Series predictions proved incorrect.[65] He forecast that "seven" players on the White Sox would "not be there" when spring training commenced the following spring. He wrote that the Reds were not the better club, and mentioned the "suspicions" that arose during the games. Controversial to say the least, his words drew fire from all corners of the baseball world because of his lack of substantiation. Fullerton scrutinized every game of the Series, listened to the rumors, and spoke under the umbrella of confidentiality with people who didn't want to be on the record. The man who told him about the "seven men" was Charles A. Comiskey himself.[66] Comiskey didn't have proof of the scam, but his suspicions were swelling by the day.

Additionally, Fullerton was given advice from Burns the morning of the opening game between the Sox and Reds, telling him to "Get wise, the Reds are in already." There were others who preached inside information about a fix, but nothing was more convincing to Fullerton than seeing the games themselves and watching players such as Felsch and Cicotte, always steady in their on-field actions, collapse in inexplicable fashion.

Comiskey observed it as well. It was a devastating display of ineptitude, and the rumors were a dagger to his heart. Maybe he wished it was all a dream that he'd wake up from, but the agony never disappeared.

As for the crooked players themselves, after game one, they were locked into a constant back-and-forth struggle with their benefactors; not a baseball owner, but an ill-reputed gambler. This wasn't something they could take to the National Commission or the press, and whatever happened had to stay under lock and key. But they quickly learned that when playing with fire, they were apt to get burned. And they did, repeatedly.

ENDNOTES

1 Fullerton predicted that the Sox would win the Series with five victories in eight games. *Chicago Herald and Examiner,* October 1, 1919, p. 17.

2 *Chicago Herald and Examiner,* September 26, 1919, p. 17.

3 *Chicago Herald and Examiner,* September 27, 1919, p. 15.
  There were 31 total hits and 12 errors, 8 committed by Detroit.

4 *Chicago Daily Tribune,* September 19, 1919, p. 19.

5 *Chicago Herald and Examiner,* September 30, 1919, p. 11.
  The newspaper listed many of people traveling on the Woodland Bards Special to Cincinnati. On the list were Charles, William, and Ray Tennes, plus an "L.M." Tennes. The latter may have been Mont Jacob Tennes, whose national reputation as a gambler might have warranted a slight change of his first name initials by protective Joe Farrell for the press report. Tennes was known to have attended the first two games in Cincinnati.

6 *Chicago Daily News,* September 30, 1919, p. 2.

7 *Chicago American,* October 1, 1919, p. 10.

8 *Chicago Herald and Examiner,* October 1, 1919, p. 16.

9 *Chicago Herald and Examiner,* September 14, 1919, p. 8.

Heeman, who was Secretary of the Woodland Bards, was credited with saying that he, along with his pals, had plenty of money to bet on the White Sox. They received an $8,000 offer from Milwaukee gamblers and Heeman promptly took it. *Chicago American*, October 1, 1919, p. 10.

10 *Chicago Daily News*, September 30, 1919, p. 1.

11 *Collyer's Eye*, October 4, 1919, p. 1.

12 *Chicago Herald and Examiner*, October 7, 1919, p. 11.

13 *Chicago Daily News*, October 1, 1919, p. 1.

14 *Milwaukee Journal Final*, January 31, 1924, p. 1.

15 Baseball historian Bob Hoie adds that Tennes told O'Neill that from the way the betting shifted from the White Sox being 7/5 favorites the night before the first game, to Cincinnati being 7/5 favorites immediately before the game started was evidence that something was wrong. Tennes believed from his experience that the "White Sox had been reached," according to Hoie.

16 *Milwaukee Journal Final*, January 31, 1924, p. 1.

17 *Sporting News*, July 17, 1919, p. 4.
It was explained that Burns used to fall asleep on the bench during his playing days, thus the nickname, "Sleepy."

18 *Sporting News*, July 17, 1919, p. 4.
Burns was reportedly offered $60,000 for his oil property in 1919, but that figure can't be confirmed. The amount might have been a tall tale told by Burns to the press.

19 *Sporting News*, November 11, 1920, p. 8.
McGraw admitted that he gave an unconditional release to pitcher Jean Dubuc because Dubuc regularly associated with Burns during the 1919 season. McGraw took steps to forcibly retire both Zimmerman and Chase by sending them 1920 contracts with low salary figures, knowing that they'd refuse to sign. Additionally, he believed that Zimmerman didn't give his best in the 1917 World Series against Chicago. Rube Benton told the Cook County Grand Jury that Burns was indeed hanging around Dubuc at the Ansonia Hotel weeks prior to the Series. He said Dubuc received a telegram telling him to bet on Cincinnati, and thought it was sent by Burns. Hal Chase, he noted, was also getting "lots" of telegrams at that time. *Chicago Daily Tribune*, September 24, 1920, p. 2. Baseball historian Bob Hoie noted that Chase's 1920 contract was for $6,500, $500 more than what he received in 1919.

20 *Eight Men Out* by Eliot Asinof depicts the animosity of Sox players toward Comiskey as being a motivational factor in what would ultimately become the first stage of the controversy—when Gandil met with "Sport" Sullivan in Boston. In fact, Gandil has long been accepted as the "father" of the entire episode. There seems to be as much evidence supporting the theory that the Chase-Burns faction conceptualized their own vision for throwing the World Series, and then gained a foothold on the Sox through Cicotte and Gandil. The *Sporting News* acknowledged the claims that Sox players made the initial proposition to Burns, while, at the same time, noting that Cicotte and several others said just the reverse—that it was Burns who offered up the idea for the fix. Burns might have

flaunted imaginary wealth, supposedly millions of dollars, when he was worth much less. But the effect was all too real on the impressionable members of the White Sox, and helped him garner their allegiance in the scam. *Sporting News*, October 21, 1920, p. 7.

21 *Washington Post*, October 23, 1920, p. 10.

According to this article, Chase approached Abe Attell, "Sport" Sullivan, and Bill Burns with the idea of throwing the 1919 World Series.

22 *Sporting News*, April 23, 1947, p. 5.

A month before he died, Chase emphatically denied that he was the architect of the 1919 Series scheme, but that he was approached by Bill Burns and a "well-known sports figure of that time," which the article purposefully declined to name. He did admit that he knew about the plot beforehand and expressed regret that he didn't contact National League President John Heydler about it. He claimed he never received a cent "from any player or gambler" regarding the fix. Stories in the press that disseminated in the 1920–21 time frame reported the Chase made as much as $40,000 in gambling winnings on the Series.

23 Gamblers were making headway in all types of professional athletics, including baseball, making friends and contacts throughout the sport. For years, Ban Johnson was on record trying to combat the growing influence of bettors. All things considered, it was naïve to think gamblers wouldn't be trying to influence the annual World Series in one way or another.

24 There were two meetings between Burns and Cicotte at the Ansonia Hotel, the initial on September 16, which very little was said, and the second on the morning of September 18. During the latter conference, the idea was fully discussed, and a demand for $100,000 to throw the Series was reportedly made. *Chicago Daily Tribune*, July 20, 1921, p. 2, *Chicago Daily Tribune*, July 22, 1921, p. 1.

25 Cicotte admitted to talking about throwing the Series in his 1920 deposition to attorney Alfred Austrian. However, his discussion aboard the train was just small talk at the time. Cicotte later explained that despite conversing about the idea with teammates, he needed time to be convinced to actually participate. Throwing away his dignity for money was not something he decided on a whim. After all, he was risking everything after fifteen years of playing Organized Baseball. blog.chicagohistory.org/index.php/2011/04/did-the-cubs-lose-the-1918-ws-on-purpose

26 *Chicago American*, August 6, 1919, p. 9.

27 Many depictions of this story downplay McMullin's role in the fix to the point in which it is said he simply overheard a discussion by Gandil and/or Risberg, and finagled his way into the deal. He wasn't going to be a factor in the Series, so his involvement was not necessary to throw actual games on the field. Off the field, McMullin might have been a substantial player as a lieutenant of Gandil along with Risberg. During one of the earliest meetings, McMullin and Gandil reportedly took the players aside, one-by-one, and asked them what their price was to participate in the plot. This shows much more than a passing involvement in the administration of the affair, at least how it related to the White Sox.

28 1910 U.S. Federal Census, U.S. World War II Draft Registration Cards, Ancestry.
    com.

29 *Sporting News*, November 14, 1918, p. 4.

30 *Sporting News*, March 13, 1919, p. 1. Risberg's second child, Lawrence, was born
    on October 22, 1919. Also, there are reports that allude to an extramarital affair
    Risberg was having and the combined circumstances of having a young family—
    plus a mistress and possibly facing a divorce—may have added to his financial
    worries leading up to his fateful decision in 1919. blog.chicagohistory.org/
    index.php/2011/04/did-the-cubs-lose-the-1918-ws-on-purpose

31 U.S. Federal Census records for 1910 and 1920, Ancestry.com. McMullin and his
    wife Delia had a young son in 1919, William, who was born on November 23,
    1916. Read the comprehensive biography on McMullin at the sabr.org website
    written by Jacob Pomrenke.

32 *Sporting News*, June 19, 1919, p. 1.

33 *Philadelphia Inquirer*, September 26, 1920, p. 18.
    According to a member of the Cook County Grand Jury, which was early in its
    investigation of baseball's shenanigans, McMullin was a "fixer" of the crooked
    plot. He apparently connected with gamblers while spying on the Reds in Cin-
    cinnati before the Series. It was also said that he was a friend of Abe Attell.

34 *New York Evening World*, September 29, 1920, p. 1.

35 Baseball-reference.com.

36 1940 U.S. Federal Census, Ancestry.com.

37 *Chicago Daily Tribune*, July 26, 1919, p. 11.

38 *New York Evening World*, September 29, 1920, p. 1.

39 U.S. Federal Census records for 1900 and 1910, Ancestry.com.

40 In Chick Gandil's infamous 1956 *Sports Illustrated* article, he claimed that Sulli-
    van approached him and Cicotte outside of their hotel, about a week before the
    Series. He said that Sullivan "suggested" the players form a unit of about seven
    or eight players to purposely lose the Series, and that Sullivan offered to pay
    each athlete, $10,000. *Sports Illustrated*, September 17, 1956. Gandil's story com-
    pletely disregards the fact that the proposal had already been discussed in New
    York, days before the Sox were in Boston for the series against the Red Sox. Also,
    if Sullivan approached Gandil and Cicotte like Gandil said, it might lend credi-
    bility to Sullivan having already been informed of a potential fix by Hal Chase
    via phone call from New York, as mentioned in the *Washington Post*, October 23,
    1920, p. 10.

41 Asinof, Eliot, *Eight Men Out*, p. 6.

42 *Chicago Daily Tribune*, July 29, 1919, p. 14, *Philadelphia Inquirer*, July 31, 1919, p.
    14, *Chicago American*, August 6, 1919, p. 9.
    It is impossible to know with any certainty if Gandil and Sullivan talked in per-
    son about a possible fix prior to August-September 1919, or if they communi-
    cated by another means at any time.

43 *Rockford Republic*, October 1, 1920, p. 22.
    The Boston series began on September 19 and included a doubleheader on
    September 20. After putting in an appearance on September 19, Cicotte was

given special permission to go home to Detroit, according to the September 20, 1919, edition of the *Chicago Daily Tribune*. That narrows a meeting involving Cicotte with Sullivan to the evening of September 18, if the Sox arrived that night, or earlier on September 19.

44 *New York Tribune*, September 28, 1920, p. 1.

45 *Chicago Daily Tribune*, July 20, 1921, p. 1.

46 *New York Tribune*, September 30, 1920, p. 2.

Others at the Hotel Astor meeting were private detective Valerian "Val" O'Farrell and a gambler named "Orbie" from Long Island. Orbie reportedly entered the lobby with Kauff and Burns, according to O'Farrell's version of the story, and was a friend of Abe Attell. Maharg told of a meeting with Rothstein at the Astor, in which Rothstein simply said he didn't think the scheme would work.

47 *Chicago Daily Tribune*, July 22, 1921, p. 1, 8.

During the Cook County Grand Jury investigation in 1920, it was speculated that Chase was the first man to contact Attell.

48 Pietrusza, David, *Rothstein*, p. 150–155.

49 *Boston Herald*, September 30, 1920, p. 15.

50 *New York Evening World*, September 29, 1920, p. 2.

The meeting was held in Cicotte's room and was said to have been "three or four days" before the Series.

51 *New York Evening World*, September 29, 1920, p. 1.

Williams said that Sullivan and Brown offered $5,000 to each member of the Sox. This amount conflicted with Gandil's statement back in New York, which had the sum for throwing the Series at $20,000 per man. That had been the price under the Burns agreement. It should be noted that it was originally supposed to be $100,000 for five players, each getting $20,000. That was what Williams and Joe Jackson, specifically, were led to believe by Gandil, and Jackson admitted such during his grand jury testimony.

52 *Chicago Daily Tribune*, July 20, 1921, p. 2.

Jackson, according to various reports, might not have attended any of the meetings in which the plot was discussed.

53 *Chicago Daily Tribune*, July 20, 1921, p. 2. Cicotte's role in the origins of the fix is perplexing. Admittedly, in his 1920 deposition, he discussed the idea of throwing the World Series and talked about the money that could be obtained by such a swindle. Burns was adamant that Cicotte came to him with the idea first, but at the same time Burns made those claims, he was holding a deep grudge against all of the tainted Sox players. When Cicotte himself confessed to the fix, he appeared to display a deep personal remorse for his actions and was emotionally distraught, admitting that, "Risberg and Gandil and McMillin were at me for a week before the World's Series started." So it appears that while he did openly converse about throwing the Series during a train ride east in September 1919, he didn't immediately sign on to participate when the deal was being brokered. Apparently, he needed more time to properly digest the scope of what he was about to do. If he had to be convinced to participate, does it sound like he was an enthusiastic member of the scheme? His statement and the evidence found are not enough to

definitively say one way or another. These men wanted to protect themselves from legalities, and it is unknown whether they curbed their statements to do just that. For Cicotte's quotes, see *New York Evening World*, September 29, 1920, p. 2.

Eight Men Out has Gandil as the originator, coordinating with Sullivan and Cicotte on his own, and then Burns learning about the plot from Cicotte. Asinof, Eliot, *Eight Men Out*, p. 6–9, 15–17, 22–23.

Also see: Cicotte's 1920 deposition: blog.chicagohistory.org/index.php/2011/04/did-the-cubs-lose-the-1918-ws-on-purpose

54 *Chicago Daily News*, October 1, 1919, p. 2, *Boston Herald*, October 2, 1919, p. 16. The *Herald* article was also notable because it mentioned a rumor that Cicotte had bet $5,000 on himself to win the initial game of the Series, noting that it was "bunk."

55 *Chicago Herald and Examiner*, October 3, 1919, p. 10.

56 *Chicago American*, October 4, 1919, p. 1, 6.
An *American* reporter made mention to a Louis Comiskey-Buck Weaver conversation under the grandstand before the game. In ominous fashion, Comiskey bet Weaver a pair of shoes that Cincinnati would win the game, and Weaver took the bet. The writer documented that the prediction caused "much astonishment."

57 Joe Jackson, after his Grand Jury confession in September 1920, talked to the press. He mentioned game three of the Series, saying that "The eight of us did our best to kick it and little Dick Kerr won the game by his pitching." He added that, "Because he won it, these gamblers double crossed us for double crossing them." *Chicago Daily Tribune*, September 29, 1920, p. 2. It was said that the crooked Sox weren't going to play to win behind the "busher," Kerr. Another report claimed that Sox players double crossed the gamblers in the third game because they hadn't been paid the money they were promised. They told them they were going to lose, and then worked doubly hard to win.

58 *Chicago Herald and Examiner*, October 5, 1919, p. 1.
The *Tribune* reported that Cicotte was cheered in spite of his errors. *Chicago Daily Tribune*, October 5, 1919, p. A2.

59 *Chicago Daily Tribune*, October 6, 1919, p. 23.
The two players engaged in the card game were Lefty Sullivan and Grover Lowdermilk.

60 *Chicago Herald and Examiner*, October 7, 1919, p. 10.

61 *Chicago American*, October 8, 1919, p. 1.

62 *Chicago American*, October 9, 1919, p. 1.
The newspaper stated that the Sox looked like champions in this appearance and Cicotte had outstanding control early in the game. Where over 30,000 people were expected to see the spectacle in Cincinnati, the number was closer to 14,000.

63 *Chicago American*, October 10, 1919, p. 1.

64 *Chicago Herald and Examiner*, October 10, 1919, p. 11.

65 *Chicago Herald and Examiner*, October 10, 1919, p. 11.

66 *New York Evening World*, September 29, 1920, p. 1.

17

NOT HEARSAY, BUT LEGAL EVIDENCE

One of the greatest pure hitters of his generation, Joeseph Jefferson ("Shoeless Joe") Jackson batted .375 in the 1919 World Series. He was specifically complimented by fellow teammates Eddie Collins and Ray Schalk after the games, and Oscar C. Reichow of the *Chicago Daily News* wrote that Jackson "played up to his standard."[1] [2] This after batting .351 during the regular season, Jackson had demonstrated unequivocally that he was on par with the best in the business. He was at such a level that his annual salary should have reflected five figures, but the reasoning that it did not was complex, and much more than just Charles Comiskey being a terrible club owner.[3]

In August of 1915, just days before his sale to the White Sox, Jackson signed a three-year contract with the Cleveland Indians calling for an annual pay of $6,000.[4] Comiskey purchased the star outfielder and assumed his three-year contract, which covered the 1917, 1918, and 1919 seasons. That essentially meant that his terms weren't legally up for negotiation until prior to the 1920 season, and the amount was not something Comiskey personally settled upon. That was an agreement made between the Cleveland owner and Jackson himself.

Jackson's 1917 performance would certainly have earned him a reasonable increase in salary, but, surprisringly, he didn't clamor for a new deal going into 1918. Some months after the Sox won the World Series, Jackson was faced with a dire situation as the war was building overseas. His draft status had changed, and he made a decision that shattered the sense of loyalty between him and Comiskey by jumping to a shipbuilding company. Jackson wasn't acting spitefully to harm the Sox or his teammates, but had made a conscience decision to protect his family. Comiskey didn't see it that way, and raged, condemning Jackson in nearly every way possible. He held devotion to the club in such a high regard that Jackson simply betrayed him and the fans, and there was no other way about it.

Kid Gleason, when he rejoined to manage the Sox early in 1919, favored the return of Jackson and brokered a resolution between the owner and player. Jackson's previous three-year contract had been broken when he left the team, and in February 1919, he signed a new, one-year deal valued at $6,000, the same salary he would have received had he not walked away from the team. Considering that Comiskey didn't want Jackson ever to return, a $6,000 contract was a definite compromise, and some might have looked at the situation and said he was lucky to get that.

But Joe Jackson's breach of loyalty to Comiskey and Organized Baseball took an entirely new appearance when he coordinated his efforts with a crooked gang of White Sox players. Regardless of his batting average, the compliments of fellow teammates, or the comments of sportswriters, Jackson was forever connected to the conspiracy, and allegedly expected to be paid $20,000 for his participation. Jackson was smarter than people gave him credit for, despite his inability to read or write, and he knew the ins and outs of baseball. He was aware that his salary was to be renegotiated in 1920, and his performance in the World Series was going to give him the leverage he needed to garner more money.

Any specific instances of Jackson playing to lose in the Series can be endlessly debated, but never proven. His batting average can be shown as evidence of his hard work, but he still took $5,000 of gambling money. Reports that he tried to inform and effectively confess to Comiskey have surfaced, but if Jackson wanted to break open the story after the fourth game—when he received the cash—or at any other time, he didn't need Comiskey to do so. Instead, he could have reached out to any of the baseball officials at the Series, a sportswriter, or even his manager, Kid Gleason. A confession to the press in 1919 would have changed history.

Needless to say, the members of the infamous "Black Sox" didn't achieve the fortunes they expected when they first agreed to the plot. Outside of Chick Gandil, who may have pocketed more than $30,000, and Eddie Cicotte, who received $10,000, the others were assumed to have been given the shaft. Jackson, Lefty Williams, and Happy Felsch each received $5,000, and Swede Risberg and Fred McMullin got anywhere from $5,000 to $15,000 apiece. Buck Weaver, the hero of game six, reportedly didn't receive a penny because he never agreed to participate in the first place.

The conspiracy itself was a complete mess from beginning to end. Abe Attell, "Sport" Sullivan, and the rest were as dishonorable as humanly possible, and the players were naïve to think they'd be treated fairly by such a crew. Bill Burns, as a middleman, was stuck between two entities, and took the brunt of the players' animosity for reneging on payments. When the Sox won game three, the gambling contingent perceived it to be a double cross by the players, and Burns himself lost all of his winnings from the first two games. All of the friendliness that existed before the Series began was lost along the way, and Gandil reportedly told Burns to go "to hell" at one juncture.[5]

Williams later admitted that he and Cicotte talked about playing to win "on the second trip to Cincinnati," around game six, which the Sox won with Dick Kerr pitching.[6] Cicotte then won game seven on October 8, leaving the Series at 4–3 in favor of the Reds as the focus shifted back to Chicago. Modern depictions of the story tell of a physical threat to Williams that motivated him to blow the final game, as gamblers had wagered significant amounts on Cincinnati to win outright and were in fear of a White Sox comeback. Williams never spoke publicly about such a threat, but his game eight Series performance was abysmal and left the Sox no hope of coming back.

Initially, none of the players broke their silence about the fix and went to their respective homes following the "historic downfall," as Harold Johnson of the *Chicago American* explained it, as if nothing had happened.[7] The winning share of the Series pot, which had yet to be distributed, equaled $5,207.01, and amounted to more than what several conspirators received for their participation in the fix.[8] The Sox end was $3,254.36.

Comiskey acknowledged that Cincinnati had a "better ball club" on that particular week, but added that he felt "I had the greatest ball team that ever went into a World's Series." Had Red Faber or Jack Quinn been amongst his pitching staff, things might have turned out much differently. He admitted that the Sox were a "terrible disappointment," but despite that, "it was a wonderful crowd and a wonderful tribute to a ball team" in the final game.[9]

Since none of the players or gamblers directly involved in the scandal confessed, Comiskey, Gleason, and the legion of eager sportswriters were left to their speculation and, if they dared to write about the subject, had to be careful in how they did it. At this point, everything was just gossip. Comiskey addressed the stories by saying, "If there was anything of this nature in connection with the Series, I am ignorant of it. If anybody has any information or evidence along this line, I will pay liberally for the same. I have often heard rumors in connection with World Series, but I never in all my long connection with the national game ever found anybody who could produce evidence to back up their charges."[10]

He wanted to see the guilty punished, should proof verify the rumors, and offered up to $10,000 cash as a bounty for evidence.[11]

Gleason told the press that "something was wrong" with the entire situation. "I didn't like the betting odds," he explained. "I wish no one had ever bet a dollar on the team."[12]

Within days of the final Series game, Gleason and "Tip" O'Neill went to St. Louis to meet with forty-four-year-old Harry Redmon, a theater operator, and followed up on a report that he had inside information of a gambling ring that had influenced the outcome of the championship.[13] Redmon wanted to share his knowledge in exchange for the $6,500 he lost gambling on the Sox, but all that was garnered from the meeting was hearsay stories.

Louis Comiskey was recovering from his appendicitis threat and went to Excelsior Springs, Missouri, with his wife Grace and mother Nan. Charles joined them after Gleason returned from St. Louis with his findings, and tried to get in some much needed relaxation. Stress was a perpetual menace, and the Sox owner needed to find a little breathing room away from the baseball environment. His usual excursion to his Wisconsin camp was no longer an option, as an internal squabble with members of the Jerome Fishing and Hunting Club ended up in the courts, ending the friendly association.[14] The grounds were later sold.[15]

The camp meant a great deal to Comiskey. It was his home away from home; a place where he could unwind from the constant demands of business. Talk of baseball at Camp Jerome was prohibited. Anyone who brought up the subject was "punished" by being disqualified from having a drink for the rest of the day.[16] Always surrounded by friends, Comiskey relished the refreshing environment of the woods and thoroughly enjoyed spending time there after each season. It was his routine for almost two decades, and now that he needed it the most, it was missing from his life. Comiskey needed a new sanctuary, and fast.

Baseball politics remained at a heightened state of concern, especially when there was mention of a potential third major league sprouting up as a result of the American League Civil War. The concept was unpopular, and again pointed to Comiskey's anti-establishment role in the organization. His minority stance was unusual, turning opinions against him, and would eventually intensify the spotlight on his every action—or inaction—regarding the Series fix.[17] When asked about the new league, Comiskey said "It could be done," but refused to say any more.[18]

Secession from the American League for the White Sox, Yankees, and Red Sox was the threat directed at President Ban Johnson. Comiskey, in November of 1919, participated in two board of directors meetings in New York, only attended by his like-minded associates, and issued a powerful statement, saying that Johnson was endangering the integrity of baseball.[19] [20] On top of that, he was imperiling the value of their clubs, and Comiskey affirmed their core desire to eliminate Johnson from the baseball world.

The majority of the board of directors, made up of Comiskey, Harry Frazee of Boston, and Jacob Ruppert of New York, called for the annual league meeting to be staged at a hotel in Manhattan. Johnson ignored that ruling and announced the conference would be held in Chicago instead— surely to be attended by the other five owners. Every maneuver was a bone of contention and every spoken word added to the vitriol of the feud. Fueling the fire was a controversy surrounding the third place World Series payment, which was being tied up by the National Commission in a dispute between the Yankees and Detroit Tigers, of which the Board demanded the immediate release of the money to New York.

At a time in which the American League should have been united to combat the imposing menace of influential gamblers on the sport and ferreting out the rumors of the last World Series, the owners were locked into an exhausting and mostly trivial squabble with no end in sight. Too many personal feelings had been interjected into the conflict, and it wasn't about business or baseball at the heart of the matter.[21] It was about Ban Johnson and Ban Johnson alone.

There were several members of the pro-Johnson faction ready to go to war with a third league. Phil Ball of the St. Louis Browns was the point-man in the establishment of a new Chicago American League franchise in the case that Comiskey launched an outlaw faction. Ball coordinated with Chicago banker Lemuel B. Patterson and James K. Crawford, an oilman from Tulsa, to potentially represent the Johnson-led organization if the worst case scenario erupted. Johnson also tried to invoke political pressure to force Frazee out in Boston by actively searching for new owners.

Rather than continue the farce, Johnson called off his Chicago meeting and went to New York with his five-allied owners to face down the Comiskey group in December of 1919.[22] The two sides engaged in heated discussion, but Johnson gained the upper hand when his supporters voted to create a new board of directors made up of all pro-Johnson magnates. For good measure, they also removed Comiskey from his station as league vice president, replacing him with Frank Navin of Detroit. Comiskey tried to work his old magic, striving to persuade his adversaries to join his cause, but it accomplished little. The overall actions left the rebels in a weakened spot and with little recourse. Bitterness on both sides increased, and even before the meetings had concluded, Comiskey walked out in disgust and returned to Chicago.

Philadelphia sportswriter James C. Isaminger watched Comiskey intently during the league conference and noticed a few peculiarities. He saw Comiskey as having aged ten years in the last twelve months, and that he seemed "to have lost his former superb composure and was restless and nervous during the proceedings." Just "one word" by Comiskey, Isaminger felt, would have resolved the difficulties.[23]

Comiskey was adamant in his grievances. A brief time after the meeting, he told the press that the conditions in the league were "awful," and that it would be lucky to survive past July 4 if a change in the presidency did not occur.[24] His rivals repudiated the statement wholeheartedly.

The prevailing sentiment surrounding Comiskey was less than joyous, and his gloomy outlook for the future of the American League was drastically different from the days when he appeared the eternal optimist. Once more, the transformation of his personality under the weight of constant bombardment was showing through.[25] And the most terrible aspects of concern were yet to become entirely apparent.

In the *Sporting News*, correspondent Joe Vila said that owners needed to end their petty arguments and focus on the vast rumors surrounding the World Series.[26] He mentioned that if there were any magnates "opposed to a disclosure of what has been going on, wishing the public to be kept in ignorance, he should be exposed." The gist of his declaration was perfectly clear, and Comiskey himself had to step up to ensure that a full and complete investigation of the Series had occurred. The press, and public for that matter, demanded it.

Full of pride, Comiskey wanted to avoid public embarrassment, and the league war already left him in a diminished light. But there was no escaping the truth from being known. It was virtually impossible to contain the enormity of players fixing the World Series, and even a man with all the money in the world and limitless power was going to be at the mercy of verifiable facts. In this case, that was particularly true because so many different people were involved and knew the inside scoop. The information that Comiskey had gathered by mid-December 1919 barely touched the surface of the scam, and there was one constant fact: he still had zero legal proof to condemn the crooked members of the White Sox.

In that same amount of time, who did successfully turn up evidence?

Garry Herrmann, head of the National Baseball Commission, said: "As to the charges that the World's Series were framed or fixed by gamblers, I have seen no proof, and must in the absence of such proof refuse to believe such charge could be true."[27]

American League President Ban Johnson stated: "I have heard rumors myself, but I have been unable to learn anything definite as to the identity of the men who are alleged to have approached ball players. If any men in our league are guilty of dishonesty, they should be barred from baseball forever. I would welcome any evidence and, in fact, have tried to obtain it, but so far as I can learn, all this is rumor."[28]

Every baseball writer in the business knew that this story had the potential of being the biggest in history, and they each wanted to break the news to the public. They wanted the glory. In the two months following the Series, these scribes looked high and low, low and high, and flipped over nearly every available rock to find out the exciting scoop. The 200-odd members of the Baseball Writers' Association had an enormous reach in terms of seeking out information.

But the eager contingent of writers found nothing in terms of proof. Johnson was independently pursuing leads, but did not call Sox players before him to provide statements or affidavits regarding their knowledge of a possible fix. Comiskey didn't either. On December 14, 1919, the Sox owner made the following declaration: "I am now very happy to state that we have discovered nothing to indicate any member of my team double crossed me or the public last fall."[29]

It was wishful thinking to the maximum degree. But it was also true that his investigation, which entailed the hiring of an experienced private detective agency, revealed no legal evidence to date.[30]

Additionally, Comiskey's senior advisor was attorney Alfred Austrian, a forty-nine-year-old Harvard graduate with over twenty-five years experience.[31] Austrian counseled him at great length, presenting the various options and relayed his extensive knowledge of the legal system. He knew that slander laws explicitly prevented the White Sox from defaming the reputations of any of the alleged players, and Comiskey had a lot to lose if he stepped over the line. In fact, he would have been unmercifully targeted in lawsuits that might have crippled him, not only financially, but mentally and physically as well. He couldn't act any differently toward the accused seven or eight members of the Sox than he would otherwise, or the public and scribes would have immediately picked up on it.

Austrian, based on his terrific comprehension of the facts in the case, recommended to Comiskey a composed and undeviating trajectory. The inadequate potency of information left no other option but to enter the 1920 baseball season like all previous years. That meant contracts were sent out to the entire White Sox roster, including the allegedly tainted eight players—incredibly, with salary raises.[32]

For that reason, there would develop a major controversy in the way Comiskey was seen in handling the aftermath of the 1919 Series. His perceived inaction and the way his team would nearly mirror that of the fateful season in 1920 turned into the illusion of a cover-up, more distasteful to some pundits and fans than the shameful players themselves.

The propagated allegation of concealment was leveled at the feet of Comiskey in an effort to portray him in the most negative light possible. He was alleged to have wanted to hide the shenanigans of his players to keep his powerful team together, which ignored his decades of fine sportsmanship and displays of integrity. This claim added to the accusation that Comiskey's underpayment of his athletes spawned discontent in the ranks to the point in which it initiated the fix. These two charges were a double-barreled attack of the worst kind.

His critics didn't bother to evaluate the legal ramifications of persecuting the reportedly corrupt players without proof. Those writers who'd taken an anti-Comiskey stance stemming from the American League Civil War and the feud with Ban Johnson seemed to take delight in the downfall of Comiskey. The polluted commentary was also perpetuated by writers who dramatized the scandal and willfully portrayed Comiskey as the villain.

However, Comiskey related more to the victim than the villain. But there was no way for him to evade the tarnish of his crooked athletes.

As 1919 was coming to a close, there were a few outstandingly motivated people working to uncover the truth. Bert Ernest Collyer, publisher of the sensationalistic *Collyer's Eye* newspaper, was one of those individuals.[33] Shortly after the final Series game was played, his paper mentioned that "seven members" of the Sox were "under suspicion." Like Comiskey and Hugh Fullerton, Collyer heard the gossip and rushed to the press with the breaking news, sans any intricate details or names. Two months later, the newspaper attributed comments to catcher Schalk, and specifically named Jackson, Cicotte, Williams, Felsch, Risberg, McMullin, and Gandil as players who wouldn't be returning in 1920.[34]

Despite the fact that Collyer was extremely motivated to break open the plot for the public's consumption, he was still limited by the same problematic criteria that hindered Comiskey and Fullerton. In the absence of verifiable proof, more and more time was passing, and people were becoming antsy. They wanted answers to the allegations, one way or another.

In a stark contrast to all the gloom, a biography was released in late 1919 by a Chicago publishing house entitled, *Commy: The Life Story of Charles A. Comiskey*. Written by longtime newspaperman Gustave W. Axelson, the book was a positive portrait of the Sox owner and recited a somewhat censored version of his history.[35] Many contentious topics were left out, and because of the timing of its publication, the book did not cover the "Black Sox" scandal. Comiskey contributed the final chapter, and he expressed his gratitude toward the people of Chicago, and ironically predicted that 1919 would be the "greatest season of them all."

Needless to say, 1919 was the worst year of his baseball career.

No sportswriter, including Axelson and others in the Chicago area, managed to tackle Comiskey's complicated evolution like St. Louis scribe, John B. Sheridan.[36] In an illuminating expose featured in the *Sporting News* on December 18, 1919, Sheridan discussed the Comiskey he knew years earlier, the guy he "worshipped" as a player, and the man full of hate that he'd become.

When Comiskey was at his finest, he was socially adept for every occasion; full of life and always thoughtful. Sheridan spent time with him and saw firsthand that he possessed "a personal magnetism and charm that is given to few men." He added that Comiskey was possibly "loved for himself as much as any man ever has been loved for himself." It was "easy" for people to love Comiskey, "and he probably has had as few fair weather friends as any man."

Notably, the friendships in Comiskey's life, Sheridan wrote, were not what they once were. Ban Johnson, whose status was clear, and Ted Sullivan were two of Comiskey's oldest friends, and Sheridan had heard "a coolness" had erupted between the latter duo. "There is no better indication of a man's worth than that he sticks to his old friends," Sheridan added, "and that his old friends stick to him."

But now, Comiskey was displaying an outward hatred. Sheridan wrote, "If so gentle and generous a nature as that of Charley Comiskey can hate, his hatred will hurt not the objects of it, but himself." And that Comiskey was "too old a man to hate." Sheridan was personal in his words, mentioning Comiskey's wife Nan and son Louis, and expressed the relative insignificance of the current quarrels when observed in the big picture. It was a poignant expression of the facts, and altogether true that the pettiness of Comiskey's feud with Johnson was detrimental to the sport. But more importantly, it was costing them rewarding moments at a time in their lives in which every minute counted.

Comiskey got some needed vacation at St. Augustine, Florida, and perhaps was able to put things in perspective. At the February 1920 league meetings in Chicago, he shared a few nice words with Johnson, telling his old friend: "Ban, I hope your health is good. I regretted last December to learn that you contracted blood poisoning of the toe. I hope it is quite disappeared."[37]

Johnson replied: "Quite, Commy, thank you. I am glad to note that though you look thin, you seem to be hard as nails. I have heard that Mrs. Comiskey is in much improved health. I am delighted to know it. Her illness had a very depressing effect upon you and upon all of us."

Their conversation, in addition to the end of the American League war, was a sign of positivity, and although Comiskey and Johnson were not yet buddies again, the initial layer of ice was broken. Things could still go either way.

For the crooked alliance of Sox players, the post-1919 Series was anything but enjoyable. The shadow created by the allegations was considerable, and some people wondered why the athletes themselves didn't break free from the suspicion by vehemently denying the rumors and demanding evidence to the charges. Of the players involved, few spoke out about the allegations, and they mainly went about their normal lives. Williams kept busy by returning to the shipyard in Wilmington, Delaware, and worked on boilers.[38] Cicotte paid off his $4,000 farm in cash, but suffered the loss of his garage in an explosion.[39] Thirty-four of his automobiles were destroyed.

Out in California, Chick Gandil was operated on for a broken ligament in his left hand. He also displayed a bit of his sizable bankroll when he bought a new house on Chesley Avenue in Los Angeles and ventured to San Diego for a few days vacation with his wife and daughter, traveling in his new car.[40] Contradictory press reports surrounded Gandil ever since the conclusion of the Series, beginning with a statement that when he left Chicago to have his appendix dealt with, he predicted he'd be in condition by the time spring training came along.[41] He changed his mind by November of 1919, saying he was done with the White Sox and specifically brought up that his World Series pay had been withheld.

The holding up of Series compensation for the players alleged to have participated in the conspiracy was another tactic Comiskey used during his investigation.[42] Not surprisingly, Gandil was one of three men, along with Cicotte and McMullin, to protest the stalled payment to President Johnson.[43] Gandil told a journalist that he believed Comiskey was being influenced by gambling sore losers who were spreading the reprehensible gossip about a Series fix.[44] He admitted that at times, Comiskey could be the "best fellow in the world," but at others, he was "very difficult to please." He knew he'd given the Sox his "best at all times," and constantly played through injuries.

Eddie Collins, whose five-year contract recently concluded, signed a new deal in early February of 1920, and admitted that Comiskey had given him a bonus for his efforts the year prior.[45] The added money, "unsolicited and wholly gratuitously," contributed to Collins' belief that Comiskey was "one of the most liberal employers in baseball."

Conspirators Cicotte, Jackson, and their mum teammate Weaver, were not as pleased with Comiskey as Collins was. Jackson corresponded with Comiskey over a period of months and was steadfast in his desire for an annual pay of $10,000 for three years. Comiskey offered $7,000, and then compromised to $8,000 when Secretary Harry Grabiner went to Savannah to see Jackson in person.[46] Jackson acquiesced and reported to the team normally.[47]

Weaver was a strange case. In November of 1919, he spent time in California with slugger Babe Ruth, who announced he was breaking his three-year contract with the Boston Red Sox at $10,000 a year and demanding an annual salary of $20,000.[48] [49] The boisterous attitude of Ruth seemed to have an impression of Weaver, and the latter tried to back out of his contract in an effort to get more money or be traded to the Yankees.[50] After realizing he had no leverage and was not comparable to Ruth in terms of value, he rejoined the club. Cicotte went to camp without a contract, but soon agreed to a $10,000 a year deal. Risberg also fell into line after threatening to retire and operate a San Francisco restaurant.

Gandil stuck to his word and never returned to the Sox. Spring training at Waco, Texas, went on without him, and first base was played by Ted Jourdan and Shano Collins. Camp was loaded with rookie prospects, including over fifteen pitchers. One of the key positives going into the 1920 season was the expected return to form of Red Faber, which thrilled manager Kid Gleason. His pitching staff included four men of ability, Cicotte, Williams, Faber, and Kerr, and despite early predictions that the Sox were headed for the doldrums, the players were full of confidence and ready to repeat as league champions.

The unresolved rumors remained mighty prevalent when the Sox opened things up at Comiskey Park on April 14, 1920, but the audience of 25,000 enjoyed a 3–2 win in 11 innings anyway.[51] Over the following weeks, there were many bumps and bruises, including injuries to Cicotte and Jourdan, and the Sox were pushed back to third in the standings. They were unwilling to relent in the slightest, fighting to keep pace with Cleveland and New York in a scorching race. Getting great pitching and .300-plus hitting from Jackson, Weaver, and Eddie Collins, Chicago was not in the chaotic condition pundits thought they were in.[52] Still owning a mishmash of jumbled personalities, the Sox were able to function as a balanced unit on the field.

After winning 9 of 10 to finish the month of June, the Sox had won 12 of 15 by early July and were streaking toward first place.[53] Much of the sporting community was focused on the astronomical power hitting of Babe Ruth and his amazing home run feats were a splendid box office draw. At Comiskey Park, fans were said to have been "gratified" by the sight of his 38th smash of the year on August 2, and it wasn't abnormal to see rivaling crowds cheer Ruth as he ran the bases.[54] In Cleveland, Tris Speaker's Indians were playing remarkable ball and getting timely victories from the pitching trio of Jim Bagby, Stan Coveleski, and Ray Caldwell, but then became sentimental favorites following the death of shortstop Ray Chapman on August 17, 1920.[55] Chapman, while at the plate at New York the day before, was hit in the head by a pitch thrown by Carl Mays and suffered a fractured skull. His loss to the Indians and to the baseball world was immeasurable.

Throughout 1920, Comiskey suffered from increased health concerns, and it grew in severity to the point in which his doctors advised him to completely refrain from watching any ballgames, as the stress was too much for him to handle.[56] His heart was ailing, as well as his nerves, and the rumors of dishonesty amongst the roster of his prized club was crippling. Adding to his anxiety was the news that a violent group of young Chicago thugs had planned to rob the White Sox ticket offices during the next sellout appearance of Babe Ruth.[57] It was a stroke of fortune that they were captured on August 26, 1920, as they tried a $40,000 heist of a stockyards company. Having already murdered a police sergeant, the men were confirmed killers, and it was explained in their confession that they planned to slay Comiskey and others to eliminate all witnesses.

The American League pennant chase was unrelenting in its competitiveness going into the final weeks of the season. Simultaneously, there was a huge surge of pressure from various sources, including the public, completely adamant about launching an inquiry into the sport's many alleged impurities. Columnist Joe Vila wrote a syndicated article with more accusations about the recent Series, and Lou Comiskey immediately requested that Vila produce his "evidence" before the newly instituted Grand Jury of Cook County (IL), organized to formally investigate baseball.[58] Vila, of course, didn't step forward because his proof was lacking.[59] He was relying upon the same backroom gossip that proved worthless months before.

But this time, the rumors were receiving much more consideration by officials, and the deployment of the grand jury to study baseball was a clear shift to cultivating real answers. The threat of legal ramifications and potential jail time was a legitimately frightening thought to several key participants of the Series scandal, and their confidence in their ability to get away with it wavered. In actuality, for Comiskey, major league baseball, and the public to obtain the evidence it needed to crack the case once and for all, they needed the voices of the conspirators themselves to admit what they had done. There was nothing more and nothing less. Comiskey, with all of his wealth and power, was incapable of producing any tangible information that would legally suffice.

To maintain the integrity of baseball, the sport needed a confession. Eddie Cicotte, who claimed it took a week for him to be convinced to participate in the crooked scheme, was beyond distraught by guilt.[60] He was prepared to own up to his dishonest actions and reveal to the world that the

White Sox had purposely thrown the 1919 World Series to the Cincinnati Reds. The house of cards the "Black Sox" had built were finally going to collapse.

ENDNOTES

1 *Chicago Daily News*, October 10, 1919, p. 2.

2 *Chicago Daily News*, October 11, 1919, p. 2.

3 Some baseball pundits have chosen to criticize Comiskey based on their perception that he was purposely underpaying Jackson. It draws on the conclusion that Comiskey was a spitefully mean club owner and that he bullied his players into unrealistic contracts. This fictional story has served to draw up sympathy for Jackson and vilify Comiskey at the same time, while making Jackson's participation in the Series fix somewhat comprehendible or even acceptable.

4 *Chicago Daily Tribune*, August 21, 1915, p. 9. Jackson's new contract covered the 1917–19 seasons, and he was already signed for 1916 as well, stemming from an earlier deal.

5 *Cleveland Plain Dealer*, July 21, 1921, p. 14.

6 *New York Evening World*, September 29, 1920, p. 1.

7 *Chicago American*, October 11, 1919, p. 7.

8 *Chicago American*, October 11, 1919, p. 7.

9 *Chicago Daily News*, October 16, 1919, p. 2.

10 *Chicago American*, October 11, 1919, p. 7.

11 *Chicago Daily Tribune*, October 11, 1919, p. 15.
An incorrect report of a $20,000 offer by Comiskey for evidence of the fix was unleashed along the wire services and printed in newspapers across the nation. When it was later assumed to have been "reduced" to $10,000, writers have used it as another dig at Comiskey's so-called cheapness. The *Tribune* reported on October 11, two days after the Series ended, that the offer was $10,000. That amount was also listed in the *Sporting News*, October 16, 1919, p. 4.

12 *Chicago Daily Tribune*, October 10, 1919, p. 19.

13 *Washington Post*, October 28, 1920, p. 12.
Redmon was the owner of the Majestic Theater in East St. Louis, Illinois. Joining Gleason and O'Neill on their trip was Clyde Elliott of the Greater Stars Production Company. It isn't known whether Redmon received the $6,500 or $5,500, depending on the source, or whether he lost gambling in exchange for his "insider" knowledge. It was also reported that Gleason met with area gamblers Joe Pesch and Carl Zork. *Chicago American*, October 17, 1919, p. 7. At the time of the journey to St. Louis, the trip was publically acknowledged as anything but an investigation of the rumors, but newspaper writers saw through the thin veil. Redmon personally met with Comiskey on December 29, 1919, in Chicago and discussed what he knew. Since he was at least two people removed from any Sox player and couldn't possibly incriminate anyone, Redmon's comments didn't fit the category of evidence. Writer James Crusinberry addressed a St. Louis report

that three members of the Sox talked to either Redmon or Joe Pesch about throwing a ball game a week during the season for $600. *Chicago Daily Tribune,* December 30, 1919, p. 11.

14 *Chicago Daily Tribune,* July 16, 1919, p. 17.
Comiskey tried to gain complete control of Camp Jerome through the courts, but ended up withdrawing his suit.

15 *Chicago American,* August 19, 1919, p. 7.

16 *Sporting News,* December 3, 1942, p. 6.

17 *Sporting News,* November 27, 1919, p. 1.
Paul W. Eaton wrote that Comiskey's actions in connection with the "upsetters of baseball" [Frazee/Ruppert] were "hard to understand," and that this was "about the first time he ever ran contrary to public opinion." In that same publication, Joe Vila hammered the actions the Comiskey group, citing the series of efforts to discredit Johnson as "childish and amusing." He mentioned that Comiskey was showing a little inconsistency by stating that Johnson had no property interest in the American League, then claiming that Johnson was part owner of the Cleveland Indians. *Sporting News,* December 4, 1919, p. 1.

18 *Chicago Herald and Examiner,* November 8, 1919, p. 11.
Aside from a new third league, there had been mention of the White Sox, Red Sox, and Yankees crossing over to join a reorganized twelve-member National League.

19 *Chicago Daily Tribune,* November 5, 1919, p. 15, *Chicago Daily Tribune,* November 20, 1919, p. 14.
Johnson did not attend the meetings in New York, citing an infected toe as the reason.

20 *Chicago Herald and Examiner,* November 22, 1919, p. 10.

21 *Sporting News,* November 27, 1919, p. 1.
Oscar C. Reichow mentioned the stated sentiment about Johnson being detrimental to baseball by the rebellious group in the American League, but added, "I think, however, there is some other motive that the owner of the White Sox refuses to disclose." Reichow said Comiskey told him that he thought Johnson had assumed too much power, and the writer explained, "probably he did," but added that the American League was like a "son" to him. He concluded that the conflict between the former friends appeared to him to be "child's play."

22 *Chicago Daily Tribune,* December 9-12, 1919.
Several compromises were proposed at the annual American League meeting, including a new 50-50 board of directors with Navin and Mack on one side and Comiskey and Ruppert on the other. Each of them was declined by the Johnson faction.

23 *Sporting News,* December 18, 1919, p. 1.

24 *Chicago Daily Tribune,* December 13, 1919, p. 19.

25 The strain of the games themselves, the pressure of appeasing his home audience, the constant rumors, and the illnesses of his wife and son were overwhelming factors when considered. His own health was compromised within days of the Series' end. *Philadelphia Inquirer,* October 13, 1919, p. 12. Comiskey told a

Milwaukee courtroom in 1924 that he was "awful sick when he got back to Chicago from Cincinnati [in October 1919] and had been sick ever since." *Milwaukee Sentinel*, February 1, 1924, p. 6.

26 *Sporting News*, December 11, 1919, p. 1.

27 *Chicago American*, December 19, 1919, p. 6.

28 *Chicago American*, December 20, 1919, p. 7.

It should be mentioned that neither Herrmann, who was being pushed out by a pro-Judge Kenesaw Landis faction backed by Comiskey, or Johnson had any responsibility to protect Comiskey in any shape or form.

29 *Chicago Daily Tribune*, December 15, 1919, p. 21.

30 Comiskey, through his attorney Alfred Austrian, hired John R. Hunter, owner of Hunter's Secret Service of Illinois, a private detective agency. Hunter, a fifty-seven-year-old Canadian, was an experienced investigator, and with his team, followed up on leads from Chicago to San Francisco. They examined some of the accused players and continued their scrutiny in one way or another from November 1, 1919 to May 18, 1920. *Milwaukee Evening Sentinel*, February 11, 1924, p. 2. Whereas there have been claims, reportedly said by Comiskey himself, that he shelled out $10,000 or more for this investigation, Comiskey gave out a completely different figure in 1920. He said, "I employed a large force of detectives to run down every clue and paid them more than $4,000 for their services in running down every clue imaginable but could get nothing tangible." *Philadelphia Inquirer*, September 25, 1920, p. 14.

31 *Chicago Daily Tribune*, January 26, 1932, p. 1.

32 *New York Evening World*, September 29, 1920, p. 1.

Hugh Fullerton wrote, "On advice of friends and his lawyer, and torn by doubts, [Comiskey] allowed all save one to return to the team." During the 1924 trial in Milwaukee, Comiskey talked about re-signing the alleged crooks. *Chicago Daily Tribune*, February 13, 1924, p. 27. Grabiner was alleged to have recommended giving raises to the players "so that it would appear the Sox were paying living salaries." *Collyer's Eye*, March 15, 1924, p. 4. Salaries were expected to rise in 1920 because the season was lengthened back to 154 games from 140 in 1919.

33 *Collyer's Eye*, October 18, 1919, p. 1.

Collyer was forty-three years old in 1919, and was originally from Durham, Ontario, Canada. His publication took great pride in reporting the major sporting scandals of the day, and also featured the stock markets, general finances, oil news, and gambling. It often gave front page headline space to rumors, such as Comiskey purchasing Ty Cobb for $50,000. *Collyer's Eye*, October 16, 1920, p. 1.

34 *Collyer's Eye*, December 13, 1919, p. 1. This same article made mention of the alleged $10,000 bonus Comiskey promised Cicotte if he won 30 games, and claimed that Cicotte had, in fact, achieved that milestone, when he actually had not. He finished the season with 29 victories. Schalk denied he ever said that seven players would not return. *Sporting News*, January 8, 1920, p. 1.

35 Biographer Gustave Axelson was born in Sweden in 1869 and was a veteran reporter and editor in Chicago, having worked for the *Record-Herald* and *Journal*. His first name has also been spelled, "Gustaf," but he mainly went by his first and

middle initials, "G.W." Axelson was a member of the Woodland Bards, having attended the annual pilgrimage to Wisconsin in 1907. He passed away on February 2, 1927. The Comiskey biography was published by Reilly and Lee Company and sold for $1.50. *Chicago Daily Tribune*, November 9, 1919, p. A4, February 2, 1927, p. 27. John Sheridan read the biography and said it was "quite accurate" with "one or two petty" mistakes. *Sporting News*, December 4, 1919, p. 6.

36 *Sporting News*, December 18, 1919, p. 6.

Sheridan wrote a second telling column about Comiskey in the same publication a week later. He added comments about the special atmosphere he naturally created at his home stadium by "being simply Comiskey." Around 1917, though, "he ceased to be Comiskey," and as of late, had become "impatient, even irascible." He'd hate to hear that the charming man who he adored was now "crabbed and sour." *Sporting News*, December 25, 1919, p. 6.

37 *Sporting News*, February 19, 1920, p. 7.

38 *Sporting News*, December 25, 1919, p. 1.

39 *Chicago Herald and Examiner*, November 19, 1919, p. 15.

40 *San Diego Evening Tribune*, November 1, 1919, p. 7.

Also see: 1920 U.S. Federal Census records, Ancestry.com.

41 *Chicago Herald and Examiner*, October 11, 1919, p. 15.

Gandil was threatened with appendicitis during the 1919 season and it was reported that he was going to have surgery in Los Angeles soon after the Series. According to reports, the operation didn't happen until September 1920. *Chicago Daily Tribune*, September 30, 1920, p. 1.

42 *Philadelphia Inquirer*, September 25, 1920, p. 14.

Comiskey also talked about the withholding of Series money in the Milwaukee trial against Jackson. *Milwaukee Sentinel*, February 1, 1924, p. 6. He said: "I stopped payment to the eight suspected men for a good reason. I wanted to find out if they had played honestly."

43 *Chicago Daily Tribune*, September 24, 1920, p. 1.

44 *Portland Oregonian*, November 23, 1919, p. 7.

45 *Sporting News*, January 1, 1920 , p. 1.

Chicago Daily Tribune, February 7, 1920, p. 13. The terms of Collins' new deal was not reported.

46 Grabiner going to Savannah to negotiate with Jackson was a major issue of the 1924 Milwaukee trial between Jackson and the Chicago White Sox over back pay. Grabiner being on the road to get contract signatures was not unusual. He also dropped into Paris, Texas, to see Dick Kerr, and signed him as well. *Sporting News*, February 26, 1920, p. 1.

47 *Chicago Daily Tribune*, March 9, 1920, p. 15.

48 *Chicago American*, November 17, 1919, p. 9.

49 *Chicago American*, October 27, 1919, p. 9, *Washington Post*, October 27, 1919, p. 9.

50 *Chicago Daily Tribune*, March 26, 1920, p. 13, *Sporting News*, April 1, 1920, p. 1.

51 *Chicago Daily Tribune*, April 15, 1920, p. 9.

52 *Sporting News*, May 13, 1920, p. 1.

53 *Sporting News*, July 8, 1920, p. 1.

54 *Chicago Daily Tribune*, August 3, 1920, p. 13.
   Babe Ruth was credited with the revival of baseball's popularity in the aftermath of the "Black Sox" scandal.
55 *Sporting News*, August 19, 1920, p. 1.
   In the aftermath of Chapman's death, there were calls to strike against the pitching of Carl Mays, but Kid Gleason and the White Sox refused to do so. *Sporting News*, September 2, 1920, p. 1.
56 *Kalamazoo Gazette*, September 1, 1920, p. 10.
   It was explained that Comiskey had witnessed only about a "dozen games" up until this point in the 1920 season, and that he'd been under the watchful eye of a doctor "almost daily" since the fall of 1919. Comiskey was quoted as saying, "I am going to win this battle for better health, although I know it means a terrific fight." The newspaper described his condition as a "nervous breakdown."
57 *Chicago Daily Tribune*, August 27, 1920, p. 3.
   Also see: *Washington Post*, August 28, 1920, p. 3.
58 *Philadelphia Inquirer*, September 11, 1920, p. 17, *Chicago Daily Tribune*, September 14, 1920, p. 17.
59 *Chicago Daily Tribune*, September 17, 1920, p. 15.
   Vila blamed his unavailability on "business engagements." It was apparent that he was comfortable writing roundabout allegations regarding the fix, based on his insider knowledge, but unwilling to share the evidence needed to break the case open.
60 *New York Evening World*, September 29, 1920, p. 2.

18

UNRAVELING THE CONSPIRACY

The investigation of the Cook County Grand Jury under the authority of Chief Justice Charles A. McDonald of the Criminal Court was comprehensive.[1] Charles Comiskey, Ban Johnson, John Heydler, Arnold Rothstein, and a slew of others appeared as witnesses to answer questions relating to suspicions of fixed games and corrupt ballplayers. Hearsay was rampant, as expected, but a common theme became apparent surrounding a growing list of White Sox players purportedly involved in dishonest work. Pitcher Rube Benton was one of the more revealing characters to speak before the jury. As a member of a notorious New York Giants crew, he hung out with Hal Chase, Benny Kauff, and Heinie Zimmerman, and was, at least, familiar with Bill Burns, who spent time in New York late in the summer of 1919.

In testimony, it was found that Benton told two fellow players that he was tipped off by Chase about the Sox losing the first two games of the Series.[2] Benton admitted seeing a telegram, but thought it was sent by Burns.[3] He noted that Chase was receiving telegrams as well, and it was generally believed that they were regarding the status of the fix. He thought Chase won maybe $20,000 in gambling on the games, but didn't know for sure. The evocation of the name "Bill Burns" was infringing on previously protected territory. While his name might have been bandied about, this was the first time his name was taken seriously as being a participant, and he was, literally, one physical step away from the players themselves. He knew exactly which members of the Sox were involved.

For those still trying to remain concealed, the suggestion of Burns was too close for comfort. Nevertheless, the investigation continued, and during the proceedings, the names Eddie Cicotte, Chick Gandil, Lefty Williams, and Happy Felsch were produced as being conspirators, albeit unconfirmed by anyone with tangible proof.[4] Comiskey's holding up of Series checks for eight Sox players was also made public, and that only widened suspicions.[5]

The biggest bombshell to date came from Billy Maharg, and his disclosures were considered a primary source. He was induced to talk by dedicated Philadelphia sportswriter Jimmy Isaminger and, as Burns' cohort, knew all the dirty secrets of the Series fix.[6] Both Maharg and Burns were broken financially during the scam after dropping their big winnings from the first two games on the unexpected Sox victory in game three. He mentioned the importance of Abe Attell in the scheme and said that he double crossed the players by not paying them the money he agreed to during the pre-Series negotiations. Maharg felt the players, in turn, double crossed him and Burns by winning game three after specifically saying that they wouldn't win for Kerr.

There were very few loyalties among the various factions, and whatever goodwill was prevalent before the 1919 Series was erased by 1920. Maharg and Burns remained friends and were entirely in concert with each other when it came to telling their version of what happened. In part, it was so they could deflect any potentially incriminating elements away from them, and especially the part about who came up with the concept first. Maharg told Isaminger that Cicotte volunteered the idea in New York, making him ground zero for the plot.

Within twenty-four hours of Maharg's statements, Cicotte was reeled in by Kid Gleason and delivered to Comiskey on a silver platter. Riddled with remorse, shame, and emotion, he told his boss of the last nine years, "I don't know what you'll think of me, but I got to tell you how I double crossed you, Mr. Comiskey, I did double cross you. I'm a crook. I got $10,000 for being a crook."[7]

"Don't tell it to me," said Comiskey, disgusted by the admission. "Tell it to the grand jury."

And Cicotte did.

Later that day, he appeared before Judge McDonald and the members of the jury panel and told his story with tears in his eyes. In contrast to Maharg's version, he said he was worked on for a week by Gandil, Risberg, and McMullin before agreeing to participate. He said he wasn't sure initially, but needed the money because of his family and for the farm he'd just bought (which he paid off in cash with the money). Ever since, though, he was living with an "unclean mind," and going through his own personal "hell" while "going along with the boys who had stayed straight and clean and honest."

That same day, Joe Jackson, fearful of being ostracized for his silence, stepped forward and also confessed to receiving $5,000 of crooked money.[8] He was followed by Lefty Williams and an "unofficial" admission by Happy Felsch.[9] [10] For White Sox fans and baseball enthusiasts everywhere, it was an upsetting display of honesty. Their heroes of the diamond, idols in the purest sense, were complete and utter frauds. The grand jury voted to indict all eight players for conspiracy to commit an illegal act and officials studied the case to locate other possible charges.[11]

Comiskey, now in possession of the legal evidence he needed to act, formally suspended seven of the alleged conspirators.[12] He indicated that if any of the men were proven innocent, they would be reinstated, but if they were guilty, he'd see to it that they were "retired from Organized Baseball for the rest of [their] lives." For the honest members of the Sox, Comiskey dispensed an extra $1,500 to each man—a round figure meant to bridge the gap between the losers' and winners' pay for the 1919 Series.[13] The deed, in essence, was a symbolic reward to his loyal players.

At the time of the indictments, there were several different perceptions of Comiskey. His friends and supporters were awed by his courage in doing what was right for baseball by encouraging the confessions of Cicotte and Jackson and issuing swift suspensions.[14] Others were not so sympathetic. They tended to focus on the fact that Comiskey had used tainted players during the 1920 season in spite of having the knowledge that they were potentially guilty of being dishonest. This belief tended to accept the theory that Comiskey would do anything to win another championship; even look the other way to a World Series fix.

The necessity of legitimate proof apparently wasn't considered by those who perpetuated that venomous line of attack. A few years later, Frank G. Menke wrote a collection of syndicated articles that crucified Comiskey for his behavior in and around the 1919 Series.[15] He regurgitated the idea that the Sox owner looked the other way despite knowing about what transpired, just because he wanted to keep his winning team intact. In fact, as this line of thought became the popular trend, Comiskey's actions were considered to be part of a shrewd "cover up."[16] Ironically, Comiskey was a man who in 1920 was warned to stay away from baseball games entirely because his health couldn't weather the stress, but, according to these believers, he was seemingly plotting and planning a huge scale cover up to protect his high-profile club.

Too much erroneous credit was afforded Comiskey in these instances. Most of the time, he relied upon his lawyer Alfred Austrian and team secretary Harry Grabiner to coordinate efforts and essentially manage the team in his absence.[17][18] How a single man, or a single franchise, could effectively pull the wool over the eyes of the entire baseball community to obscure genuine facts was impossible—particularly in a case like this when all eyes were trained to spot irregularities. Comiskey, if anything, realized that he needed a team to play the 1920 season, and had to boost salaries to re-sign his men— and did so. They were, after all, uncompromised by any legitimate information. Until proof was delivered to his doorstep, he was forced to go forward as if nothing had transpired. The other options were few and far between.

In September of 1920, the evidence was presented and he suspended seven of his stars without hesitation. Although he was keenly aware and sensitive of the public's perception of himself, there was little he could do to prevent critics from lambasting his decisions. In a way, he was dammed if he did and dammed if he didn't. He listened to his attorney and took the less painful legal route, avoiding a ton of defamation lawsuits.

Another commentary related to Comiskey's war with Ban Johnson and how he was purposefully trying to outshine his former friend by being the one to uncover the truth about the scandal. Their conflict was often based on mindless principles, and the levels of volatility appeared to fluctuate daily. It wasn't out of the question for Comiskey or Johnson to descend into immaturity when dealing with each other, and the common good of baseball was put aside to continue their wasteful feud. Comiskey took regular potshots at Johnson. He claimed that he was out for "personal gain" in the grand jury investigation, where Johnson responded that Comiskey was "grasping at straws to purify his position with the public."[19]

Of course, Comiskey was enraged when Johnson told the press that he "heard statements that the White Sox would not dare to win the 1920 pennant because the managers of a gambling syndicate, alleged to have certain players in their power, had forbidden it."[20]

The 1920 race ended with the Sox finishing two games behind Cleveland.[21] Just before the season concluded, Comiskey received a kindhearted gesture from Jacob C. Ruppert and T. L'H. Huston of New York, who offered him any of their Yankees players, including Babe Ruth, to allow him to finish the season with quality replacements.[22] Comiskey appreciated the offer, but believed the rules of the league prevented him from taking them up on it and used his own backup players. Although he was stripped of many of his top stars, he remained upbeat on the prospects of his team's ability to be competitive in the future without men like Cicotte and Jackson. Ted Sullivan, as he was accustomed, was constantly scouting for talent and the Sox also picked up veteran Amos Strunk.[23]

Baseball politics resumed in its usual manner after the completion of the regular season and World Series. Comiskey found a new way to reduce the influence of Johnson by joining a movement to reorganize the National Commission into a three-man board of control.[24] As it currently stood, Johnson, with his ties to the Cleveland club, was a member of the Commission, and his financial interest in a team was considered unethical to some people. Under the proposal, dubbed the "Lasker Plan" for its originator, Albert D. Lasker of the Chicago Cubs, the members of the board of control would be unaffiliated to any franchise. Sides were drawn in the sand, as usual, and the five loyal American League owners to Johnson were against the change. Comiskey was again partnered with his allies in New York and Boston, and was in the majority because all of the National League owners were behind his idea.

Threatening another war, the "Lasker Plan" boosters discussed the creation of a twelve-team organization made up of all eight existing National League clubs, plus the White Sox, Red Sox, Yankees, and a fourth, undetermined franchise. Finally, on November 12, 1920, after fine tuning the original plan into an agreeable compromise, all sixteen owners of the Major Leagues agreed to name Judge Kenesaw Mountain Landis the supreme commissioner of baseball.[25] His appointment replaced the board of control concept and the National Baseball Commission, and made him the final arbitrator for all internal baseball debates. After fifteen years as a Chicago Federal Judge, Landis was highly respected, and his knowledge of baseball was considered vast. He was a regular at Comiskey Park and always took the game exceptionally serious.

Redeeming the honor of the sport in light of recent developments was incredibly important to all owners—particularly Comiskey—as he later declared: "I would rather close my ball park than send nine men on the field with one of them holding a dishonest thought toward clean baseball."[26]

The *Chicago Daily Tribune* called Comiskey a "broken man" following the disclosures to the grand jury and other newspapers referred to his condition as a "nervous breakdown."[27] He battled a cold in December of 1920, and despite rumors that he was going to sell his franchise, he completely denied it.[28] [29] The gossip, naturally, was attributed to Johnson's handiwork.[30] In an attempt to settle his nerves, Comiskey found new hunting grounds in Wisconsin and spent a lot of time in the quietness of the wild.[31] Between January and March of 1921, Charles and Nan sought improved health at resorts in St. Augustine, Florida, and Paso Robles, California. After staying at the former location, Comiskey declared, "I never felt better in my life." He'd gained twenty-five pounds and was excited for the new season to start.[32]

Optimism was a great quality, but there was just no replacing the talent lost to suspension. Kid Gleason stocked his team with Earl Sheely at first base, Ernie Johnson at short, Eddie Mulligan at third, and an outfield made up of Strunk, Johnny Mostil, and Bibb Falk. In early March 1921, Sox veterans Shano Collins and Nemo Leibold were traded to the Boston Red Sox for future Hall of Famer Harry Hooper.[33] Searching for other opportunities to swap players or purchase outright, Comiskey received no considerations from his American League colleagues.[34]

Essentially, the Sox were blacklisted by the pro-Johnson sect in terms of cooperation, eliminating all potential business transactions. The other owners would rather see Comiskey fail than help his team recover, and their vengeful methods were going to continue well into the next decade.

The Yankees and Red Sox were still on friendly terms, but there were only so many deals available to Comiskey. His primary source for talent was the minors, and his scouts worked overtime searching for the cream of the crop. More than fifteen recruits turned out at their Waxahachie, Texas, training camp, but most were unfit for major league duty.

Back in Chicago, the conspiracy trial against the indicted Sox players was scheduled to begin on March 14, 1921, but was delayed after the prosecution lost their key witnesses, Cicotte, Jackson, and Williams, each of whom had confessed to the grand jury.[35] Upon examination of what was shaping up to be a weak case without their testimony, the three men decided not to incriminate themselves by testifying on behalf of the prosecution and effectively repudiated their previous confessions. With a hope to avoid jail and one day return to Organized Baseball, they recognized that silence was paramount in their defense.

Reeling from the defections, the prosecution was denied a postponement of trial to get their house in order and the entire case was dismissed in Cook County Court.[36] On March 26, new indictments were issued by the grand jury, and a plan was devised to combat the mum players.[37] The Illinois State's Attorney's office still planned to use the confessions against them. Additionally, the admissions of Bill Burns and Billy Maharg were going to be instrumental in framing the conspiracy since they were the only two "inside" gamblers to reveal secrets of the plot.

Included in the eight counts being brought against the eighteen defendants were charges of conspiracy to injure, cheat, and defraud the Chicago White Sox, and to obtain money from the public by means of a confidence game. The severest penalty was a five-year term in the state penitentiary, but it was a mighty difficult chore to achieve guilty verdicts for conspiracy, especially under these circumstances.[38]

One of the most significant factors the prosecution had to be weary of when it came time to select a jury panel was that the members of the Sox were well-known and admired celebrities. Despite their alleged crooked behavior, people were awed by the likes of "Shoeless Joe," Buck Weaver, and the rest. They had to seriously scrutinize candidates to ensure an unbiased jury was selected, capable of convicting the heroes of the diamond if the evidence proved them guilty.

Shortly before the 1921 season opened at Comiskey Park, a strange occurrence happened when a "mysterious" fire broke out in a wooden structure underneath the scoreboard.[39] Little damage was done, but the conflagration was added to three other puzzling blazes at the park that occurred the September before, causing various degrees of destruction.[40] Officials brushed off any talk of an arsonist purposefully trying to destroy the stadium, but the string of fires were suspect to say the least.

The high expectations for the remodeled White Sox were lowered measurably once the pennant chase began, and it was clear they were weak in several areas. But once the team fell out of contention, the real spotlight shined on the Criminal Court Building in downtown Chicago. After months of legal wrangling, the trial was finally brought before Judge Hugo M. Friend in July of 1921, and an extensive selection process screened over 500 individuals before settling on twelve jurists. The original list of eighteen defendants was narrowed to eleven, excluding "Black Sox" utilityman Fred McMullin, who remained in the safe confines of California.

Assistant State's Attorney George E. Gorman, in charge of the case for the State of Illinois, realized very early in the proceedings that the lawyers representing the players and gamblers were going to resort to a number of cunning maneuvers to get their clients off.[41] Their intention was to distract the jury and win them over by inspiring sympathy for the "downtrodden" and "put upon" athletes. Rather than focus on the charges of conspiracy and crookedness, they wanted the jury to feel the "pain" of the players in their plight against their overbearing and cheap boss, Charles Comiskey.

There was no legitimate way to defend the actions of the players in a straight case. Three of them confessed before the grand jury and another admitted to wrongdoing. For the defense team, it was crucial to turn the tables and attack where they could, and Comiskey was obviously target number one. The depiction of Comiskey as a tightfisted ogre developed before the jury over a period of days. Lawyers revealed that the Sox charged players 50 cents each to have their uniforms laundered, which caused a measure of resentment, and that many times the athletes went onto the field in dirty suits because they refused to pay up.[42] They also asserted that Comiskey paid unfair wages; much less than what people assumed for superstar caliber athletes.

Comiskey was Gorman's first witness on July 18, and was cordially responding to all questions until defense attorney Benedict Short turned up the heat in a memorable cross-examination.[43] The environment deteriorated very quickly when Short inferred that Comiskey had broken a contract when he left the Brotherhood for the National League in 1890, and the two men shouted words at each other in anger.

"I've never broken a contract," Comiskey declared, waiving his forefinger in Short's face. "I haven't broken any or jumped any. You can't get away with that with me."

Next, Short wanted to delve into the finances of the Sox to show that Comiskey's team hadn't been injured by the actions of his clients. By exposing the records, he wanted to make it known that the Sox had actually done better in 1920 than in 1919, and that Comiskey's business had not been damaged by the widespread rumors of crookedness. Judge Friend blocked his attempt, and Short responded by asking Comiskey, "Isn't it a fact that you only paid your players $3 a day board?"[44] Following an objection, the question was again sustained by the judge.

A major hindrance for Gorman was that the original documentation for the confessions of Cicotte, Jackson, and Williams was stolen months before. It was discovered several days into the trial that the immunity waivers that were going to prove the trio had given their admissions voluntarily were also missing.[45] Allegations were made that Arnold Rothstein paid to have

the documents lifted from the State's Attorney's office because he was concerned that he was going to be implicated in the scandal.[46] Word eventually
got around that the confessions were on the open market to the highest
bidder, and no one knows how many copies were distributed.

Links between Rothstein and Comiskey's lawyer Alfred Austrian were
publicized, as were claims that Austrian acted on behalf of Rothstein during
the latter's Chicago grand jury appearance in October of 1920. When on
the stand during the trial, Austrian denied it under oath, but that didn't
stop conspiracy theorists from connecting the dots from Rothstein to Austrian to Comiskey, creating a scenario of the strangest of bedfellows.
Although Comiskey was a mover and shaker in his prime, and mingled
amongst people of all backgrounds, he was never linked to gambling or
organized crime in any way.

For literally decades, Comiskey had distanced himself from disreputable
characters and strived to maintain a clean image, including purposefully
eliminating a questionable bar from his ballpark because it cast a shadow
over the integrity of his good name. His first and foremost concern was the
safety and enjoyment of his patrons. Turning on a dime to work hand-in-
hand with Rothstein was the opposite of his known character.

But now, there were allegations connecting him to illegal doings, stolen
documents, and people characterizing him as a conspirator in his own
right. Reporters covering Comiskey throughout this time period were more
apt to say he was either ill or on the verge of a "nervous breakdown," dia-
metrically opposite to the kind of guy brokering sneaking schemes with
gambling kingpins.

The fact that Rothstein was avoided by Gorman's prosecutors was not
lost on the defense team. They pointed out that the financers of the scheme,
the big-wigs who organized the plot and manipulated the pawns—including Abe Attell and "Sport" Sullivan—were getting away scot-free. And they
were exactly right. The grand jury testimony of Rothstein was apparently so
convincing that the State's Attorney's office decided not to indict him or
pursue any further action. Attell and Sullivan skipped the country, it was
reported, avoiding capture and refusing to cooperate. When it came time
to make their final argument before the jury, the defense clearly empha-
sized the State's failure to go after the real "masterminds" of the plot,
instead targeting "underpaid ball players and penny ante gamblers."

The testimony of Bill Burns for the prosecution was everything it was
expected to be and more.[47] [48] He exposed the various double crosses, first

by Attell and then by the players when the latter didn't get the money they were promised. Having suffered financially by the suspected double cross in game three of the 1919 Series, Burns was resentful and bitter toward the Sox. His personal feelings might have made testifying against them easier, especially when he pinned the origin of the entire scheme on Eddie Cicotte and Chick Gandil. That charge negated any of Burns' previous discussions and dealings with Hal Chase and others in New York, all of which would likely have predated his first conversation with either member of the Sox.

It was exactly what Gorman, Comiskey, and Johnson wanted: a direct accusation to demonstrate the complete and total guilt of the player-conspirators. Burns' incrimination of the "Black Sox" was done in a way to minimize his own culpability, but as the defendants saw the "truth" differently, the absolute genuineness of the story was unattainable.

Deliberations took just two hours and forty-seven minutes, and the jury utilized only a single ballot before reaching a unified conclusion on August 2, 1921.[49] All twelve jurists declared the seven former members of the White Sox not guilty. In an astonishing display, the courtroom erupted into cheers upon the verdict's pronouncement, and all, even the judge and bailiffs, were drawn into the excitement with smiles and outward happiness for the result. The ecstatic players, their lawyers, and the jurymen shifted their celebration from the courtroom to a nearby café, where they continued to rejoice in the acquittal.[50]

Commissioner Landis was the opposite of happy. As the custodian of baseball's integrity, he issued a statement permanently banning all eight of the "Black Sox" forever.[51] They might have beaten the conspiracy charge, but their crooked actions and collusion with gamblers earned them an eternal seat on the bench.

On the field, Kid Gleason was unable to salvage the 1921 baseball season, and the Sox finished in seventh place with a 62–92 record. On October 10, however, the team gained a little satisfaction by taking five straight victories from the Cubs in the City Series and capturing the Chicago championship.[52] A few months later, the Sox signed the deposed Cubs manager, Johnny Evers, to work as a coach alongside Gleason.[53] Evers was a proven winner, a future Hall of Famer, and someone the young players could look up to and admire. The combination of Gleason and Evers was first-rate and a step in the right direction to rebuilding the broken spirit of the Sox.

Hawaii was the target for Comiskey and his wife over the winter months, but Nan's weakened health condition caused the two to remain in California.[54] Grabiner administered team business, organizing a new training camp at Seguin, Texas, and successfully collected contracts from all the regulars with one major exception: Dick Kerr.[55] On account of his 1921 numbers, including an ERA of 4.72, Grabiner refused to give Kerr the $8,500 he was looking for despite his important contributions the two years prior.[56] Kerr wouldn't compromise and jumped to a semi-professional team, earning a prompt suspension from Landis.

Desperate for new faces in the Sox lineup, Comiskey got word from his West Coast scout, Danny Long, about a promising twenty-two-year-old third baseman named Willie Kamm of the Pacific Coast League. He refused to be outbid, committing $100,000 for Kamm's services, and establishing a new record for money paid to a minor leaguer.[57] Unfortunately, Kamm wouldn't be available until 1923, so the Sox had to make do with their existing roster of veterans and rookies. The production of Johnny Mostil, Harry Hooper, and Bibb Falk added nicely to the faithful offensive numbers put up by Eddie Collins, and the Sox occasionally garnered big wins over top teams. But mostly, they failed to hit in the clutch, and their pitchers were often batted all over the field.

One twenty-six-year-old right hander made history in the midst of the mediocrity and pitched baseball's first perfect game since 1908, when the Sox were blanked by Addie Joss of the Cleveland Naps.[58] Charlie Robertson, a rookie upstart for the Sox, faced the minimum 27 men at Detroit, and led his team to a 2–0 victory on April 30, 1922. It would be thirty-four years before perfection struck again, and that was Don Larsen's Herculean effort in the 1956 World Series for the Yankees.

As his team faded in the standings, Comiskey was admitted to Mercy Hospital and remained there for nearly a month.[59] He was released prior to his sixty-third birthday on August 15, and spent precious time with his family. From the comfort of his home, he followed the Sox through the end of the season, and was again disappointed by a fifth place finish. Then, in seven games, his club was topped by the Cubs in the City Series, the first such occurrence in thirteen years.[60] But his team's standing and the loss to the Northsiders meant very little in the grand scheme of things. The real importance to Charles Comiskey was his wife Nan and her well-being.

Since 1917, Nan had been engaged in a struggle for health, battling artery and kidney problems almost continuously.[61] Her condition worsened in September, and she succumbed to coronary thrombosis on October 23, 1922, at their home.

Charles lost his best friend, his constant companion, and part of his heart died that day in October. When he described first meeting Nan in 1879, he admitted it was "love at first sight," and although she wasn't naturally a baseball fan, she took to the sport with enthusiasm.[62] She enjoyed traveling with her husband to spring training and during those moments when the stress of the big leagues got to him, she was the voice of reason. Her calming presence was now gone.

Rumors flew wildly in late 1922 about a pending deal between the Sox and New York.[63] The Yankees wanted Eddie Collins and Grabiner tried to work a multi-player agreement, specifically to obtain pitcher Waite Hoyt, but it fell through despite extensive talks. Going into spring training in 1923, Kid Gleason was overburdened with the responsibility of assessing an increasing number of recruits. The downside to the explosion of young players was that most of them required exhaustive coaching to improve their abilities. Gleason was stretched thin by the job and needed more veterans to balance the composition of the team.

Behind the scenes, Gleason was also becoming frustrated by the unique friction being created in Comiskey's absence. By this point, it was generally accepted that Comiskey was at least semi-retired because of his health, and that the day-to-day operations were being handled by his son Lou, Secretary Grabiner, and right-hand man, Tip O'Neill.[64] In normal operations, Gleason, as the manager, would put his two cents in about which minor leaguers to sign and make recommendations regarding trades . . . but that wasn't happening. Grabiner was signing players without consulting Gleason, thus creating an awkward roster of names and faces that didn't mesh well together.

Lou Comiskey took a passive role, leaving Grabiner to dictate instructions and O'Neill and traveling secretary Lou Barbour to follow them. No one wanted to flatly acknowledge the truth of what was happening, but a detrimental interference was being caused, encumbering Gleason and casting a further shadow over the franchise.

Following his wife's death, Comiskey became more and more isolated. He spent most of his time in either Wisconsin, Florida, or on long road trips, which gave him the opportunity to see the countryside. He received daily reports about the play of the Sox during the season and offered his advice and strategies via long distance telephone. Rarely attending ball games, he spent little to no time around the stadium or in the company of his manager and players. Amos Strunk, in 1922, declared that in his year-and-a-half with the team, he never once met Comiskey.[65] It was a stark difference from the days when Comiskey couldn't be dragged away from the park and was constantly interacting with his athletes.

The inspired and joyful camaraderie of the Woodland Bards was a distant memory. Guys like John Agnew, John Burns, James Dunn, and Joe Farrell were either deceased, sick, or had moved on to other passions. The once lively Bards' room at Comiskey Park was vacant of the personalities that made it famous, and the friendly atmosphere that Comiskey created at his stadium, savored by everyone, was disappearing a little at a time.

Even a win of another World Series would never recover Comiskey's lost pride, and the death of his wife was expected to be the final nail in his own coffin.

ENDNOTES

1 Considering the way the grand jury inquiry was launched, and how it was managed, it is a wonder why leaders within the American and National League didn't push for the investigation nine months earlier, well before the 1920 season began. In relation to the 1919 World Series scandal, not much more was known in early September 1920 than in December 1919 or January 1920. The names of the alleged participations were exactly the same. However, it appears that any delay of time could not necessarily be pinned to the dereliction of duty of any single individual, from Johnson to Heydler to Comiskey. A specific breakthrough in the mysterious happenings surrounding the Series did not cause the grand jury to convene when it finally did, but it was a combination of factors and allegations. It wasn't until after the jury began investigating that Benton, Maharg, and eventually Cicotte revealed their stories.

2 *Chicago Daily Tribune*, September 23, 1920, p. 1.
Ballplayers Art Wilson and N. D. "Tony" Boeckel provided affidavits that Benton had told them that he'd received a telegram from Chase, advising him to bet on Cincinnati for the first two games of the Series.

3 *Chicago Daily Tribune*, September 24, 1920, p. 2.
Another report claimed Chase won $40,000 on the Series. *Sporting News*, September 30, 1920, p. 2.

4 *Chicago Daily Tribune,* September 25, 1920, p. 1.
Benton revealed that a Cincinnati man named Philip Hahn, who was associated with gambling, told him about the four Sox players and didn't know the name of a fifth. He said that the Sox threw the Series for $100,000. Hahn renounced Benton's assertions.

5 *Chicago Daily Tribune,* September 19, 1920, p. A1.

6 Isaminger's report of his exclusive interview with Maharg was initially featured in his base newspaper, the *Philadelphia North American,* and then reprinted throughout the country. A detailed synopsis was featured on the front page of the *Chicago Daily Tribune,* September 28, 1920. This was the first time Maharg was publicly tagged as being involved with the Series swindle. Isaminger broached the conversation with the ex-boxer after receiving a hot tip from Philadelphia sports figure Walter Schlichter, and he'd forever be credited with helping uncover the truth about the fix. *Sporting News,* June 26, 1946, p. 14.

7 *Chicago Daily Tribune,* September 29, 1920, p. 1.
Over time, a more sinister picture developed of the circumstances surrounding the confessions of Cicotte and Jackson, promoted by supporters of the banned players. These individuals were convinced that Alfred Austrian, Comiskey's lawyer, finagled the admissions by promises of immunity. Led to believe that Austrian was protecting their interests, they broke down and confessed, even signing immunity waivers, allegedly without being told what they were agreeing to. Like many of the stories that have been dramatized and changed through the years, this version is unverifiable. In Comiskey's 1924 testimony in Milwaukee, he explained that it was Eddie Collins who suggested that they bring Cicotte in to discuss dishonest playing and that Collins believed Cicotte was not playing up to form during the 1920 pennant chase. Gleason believed it was because Cicotte was nervous, Comiskey said, and shortly thereafter, Cicotte confessed about the conspiracy plot. *Milwaukee Sentinel,* February 13, 1924, p. 5.

8 *Chicago Daily Tribune,* September 29, 1920, p. 2.
Some Jackson devotees believe that he was coached by Austrian prior to his confession and was told not to verbally injure the Sox franchise when he spoke before the grand jury.

9 *New York Evening World,* September 29, 1920, p. 1.
Williams became the third Sox player to confess to the grand jury, revealing his story on September 29.

10 *Chicago Daily Tribune,* September 30, 1920, p. 1.
Felsch made his revelation to a sportswriter, not to the grand jury.

11 The eight players were Gandil, Cicotte, Williams, Risberg, McMullin, Felsch, Jackson, and Weaver. As far as it has been revealed, no other members of the Sox team were ever considered suspects in the fix.

12 *Chicago Daily Tribune,* September 29, 1920, p. 1.
The eighth player was Chick Gandil, already suspended for refusing to join the White Sox earlier in 1920. Comiskey estimated that the seven players' sellable value, collectively, and had they not been indicted for being crooked, was about $230,000. The breakdown was as follows: Jackson $50,000, Weaver $50,000,

Felsch $50,000, Cicotte $25,000, Williams $25,000, Risberg $20,000, and McMullin $10,000. *New York Evening World*, September 29, 1920, p. 1.

13 *Sporting News*, October 7, 1920, p. 1.

14 Business tycoon J. Ogden Armour declared Comiskey "Chicago's biggest man" for standing up against baseball's crookedness and signed a testimonial put together by the Chicago Board of Trade. 365 members endorsed the letter. *Chicago Daily Tribune*, October 6, 1920, p. 15. William Smith Jr. of the American Association said Comiskey did the "greatest thing ever heard of in baseball," by punishing his players for the fix. He offered Comiskey the use of any of his Indianapolis ballplayers for the remainder of the 1920 season. *New York Tribune*, September 29, 1920, p. 2. Hugh S. Fullerton wrote that Comiskey was "the man who saved baseball." *New York Evening World*, October 1, 1920, p. 2.

15 The first of several syndicated articles by Menke was reprinted in the *Sporting News*, April 10, 1924, p. 7. Menke focused on the fact that Comiskey knew his players had thrown the World Series only days after the games had concluded, and then "permitted" them to rejoin the White Sox for the 1920 season.

16 The theory of a "cover up" was broached at length in Gene Carney's 2007 book, *Burying the Black Sox*.

17 Comiskey and his advisors made several key moves in November 1919 and in January 1920, undoubtedly realizing that a rocky road was ahead. The American League Baseball Club of Chicago necessitated annual documents filed in its state of incorporation, Wisconsin, but failed to submit paperwork in 1908 and "corporate rights and privileges" were forfeited under state laws on January 1, 1909. However, knowing that potential lawsuits and other problems could be spawned by the alleged conspiracy of the 1919 World Series, Austrian moved to protect Comiskey's business by filing new documentation in Wisconsin to clear up the previously declared forfeiture of rights. On November 26, 1919, an annual report was filed listing Comiskey as president, J. Louis Comiskey as vice president and treasurer, and Harry Grabiner as secretary. Less than two months later, their 1920 annual report was submitted with an important change: Listed as vice presidents for the corporation were attorneys Austrian and Carey W. Rhodes, also of Mayer, Meyer, Austrian, and Platt. As officers of the White Sox, Austrian and Rhodes were authorized to attend league meetings and properly defend Comiskey's interests from nefarious dealings. For instance, Austrian attended a league schedule meeting in February 1920 that brought considerable shock to others in attendance. *Washington Herald*, February 11, 1920, p. 9. Notably, Austrian was a member of the special committee pushing for reorganization of baseball under the "Lasker Plan" in October 1920. Corporation documents for the American League Baseball Club of Chicago were reviewed. These materials were provided by the Wisconsin Historical Society at Madison, Wisconsin, with help by ARC-circulation coordinator, Matt Tischer. The American League Baseball Club of Chicago was incorporated in Illinois on October 8, 1923 and with a capital value of $750,000. *Chicago Daily Tribune*, October 9, 1923, p. 25. The company's Wisconsin charter dissolved on December 6, 1923. *Chicago Daily Tribune*, December 7, 1923, p. 27.

18 Grabiner, along with Austrian and others attached to the management of the Sox, were exceedingly sensitive to the feelings of Comiskey and worked hard to shield him from irritants. Their job became even more crucial after Comiskey became seriously ill in the 1919–20 time frame, and they managed the public relations side of the scandal. Grabiner, who'd been with the club since he was a teenager, eventually rose up the ladder to become vice president and general manager. By 1931, Grabiner owned fifty shares of team stock valued at $100 each. He remained with the Sox until December 15, 1945, when he resigned, and soon joined the Cleveland Indians. He died a couple years later. *Chicago Daily Tribune*, October 25, 1948, p. C1.

19 *Sporting News*, September 30, 1920, p. 2.

20 *Chicago Daily Tribune*, September 24, 1920, p. 1. It was claimed that gamblers threatened to reveal the secrets of the 1919 Series if the Sox won the 1920 pennant. Johnson's statement was made prior to Cicotte's confession, and, at the time, Kid Gleason responded by saying, "There's nothing to it. It is all hearsay. That is what the entire mess has been. If Johnson has anything concrete it is up to him to come out and give it cold turkey. They have not got a thing. If they had it would have been aired long before this." *Philadelphia Inquirer*, September 25, 1920, p. 14.

21 The White Sox finished in second place with a 96–58 record with the New York Yankees right behind them at 95–59. Cleveland went on to win the World Series, defeating Brooklyn. Baseball-reference.com.

22 *Chicago Daily Tribune*, September 29, 1920, p. 2.

23 Among the new signees were Bibb Falk of Texas, a promising athlete who'd star in the outfield for the Sox throughout most of the 1920s, and Ernie Johnson and Earl Sheely of the Pacific Coast League. Amidst Chicago's large importation of talent, there were rumors that Comiskey had bid $50,000 for three Baltimore players and another $30,000 for two from St. Paul. *Chicago Daily Tribune*, October 20, 1920, p. 15.

24 *Chicago Daily Tribune*, October 19, 1920, p. 19.

25 *New York Times*, November 13, 1920, p. 1.

26 *New York Tribune*, September 29, 1920, p. 2.

27 *Chicago Daily Tribune*, September 29, 1920, p. 3.

28 *Chicago Daily Tribune*, December 17, 1920, p. 22.

29 *Chicago Daily Tribune*, December 22, 1920, p. 21. He told the press: "Baseball has been my life ever since I was old enough to play it. It will continue to be my life as long as I live and it is my greatest ambition to leave to the fans of Chicago the White Sox Park as a monument to the name of Comiskey."

30 *Chicago Daily Tribune*, December 26, 1920, p. A1.

31 Comiskey procured a new estate in Oneida County, Wisconsin near Dam Lake, southwest of Eagle River. He made two land purchases from Ernest L. Burrell on April 16, 1920 at Township 39 North, Range 9 East, near Dam Lake. The area was "improved with two frame dwelling houses, tool house, barn and ice house," according to his inventory of personal property, Probate Court Records for Charles A. Comiskey, File No. 170375, obtained from the Archives Department

of the Clerk of the Circuit Court, Cook County, Illinois. This property was often referred to as his "summer home."

32 *Daily Illinois State Journal,* February 6, 1921, p. 8.

33 *Boston Herald,* March 5, 1921, p. 8.

34 *Chicago Daily Tribune,* January 29, 1921, p. 15.

Eight years later, in 1929, Comiskey talked about his inability to make trades, saying: "In recent years, old animosities have prevented our participating in trading deals, but many of the old situations have been altered and I am confident that in the future our reconstruction plans will not be blocked through malice." *Chicago Daily Tribune,* September 17, 1929, p. 25.

35 *Chicago Daily Tribune,* March 14, 1921, p. 13.

36 *Chicago Daily Tribune,* March 18, 1921, p. 20.

37 *Chicago Daily Tribune,* March 27, 1921, p. A1.

Eighteen people in total were indicted by the grand jury the second time around, including five new individuals who were affiliated on the gambling end of things: Ben and Louis Levi, David Zelcer, Ben Franklin, and Carl Zork.

38 Prosecutors were tasked with the job of building a case against the crooked ballplayers, but there were no laws on the books specifically dealing with dishonesty in professional sports. With pressure from the public and from within baseball to punish the offenders, the Illinois State's Attorney's office lumped everything into a complicated "conspiracy" rap, hoping to nail all the various participants in one shot.

39 *Chicago Daily Tribune,* March 20, 1921, p. A1.

40 *Cleveland Plain Dealer,* September 21, 1920, p. 22.

41 *Sporting News,* July 14, 1921, p. 4.

42 *Chicago Daily Tribune,* July 12, 1921, p. 3.

It was also disclosed that after the players refused to pay the 50 cents to launder their uniforms, officials removed them from their lockers anyway, and deducted it from their wages. This was likely a psychological tactic. It was reported that he was done being a "big brother" to his players and was going to "treat 'em rough" in the future. *Sporting News,* March 4, 1920, p. 8. Another article talked about his frustrations with holdouts and other problems with players. *Chicago Daily Tribune,* March 27, 1920, p. 13. Interestingly, one sportswriter commented that Comiskey took a lot of care of the members of his 1906 squad, and "hasn't treated any of his players so well since." *Sporting News,* July 8, 1920, p. 4.

43 *Chicago Daily Tribune,* July 19, 1921, p. 2.

Comiskey was said to have been "near a state of physical collapse" following his dramatic testimony. *Sporting News,* July 21, 1921, p. 1.

44 In the 1919 time frame, the average daily hotel rates for ball players was between $3 and $5.50 a day, per man, entirely paid for by the club. The allotment for board by the White Sox in 1919 is unknown, but likely varied from city to city, depending on the hotel. The expenses of the White Sox, to include traveling, hotels, meals, salaries, and maintenance of Comiskey Park, was almost $500,000 for the 1919 season, as revealed during the trial. With that kind of overhead, it

is hard to imagine that the Sox were overly stingy with their per night hotel rates. *The Washington Post,* July 29, 1921, p. 1.

45 *Chicago Daily Tribune,* July 23, 1921, p. 11.

46 *Sporting News,* July 28, 1921, p. 1.

Rothstein was said to have paid $10,000 for the confessions and immunity waivers. His attorney William Fallon admitted getting the confessions from his "Chicago representative," Henry A. Berger, who had worked previously in the office of the State's Attorney. Berger denied being in collusion with Fallon. *Chicago Daily Tribune,* July 27, 1921, p. 13. Interestingly, Berger had become a defense attorney and was involved in the "Black Sox" trial representing Oscar Felsch and Carl Zork. Two additional bits of information were located in the *Sporting News,* August 4, 1921, p. 1, 4., adding to the intrigue of this story. A mention was made that an unnamed lawyer representing one (or more) of the defendants had somehow obtained copies of the confessions, but that fact was glossed over. Also that Comiskey's attorney Alfred Austrian admitted that he had Williams' confession in his office, but it too disappeared without a trace.

47 *Chicago Daily Tribune,* July 20, 1921, p. 1, 2.

After the trial, Gandil said Maharg and Burns were "liars." *New York Times,* August 4, 1921, p. 1.

48 Burns, after he was indicted, fled to Mexico. Ban Johnson, with the help of Billy Maharg, located Burns and convinced him to testify in the "Black Sox" trial. *Chicago Daily Tribune,* July 21, 1921, p. 1. One report claimed that Johnson met Burns and Maharg at Del Rio, Texas, in March 1921. *Chicago Daily Tribune,* March 10, 1929, p. A3.

49 *Chicago Daily Tribune,* August 3, 1921, p. 1.

Only nine defendants remained by the end of the trial. Judge Friend discharged the complaints against Ben and Louis Levi, and reportedly was going to do the same for Carl Zork, but upon reviewing the case file, it was found that the jury did vote to acquit Zork with the others. The judge also considered instructing the jury beforehand to exonerate both Felsch and Weaver, presumably because there wasn't enough evidence presented to convict either. *Chicago Daily Tribune,* August 1, 1921, p. 12. However, the jury did acquit them by a vote along with Gandil, Williams, Risberg, Cicotte, Jackson, and gambler David Zelcer. Documents from the case file of *The People of the State of Illinois v. Edward B. Cicotte, et al., Criminal Court of Cook County, Case No. 21868, 23912,* were obtained from the Archives Department of the Clerk of the Circuit Court, Cook County, Illinois.

50 *Sporting News,* August 11, 1921, p. 4.

51 *New York Times,* August 4, 1921, p. 1.

52 *Chicago Daily Tribune,* October 11, 1921, p. 15.

53 *New York Times,* February 2, 1922, p. 22.

54 *Chicago Daily Tribune,* January 27, 1922, p. 10.

55 *Chicago Daily Tribune,* April 16, 1922, p. A1.

Kerr talked about the situation in the *Sporting News,* February 25, 1937, p. 5. Grabiner told the press that Kerr jumped to an outlaw team even before engaging the Sox in negotiations. *Chicago Daily Tribune*, August 5, 1925, p. 25. In 1925, Kerr made his comeback after being reinstated by Commissioner Landis and pitched in twelve games for the Sox.

56 Starting his career with the White Sox in 1919, Kerr had 34 wins to 16 losses in his first two years with the club with a combined ERA of 3.15.

57 *Chicago Daily Tribune*, May 30, 1922, p. 17.

The Sox paid the San Francisco franchise $100,000 in cash plus two pitchers valued at $25,000 for Kamm. The *Tribune* noted that the only financially heavy deal in baseball history that surpassed this one was the transaction that sent Babe Ruth to the Yankees involving $125,000.

58 *New York Times*, May 1, 1922, p. 20.

59 *Chicago Daily Tribune*, August 15, 1922, p. 15.

60 *Chicago Daily Tribune*, October 16, 1922, p. 1.

61 State of Illinois Department of Public Health, Division of Vital Statistics Certificate of Death for Nan Comiskey.

Also see: *Chicago Daily Tribune*, October 24, 1922, p. 23. Mrs. Comiskey was fifty-eight years old at the time of her death.

62 *Sporting News*, January 4, 1917, p. 7.

63 *Chicago Daily Tribune*, December 13, 1922, p. 26, *Collyer's Eye*, October 14, 1922, p. 1.

Among the other players being discussed were Ray Schalk, Ted Blankenship, and the ineligible Dick Kerr.

64 *Collyer's Eye*, April 15, 1922, p. 1.

This publication inaccurately declared Comiskey out as White Sox president, but noted that he had "practically no interest in the club for two years." It was also said that his physical features were "hardly recognizable" in comparison to the old Comiskey people were so well acquainted with.

65 *Chicago Daily Tribune*, February 7, 1922, p. 14.

19

A SORROWFUL AFTERMATH

In the wake of the "Black Sox" scandal, the lives of the banned players were irrevocably altered. Never again would they experience the rush of being greeted by thousands of cheering fans as they sprinted onto the field for a game at Comiskey Park. Sure, they'd be recognized for the rest of their lives and repeatedly asked about the fateful 1919 season, but they were forever tarnished, linked to dishonesty and crookedness, and shunned by major league baseball.

For Buck Weaver, it was akin to a prison sentence. He lived for baseball, was an excellent athlete, and one day would be likely be enshrined among the greatest to have ever played the game. From day one he maintained his innocence. He didn't arrange, scheme, or participate in any conspiracy to throw the World Series. His crime was in his complicity, regardless of any active contributions. Eddie Cicotte, in his confession, named Weaver as being on board with the plot and Lefty Williams said that Weaver attended a meeting with eastern gamblers at the Warner Hotel in Chicago. Most reports claimed he didn't get a dime of crooked money, nor was evidence presented in the conspiracy trial that directly implicated him in any malfeasants.[1]

A month after the trial ended, Weaver set out to clear his name, and if any of the "Black Sox" had real justification to do so, it was him. He went right to the office of Commissioner Landis, but was dismissed without a meeting.[2] He then sought out Charles Comiskey, but the latter was in Wisconsin convalescing. Frustrated, Weaver instigated legal proceedings in Chicago Municipal Court for back salary amounting to $20,000, but his real objective was reinstatement.[3] He wanted to return to the field, whether for the White Sox or a different team.

In January of 1922, he finally got an audience with Landis and argued his merits.[4] One of the more interesting factors of his case was that he was eager to testify before the jury in the conspiracy trial, but was advised against it and/or even blocked by the defense team. They didn't want him proclaiming his purity, while at the same time possibly implicating their other clients. Landis listened to Weaver's statement, considered the facts, and ultimately refused to change his mind on the player's status. As far as he was concerned, Weaver was to be banned forever, and to this day, his word has reigned as final.

Before fading away into the sunset, Weaver went out of his way to assail the damaged reputation of the White Sox by alleging that teammates collaborated to buy victories from the Detroit Tigers during the 1917 pennant race.[5] He asserted that several of the "clean" Sox participated in the scam and that Detroit players received cash for purposefully losing six of seven games in September for Chicago to beat out the Red Sox.

As might be expected, the accusation caused uproar and added a Comiskey connection when Happy Felsch, who was next to file a lawsuit against the Sox boss, insinuated that Comiskey participated in the Detroit arrangement.[6] Officials from the Tigers denied the charges. On the other hand, Ban Johnson said he heard a report of money exchanging between the Sox and Detroit, but believed it was as an inducement for the Tigers to beat Boston, not to throw games against the Sox.[7]

Joe Jackson was the most desirous when it came to seeking financial compensation from Comiskey. He wanted $119,000, including $100,000 for slander.[8] Of all the lawsuits filed by "Black Sox" players, the Jackson case was the only one to develop into a courtroom drama. On the heels of another disastrous season for his club, Comiskey went into 1924 with a pending appearance before Judge John J. Gregory in Milwaukee Circuit Court.[9]

"I do not see," Comiskey told a reporter before the trial began, "how Mr. Jackson can hope to receive anything in view of the statements he made before the grand jury in Chicago."[10]

As demonstrated by the debacle at the end of the conspiracy case, marked by joint celebrating by awestruck jurists and the defendants themselves, Comiskey's lawyers wanted to prevent mesmerized baseball fans from deciding the verdict. That led to an extended interrogation of the jury pool and "sharp verbal exchanges" between rival attorneys.[11] A panel of ten men and two women were agreed upon on January 28, 1924, and from there, the trial moved into the next phase of dispute.[12]

Jackson earned sympathy points early on when his lawyer talked about his difficult upbringing and how he had to go to work at age twelve to help his family, forsaking any education. The other side talked about his fraudulent commitment to the Sox during the 1919 Series and explained that he received $5,000 of dirty money. On the stand, Jackson was impressive, but he began to tread on shaky ground when his story deviated from the one he told the grand jury in 1920. He explained that it wasn't until after the Series had concluded that Lefty Williams gave him an envelope containing the cash, differing from his previous statement and the account of Williams before the grand jury.[13] Both men, at that time, said that the $5,000 was distributed after game four.

The Milwaukee audience heard Jackson say that he didn't know what was in the envelope when it was given to him and that he never agreed to participate or authorized Williams to use his name in connection with the plot. He went on to declare that he tried to meet with Comiskey the day after receiving the money, but was turned away. On cross-examination, Jackson made umpteen denials, including aspects from the official record of the Chicago trial and the grand jury transcript.[14] [15] Comiskey himself withstood questioning for three hours. His stamina and poise was tested and he was driven to yell at his examiner at least once.[16]

A deposition from Bill Burns aided Comiskey, and Grabiner, Alfred Austrian, and private detective John R. Hunter offered testimony.[17] On February 12, 1924, Happy Felsch was called to the stand as a witness for Jackson, and instead of helping his former teammate, he missed the mark entirely.[18] In fact, Felsch's appearance became a spectacle leading to his arrest for perjury the next morning. The way it happened was strange, and all Judge Gregory and the attentive courtroom could do was watch in bewilderment as Felsch denied that the signature on his 1920 White Sox contract was his. The judge, attorneys, and likely even Felsch himself knew that the signature was genuine because it was the agreement that he played the 1920 season under. Additionally, it was the contract at the center of his personal legal suit against the Sox. If he claimed that the signature wasn't his, he had no contract at all, and no lawsuit.

Judge Gregory wasn't through yet. Once the jury had been given the case and began deliberations, he shocked onlookers by ordering Jackson to be arrested, also on perjury charges.[19] Finally, he rejected the decision of the jury in awarding Jackson a victory, set aside the verdict of $16,711, and dismissed the case. "The testimony of the plaintiff is perjured," the Judge declared.

"Jackson either lied here or in Chicago, and my opinion is that he lied here. I will not permit any witness to commit perjury and get away with it."[20]

Comiskey left Milwaukee before the case was determined and was in the grip of unyielding illness. Since the end of the 1923 season, his ball club was in a state of flux, beginning with Kid Gleason's decision to resign as manager of the Sox. Gleason was perhaps the most loyal employee Comiskey ever had, and before walking away, "Kid" was determined to give his boss a last championship in the City Series. In October of 1923, he accomplished his goal when the Sox beat the Cubs in six games.[21] The following day, he met with Comiskey, and in an emotional moment, officially ended his time with Chicago.[22]

The "Peerless Leader" Frank Chance, who was the mastermind behind the success of the Cubs years earlier and was admired by Comiskey, signed to take charge of the club. His appointment drummed up new excitement in the White Sox, and there was reason to believe that a real transformation was going to take place, fashioning the team into a competitor. While in Chicago in December, Chance contracted a cold that morphed into a full blown bronchial condition. He was in such bad shape by February of 1924, that he sent his resignation to the Sox because he was unable to fulfill his managerial duties.[23] Comiskey denied his resignation, wanting him to join the team as soon as his condition improved, and in the meantime, the players would be under the leadership of coaches Johnny Evers and Ed Walsh.[24]

Gallstones were one of Comiskey's most nagging health concerns, and on March 20, 1924, he underwent an operation at Mercy Hospital to remove three small stones.[25] The *Chicago Daily Tribune* explained that he'd been ill "for the last eighteen months," but made remarkable strides in his recuperation following the surgery.[26] Chance was on the fast track to recovery as well. Although he missed spring training, he traveled straight to Chicago from his home in California and was optimistic about the team's prospects.[27] Pundits predicted his outfit was a fifth place team, but Comiskey felt differently, saying "The White Sox will be battling for the championship."[28]

The trip and the weather in Chicago was not kind to Chance, and his bronchial asthma flared up. He was quickly confined to Mercy Hospital, where Comiskey was still a patient, and placed under the care of the team's doctor. It was determined that for the sake of his health, he was going to return to a better climate in Los Angeles and not manage the Sox in 1924.[29] Chance was a fighter, but his heart failed him on September 15, and he passed away at the age of forty-eight, just six days after his birthday.

The constant turmoil both on and off the field did not help the morale of the team either. With Evers assuming the managerial role, the Sox were no better on the field than they had been in 1923. Talk of trading Eddie Collins was a detriment, despite claims otherwise, and the meddling of Grabiner continued unabated. Youngsters Maurice Archdeacon, a fast outfielder, and twenty-three-year-old Ted Lyons, a future Hall of Fame pitcher, were the top recruits on a disjointed team. Over fifteen hurlers would be used during the 1924 season, and three of the regulars, Mike Cvengros, Charlie Robertson, and Red Faber, produced more losses than wins.[30] The infield was weakened significantly by the loss of Hervey McClellan to illness, and Evers also was unavailable for a time because of appendicitis.[31]

Injuries and discipline problems doomed the Sox and, on occasion, weekday crowds at Comiskey Park fell below 500 people.[32] The standings at the close of the American League season saw Chicago in dead last with a 66–87 record. Somehow they managed to be productive in the City Series against the Cubs and win the local championship.[33]

Comiskey, along with John McGraw of the New York Giants, made arrangements for a baseball tour of Europe; a smaller scale effort of their global travels a decade earlier.[34] Like last time, the journey was part sightseeing and part business, but all in the nature of spreading baseball and American goodwill to foreign countries. Joined by his son and his family, plus Grabiner and his relatives, Comiskey was content to sail abroad and felt his health could be sustained. He used a cane to walk and there was some speculation that he planned to remain in France at a resort to convalesce, but after a few weeks of feeling well, he decided against that idea and decided to return home with his team.[35]

The international venture took members of the White Sox and Giants from Quebec to Liverpool, and continued onto Paris. During their stay in London, King George heartily enjoyed a baseball exhibition and thousands of spectators found the sport to be an entertaining presentation of athleticism.[36] In Paris, crowds were smaller, and some sportswriters called the trip a "failure," because of the lack of interest. Neither Comiskey nor McGraw was affected by the claims, and they made the most of the experience. They coordinated an effort for several hundred children to see their November 13, 1924, contest in Paris and spread baseball to places that had never seen the game before.[37] For those reasons, they thought the trip was a success.

Baseball politics burst into controversy in late 1924, and the longtime Comiskey-Johnson feud once again took center stage. It was rekindled when Comiskey called a recommendation by Johnson about the recent World Series "idiotic," and the latter was in no mood to play their customary games.[38]

"If any man ever talked out of turn when the question of baseball integrity was involved, then Comiskey is the man," Johnson explained. "Mr. Comiskey, in my opinion, is an incompetent witness when it comes to any sort of testimony or statement regarding the stand to be taken when the safety of the national game is at stake."

Johnson added that he believed that his old friend "plainly holds the dollar paramount to the integrity of baseball."

Comiskey was less than thrilled by Johnson's comments, and in spite of his strenuous travels in recent weeks, felt good enough to attend the American League meeting at New York in December. There Comiskey made an impassioned speech in front of Johnson and his colleagues, relating his version of events surrounding the 1919 Series scandal, much of which was previously unshared information.[39] More important than Comiskey's war against Johnson was the conflict between Johnson and Judge Landis. Their rivalry reached a boiling point when Johnson called the commissioner a "wild-eyed nut," and told a reporter he wanted to drive him out of baseball completely.[40]

That opinion was unpopular. No one wanted to see Landis leave Organized Baseball because of his animosities with the American League president, but that option was on the table. With those comments, Johnson suddenly found himself without the support of a majority of American League owners.

In a special session, seven of the eight magnates voted to formally restrain him going into the future, limiting his actions to only league operations.[41] They also promised Landis that Johnson would be removed from office if he overstepped his bounds again. Three of Johnson's former supporters, Connie Mack, Thomas Shibe, and Clark Griffith, were loud critics of his behavior and were adamant in their sponsorship of Landis.[42]

Lost in the immediate moment were all of Johnson's tremendous contributions to the American League and baseball in general. But owners were steadfast in the conviction that Landis was restoring the sport's integrity and they didn't want him to resign because of Johnson's miscalculated remarks. The entire situation proved to be a quiet victory for Comiskey.

Eddie Collins received a justified promotion to White Sox manager in 1925, and was confident after a successful spring exhibition schedule.[43] The team appeared to be more rounded with a strong mix of regulars and utility players, and prospects were higher than in previous years. Early in the season, the Sox garnered the largest attendance for a baseball game in Chicago, when an estimated 44,000 turned out to see a contest against Cleveland.[44] Over 7,000 of the people were in roped off sections on the field, and their excitement was such that as soon as it appeared that the game had ended in the bottom of the ninth, they rabidly rushed onto the field. But the problem was that the game was not over; a Sox runner had been deemed safe by the umpire in a close play. Unable to regain control over the crowd, Clarence Rowland, former Sox manager turned umpire, called the game and awarded it to Cleveland by forfeit.

With Collins in charge, the team showed a renewed spirit and willingness to fight for victories into the late innings, taking many games they normally would have lost in seasons previous. They pulled off a seven game win streak in June, and Ted Lyons stepped up to become the ace of the pitching staff. Earl Sheely, Johnny Mostil, and Bibb Falk displayed championship caliber hitting at times, and Buck Crouse and Bill Barrett did a fine job in back-up roles. While many players excelled, some others failed to live up to expectations, including pitchers Charlie Robertson, Mike Cvengros, George "Sarge" Connally, and Hollis "Sloppy" Thurston. Along the line and under pressure the sustained team effort veered off course and the Sox were unable to maintain a position above fifth place. While the season was again a disappointment, the team did achieve its first winning season in five years with a record of 79–75.[45]

Comiskey escaped to warmer climates prior to the holidays and spent more than two months enjoying a leisurely road trip to California.[46] He was fond of an idea, shared by John McGraw, to make the next international journey to South America. Ted Sullivan had actually pushed for the trip many years earlier, but for whatever reason, it didn't come to fruition. This time, more progress was made in planning, but again, the excursion never left U.S. shores.

Back in Chicago, other changes in the lineup were made in the hopes of improving the team. The acquisition of veteran Everett Scott was big in terms of filling the shortstop position prior to the start of the 1926 campaign. In addition, the Sox had an option to pick any player from the Baltimore franchise of the International League in return from the deal that sent outfielder Maurice Archdeacon to that club.[47] Pitcher Alphonse "Tommy" Thomas was chosen. Thomas was a 30-game winner for the Orioles and possessed a feared curveball. He was the kind of winner the Sox needed to complete its roster, and fans anticipated big things from him.

Before leaving for training camp at Shreveport, Collins spent a couple hours discussing strategies with Comiskey in a scene reminiscent of bygone days.[48] Comiskey's mind was still sharp as a tack, and he could recite dates, names, and even memorable plays from decades earlier. They both were enthusiastic about the changes made to team, and it was definitely felt that 1926 was the year for the Sox to graduate from the second division into the first.

Rookie Bill Hunnefield turned out to be a bigger impact player than Everett Scott and filled in at third for the injured Willie Kamm. After continued success, they shifted him to shortstop, putting Scott out of a job. Surprisingly, the Sox were in second place in June and trying to threaten the league leading Yankees, but in the end, the competition was too tough for their blood. They faltered and faltered again, dropping out of contention and ending up in a fight with Washington for fourth place, which they eventually lost.[49]

Two big changes happened in the realm of Charles Comiskey during the offseason. First, the H. F. Friestedt Company was contracted to enlarge the capacity of Comiskey Park by expanding the current double deck seating to completely surround the field.[50] The construction would make it possible for as many as 70,000 people to witness a game at a cost of $750,000.[51] [52] It was a massive undertaking, but in concordance with Comiskey's longtime vision for the stadium.

The second modification was to the management of the club. Collins was, to a degree, successful, but the consecutive fifth place finishes were unsatisfactory to team officials. The fact that he had given up his spot on the field to manage from the bench was considered a weakness, and hampered the Sox rather than helped. In November of 1926, Collins was unceremoniously dumped and replaced by the team's other legend, Ray Schalk.[53] Schalk, an incomparable catcher, had been with Comiskey since 1912, and year after year gave his heart and soul to the cause of the team. He was the true backbone of the squad and a natural replacement for Collins.

Out of the woodwork appeared accomplices of the "Black Sox" scandal in early 1927, trying to rehash the controversy involving an alleged payment to Detroit players for thrown games in 1917.[54] Swede Risberg, Happy Felsch, and Chick Gandil were among those to speak out about the scandal, and it garnered plenty of news attention. But the shock value of the claims was significantly reduced because the story had already broken five years earlier. Those with motives to disparage people like Collins and Schalk, and of course Comiskey, pushed to have the case investigated by Commissioner Landis. Ultimately, the situation did little more than fill a few weeks with scandalous headlines.

Through trades, the Sox obtained second baseman Aaron Ward and shortstop Roger Peckinpaugh to strengthen their infield. Willie Kamm assumed the captainship of the team with Collins being gone, and at camp in Shreveport, Louisiana, Schalk worked to put the right combination of players together. On March 8, 1927, disaster struck when outfielder Johnny Mostil, in the clutches of a severe depression, attempted suicide at the team hotel.[55] Initially expected to pass away from his wounds, last rites were performed, but Mostil received pivotal medical attention and miraculously survived. His condition, in the days and weeks following, improved steadily, and he returned to baseball for the Sox in early September.

With the revamped stadium ready in time for the new season to begin, there was ample interest in what the White Sox were doing on the South Side of Chicago. A motivated rooters' organization sprouted up to add festiveness to home games and Schalk was doing the best he could under the circumstances.[56] The loss of Mostil was crucial and once the race began, the Sox quickly fell to the bottom of the pack. That all changed when the team experienced a hot streak in May (winning 18 of 28 games in the month) and jumped all the way to second in the standings. Schalk, who rarely played, was keenly in tune with his athletes and wasn't afraid to shake up the batting order in search of better results. His leadoff man, Californian Alex Metzler, in his first full season as a big leaguer, was providing a much needed spark that seemed to aid his teammates when they needed it the most.

On the road at the beginning of June, the Sox were only one game out of first place, and entered New York with star pitchers Ted Lyons and Tommy Thomas in top form. They matched up against the Yankees on June 8, 1927, and held an 11–6 lead after scoring two runs in the top of the 9th.[57] In an instant, the momentum of the Sox imploded as they gave up five runs, and then lost the game in the eleventh inning after Cedric Durst tripled and later scored on a single by Ray Morehart. Not only did this one defeat affect the Sox during their stay in the east, but was a constant reminder for players the rest of the year. However, the Yankees, as a team, were well out of their league and literally were one of the greatest clubs ever put together. On the backs of Babe Ruth and Lou Gehrig, they won 110 games and captured the World Series title after sweeping the Pittsburgh Pirates.

Also in New York, American League owners gathered on July 8, 1927, but Comiskey was on the mend in Wisconsin and unable to make the trip.[58] Grabiner was sick, leaving Alfred Austrian to represent the franchise in what was going to be a historic meeting.

Months earlier, Ban Johnson was engaged in yet another confrontational episode with Commissioner Landis.[59] Yearning to extinguish the flames before any kind of detrimental eruption, league owners voted to give Johnson a leave of absence, temporarily sidelining him as he dealt with some health problems. Upon returning to his position, he was stimulated to make his presence felt, and his increased vigor bothered influential members of the league. Johnson said he wasn't going to resign, but that's exactly what he did in New York, and effective November 1, his twenty-seven-year tenure as American League president came to a close.[60] Regardless of how Comiskey, Landis, or any individual owner felt about Johnson personally, his exit from Organized Baseball was a blow to the sport.

In the midst of freefalling from second to fifth place—where they'd eventually finish—the Sox direly needed new talent, and made a $100,000 bid for infielder Lynford Lary of the Pacific Coast League.[61] The offer was apparently declined, and Lary was shipped off to the Yankees instead. Schalk was left with a weakened pitching staff, an unbalanced infield, and a series of disappointing results. At the end of the season, the Sox were 70–83.

Plenty of analysis was conducted by sportswriters speculating about their continued inability to be competitive. Irving Vaughan of the *Tribune* mentioned that he'd heard murmurs about some players being unhappy because of low salaries, but admitted that there was "no proof" to such an allegation.[62] Ed Burns, for the same publication, specifically named Bibb Falk as being "dissatisfied," apparently because of a reduction in wages.[63] There is no way to know why Chicago cut his salary, but Falk's performance prior to the reduction in 1927 was consistent with a top-level player, when he batted .345 in 1926 with 195 hits. Burns believed that Falk, because of whatever was troubling him, was "unwilling to exert himself."

The long reported claims of administrative interference by Grabiner, Tip O'Neill, or others remained as prominent in 1927 as it had been earlier in the decade during the Kid Gleason regime. Burns blamed Comiskey for not "letting a manager be the real boss of the team," and thought that day-to-day instructions were coming all the way from the top.[64] He reiterated that "nightly" telegrams were sent to the "home office," telling the higher-ups about the happenings of the club. This system didn't show faith in the manager, no matter if it was Schalk, Collins, or Gleason.

The true force behind the White Sox in 1927, and throughout this entire time frame, was not Comiskey, but Grabiner.[65] He ran the team, controlled what information went up the ladder to Comiskey, and the latter had 100 percent confidence in Grabiner's ability to direct operations. Why? Because he was the man who taught Grabiner everything he knew about baseball. From the time he was a teenage prodigy in the Sox organization to a dedicated team secretary in his thirties, Grabiner was all eyes and ears, studying Comiskey's formulas and ensuring that his policies were adhered to. He was well liked throughout the industry and was extremely competent in his job. He could be a pit bull when necessary, and with Comiskey behind him, he had the confidence to resort to hardball tactics with players if need be. That included any salary adjustments at contract time.

Grabiner was not going to be bullied by any of his athletes. He supervised Schalk, dealt with scouts and personnel issues, and coordinated the efforts of the Sox in a direct fashion. Regularly, he consulted with Comiskey, but with the "boss" in an entirely different state most of the baseball season, he alone reigned supreme.

Schalk ventured to Comiskey's Wisconsin retreat in October of 1927 in what amounted to a business vacation, but oddly, the Sox delayed announcing his return as manager.[66] That declaration came in December, right around the time most fans were digesting the news of a major investment in a Pacific Coast League player.[67] As much as $123,000 in cash and talent was traded for Chalmer "Bill" Cissell, a twenty-four-year-old Missouri-born shortstop.[68] With Bud Clancy at first base, the Sox released Earl Sheely, and training camp at Shreveport was again packed with recruits looking for a spot on the team.[69] Of all the young athletes in the grind for a permanent position, outfielder Carl Reynolds of Texas was the standout.

The season of 1928 was another year of underperformance for the White Sox. Old favorites Ted Lyons, Tommy Thomas, and Red Faber struggled because of weak run support, and guys like Johnny Mostil, and Bud

Clancy were lackluster at the plate (hitting .270 and .271 respectively). But behind every complication, and almost every loss, there was an alibi. Injuries, illnesses, and general poor play were routine impediments, and Schalk benched regulars when they failed to help the team. By July, the Sox were 12 games under .500 and in seventh place. Their dreary efforts prompted Schalk to resign as manager on July 4, 1928, and cited the constant "bad luck" as an aggravating factor in the club's lack of success.[70]

His midseason replacement was Lena Blackburne, a former player first signed by Comiskey in 1909. Blackburne had more recently acted as a coach for the Sox, and he implemented a different approach than Schalk, which prioritized discipline. He tried to motivate his players by talking about the money to be made if their individual numbers improved or if the team garnered any of the World Series pot. Blackburne led the charge as the team battled into fourth place and won six straight into early August. He placed rookie Art Shires at first and Karl Swanson at second and toyed with the lineup to maximize the output.

Late in the season, the team captured two of three from the Yankees in an impressive showing, but the Sox still finished ten games under .500.[71] The position in the standings, of course, was fifth place.

The dramatic upswings and downslides of illness were unfailing in Comiskey's life. Prior to his sixty-ninth birthday in August, he was in rough shape, but regained strength and enjoyed hearing from friends to wish him well.[72] In January of 1929, he showed his spunk by gathering a few close friends and hitting the road for a vacation in Florida.[73]

Dallas, Texas, was selected as the training location for Blackburne's 1929 outfit, and the normal bumps and bruises were being dealt with as the athletes worked to get back into form. Team morale dipped and open "dissension" was publicized on the back of two notable conduct infractions by Bill Cissell and Art Shires.[74] The two men, in separate incidents, were caught under in the influence of alcohol and penalized. Players felt that Blackburne was worrying too much about discipline and sending them out against "fourth rate" ball teams in exhibitions rather than turning them into a promising squad ready for major league competition.

Bibb Falk was traded away to Cleveland and Bill Barrett was sent to the Red Sox.[75] The new Chicago outfield consisted of Alex Metzler, Carl Reynolds, and Clarence "Dutch" Hoffman, with Johnny Watwood serving as a backup. The various roster changes, imports, and releases unaffected the standings in a positive way, and the team remained firmly in the bottom four. Not one member of the regular pitching staff achieved a winning record (Red Faber finished 13–13, and had the best record on the team), and all the forward progress in rebuilding a championship contender seemed to be reversed. Ed Burns of the *Tribune*, in September of 1929, tried once again to explain the problems of the Sox.[76] He called the players disgruntled, disorganized, and said they didn't respect Blackburne as a manager.

The list went on and on. Ironically, there were scores of potential reasons why the White Sox were completely uncompetitive against real ball clubs. It was Grabiner's fault, Comiskey's, the fact that the ownership was cheap, and so on and so forth. Burns flatly addressed the latter statement in writing, stating that "The club isn't cheap and Comiskey isn't cheap." He made an honest reference to the "folklore" of complaints by Sox players, and how year after year, the grievances spread from veteran to rookie and so on. And even if the rookie had no basis to complain, he started to because it was ingrained in his attitude from day one in the clubhouse. The patterns were almost rituals for the team roster and it condemned Chicago annually.

Comiskey, who on July 5, 1929, lost his longtime best friend, Ted Sullivan (at the age of seventy-eight), was tired of the same old story.[77] His lengthy recuperation had him feeling the best he had in years, and he wanted to return to the helm of the Sox to aid in its rebirth into a winner.[78] Having recently turned seventy, Comiskey was feeling invigorated and believed he now had the physical prowess to act on the ideas he had to turn things around.

Breaking his silence, he opened up about the worst episode in his professional career. "That team," Comiskey told a reporter, "or the eight crooks that were on it, gave me the worst shock that ever a man suffered in baseball. I don't think the public realizes what a crushing blow those 'Black Sox' gave to the proudest owner that ever built up a ball club. The years haven't healed the wounds completely, and I am sad when I recall the reaction to my pride of just ten years ago, but I've suffered long enough. I'm coming back to Chicago to start in on a lot of new happiness."[79]

Part of his rejuvenation was the release of bitterness that he carried for far too long. "God has spared me," Comiskey said, referring to his health. And because of that, he wanted to live as much life as possible with the time he had left.

The Sox finished the 1929 season with a 59–93 record, in seventh place, and Comiskey promptly released Blackburne and signed former Detroit Tigers star Donie Bush as manager.[80] Bush's credentials spoke for themselves and he was respected by players for his accomplishments. For that reason, he didn't expect to deal with the disciplinary problems Blackburne had faced.

Bush's vision of a balanced roster didn't include Johnny Mostil, Buck Crouse, or Dutch Hoffman, and he figured out a way to rid the Sox of their services while signing power-hitter Smead Jolley from the Pacific Coast League.

Comiskey spent a few weeks in Miami in early 1930, but the wear and tear of travel burned him out.[81] It was obvious that his mind wanted to do things that his body couldn't keep pace with, and he wore out easily. He did correspond with Art Shires in a successful effort to resolve the lingering differences between the player and team.[82] From a safe distance, he watched Bush struggle unmercifully in the championship campaign, and the Sox were not in fourth place as some people predicted, but rather in seventh. Vague glimpses of budding cohesion appeared, but faded almost as fast.

Yearning for better players, Bush reached out to other clubs for trades and continued to stock up on young talent. It seemed that out of every hundred recruits, one stood out as a superstar in the making. In the latest batch, Luke Appling was picked up from the Atlanta Crackers of the Southern Association, and his inborn abilities in the field as well as at the plate were considered noteworthy for the future. Everything they did appeared to be for the future because in the moment, it seemed virtually impossible to improve. The Sox won only three games more in 1930 than they did the year before, finishing with a 62–92 record and again in the inglorious seventh position.

All the usual, tried and true methods that Bush and Comiskey were acquainted with were being applied in the reconstruction of a broken club. Their combined experience was more than enough to lay out a clear blueprint, but getting their men to actually win with regularity was proving to be out of reach.

In January of 1931, Comiskey made his annual getaway—this time to California and Arizona—and then drove to San Antonio, Texas, to attend his first Sox training camp since 1918.[83] He rested comfortably in the front seat of his limousine and watched his athletes prepare for the long season ahead. His chief concerns related to the condition of the field, which was indicative of his attention to detail and understanding the importance of professional grounds to train. When prediction time came around, optimists thought fourth place for the Sox sounded good, but how reasonable it was still remained a question, as the team hadn't finished that high since 1920, when they finished second to Cleveland.

American League President Ernest S. Barnard unexpectedly passed away on the evening of March 27, 1931, and the next day, his predecessor, Ban Johnson died in a St. Louis hospital.[84] Johnson's long term illness was well documented, and he put up a gallant fight against diabetes. Friend and foe, Johnson and Comiskey were revolutionaries in the creation of the American League and in shaping modern day baseball. At their height they were bosom buddies, and together they could have accomplished anything they set their minds to. But their cruel decline into rivalry cost them each a prized friendship. Many times, they fought for reasons that were absolutely meaningless.

The lives of Comiskey and Johnson and their families would have been so much improved had they just put things into perspective, not taken each other so seriously, and been able to laugh off whatever petty argument that seemed so important that day. In a telegram to Johnson's widow Jennie, Comiskey said: "Most sorry to hear of Ban's passing and extend deepest and sincerest sympathy to you from family and self."[85]

Lou Comiskey represented the club at Barnard's funeral in Cleveland, and, acknowledging the long history between his family and the Johnsons, called his father to see if it would be appropriate to attend Ban's services in Indiana.[86] Charles advised him to go, and Lou went directly to Spencer to pay his respects. As soon as Jennie saw him walk in, she burst into tears and said, her words full of emotion, "Oh, Lou." The hatchet was buried between the families, but unfortunately, it took one of the patriarchs to die before this was accomplished.[87]

Bush's 1931 pitching staff of Tommy Thomas, Ted Lyons, Red Faber, Vic Frazier, and Pat Caraway was considered to be first-class. Twenty-year-old Billy Sullivan Jr., the namesake of the famous Sox catcher, joined the team as an infielder, as did veteran Lu Blue. Willie Kamm was traded to the Indians for Lew Fonseca, and Mel Simons was purchased for upwards of $30,000 in cash and players. These transactions were logical maneuvers in attempt to give Sox fans something to finally cheer for.

Once the season got underway, few people found enjoyment in their performance. The stability of the team's pitching crumbled under injury and illness, leaving Bush severely handicapped on the mound.[88] In crisis mode, he prodded management for added support, but options were scarce.[89] It was a losing cause on a sinking ship; straight to the cellar of the American League. High dollar investments went bust and shoddy teamwork all around landed the Sox in eighth place with only 56 victories to 97 losses. For a club with so many good intentions early in the year, Chicago was confronted by insurmountable challenges and ended up with yet another disappointment.

Charles Comiskey moved to the upscale Jackson Towers in the Hyde Park neighborhood of Chicago's South Side around May of 1931.[90] His seventy-second birthday was celebrated on August 15, 1931, and he announced his goal to win another baseball championship.[91] Out at his stadium, more than 53,000 people witnessed the Sox and Yankees, including an exhibition by Babe Ruth on August 23.[92] In a high-profile charity game for the Governor's Unemployment Fund on September 9, 34,865 turned out to see the Cubs win over the Sox, 3–0.[93]

On September 20, 1931, at 2:00 in the morning, Dr. Russell A. Oldfield of Eagle River was summoned to Comiskey's Wisconsin residence.[94] Charles was suffering from combined heart and kidney problems and his prognosis was uncertain. The physician attended to Comiskey over a dozen times in the next four weeks and Dr. Philip H. Kreuscher, the Sox team doctor, traveled to see him as his condition worsened. News reports claimed he was doing better, but the reality of the situation was that it all was touch and go.[95] Sluggish improvements were made as he strived to recover, but he lapsed into a coma, and at 1:25 a.m. on October 26, 1931, Charles Albert Comiskey passed away as the age of seventy-two.[96]

Baseball's grand "Old Roman" was now gone forever.

ENDNOTES

1 In the 1919 World Series, Weaver would hit .324 and scored four runs, which were both second best on the team behind Joe Jackson.
2 *Dallas Morning News*, September 5, 1921, p. 8.
3 *Chicago Daily Tribune*, October 19, 1921, p. 4.
4 *Kansas City Star*, January 12, 1922, p. 14.
5 *San Diego Evening Tribune*, May 12, 1922, p. 22.
   Weaver's story was told to James L. Kilgallen of the International News Service and appeared in newspapers far and wide.
6 *Chicago Daily Tribune*, May 12, 1922, p. 1, 17.

Felsch filed his suit in Milwaukee through attorney Raymond J. Cannon seeking unpaid wages and a promised bonus from 1920. Also, he was looking to be rewarded damages for his injured reputation. Cannon planned similar action on behalf of Weaver, Risberg, Cicotte, and Jackson.

7 *Chicago Daily Tribune*, May 13, 1922, p. 10.

8 *Chicago Daily Tribune*, April 10, 1923, p. 19.

By January of 1924, most newspapers pegged the amount Jackson wanted to be somewhere in the neighborhood of $18,000 to $20,000. The total would have included his pay for the remainder of 1920 after the time he was suspended, annual salary of $8,000 for the years 1921 and 1922, and a $1,500 bonus promised from the 1917 World Series.

9 The White Sox finished the 1923 season with a 69–85 record, in seventh place in the American League. Nearly forty players were on the club roster at different points during the season and a knee injury to Eddie Collins in July was considered one of the turning points in their collapse.

10 *Milwaukee Sentinel*, January 28, 1924, p. 4.

11 Ibid, p. 10.

12 *Milwaukee Sentinel*, January 29, 1924, p. 4.

Both women on the jury admitted to never having heard of Joe Jackson.

13 *Milwaukee Sentinel*, January 30, 1924, p. 1, 9.

14 *Milwaukee Sentinel*, January 31, 1924, p. 1, 6.

A major point of discussion during the trial was Grabiner's 1920 visit to Savannah in attempt to obtain Jackson's signature on a contract. Jackson had been holding out for a three-year deal worth $10,000 a season, but Grabiner offered $8,000. The latter was supremely persuasive, according to Jackson, and got the outfielder to sign on the steering wheel of his car without his wife being present. Unable to read, Jackson didn't know that the contract contained the ten-day clause, a rule favorable to owners, granting them the power to release a player on ten-days notice. Jackson also said that Grabiner surprisingly acknowledged the scandal itself, mentioning the $5,000 he received, but seemed more interested in getting the contract signed than discussing the Series. Grabiner denied Jackson's claim that the contract was signed in the car, and said it had been done in Jackson's living room with his wife present. *Milwaukee Sentinel*, February 12, 1924, p. 4.

15 The grand jury documentation and testimony was reportedly stolen from the Illinois State's Attorney's office prior to the 1921 conspiracy trial, and the theft was purportedly tied to Arnold Rothstein of New York. During the Milwaukee proceedings, Comiskey's lawyers produced Jackson's grand jury transcript, and just how they obtained the records was questioned. It was never said, however, that they had the original copy of the transcript, and it was likely just a reproduction, perhaps obtained from Rothstein or whoever had eventually purchased the testimony when the latter put it up for sale. *Milwaukee Journal Final*, February 4, 1924, p. 1.

16 *Milwaukee Sentinel*, February 1, 1924, p. 1, 6.

17 *Milwaukee Journal*, February 4, 1924, p. 1.

Later that year, Ban Johnson admitted to helping Comiskey by arranging for Burns to travel to Chicago for a deposition, taken around 1922. The maneuver was in aid against the various lawsuits brought by "Black Sox" players. *Chicago Daily Tribune*, November 12, 1924, p. 28. Johnson had reportedly spent $37,500 out of the American League treasury in his search for evidence and Comiskey wanted Johnson to produce the resultant evidence in the Milwaukee trial. He believed he was entitled to the support since he was paying into the treasury to finance Johnson's hunt. *Chicago Daily Tribune*, December 13, 1924, p. 13.

18 *Milwaukee Sentinel*, February 13, 1924, p. 1, 5.

In his testimony, Felsch also denied any participation in the 1919 Series plot. He was promptly arrested upon his appearance the next day, taken to Milwaukee County Jail, and bailed out that afternoon for $2,000. In an announcement from the Court, it was stated that Felsch's actions were a "malicious and vindictive case of perjury." Comiskey added that he was "very sorry" for Felsch, noting that he was a "great baseball player." *Milwaukee Sentinel*, February 14, 1924, p. 16.

19 *Milwaukee Sentinel*, February 15, 1924, p. 1.

Jackson was released a few hours later on $5,000 bail.

20 Ibid, p. 1, 4.

The jury answered all ten questions in favor of Jackson, but Judge Gregory responded by saying, "How you could answer some of those questions in the manner you have, the court can't understand." He told the jury, "You have failed in the discharge of your duty," and said that Jackson's evidence reeked with "perjury." Jackson's lawyer Raymond Cannon, according to the newspaper report, was "jubilant over the verdict," and said it was "one of the most wonderful victories that the players in Organized Baseball have ever achieved, in view of the odds that they had to contend with."

21 *Chicago Daily Tribune*, October 17, 1923, p. 17.

22 *Chicago Daily Tribune*, October 18, 1923, p. 25.

It was acknowledged that there were "tears in the eyes of both" men. Gleason continued his baseball career as a coach for his hometown Philadelphia Athletics and died in 1933.

23 *Chicago Daily Tribune*, February 17, 1924, p. A1.

24 *Chicago Daily Tribune*, February 18, 1924, p. 24.

25 *Chicago Daily Tribune*, March 21, 1924, p. 19.

26 *Chicago Daily Tribune*, March 22, 1924, p. 15.

27 *Chicago Daily Tribune*, April 12, 1924, p. 15.

28 *Chicago Daily Tribune*, April 13, 1924, p. A1.

Comiskey told the press that "money will be no object in building up the Sox," and that "Chance can have any player he wants whom it is possible to purchase."

29 *Chicago Daily Tribune*, April 20, 1924, p. A1.

It was said that Chance was still the official manager of the White Sox and, when he was ready to return, would assume the position as team leader. Evers was said to have full management in late July. *Chicago Daily Tribune*, July 29, 1924, p. 9.

30 While Sloppy Thurston had 20 wins for the 1924 White Sox (30 percent of the team's wins), he also had 14 losses, and along with Mike Cvengros (3–12), and Sage Connally (7–13), they combined for 45 percent of the teams losses.

31 *Chicago Daily Tribune,* June 3, 1924, p. 19.
McClellan had been with the Sox since 1919 and was the regular shortstop. He suffered from ulcers and gallstones and played only 32 games in 1924. He died on November 6, 1925 at the age of thirty.

32 *Chicago Daily Tribune,* September 30, 1924, p. 19.

33 *Chicago Daily Tribune,* October 7, 1924, p. 21.

34 *Chicago Daily Tribune,* September 23, 1924, p. 25.

35 *Chicago Daily Tribune,* November 8, 1924, p. 16.

36 *San Diego Evening Tribune,* November 7, 1924, p. 20.

37 *Chicago Daily Tribune,* December 3, 1924, p. 23.

38 *Chicago Daily Tribune,* November 12, 1924, p. 28.

39 *Chicago Daily Tribune,* December 13, 1924, p. 13.
Comiskey's appearance was his first at a league meeting in years.

40 *Dallas Morning News,* October 4, 1924, p. 10.

41 *Chicago Daily Tribune,* December 18, 1924, p. 1.
Phil Ball of St. Louis was the only owner to vote against the resolution.

42 *Chicago Daily Tribune,* December 19, 1924, p. 29.

43 *Chicago Daily Tribune,* December 12, 1924, p. 21.

44 *Chicago Daily Tribune,* April 27, 1925, p. 17.
When the audience ran onto the field in the ninth, Cleveland was leading the game, 7–2.

45 Following the season, the Sox were defeated by the Cubs in the City Series. *Chicago Daily Tribune,* October 14, 1925, p. 29.

46 *Chicago Daily Tribune,* January 22, 1926, p. 21.

47 *Chicago Daily Tribune,* December 28, 1925, p. 25.

48 *Chicago Daily Tribune,* February 27, 1926, p. 13.

49 The Sox finished with a record of 81–72 in 1926, and it would end up being the highest win total Comiskey's team would achieve before his death. In the City Series, the Sox prevailed in seven games. *Chicago Daily Tribune,* October 8, 1926, p. 25.

50 *Chicago Daily Tribune,* September 12, 1926, p. A5.

51 *Chicago Daily Tribune,* March 3, 1927, p. 17.
This figure included standing room only spectators.

52 *Chicago Daily Tribune,* February 11, 1927, p. 22.
Comiskey Park maintained one of the largest playing grounds in the majors, with 365 feet along both foul lines and 455 in dead centerfield. In comparison, Wrigley Field was 348 feet in left, 318 in right and 447 in center. *Sporting News,* July 18, 1929, p. 4. The revamped stadium would include three scoreboards, and improvements were made all around the park, from the style of seats to rest rooms. It was reported that the scoreboard was "an innovation" because it ran on electric power. *Chicago Daily Tribune,* April 17, 1927, p. A2.

53 *Chicago Daily Tribune,* November 12, 1926, p. 23.

Collins was unaware of his dismissal when the announcement was made in the press. He reportedly was faced with many of the same problems his predecessors dealt with, including being bogged down with fresh recruits who had little ability to help turn the team around. In an interesting side note, after the 1926 season, five of the eight American League teams changed managers. Four of the leaders were future Hall of Famers: Collins, Ty Cobb, George Sisler, and Tris Speaker. Collins joined Philadelphia and a special "Eddie Collins Day" was celebrated at Comiskey Park when the Athletics came to town on July 13, 1927. In honor of his many contributions in Chicago, Collins was presented with an automobile by his local friends. *Chicago Daily Tribune,* July 14, 1927, p. 17.

54 *Chicago Daily Tribune,* January 2, 1927, p. A1.
55 *Chicago Daily Tribune,* March 9, 1927, p. 1.
Lou Comiskey accompanied Mostil to the hospital in the ambulance.
56 *Chicago Daily Tribune,* April 12, 1927, p. 29.
57 *Chicago Daily Tribune,* June 9, 1927, p. 17.
The Yankees' Tony Lazzeri hit three home runs, including one in the bottom of the ninth that tied the game. The final score was 12–11.
58 *Chicago Daily Tribune,* July 8, 1927, p. 17.
59 *Chicago Daily Tribune,* January 24, 1927, p. 23.
60 *Chicago Daily Tribune,* July 9, 1927, p. 11.
Before leaving office, Johnson complained about the "childish" acts of White Sox officers for returning mail to him unopened and the back-and-forth verbal quips continued from both sides in the feud. *Chicago Daily Tribune,* October 1, 1927, p. 21. Johnson left office on October 17. Interestingly, after Johnson departed from the American League, Comiskey was added to the organization's board of directors in December 1927, along with Col. Jacob Ruppert, two men Johnson blocked from directorship following the Mays case.
61 *Chicago Daily Tribune,* August 2, 1927, p. 19.
62 *Chicago Daily Tribune,* August 14, 1927, p. A2.
63 *Chicago Daily Tribune,* August 17, 1927, p. 19.
64 *Chicago Daily Tribune,* August 17, 1927, p. 19.
The *Tribune* declared the Sox season a "failure." No City Series was staged in 1927.
65 Sportswriter Ed Burns called Grabiner "one of the shrewdest baseball men in the business." *Chicago Daily Tribune,* February 12, 1928, p. A2. Comiskey had a history of micromanaging his teams, and taught Grabiner to do the same thing.
66 *Chicago Daily Tribune,* October 11, 1927, p. 25.
67 *Chicago Daily Tribune,* December 2, 1927, p. 27.
68 *Chicago Daily Tribune,* November 6, 1927, p. A1.
Bert Cole, Ike Davis, and Ike Boone were sent to Portland to complete the deal for Cissell.
69 *Chicago Daily Tribune,* January 21, 1928, p. 17.
70 *Chicago Daily Tribune,* July 5, 1928, p. 21.
Schalk made nice comments about Comiskey and the club following his stepping down, admitting that he always had "been friendly with Comiskey." By the

end of July, his opinion changed after his salary was cut from $25,000 for his managerial job to $6,000 to be a standard, backup catcher. The situation wasn't optimal, but realistic considering Schalk's value as a player at age thirty-five. His best years were behind him, but Cooperstown would one day call and acknowledge his extraordinary accomplishments.

71 At the close of the 1928 season, their record was 72–82. In the City Series, the Cubs beat the Sox in seven games. *Chicago Daily Tribune*, October 10, 1928, p. 27.

72 *Chicago Daily Tribune*, August 16, 1928, p. 18.
During the summers, he spent time with his grandchildren and their friends at his Wisconsin sanctuary.

73 *Chicago Daily Tribune*, January 26, 1929, p. 19.
Along for the trip were Joe Barry and his wife and Harry Grabiner. Barry was Lou Comiskey's brother-in-law and a former Chicago police officer. In 1931, he'd be named traveling secretary for the Sox.

74 *Chicago Daily Tribune*, April 2-3, 1929.
Blackburne would engage in two physical altercations with Shires and the latter was considered a troublemaker, affecting the entire club.
Also see: *Chicago Daily Tribune*, May 17, 1929, p. 25. Shires, after the 1929 season, became a professional boxer and refused to sign a new Sox contract until his $25,000 demand was met. He eventually compromised.

75 *Chicago Daily Tribune*, February 28, 1929, p. 17.
The Sox received catcher Martin "Chick" Autry in return.

76 *Chicago Daily Tribune*, September 15, 1929, p. A2.

77 *Sporting News*, July 11, 1929, p. 3.
Sullivan died in Washington, D.C., and was brought to his hometown of Milwaukee for burial. A longtime friend, associate, and scout for Comiskey, it was once said that he was a "part-owner" of the Sox. *Sporting News*, October 30, 1919, p. 2.

78 *Chicago Daily Tribune*, September 17, 1929, p. 25.

79 Ibid.

80 *Chicago Daily Tribune*, October 1, 1929, p. 31.

81 *Chicago Daily Tribune*, March 12, 1930, p. 23.

82 *Chicago Daily Tribune*, March 26, 1930, p. 17.
Shires was traded to Washington in June.

83 *Chicago Daily Tribune*, January 31, 1931, p. 20.

84 *Chicago Daily Tribune*, March 29, 1931, p. A1.
A lengthy, multipart biography of Johnson ran in various newspapers in 1929. It was featured in the *Tribune* beginning on February 24, 1929.

85 Ibid.

86 *Sporting News*, April 9, 1931, p. 5.

87 Through the tenure of the Comiskey-Johnson feud, there were umpteen reasons mentioned in the press of why they were at odds with each other. But maybe the most important reason for their rivalry was never revealed publicly. Harvey T. Woodruff of the *Tribune* mentioned that he once got the alleged real scoop from an inside source who later regretted telling him. The story was relayed in secret and Woodruff never revealed what it was, but based on its seriousness,

understood how their friendship "never could be healed." *Chicago Daily Tribune*, March 31, 1931, p. 23.

88 *Chicago Daily Tribune*, July 27, 1931, p. 21.

89 *Chicago Daily Tribune*, July 28, 1931, p. 17.

90 The building was at 5555 Everett Avenue and he inhabited apartment A-11-12. His monthly rent was $833.33. Jackson Towers statement of account for December 1931, Probate Court Records for Charles A. Comiskey, File No. 170375, obtained from the Archives Department of the Clerk of the Circuit Court, Cook County, Illinois.

Also see: *Chicago Daily Tribune*, May 24, 1931, pg. A11. Comiskey, previous to this move, lived at 5131 South Michigan, having settled there in May 1922. *Chicago Daily Tribune*, May 3, 1922, p. 28.

91 *Chicago Daily Tribune*, August 15, 1931, p. 13.

92 *Chicago Daily Tribune*, August 24, 1931, p. 21.

93 *Chicago Daily Tribune*, September 10, 1931, p. 21.

94 Dr. Oldfield's statement for services rendered, Probate Court Records for Charles A. Comiskey, File No. 170375, obtained from the Archives Department of the Clerk of the Circuit Court, Cook County, Illinois. Dr. Oldfield also attended to Louis Comiskey in 1939.

95 *Chicago Daily Tribune*, September 26, 1931, p. 19.

96 *Chicago Daily Tribune*, October 26, 1931, p. 1, 26.

Also see: *Sporting News*, October 29, 1931, p. 1, 3.

20

SETTING THE RECORD STRAIGHT

The solid baseball stadium at the corner of Shields and 35th Streets on the South Side of Chicago rested quiet on the morning of October 29, 1931. From the empty field, only the cool whipping winds were audible, and the American flag, which usually stood tall at the top of the structure, was lowered to half mast in honor of Charles A. Comiskey, the ballpark's namesake, who had died three days before. For decades, the venue hosted millions of fans in the celebration of the nation's pastime and game-day was always an exciting adventure for families. But from that point on, it was known that the dedicated baseball leader, the man who started it all by ushering in the era of the White Sox, was gone.

That same day, also on the South Side, baseball dignitaries and friends from all walks of life converged on St. Thomas the Apostle Roman Catholic Church to attend his services.[1] Among the 1,500 people crowded into the cathedral were Commissioner Landis, Clark Griffith, Ray Schalk, Urban "Red" Faber, William Wrigley, John Heydler, and William Harridge. Reverend James Leddy performed the funeral sermon and told the mourners that Charles had "set a good example for America's boyhood and manhood with his honesty and love of good, clean sport.

"Yet he died of a broken heart," Reverend Leddy proclaimed, his voice bounding to all corners of the church. "He built up one of the greatest baseball clubs the game ever saw, pinned his faith and trust in his boys, and then saw his mighty structure crash with the weight of disloyalty of those same players. The edifice, which he had built up through the years of endeavor, in a few days, was torn down in a heap of ruins at his feet. Yet he took up the burden once more, and attempted to build a new, but the effort was too great in his declining years."

More than 200 automobiles drove in procession to Calvary Cemetery in Evanston, Illinois, where Charles was laid to rest next to his wife Nan.

The somberness of the occasion drudged up memories and thoughts of all kinds. Looking back over his fifty-five-year involvement in baseball, it was difficult not to be greatly impressed by his contributions to the advancement of the sport. His innovations as a player and manager were lauded, his accomplishments revered, and the people of Chicago were ever loyal for his dedication to the prosperity of the White Sox. As a civic leader, he was always willing to lend a hand; from aid to military soldiers and the Red Cross during World War I to supporting the women's suffrage movement.[2] Of course, it was hard not to reflect on the caustic 1919 World Series, and Reverend Leddy's comments were a reminder of Comiskey's difficulties in the scandal's aftermath.

Between 1917 and 1920, Comiskey became one of the most polarizing individuals in professional sports. In a way, he transitioned from a man who had a "reputation of bringing sunshine wherever he went" and "by long odds, the most popular and best known man in baseball," to overbearingly controversial.[3] [4] It was a stunning metamorphosis brought on by four factors: The devastating illness of his beloved wife, his own nagging health problems, his unrelenting stubbornness, and the "Black Sox" scandal. These were listed in no particular order, but it is evident that most of the elements that caused the dramatic change to Comiskey's personality were out of his hands, while the ramifications of his mulishness was, of course, brought on himself.

Several years before the downfall started, talented author Hugh C. Weir contributed a revealing article about Comiskey in *Baseball Magazine*.[5] The piece was fittingly titled, "The Real Comiskey," and Weir attempted to look past the typical depictions to describe the true man underneath the constant deluge of admiration. The truth of the matter was that Comiskey was indeed baseball royalty. He was lauded by his compatriots, looked to for counsel, and along with Ban Johnson, solved many a crisis. At home in Chicago, he was beloved by his faithful supporters for his down-to-earth and friendly policies, which made Comiskey Park a home away from home.

"Consideration for patrons is one of the reasons why Comiskey is almost a popular idol in Chicago," Weir wrote, "at a time when other magnates are being grilled in the daily press for their greed. [The] White Sox are known as the most loyally supported baseball club in the country."

Beginning with his arrival on the South Side in 1900, Comiskey specifically went out of his way to cater to his audience. He took time to address the concerns of a visitor to his ballpark, creating manageable entrances and exits and boosting concessions to keep patrons from having to stand in long lines. He relished his bleacher supporters and knew that the fans that paid 25 cents to see Sox games were the backbone of his franchise. Time and again, he flatly refused to boost ticket prices, brushing off the recommendations of fellow owners and fighting league directives to streamline rates across the board.[67] He was also against the raising of ticket prices each year his team was in the World Series, feeling that the fans that had supported the team throughout the season shouldn't be priced out when the team needed them most.

"When we came into Chicago," Comiskey said, "we wanted those 25 cent admissions. Those bleacherites made this big new plant possible. Baseball has grown but the pocketbooks of some of our friends haven't. Never while I am living will their space be cut down. The fellow who can pay only twenty-five cents to see a ball game always will be just as welcome at Comiskey Park as the box seat holder."[8]

Weir also noted that during rainstorms, Comiskey permitted his bleacher spectators to enter the higher-priced seating areas to get shelter; a thoughtful policy that was not the law in all ballparks. For these reasons and others, attendance at Comiskey's stadium was exceptional, even when the team was losing, and fan loyalty was arguably the best in baseball.

In studying contemporary views of Comiskey as an owner, it is evident that a high percentage of negative opinions are based on inaccurate or inadequate source material. As with any biography, there is a particular importance to analyze all sides of the individual's life, and it is purely negligent to cast any human being into a narrow representation generated from abridged research.

However, that is exactly what led to Comiskey being misunderstood.

For instance, author Eliot Asinof tackled the complexities of the "Black Sox" scandal in his 1963 book, *Eight Men Out.* Perhaps limited by space, he was unable to provide a rounded perspective of Comiskey, and centered on what he believed to be at the core of the players' alleged "bitterness and tension," essentially motivating their actions. And that bitterness circled back to Comiskey, providing the "Black Sox" athletes with someone to blame for their crookedness. To Asinof, Comiskey was a "cheap, stingy tyrant," who didn't pay his players what they were worth, betrayed them with a smile, and made them "feel like dirt."[9]

Was this the "Real Comiskey" nobody knew about?

It didn't matter, because Asinof's version was the one that was accepted by the public, especially after *Eight Men Out* was made into a major motion picture in 1988. The film version featured many popular young actors like John Cusack and Charlie Sheen, and was dramatized just right to evoke sympathy for the crooked "Black Sox." At the same time, Comiskey filled the role of the villain. Appearing heavier than he actually was in person—probably to seem gluttonous—he was portrayed in a highly unlikable fashion. He openly reneged on promises to his players, appeared to be enthusiastically callous, and thrived in his arrogance.

This was not reality, but Hollywood's version of reality.

The alibi of underpaid wages was great fodder for conversation. If the players were being paid "starvation salaries," why didn't they all hold out for more money prior to the 1919 season? The Cincinnati Reds, who the Sox played in the 1919 World Series, faced such a situation when Edd Roush, Ivy Wingo, Rube Bressler, and Hod Eller became holdouts for more greenbacks in March of 1919, raising the pressure on owner Garry Herrmann to act.[10] Similarly, prior to the 1917 season, Charles H. Ebbets of the Brooklyn Robins (later to become the Dodgers) had as many as ten unsatisfied players and was compelled to increase salaries. There was no reason why members of the Sox couldn't have done the same. That is to say, if they were actually dissatisfied.

Regardless of what was said about the reserve clause and the power of owners, the players were the real box office attractions, and Comiskey needed dividends on his investments. Had several players shown discontent and decided to hold out, Comiskey, like Herrmann and Ebbets, would have been forced to compromise to players' satisfaction up and down the line.

While the "Black Sox" scandal changed gambling and the sport forever, throwing games for money wasn't completely taboo in certain minority segments of the baseball community. It was a quick way to make money, and for the Sox players involved, the opportunity looked too good on the surface to pass up, especially since they believed they could get away with it. There is no way to know whether or not the personal principles of these men would have been stronger had they been paid a larger salary by Comiskey. It is possible that even if they had been receiving $10,000 a year each, the thrill of making $10,000 or $20,000 more by throwing Series games would still have enticed them to participate. It wasn't really about the money itself, but a question of their character, honesty, and sportsmanship.

Money was definitely heavy in the minds of ball players throughout the majors in 1919, but when scrutinizing the lives of key conspirators Ed Cicotte and Chick Gandil, it is obvious they had extraordinary financial obligations. The imminent birth of his third child, a garage business, and a new farm were constantly lingering the mind of Cicotte. For Gandil, it was the desire to remain on the California coast, where his wife wanted to live, and to provide enough money to establish a new existence away from the demands of big league ball. Both men were aware that their livelihoods in baseball were increasingly short.

Asinof added an interesting dynamic to his story by alleging that the "bitterness and tension" in the clubhouse nearly prompted a strike by players in July [of] 1919.[11] He asserted that Comiskey contributed to a baseball-wide policy by owners to "cut the ballplayers' salaries to the bone" because of the conditions during World War I, and that the Sox were "the best and were paid as poorly as the worst."

The question begs to be asked: Did Comiskey dramatically decrease his player's salaries going into the 1919 season?

The first thing that needs to be known is that owners shortened both the 1918 and 1919 seasons from the regular 154-game schedule because of the war and what was termed "retrenchment."[12] Comiskey was against the reduction and felt it was important to maintain the structure of the sport that had already proved popular with fans. Nevertheless, the changes were made, and because of the shorter season, players worked less—and thus, were paid less.

Baseball historian Bob Hoie thoroughly examined the White Sox payroll for 1919 and found that Comiskey had perhaps the highest salary list in the major leagues.[13] At around $90,000, it was competitive with the Yankees and Red Sox, and may have just edged them out for the top spot. According to Hoie, "an active imagination" was needed to believe any opposite charges.

Eight Men Out cited poor pay as affecting the overall morale of the Sox, and it was said to have driven the resentful players to turn dishonest. Dick Kerr, in 1937, talked about the scandal, and noted that in his opinion, one member of the Sox was the ringleader, and the others followed.[14] "Some of them were pretty easily led," he added. If that was true, it wasn't a groundswell of equally angry players fighting their so-called horrible playing conditions, and just a case of follow the leader.

Three years after Kerr made his comments, Ray Schalk, who as catcher had a greater vantage point to see the fix unfold on the field than any other player, also recollected the Series.[15] He said: "Despite some of the stories about the players being disgruntled, I thought, in 1919, and I think now, that there never was a group of athletes with better morale than the White Sox of 1919. Whatever happened was not traceable to any general discontent."

Legendary baseball writer Frederick G. Lieb assessed the "Black Sox" scandal forty years after the fix, and listed five reasons why the players conspired to throw the games.[16] The first was "greed," he wrote, and the second was the "bad effect" of plot leaders on "otherwise honest players." Thirdly, he mentioned "lush money" that was being circulated by calculating "underworld" types after the Great War, and his fourth point claimed that players were well aware that Hal Chase and others had gotten away with throwing games in the past. Lieb concluded his list by citing the low salaries paid by Comiskey. He added that the insufficient pay "did not excuse" any of the Sox players, but offered insight why some felt "bitter and had larceny in their hearts."

A key element in Asinof's depiction of the scandal related to Cicotte's motivation. In the film version of *Eight Men Out*, a penetrating moment occurred when the downtrodden Cicotte went to Comiskey's office and was treated appallingly by the pompous owner. With an exaggeratedly theatrical spin, the scene captured the purported cavalier and snobbish attitude of Comiskey and awarded compassion to Cicotte as he soon agreed to throw games and go crooked.

The discussion between Cicotte and Comiskey was about a $10,000 bonus the latter reportedly offered the pitcher if he was victorious in 30 games. Ironically, the movie depicted the event as happening in 1919, while Asinof's book version stated 1917, and by and large, there is doubt that the situation took place at all.[17]

As the story goes, Comiskey told Kid Gleason to bench Cicotte so he couldn't reach his 30th win, and therefore, of course, avoided having to pay out the money. But the truth of the matter is that a $10,000 bonus for any numeric achievement in baseball was extremely rare in the late 1910s, not only for Comiskey, but any owner in baseball. For the rumor that Cicotte was "benched" in 1917 or 1919, there is evidence to the contrary. During the last month of 1917, Cicotte pitched eight games out of the twenty-five played—the most of any Sox pitcher—and won seven of them.[18] He finished the season with a record of 28–12.

In early September of 1919, Cicotte was rested for nearly two weeks after becoming ill and facing near exhaustion from his incredible workload. He returned, however, and had his final legitimate chance to win his 30th game on September 24, when he pitched seven innings against the Browns and gave up 11 hits and 5 runs, leaving with the Sox down, 5–4.[19] Kerr relieved him and was awarded the victory after the Sox scored two runs in the ninth. Four days later, Cicotte pitched his final game of the regular season, a two-inning outing that was essentially a warm up session for the Series. Cicotte finished 1919 with a 29–7 record and a 1.82 ERA in 40 games.

The yarn was another crack at Comiskey's alleged "tightfistedness." *Eight Men Out* played up the fable, and it was very effective in the movement to demonize Comiskey.

Another thing that must be acknowledged is that during the 1920 confessions of Cicotte, Jackson, Williams, and Felsch, none of the athletes directly implicated Comiskey's policies or the salaries he paid as the reason why they joined the conspiracy. If they had been driven to dishonesty by Comiskey, wouldn't he have been publicly blamed by each of them?

As was documented earlier, Comiskey had his own way of dealing with his players during contract time. Weir wrote that he'd often "surprise a player by offering more [money] than expected."[20] But business was business, and he refused to pay a dollar more than what he felt a player was worth. Based on his experience, Comiskey was much more able to assess a player's financial value than the player themselves. And if it turned out that he was mistaken and the athlete achieved greater results than expected, Comiskey recognized their contributions by way of a bonus and raise in salary the next year.

In the time and era of baseball's growth, players wanted more and more money; there never was enough. Salaries kept skyrocketing until there were seemingly no limitations, and to the point where a couple of thousand dollars a year appeared measly. The thing about Comiskey, though, was that he came from a different world than the entitled, modern-day ball player. When he began his professional career, Jesse James was still America's most wanted "outlaw." He was old school in mind and spirit, and not a star-struck rich owner who earned his fortune in another vocation. He played the game when $50 a month was acceptable and might even have played for free if the situation demanded it.

During his early days on the diamond, he was forced to be thrifty to extend every cent of his money, and was tutored by Ted Sullivan in the best ways to live cheaply and sustain his meager baseball allowance. Not only did Comiskey fine-tune the "skill" of extending his salary as far as possible, but he eventually became a saver; signifying a rare quality that only the most disciplined players demonstrated. He was a forward-thinker and figured that having padding was much more important than throwing away cash on needless things. His perspective on money—to be thrifty, but not necessarily cheap—was one of the principal lessons he passed onto his son Lou and Harry Grabiner for the management of the Sox in his absence.

While in St. Louis as a member of the Browns in the 1880s, Comiskey attained his first real education of a club's inner-workings. At first, he watched owner Chris Von der Ahe from afar, but slowly, as his position on the team grew, he became more acquainted with the responsibilities of a baseball magnate. Naturally, Comiskey was influenced by many of Von der Ahe's methods, from cutting back on expenses to implementing a Ladies' Day, where women would get into the park for free.[21] [22]

In 1887, after pitcher Nat Hudson refused to come to terms, Von der Ahe said: "Well, you know he has made a big kick for a high salary, but I've determined not to give it to him. If Hudson wants to play with the Browns this year, he will not get a cent more than $1,000 for the year's work, and if that doesn't suit him . . . well, he need not play ball at all, or he will have to do it with some other team. The fact of the matter is that I'm growing tired of the trouble I've been having with my players, and I'll warrant you that I'll have no more of it. I'll teach Mr. Hudson a lesson this time, and show him that I and not he is managing the team."[23]

Flash forward to 1909 when Ed Walsh, star pitcher for the Sox, was holding out for more salary. Comiskey said: "We will win the pennant without . . . Walsh, if necessary. I have not written Walsh and will open no communication with him, as I'm through with him. We have a splendid string of pitchers, and Walsh's return would make it harder to choose among them. Walsh has been treated pretty well by the White Sox, but he has forgotten the years we carried him along on the pay roll at a comfortable salary just to sit on the bench and learn how to pitch, when everyone else thought it was a joke to carry him."[24]

Comiskey's words were missing some of Von der Ahe's panache, but the gist was that no player, not even a star like Walsh, was going to force him to pay more salary by holding out, using threats, or hiring lawyers. It was a conversation he wanted out of the press, and when a player took a salary issue to the newspaper, Comiskey's attitude immediately turned negative.

He'd cut off contact and instruct his manager to begin searching for a replacement.

The process of playing hardball in salary duels was a stressful yet necessity evil for ball club owners. Not every athlete deserved the money they thought they were personally worth, and it was up to a discerning owner to figure out who truly merited the big bucks. The financial stability of the franchise depended on it. In terms of negotiating salaries, Comiskey thrived in one-on-one meetings, and usually always found a way to compromise.

And that's exactly what happened in 1919 when Buck Weaver wanted a raise. Weaver's holdout was important for another reason: It was one of the first noticeable moments when prominent sportswriters decried a player's wages on the White Sox. They believed Weaver was worth more than he was getting, and wanted Comiskey to quickly rectify matters. This was compounded in 1920 after roundabout salary figures were made public for the "Black Sox," and there was more talk that Comiskey was not paying sufficient wages. His enemies in the league and rival attorneys helped spread the rumors, and Comiskey's reputation as being cheap grew.

Columnist Westbrook Pegler was also extremely outspoken about the Sox owner's alleged miserliness, and, over a twenty-plus year period, wrote articles referring to his cheap ways. Without question, Pegler's remarks influenced readers for generations.[25]

Harry Grabiner faced the complaints about Comiskey's so-called penny-pinching ways all through the difficult 1920s. People wanted the Sox to spend more money to put a contender on the field, but Grabiner always defended his boss. In his desk, he kept a copy of the $100,000 check Comiskey spent for third baseman Willie Kamm, and when anyone proclaimed the Sox boss overly economical, Grabiner said: "Does this look like Mr. Comiskey was cheap?"[26]

The amounts Comiskey paid for talent over the years was astounding. He set baseball records for his $18,000 purchase of Larry Chappell, his $65,000 deal for Eddie Collins, and the $100,000 for Willie Kamm.[27] Over the last ten years of his life, Comiskey spent upwards of $50,000 each on Smead Jolley, Maurice Archdeacon, and Frank "Stubby" Mack, and another $123,000 in cash and players for Bill Cissell in 1927. And these examples were just the tip of the iceberg. There were other times when he offered clubs huge amounts to buy star players, including Joe Bush for $50,000 in 1917, and a rumor that he was after Babe Ruth in 1929.[28] [29]

Had Comiskey raised ticket prices, cut every corner known to mankind—especially in charging groups to use his park—and promoted salary limits, he might have more closely resembled the money-hungry cheapskate people said he was. Instead, he opposed ideas that would have made him more cash and even offered to pool financial resources with his peers during World War I to ensure the survival of the American League. He always gave permission to charities and organizations to hold their functions in his stadium for free.[30] On a routine basis, he helped the likes of the Off the Street Club, the House of the Good Shepherd, the Boy Scouts, and benefits for city hospitals. He supplied thousands of tickets to school children, including Sally Joy Brown's famous program, and was a big supporter of military veterans.[31]

A reversal in his approach to these regularly accepted deeds would have made Comiskey much richer, but no, that wasn't important to him. He wanted to provide these civic contributions to the city he loved. It was clear he wasn't all consumed by money.

Al Monroe of the *Chicago Defender* admitted that Comiskey was "not a philanthropist," but "gave freely when his advisors thought it necessary."[32] He added that "Half the churches on the South Side that [had] risen from store fronts to magnificent buildings [had] been aided in their climb through gifts from Mr. Comiskey."

Through his willingness to help civic programs, he became personal friends with many politicians, organizers, judges, and Chicago's social elite. His wife Nan was always just as committed to aiding worthwhile causes, and they frequently donated money to relief funds. He received faithful support from the City Council and unions, and after arriving in Chicago in 1900, because of who his father was, union contractors worked overtime to get his grandstand built in time for the season to begin.[33]

Through the years, many Sox players had deep personal respect and admiration for Comiskey. Frank Isbell, Jiggs Donahue, Jimmy Callahan, and Clark Griffith were longtime friends, and catcher Billy Sullivan was so important to Comiskey that when the former suffered blood poisoning and was in critical condition in 1910, he wept uncontrollably.[34] At times when he needed to release players to the minors, Comiskey, as a token of goodwill, gave the athletes an option of two or three teams in different cities, allowing them to choose the best option for themselves.[35] He compensated Lee Tannehill in 1912 and Chick Gandil in 1914 in situations that didn't necessarily require him to do so, and several times helped players with their children's college funds.[36]

In 1910, Comiskey picked the distinguished Ty Cobb as the greatest player of all-time.[37] In response, showing his respect, Cobb said: "President Comiskey himself has been regarded for twenty years as one of the greatest men in baseball, as player, as manager, and as club owner, and to be spoken of by him as I have been, I consider it the greatest compliment I ever received in my life—the greatest compliment any ball player could receive. I simply cannot begin to express my appreciation."

Pundits loved to dub him the "Old Roman," and the nickname seemed to fit his untouchable mystique during his heyday. There were literally half dozen or more stories about its origin. In a 1907 letter to the editor of the *Chicago Daily Tribune,* the question was posed, and the answer was that Comiskey was similar to the Romans because of the way he conquered the sport of baseball.[38] Some years before, while in St. Paul, a theatrical "spectacle" was presented on the "Fall of Pompeii," and to honor Comiskey, a large rendering of his face was integrated into the set design.[39] It wouldn't have been a stretch for someone to rib Comiskey about the depiction and instigate the nickname. But no, it went back even further than St. Paul.

One version claimed it was hatched during Comiskey's time as a manager in Cincinnati.[40] Even prior to that, in 1889, a St. Louis newspaper called him, "the noblest Roman of them all," but didn't specify why.[41] The most logical reasoning found for the nickname was his looks, specifically the prominent bridge of his nose—the "Roman nose."[42] Since the definitive answer remained unclear, some sportswriters decided it was easier to say that origin of the moniker was "lost" through the years.[43] Comiskey was never enthused about the nickname, and actually preferred to be called "Commy."[44]

The idolization of Comiskey, as well as the grandiose-style in which sportswriters affixed the name "Old Roman" to him, dissipated as he isolated himself following the 1919 scandal. His health was crippled and his pride devastated by everything that took place, and he fought to participate in the administration of the Sox on a much smaller scale. Many witnesses to the entire affair wished things would have gone differently. Had Comiskey been healthy and his friendship with Ban Johnson strong, the throwing of the World Series would likely have been handled in a much different way. The sidebar warfare between the former friends was too much of a distraction, and it proved costly in the overall scheme of things.

There are a million better case scenarios and avenues Comiskey could have taken. The same goes for the members of the infamous "Black Sox," and today, nearly a full century after the plot unfolded, the great American baseball mystery still continues to intrigue the public.

Charles A. Comiskey was a self-made man. As a kid, he dreamt that he would one day own a baseball franchise in his hometown. With an unbreakable determination, he followed through and accomplished his goal. His White Sox rose to great heights, and he was the proudest man in the sport. But in a flash his world crumbled, and his ego was fractured beyond repair. His life would have been much different if he would have escaped the 1919 World Series with the honesty of his club intact.

In his last years, from time to time, he'd quietly murmur to himself, "I can't see why they did that to me."[45]

The Comiskey Dynasty continued under the leadership of J. Louis Comiskey following his father's death. In 1939, upon the untimely demise of "Lou," his wife Grace assumed control of the Sox and worked closely with Grabiner and others in the management of the franchise. When she passed in 1956, the club entered the hands of Charles' oldest grandchild, Dorothy Comiskey Rigney, and she remained in charge for several years. Charles Comiskey II was also involved with the team in the 1950s and early sixties before he sold out completely around 1962—officially ending the family's connection to the Sox.

Some people believed the Sox were under the cloud of a powerful "curse" following the "Black Sox" conspiracy. It took the team forty years before they reached another World Series, but in 1959, after accomplishing the feat, they were defeated by the Los Angeles Dodgers, 4 games to 2. The next time Sox fans watched their favorites compete for a world championship was in 2005, and this time, in four straight games, Chicago was victorious over the Houston Astros. Eighty-eight years had gone by since the team's last title.

Comiskey Park was demolished in 1991, and a modern version of the stadium was built across the street, housing the same name. However, the new stadium was renamed U.S. Cellular Field in 2003, removing the final physical bond to the founder of the White Sox. But erasing his name from the façade of the park can't expunge his importance in the history of the South Side franchise. Now that the facts have been separated from the fiction, baseball enthusiasts can understand the real Charles Comiskey and appreciate his contributions to America's pastime. His genuine legacy has achieved him a spot in the National Baseball Hall of Fame, and no amount of revisionist history can invalidate the accomplishments he earned through more than a half century's allegiance to the sport.

ENDNOTES

1 *Chicago Daily Tribune,* October 30, 1931, p. 31.
   Also see: *Sporting News,* November 5, 1931, p. 6.
2 *Chicago Daily Tribune,* March 26, 1914, p. 3.
3 *Sporting News,* February 11, 1915, p. 1.
   Sportswriter George S. Robbins was the author of the quote, and it was relating to Comiskey's special invitation to appear with his Sox at the Panama-Pacific International Exposition in San Francisco by its president, Charles C. Moore.
4 *Chicago Daily Tribune,* February 14, 1915, p. B4. Alfred H. Spink, founder of the *Sporting News,* was being quoted.
5 *Baseball Magazine,* February 1914, p. 21–28.
6 An example of being against raising ticket prices occurred in January 1920 and the *Tribune* reported that his admission fees were "the same as it was when Comiskey started on the South side." *Chicago Daily Tribune,* January 27, 1920, p. 19. A few weeks later, owners voted on a measure eliminating the 25 cent seats, and charging 50 cents for bleacher occupancy. At some parks, owners were charging as much as a $1.00 more for box seats. *Chicago Daily Tribune,* February 12, 1920, p. 11. Again, in 1925, Comiskey blocked any ticket spike. *Chicago Daily Tribune,* January 14, 1925, p. 18. He also could have arranged for steeper prices during the 1917 World Series, but didn't. *Sporting News,* October 4, 1917, p. 3.
7 He admitted his ticket pricing plan in 1912, stating that because his fans had built the new Comiskey Park with their hard-earned money, "There isn't a seat in the ball park for which they have to pay over $1. There never will be while I live." He added: "Other club owners in both leagues have told me I made a mistake in not charging $1.25 and $1.50 for some of my box seats at the new park. I told them no. One dollar is enough to pay to see a ball game. That was the highest price at the old wooden plant on Thirty-ninth street, and just because the people of Chicago paid it often enough to let me build a new park for them, I was not going to raise the price of seats. Practically all the other clubs in the American League and some in the National League charge more than $1 for some of their box seats. I believe it is a mistake, and always will believe so." *Chicago Daily Tribune,* December 19, 1912, p. 16.
8 *Baseball Magazine,* February 1914, p. 21–28.
9 Asinof, Eliot, *Eight Men Out,* p. 20, 22.
10 *Sporting News,* March 20, 1919, p. 2.
11 Asinof, Eliot, *Eight Men Out,* p. 15–16.
12 *Philadelphia Inquirer,* January 1, 1919, p. 12.

The 140-game season would take place over a time span of about five months and ten days.

13 Bob Hoie, "1919 Baseball Salaries and the Mythically Underpaid Chicago White Sox," *Base Ball: A Journal of the Early Game*, Spring 2012.
Hoie estimated that the Sox payroll might have been around $93,051.

14 *Sporting News*, February 25, 1937, p. 5.

15 *Sporting News*, November 28, 1940, p. 10.

16 *Sporting News*, September 30, 1959, p. 11.
Lieb explained that salary cuts were agreed to upon by owners after a poor 1918 season.

17 Asinof, Eliot, *Eight Men Out*, p. 21.

18 Baseball-reference.com.

19 Ibid.
Years later, when Cicotte's great nephew Al Cicotte was breaking into the majors as a pitcher, he spoke with writer Milton Gross about his great uncle. He recited a family story that claimed Eddie was to win a "$5,000 bonus" if he annexed 30 victories. But after winning his 29th game with more than three weeks left in the season, he was benched, not getting even one start under the guise of resting him. *Sporting News*, March 18, 1953, p. 15.

20 *Baseball Magazine*, February 1914, p. 21–28.

21 Comiskey was well-known for his favorable treatment of sportswriters, and he discovered the benefits of maintaining friendly bonds with the press by watching Von der Ahe. Von der Ahe, in effort to show his appreciation for the local scribes, regularly banqueted St. Louis sportswriters. *Cleveland Leader and Herald*, July 25, 1886, p. 13. Comiskey did the same at Comiskey Park.

22 Comiskey was frequently credited with being the first owner to sponsor a Ladies' Day, and the publicity stunt was a popular happening at Comiskey Park in the early days of the Sox. Von der Ahe was admitting women free to certain games under that promotion as early as 1884, perhaps earlier. *St. Louis Post Dispatch*, July 25, 1884, p. 7.

23 *St. Louis Post Dispatch*, April 9, 1887, p. 10.

24 *Chicago Daily Tribune*, April 2, 1909, p. 6.

25 Baseball historian Bob Hoie documented Pegler's years of commentary about Comiskey in his detailed research piece, "1919 Baseball Salaries and the Mythically Underpaid Chicago White Sox," *Base Ball: A Journal of the Early Game*, Spring 2012.

26 *Sporting News*, July 21, 1954, p. 3.

27 Columnist Henry P. Edwards wrote that Comiskey's nickname should be changed to the "noblest bidder of them all" from the "noblest Roman of them all" because of the big sums of money he was paying for players. *Cleveland Plain Dealer*, December 11, 1914, p. 13.

28 *Chicago Daily Tribune*, December 28, 1917, p. 14.

29 *Chicago Daily Tribune*, July 24, 1929, p. 15. The story was that Comiskey wanted Ruth to manage the White Sox in 1930.

30 Comiskey supported innumerable functions and organizations at his stadium to include: Marshall Field & Company Field Day, the Canadian Red Cross lacrosse team, Knights of Pythias, the Elks Club, military ceremonies, church-based occasions, political rallies, various picnics, and other community-related events. Comiskey also rented his park out to boxing and wrestling promoters and staged college and professional football games.

31 An example of his generosity toward children was when he hosted nearly 15,000 people from South side public schools in June 1916. *Chicago Daily Tribune,* June 2, 1916, p. 15.

32 *Chicago Defender,* October 31, 1931, p. 8.

33 Axelson, Gustave W., *Commy: The Life Story of Charles A. Comiskey,* p. 150.
The Chicago Federation of Labor stated that Comiskey had always been fair to them, and they were going to reciprocate after issuing boycott orders on the Cleveland club for using nonunion labor to build their stadium. *Chicago Daily Tribune,* March 21, 1910, p. 7.

34 *Sporting News,* December 3, 1942, p. 6.

35 Comiskey provided this option for a number of players to include Freddie Parent, Ping Bodie, Thomas Quinlan, Jack Fournier, and Zeb Terry.

36 Comiskey paid Gandil $200 that the latter believed was owed him from his first stint with the White Sox from 1909–11. Gandil had previously protested to the National Commission and was denied. *Trenton Evening Times,* July 19, 1914, p. 27.

37 *Chicago Daily Tribune,* April 18, 1910, p. 10.

38 *Chicago Daily Tribune,* May 26, 1907, p. A2.
I. E. Sanborn of the *Chicago Daily Tribune* discussed Comiskey's participation in various baseball wars, noting that he'd seen conflict as an owner, manager, and as a player during his lengthy career. He was "always a fighter," and was against capitulation in any manner. Sanborn wrote, "and that trait on and off the diamond gave him the name 'Old Roman.'" *Chicago Daily Tribune,* January 9, 1916, p. B1.

39 *St. Paul Globe,* August 26, 1896, p. 5.

40 *Chicago Daily Tribune,* October 20, 1911, p. 11.

41 *St. Louis Post Dispatch,* February 24, 1889, p. 16.

42 This correlated with his passport application, dated November 12, 1913, where in the description of his nose, it was listed as "Roman." Ancestry.com.

43 *Trenton Evening Times,* October 26, 1931, p. 14.

44 *Chicago Defender,* October 31, 1931, p. 8.

45 *Sporting News,* October 29, 1931, p. 4.

ACKNOWLEDGMENTS

During the creation of this book, I communicated with many knowledge-able and gracious individuals who were instrumental along the way. Their combined help was crucial in allowing me to piece together and under-stand the life story of Charles Comiskey. Much of my appreciation must go to Amy Miller of the Broward County Main Library in Fort Lauderdale, Florida, for her tireless efforts in obtaining all of the Interlibrary Loan materials that I needed. I also thank the rest of the Interlibrary Loan depart-ment and the employees of the magazines and newspapers section on the third floor of the library. Their courtesies in my day-to-day research were always appreciated.

Additionally, I'd like to thank: Dr. David P. Miros of the Midwest Jesuit Archives, independent archive researcher Abigail Lambke, Brother Robert Werle of De La Salle Christian Brothers (Midwest District Archives), Don-ald Hoffman of Saint Ignatius College in Chicago, Illinois, Amy Muchmore of the Carnegie-Stout Public Library in Dubuque, Iowa, Judith Cremer of the Pottawatomie Wabaunsee Regional Library in St. Marys, Kansas, Matt Tischer of the Wisconsin Historical Society in Madison, Wisconsin, Scott M. Stroh of the Milwaukee County Historical Society in Milwaukee, Wisconsin, William R. Blohm of the Gail Borden Public Library District in Elgin, Illi-nois, historian E. C. Alft, researcher David Siegenthaler, and Phillip J. Costello of the Cook County Court in Chicago, Illinois.

Additional information was provided by archivists Katie Dishman, Mary Kay Schmidt, and Christina V. Jones of the National Archives and Records Administration, as well as to baseball historians Gabriel Schechter and Jim Nitz.

A significant amount of assistance was supplied by reference librarian Freddy Berowski and Photo Archivist Pat Kelly of the National Baseball Hall of Fame & Museum in Cooperstown, New York, Jane Winton, Curator of the Boston Public Library Print Department, Boston, Massachusetts, and Shelby Silvernell, Photographer & Imaging Specialist, Chicago Hisotry Museum, Chicago, Illinois.

Resources such as the *Sporting News* archive at paperofrecord.com and baseball-reference.com were regularly utilized, as well as the Chicago Public Library's online historical database for the *Chicago Examiner*. The community of SABR (Society for American Baseball Research) also must be lauded for their exceptional professionalism and work in chronicling the national pastime. Their combined efforts have ensured that the sport is documented for future generations to study and enjoy.

I would also like to thank baseball historian Bob Hoie, who graciously wrote the foreword to this book and added a lot of key information and fact checking. Also to Ken Samelson, for his keen eye in making sure all the information included in this work was accurate.

A special thanks to my editor Jason Katzman for his razor-sharp eye, astute observations, and encouragement. In terms of having a great collaborator, I couldn't ask for more.

This book would not have been possible without the love and support of my wife Jodi. Also, thank you to Timothy and Barbara Hornbaker, Melissa Hornbaker, Virginia Hall, Sheila Babaganov, Debbie Hopkins Gammill Kelley, Chad Porreca, Frances Miller, and John and Christine Hopkins.

SOURCES

BOOKS

Asinof, Eliot, *Eight Men Out*, New York: Holt Paperbacks, 2000.

Axelson, Gustave W., *Commy: The Life Story of Charles A. Comiskey*, Chicago, IL: The Reilly & Lee Co., 1919.

Breslin, Jimmy, *Can't Anybody Here Play This Game?*, Chicago, IL: Ivan R. Dee, 1963

Carney, Gene, *Burying the Black Sox*, Sterling, VA: Potomac Books, Inc., 2007.

Cooper, Brian E., *Ray Schalk: A Baseball Biography*, Jefferson, NC: McFarland Books, 2009.

Fleitz, David L, *Shoeless: The Life and Times of Joe Jackson*, Jefferson, NC: McFarland Books, 2001.

James, Bill, *The New Bill James Historical Baseball Abstract*, York, NY: Free Press, 2001.

Lynch, Michael T., *Harry Frazee, Ban Johnson and the Feud that Nearly Destroyed the American League*, Jefferson, NC: McFarland Books, 2008.

Macmillan, *The Baseball Encyclopedia, Eighth Edition*, New York, NY: Macmillan Publishing Company, 1990.

Pietrusza, David, *Rothstein*, New York, NY: Basic Books, 2004.

Spink, Alfred H., *The National Game* (2nd Edition), St. Louis, MO: National Game Publishing, 1911

Veeck, Bill, *The Hustler's Handbook*, Chicago, IL: Ivan R. Dee, 2009.

MAGAZINES

Baseball Magazine   *Sporting Life*   *Sports Illustrated*

Sport   *Sporting News*

NEWSPAPERS

Ann Arbor News
Baltimore Sun
Bellingham Herald
Bismarck Tribune
Boston Herald
Boston Journal
Buffalo Commercial
Chicago American
Chicago Daily News
Chicago Daily Tribune
Chicago Defender
Chicago Examiner
Chicago Herald and Examiner
Chicago Sunday Times
Chicago Tribune
Cincinnati Daily Gazette
Cincinnati Enquirer
Cincinnati Post
Cleveland Leader
Cleveland Plain Dealer
Collyer's Eye
Daily Illinois State Register
Daily Inter Ocean
Dallas Morning News

Detroit Free Press
Dubuque Daily Herald
Dubuque Daily Times
Dubuque Telegraph Herald
Duluth News-Tribune
Elgin Daily Courier
Elgin Morning Frank
Elkhart Truth
Idaho Statesman
Kalamazoo Gazette
Kansas City Star
Kansas City Times
Milwaukee Daily News
Milwaukee Journal
Milwaukee Sentinel
Muskegon Daily Chronicle
New York Evening World
New York Herald
New York Sun
New York Times
New York Tribune
Omaha World Herald
The Patriot
Pawtucket Times

Philadelphia Inquirer
Philadelphia North American
Philadelphia Record
Portland Oregonian
Richmond Times Dispatch
Rockford Daily Register
Rockford Morning Star
Rockford Republic
Salt Lake Telegram
San Diego Evening Tribune
San Diego Union
San Francisco Call
San Francisco Chronicle
St. Louis Globe Democrat
St. Louis Post Dispatch
St. Mary's Star
St. Paul Globe/Daily Globe
Trenton Evening Times
Washington, D.C. Evening Star
Washington Herald
Washington Post
Watertown Daily Times
Webster City Tribune
Wilkes-Barre Times

INTERNET SOURCES

Ancestry Databases, ancestry.com
Baseball Almanac, baseball-almanac.com
Baseball History Blog, baseballhistoryblog.com/2784/comiskey-and-the-american-league-ride-into-chicago-1900
Baseball Reference, baseball-reference.com
Chicago History Museum Blog,blog.chicagohistory.org/index.php/2011/04/did-the-cubs-lose-the-1918-ws-on-purpose
Chicago Lawyer Magazine, chicagolawyermagazine.com/Archives/2009/09/01/092009sox.aspx
Chicago Public Library Digital Resources, chipublib.org/images/index.php
Church of the Holy Family, holyfamilychicago.org/newsroom/81204ComiskeyRe-lease.htm

Cook County Circuit Court, cookcountyclerkofcourt.org/?section=RecArchiveP-
    age&RecArchivePage=black_sox
Missouri State Death Certificates, sos.mo.gov/archives/resources/deathcertificates
The Sporting News archive, paperofrecord.com
This Game of Games, thisgameofgames.blogspot.com

WIRE SERVICES

Associated Press
International News Service
Newspaper Enterprise Association
United Press International

OTHERS

Archives of St. Ignatius College, Chicago, IL
Boston Public Library, Boston, MA
Charles Comiskey File, National Baseball Library, Cooperstown, NY
Chicago Circuit Court Archives & Probate Records
Illinois Corporation Records, Office of the Illinois Secretary of State
Major League Baseball Transaction Card Collection, National Baseball Library,
    Cooperstown, NY
Midwest District Archives of De La Salle Christian Brothers
Midwest Jesuit Archives, St. Louis, MO
Wisconsin Corporation Records, Wisconsin Historical Society

INDEX

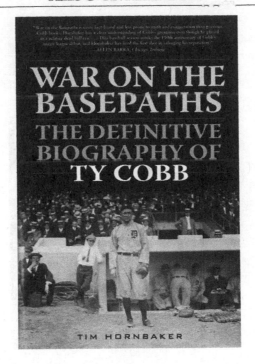

War on the Basepaths

The Definitive Biography of Ty Cobb

by Tim Hornbaker

War on the Basepaths offers a fresh look of one of the greatest players ever to grace a baseball diamond, Ty Cobb. Based on detailed research and analysis, author Tim Hornbaker offers the full story of Cobb's life and career, some of which has been lied about and mythologized for almost a century, showing who Ty Cobb really was and placing readers in box seats to view his life and career.

$16.99 Paperback • ISBN: 978-1-61321-951-5

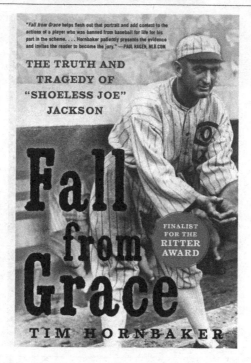

"*Fall from Grace* helps flesh out that portrait and add context to the actions of a player who was banned from baseball for life for his part in the scheme. . . . Hornbaker patiently presents the evidence and invites the reader to become the jury." —PAUL HAGEN, MLB.COM

THE TRUTH AND TRAGEDY OF "SHOELESS JOE" JACKSON

FINALIST FOR THE RITTER AWARD

Fall from Grace

TIM HORNBAKER

Fall From Grace
The Truth and Tragedy of "Shoeless Joe" Jackson

by Tim Hornbaker

Fall from Grace tells the story of the incredible life of Joseph Jefferson Jackson. From a mill boy to a baseball icon, author Tim Hornbaker breaks down the rise and fall of "Shoeless Joe," giving an inside look during baseball's Deadball Era, including Jackson's personal point of view of the "Black Sox" scandal, which has never been covered before.

$14.99 Paperback • ISBN: 978-1-68358-201-4